Deep Ecology and World Religions

SUNY series in Radical Social and Political Theory

Roger S. Gottlieb, editor

Deep Ecology and World Religions

New Essays on Sacred Grounds

Edited by

David Landis Barnhill
and
Roger S. Gottlieb

STATE UNIVERSITY OF NEW YORK PRESS

Published by
State University of New York Press, Albany

For information, address State University of New York Press,
90 State Street, Suite 700, Albany, NY 12207

Production by Kristin Milavec
Marketing by Fran Keneston

Library of Congress Cataloging-in-Publication Data

Deep ecology and world religions : new essays on sacred ground / edited by
David Landis Barnhill and Roger S. Gottlieb.
    p.   cm. — (SUNY series in radical social and political theory)
    Includes bibliographical references and index.
    ISBN 0–7914–4883–5 (hardcover : alk. paper)—ISBN 0–7914–4884–3
(pbk. : alk. paper)
        1. Deep ecology—Religious aspects.   I. Barnhill, David Landis.
II. Gottlieb, Roger S.   III. American Academy of Religion. Meeting (1997).
IV. Series.

GE195 .D437   2001
179.1—dc21
                                                                    00–030081

10 9 8 7 6 5 4 3 2 1

For my parents,
Charles Joseph Barnhill and Phyllis Grace Landis Barnhill

D. L. B.

For my children,
Anna Sarah Gottlieb and Esther Bella Greenspan

R. S. G.

Contents

Acknowledgments

This book grew out of a session on deep ecology and world religions at the 1997 national meeting of the American Academy of Religion. David did most of the work of soliciting new contributions, editing essays, prodding well-meaning but overly committed authors, and soothing the publisher when deadlines were not quite met. Roger put in his two cents on the essays, gave a lot of advice, and appreciated how much work David did.

Both of us are grateful to the authors of these fine papers, and to the support of the staff at SUNY Press. Most importantly, we thank the countless women and men who are confronting the environmental crisis, and using whatever religious, spiritual, social, economic, educational, commercial, political, and personal means they have to respond to it. We both believe that you cannot love God without loving the earth and all who dwell upon it; and that in order to find spiritual peace, we must resist the foolish violence that is being done to us all.

In safety and in bliss
May all creatures be of a blissful heart
Whatever breathing beings there may be
Frail or firm, . . . long or small
Dwelling far or near
May all creatures be of a blissful heart.

—Sutta Nipata, Buddhist Scriptures

The mother of us all,
The oldest of all,
Hard,
    Splendid as rock

Whatever there is that is of the land
   It is she
    Who nourished it,
  It is the Earth
  That I sing.

—Homer, "Hymn to the Earth"

If a person kills a tree before its time, it is like having murdered a soul.

—Rebbe Nachman of Bratslav, Eighteenth Century

The deep ecology sense of self-realization goes beyond the modern Western sense of "self" as an isolated ego striving for hedonistic gratification. . . . Self, in this sense, is experience as integrated with the whole of nature.

—Bill Devall and George Sessions, "The Development of Natural Resources and the Integrity of Nature"

The indescribable innocence and beneficence of Nature—of sun and wind and rain, of summer and winter—such health, such cheer, they afford forever. . . . Shall I not have intelligence with the earth? Am I not partly leaves and vegetable mold myself?

—Henry David Thoreau, *Walden*

Introduction

DAVID LANDIS BARNHILL AND ROGER S. GOTTLIEB

NATURE, RELIGION, HISTORY

AWE, REVERENCE, LOVE, and affection (along with fear, frustration, and grudging respect) have long marked human beings' attitude toward the natural world. In recent years the ethical and religious attitude of valuing nature for its own sake and seeing it as divine or spiritually vital has been called "deep ecology." The subject matter of this book is the relation between contemporary deep ecology and the world's religious traditions.

The simple and overwhelming reason why a new name is needed for a human attitude that may be tens of thousands of years old is that history has fundamentally altered our relationship to the surrounding, supporting Earth. Deep ecology has emerged as a response to what we have done to nature. In a sense, as Bill McKibben bleakly argued, nature has "ended." Having altered the atmosphere by thinning the ozone, affected global weather patterns, extinguished species at a rate unknown for tens of millions of years and consciously created new ones, we have put an end to that relatively autonomous realm. Of course every breath, hut building, and berry picking alters "nature." But the global effects of what we have done over the last century or so are monumentally larger than anything we might have even dreamed of before. Even if we think of "nature" as including human beings, we find that one part of nature—ourselves—is having vastly disproportionate and unsettling effects on the other parts.

Thus, at least on Earth, nature as we have known it is gone. In its place is "the environment." Every tree and river, large mammal and small fish, now exists in relation to human action, knowledge, commerce, science, technology, governmental decisions to create national parks, international campaigns to save endangered species, and (God help us) leisure lifestyle choices about mountain bikes, off-road vehicles, and sport fishing. Cell phone towers sprout like mushrooms on mountain tops, grizzly bears wear radio collars, genetic engineering produces overweight, arthritic pigs, and the children of Los Angeles slums grow up with stunted lungs because of polluted air. The world's coral reefs are bleaching a sickly, dead white; all of Japan's rivers are dammed; and the cod off Nova Scotia have been fished out.

But deep ecology embodies more than a love of and identification with nature, and a simple recognition that all of us, whether or not we flee from it in denial, live in the midst of an environmental crisis. It also purports to be the guiding philosophy of an environmental movement that seeks to slow or halt the ruin. Other philosophical or religious values guided wars of conquest or rebellion, shaped movements for national liberation or racial justice. Similarly, a renewed reverence for wilderness, endangered species or the maple tree in your front yard—not to mention an awareness of what toxic waste dumps do to people, animals, and plants alike—can shape public policy, move us to sue polluters, change the way children are educated, and lead us to resist Monsanto's chemicalized agriculture.

What sense can religions make of a world now colored by an environmental crisis—and of the deep ecological ethical and spiritual response to that crisis?

To begin with, religious spokespeople need to admit to themselves and the world that they live in history. This is, perhaps, not such an easy admission to make. Fundamental to the perspective of most religions, after all, is the notion that they embody a timeless truth, one derived either from a divine Source or from insight into an unchanging Reality. It is therefore a challenge for religions to admit that something absolutely basic to the world has changed. In response to the transition from nature to environment and the corresponding threats that are posed to humanity, religious values must themselves be closely examined.

In this light, religious traditions need to examine their own role in creating the disaster, rethinking the anthropocentrism of all our major religious traditions. Further, it must be admitted that whatever their theological attitude toward the earth, religious traditions were pretty much blind to the environmental crisis until it was pointed out to them by others. While many religious leaders were suspicious of science's claims when they conflicted with scriptural narratives, few were critical of technological advances and the threats they posed. Romantic poets, spiritual mavericks such as Thoreau, phenomenologists such as Edmund Husserl and Martin Heidegger, and Western Marxists (Karl Korch, Max Horkheimer, Theodor Adorno, Herbert Marcuse)—these were the voices that challenged the dominant Western treatment of nature, not those of ministers, priests, popes, or rabbis.

As have the rise of science, the struggle for democracy, and recent challenges to sexism and racism, the environmental crisis will alter religious sensibilities. It has already called forth explicit proclamations from almost every established religion. Whether nature is considered valuable in itself or as a part of God's creation, most religious authorities now see it as deserving of care, stewardship, and respect. In this way traditional religions are making (perhaps unconscious) common cause with deep ecologists and their kindred: radical environmentalists, ecofeminists, witches, and various tree-huggers of indeterminate self-description. An alliance between deep ecology (or, more broadly, any serious environmental philosophy) and world religion may thus have some quite significant political effects. The kind of energy religious institutions invested in the civil rights and antiwar movements, for instance, could be manifested in support of endangered species, clean energy sources, and World Bank "development" loans that don't destroy the rain forest. Religious institutions could look inward as well: making their buildings energy efficient and nontoxic, using recycled paper, and asking serious questions about where their own endowments are invested and how their wealthy secular leaders make their money. (If pornographers would not be allowed on a church's board of directors, why should polluters?)

Further, religious rituals, from church services in honor of animals to Buddhist meditations emphasizing our interdependence with the natural world, have been and will continue to be created and practiced. Considered as a technology of spiritual life, rituals allow us to celebrate even in the midst of devastation, and to express a kind of formalized, collective contrition for our ecological sins. As methods of focusing spiritual energy and moral intention, rituals are essential to a religious life that seeks to be more than a purely inner experience. Spiritual imagination and creativity are needed to continue to help us find widely meaningful ways to allow us to do this.

Finally, religions need to face how the environmental crisis changes certain basic facts about the spiritual meaning of the world around us. Considered as God's creation, nature—at least in the form of the ecosystems that make up this current phase of earth's biological development—is now subject to human intervention, alteration, and (to some extent, at least) control. No longer can God intimidate Job with talk of the whirlwind and the behemoth, not when we've hunted whales to the edge of extinction and can fly into hurricanes. No longer is the vastness of God's creation an intimation of human finitude. We might be guilty of folly in the way we use our powers, but they remain powers nevertheless.

Perhaps most painfully, the natural world is no longer an unclouded source of calm and peace, no longer a pure promise of goodness and happiness. All the religious poems and prayers that counsel us to find God in forest or field, to celebrate the simple beauty of flower or sunset, must now reckon with the toxic chemicals that permeate flora and fauna, with the increased certainty that sunshine causes skin cancer, with trees that are dying from acid rain and flowers that have strange new growing seasons because of global warming. And this new awareness might be extended to religious practices that do not explicitly concern "nature." If, as the Buddhists tell us, we should "focus on our breath" to develop a meditative awareness, we will have to be aware of what we are breathing on a humid summer day when the air pollution index is up. If we are to find Christ in a wafer, we might well wonder what pesticide residues are there as well. And our knowledge of these same residues may alter the blessings we make over wine on Sabbath eve.

In short, everything has changed—and we cannot go home again. This change may be an opportunity for increasing our self-awareness, rekindling our dedication to God, and finding an Inner Truth that is a source of blessing for Others. But these outcomes are only possible if world religions recognize and respond to this Frightening New World that humanity—and not God—has created.

It is the task of any world religion worth its salt to act openly, honestly, contritely, and (paradoxically) joyously in the face of the environmental crisis. The essays in this volume sketch some of the ways those responses have taken place and how they might unfold in the future. In particular, the essays in this book ask: what relations—of support, mutual enlightenment, creative tension, or conflict—can hold between world religions and a contemporary philosophical, ethical, and spiritual outlook that is committed to acknowledging and healing our fundamental connections to the earth?

Deep Ecology

In collecting essays about the complex phenomenon of deep ecology, we have sought a wide diversity of perspectives, approaches, and styles. Some authors see a close parallel between deep ecology and the religion being examined. Others find sharp contrasts. Some authors treat deep ecology as a way to extend and refine traditional religions. Others use that religion to reformulate deep ecology or critique its limitations. Indeed, it is not only traditional religions that are problematic. Deep ecology also is in need of ongoing rethinking, and one of the principal goals of this book is to use world religions as a framework for that task.

The very term *deep ecology* is multivalent and in dispute, and the authors in the volume use it in different ways. It may be helpful here to summarize some of the basic variations in meaning and how they relate to religion. We can follow Warwick Fox[1] and distinguish three principal meanings of the term. First, it refers to deep questioning about environmental ethics and the causes of environmental problems. Rather than simply adjusting existing policies or amending conventional values, such questioning leads to critical reflection on the fundamental world views that underlie specific attitudes and environmental practices. By probing world views, deep ecology inevitably is concerned with religious teachings and spiritual attitudes. In this sense of the term, deep ecology is a *methodological approach* to environmental philosophy and policy.

Second, deep ecology refers to a platform of basic values that a variety of environmental activists share.[2] These values include an affirmation of the intrinsic value of nature; the recognition of the importance of biodiversity; a call for a reduction of human impact on the natural world; greater concern with quality of life rather than material affluence; and a commitment to change economic policies and the dominant view of nature. Various religious world views can form the basis of these values, which can lead to a variety of different types of environmental activism and spiritual practices. In this sense, deep ecology is a unifying but pluralistic *political platform* that can bring together disparate religions and support a diversified environmental movement.

Third, deep ecology refers to different *philosophies of nature* (sometimes called ecosophies) that arise out of that deep questioning and that are in concert with the values associated with the platform. Individual ecosophies differ from each other, in part because they are often grounded in distinct religious traditions. Yet they have certain common characteristics, which are referred to generically as deep ecology, so it may be useful to begin with a list of the characteristics commonly ascribed to deep ecology. A caution, however. These are simply tendencies, and they can be found in a variety of forms and degrees in different deep ecologists, and some in fact may be absent or rejected by a particular deep ecologist. As a result, what one person praises as deep ecology may be different from what another criticizes.

With that proviso in mind, we can say that deep ecology is usually characterized by most of the following qualities:

deep ecology characteristics (handwritten margin note)

- an emphasis on the intrinsic value of nature (biocentrism or ecocentrism);
- a tendency to value all things in nature equally (biocentric egalitarianism);
- a focus on wholes, e.g., ecosystems, species, or the earth itself, rather than simply individual organisms (holism);
- an affirmation that humans are not separate from nature (there is no "ontological gap" between humans and the natural world);
- an emphasis on interrelationships;
- an identification of the self with the natural world;
- an intuitive and sensuous communion with the earth;
- a spiritual orientation that sees nature as sacred;
- a tendency to look to other cultures (especially Asian and indigenous) as sources of insight;
- a humility toward nature, in regards to our place in the natural world, our knowledge of it, and our ability to manipulate nature in a responsible way ("nature knows best");
- a stance of "letting nature be," and a celebration of wilderness and hunter-gatherer societies.

In his opening essay, Roger S. Gottlieb adopts a fourth and related meaning of deep ecology: a general *spiritual orientation* of intimacy with and reverence for the earth. As Gottlieb notes, in this inclusive sense of the term, deep ecology is the "oldest and newest religion." Rather than being limited to one school of contemporary ecophilosophy, it is a quality common throughout human cultures, and it can function as the foundation for diverse forms of contemporary spirituality. In general, the authors in this book use the term deep ecology in either the third sense (especially if it is being criticized) or this more inclusive sense.

To sharpen these different ways in which the concept of deep ecology has been used, it might help to contrast various "deep ecological" beliefs with what deep ecologists oppose. Thus, when a deep ecologist makes the *moral* claim that nature has inherent or intrinsic value, she is opposing (variously) instrumentalism and anthropocentrism. That is, the instrumental belief that the natural world exists solely to meet human needs; or the anthropocentric belief that only human beings have ethical value. For the deep ecologist, how we treat nature is a moral question, not one simply of efficiency or property rights.

When a deep ecologist makes the *metaphysical* or *psychological* claim that to be human is to be part of nature, he is opposing (again) anthropocentrism and individualism. That is, the anthropocentric view that human beings are (because of intelligence, technology, science, political life, language, the soul, etc.) categorically different from their surroundings; or the individualist view that sees people essentially as individuals, who form relationships with other beings but are not constituted by those relationships. Thus, for deep ecology our kinship with nature penetrates deeply into the essence of who we are. If as individuals and communities, we fail to realize and celebrate this fact, we will be neither truly happy nor truly sane.

When a deep ecologist advocates an "ecocentric" or "biocentric" *ethic*, he may be opposing a position that stresses individual rights. That is, for the deep ecologist the ecosystem or "life as a whole" is the unit of value, and not each particular human or animal taken as an individual possessor of rights. Thus, when authorities in California seek to kill feral cats because of their decimation of endangered birds, animal rights advocates resist and deep ecologists applaud. When property owners appeal to the absolute quality of their right to do what they want with what they own, deep ecologists argue that the value of the ecosystem takes precedence over that right.

At times, deep ecologists may express the *religious* claim that the earth, or nature, or life is "holy." Here the opponent is any religion that reserves sacredness for humans, angels, and gods, and excludes it from sea turtles, rivers, and redwoods. Here deep ecologists make happy common cause with pagans, witches, druids, and indigenous tribes. Here the environmental crisis signals a desecration and not just a terrible "mistake." (Or, as Edward Abbey remarked, we've agreed not to drive cars through our cathedrals and bedrooms, why can't we keep them out of the national parks as well!)

Finally, deep ecologists have taken a *political* or *strategic* position that makes the preservation of wilderness and the "defense of mother earth" the primary goal of the environmental movement. Here deep ecologists have a different orientation than that of social ecologists, ecosocialists, ecofeminists, or the environmental justice movement. Such groups, while not always in opposition to deep ecological positions, typically employ a different vocabulary and sensibility. They are much more likely to stress the interconnection between social relations and the human treatment of nature than are deep ecologists; and may even claim that humanity's collective treatment of nature is actually the outcome of the way different groups of human beings treat each other. For socially minded ecological groups, the environmental crisis is to a great extent the product of social forces such as racism, sexism, militarism, nationalism, and class exploitation.

Stressing these differences among environmentalists can help clarify their various approaches. But it also can be merely an academic exercise and even lead to unnecessary bickering. In some cases, a closer look at apparent differences in philosophy can reveal fundamental theoretical compatibility. In addition, theoretical disagreements about environmental philosophy often can coexist with political agreement about cleaning up the mess we've made. As in the history of other social movements—from nineteenth-century European socialism to the U.S. civil rights movement—alliances among groups with different philosophical orientations or constituencies have sometimes been essential for success. At other times, alliances have been impossible for principled reasons. And still other times coalitions have fallen apart mainly because of childish egotism or arrogance on the part of theorists or leaders. We prefer an ecosystem view of environmental thought: health is found in diversity and interdependence. Deep ecology is one among many perspectives, all of which seek to promote the earth and all who dwell upon it.

DEEP ECOLOGY AND WORLD RELIGIONS

Each essay offers insights into deep ecology and the religion being considered, but much of their value lies in the relationships among them: the parallels and divergences of interpretation, the contrasting or complementing emphases, and in some cases surprising juxtapositions. Gottlieb establishes a context for the essays by reviewing the response of contemporary religion to the Enlightenment. The enormous success of the Enlightenment has generated terrible results: a destructive technology, a consumer society devoid of community, social "progress" that has destroyed both cultures and ecosystems and created injustice. Religions have responded with renewed energy, but they face competition from secular philosophies and a wide variety of other religions and confront a growing recognition of their past sins. Such a situation is difficult for religions, because it calls for self-criticism and humility at that same time as it demands passion and commitment. In linking religion and politics, Gottlieb asks, how can a spiritual deep ecology transcend the limitations of the Enlightenment yet keep its positive accomplishments? That question must be answered incisively, for what is sacred, this earth, is under siege.

John Grim compares indigenous traditions and deep ecology in terms of conceptual foundations, politics, and religions. A central ideal of deep ecology is the development of epistemologies and world views intimately related to the local bioregion, something characteristic of indigenous traditions. For the Maori of New Zealand, the intimate connection between nature and culture (from patterns of basket making to conceptions of cosmological forces) implies that every living thing has an inherent right to its place in the world, and all food is sacred, a view that resonates with deep ecology's affirmative ecocentric approach to value and spirituality. Deep ecology also tends to share with indigenous traditions an intuitive sense of an interwoven cosmology. Differences emerge in notions such as "wilderness." Deep ecology has emphasized the destructiveness of human activity in nature and in response has idealized a state of wilderness devoid of human intervention. Indigenous traditions, on the other hand, emphasize "the covenantal character of working in and with the land." There also has been the complaint that deep ecology has appropriated Native American ritual life in an inauthentic way. Unlike most deep ecologists, indigenous peoples tend to integrate spiritual attitudes in pragmatic, subsistence activities. The link between deep ecology and indigenous traditions, then, is both real and problematic.

Christopher Key Chapple explores the complex relationship between Hinduism and deep ecology by considering scripture, meditative techniques, agricultural rituals, contemporary conservation projects, and urban consumerism. Central to his study is the notion of embedded ecology, which suggests the materiality of Hinduism's positive view of nature and its incorporation into rituals and agricultural practices. A belief in the sacrality of the five elements, for instance, forms the basis for an understanding of the body's interconnectedness with the cosmos. Agricultural rituals enact a divinization of the land and its association with human fertility. Closely related is the tradition of sacred groves, which informs current reforestation projects. Chapple also reviews a Third World critique of deep ecology that echoes criticisms by indigenous scholars of deep ecology's tendency to cordon off nature as a sacred wilderness free from human interference—and the subsistence needs of local peoples. He then offers a possible model for a Third World form of deep ecology: the Indian state of Kerala, which has a high level of health, nutrition, and education combined with low consumption. This model of concern for both material welfare and an ethical, sustainable use of the land accords with Grim's description of the lifeways of indigenous peoples, and it may help deep ecology bridge the gap between a concern for nature and for humans.

In his essay on Buddhism, David Landis Barnhill takes a more philosophical approach by analyzing the issue of holism and relationships, an issue that lies at the heart of spiritual ecophilosophies and which has caused sometimes rancorous debate between deep ecology and ecofeminism. Reviewing ecofeminist criticisms of deep ecology's emphasis on an expanded self and whole systems, he explores Huayan Buddhism's nondualistic approach as a way to overcome the division between relationality and holism. In this perspective, nature is a whole with which we can identify, but it involves neither the monistic denial of relationality nor the transcendence of the concrete world of particulars, which many ecofeminists have objected to. Instead, the whole and the part mutually imply each other, both the earth and the organism have unqualified value, and the absolute is nothing other than this concrete, phenomenal world. Barnhill proposes a new typology concerning the self and the whole, and he presents Huayan as a form of "relational holism" that incorporates many of the values found in both deep ecology and ecofeminism. Such a view could serve as a philosophical basis for the practical embodiment of valuing nature found in the state of Kerala, while the practices found there and in indigenous traditions could help to extend Huayan ideals into concrete reality.

Jordan Paper brings a sharply critical approach to the way deep ecologists have appropriated Daoism, raising the key issue of validity in using non-Western religions in modern ecophilosophy. Deep ecologists have tended to limit discussions of Daoism to two early texts, the *Daode jing* and the *Zhuang Zi*, ignoring the long ritual and spiritual tradition associated with Daoism.[3] In addition, they have followed the Western practice of artificially separating a complex but singular Chinese religion into distinct traditions of Confucianism, Daoism, and Buddhism. Paper finds portrayals of Daoism as anarchistic and uncontaminated by religion to be a romantic fantasy that is unhelpful in dealing with ongoing environmental destruction. He urges us to take a holistic view of Chinese religion and recognize its pragmatic intent, seen especially in agricultural rituals that divinize Sky and Earth and thereby provide checks against the abuse of the natural world. Paper claims that the experience of the earth as sacred, embodied in these rituals, is found in many cultures, an argument that finds support in Grim's analysis of indigenous traditions and Chapple's discussion of Hinduism.

Like Barnhill on Buddhism, Mary Evelyn Tucker analyzes the metaphysical views of Neo-Confucian philosophy. This tradition, which dominated China from 1000–1900, offers a complex and sophisticated view of nature that the West is just beginning to understand and appreciate. Neo-Confucianism displays a number of characteristics found in deep ecology and Huayan Buddhism: the intrinsic value of nature; an insistence on ontological continuity, with humans seen as fully a part of an organic universe; an emphasis on interrelatedness combined with a type of holistic view ("heaven and earth as one's body"). However, Neo-Confucianism also exhibits certain views that are normally associated with Western views, such as a sense of hierarchy, with humans having a distinctive role in the cosmos. Like Buddhism, Neo-Confucianism stresses that reality is characterized by change; like Daoism, it highlights the dynamism of nature. Its particular emphasis, however, is on each living thing's natural process toward fulfillment, which links the growth of a tomato plant and the moral development of human beings. This is one manifestation of "anthropocosmology," the perspective that the qualities and processes of nature are same as those of humans, and vice versa. Given this directional dynamism, to identify with the earth is to actively participate in this process of transformation and to help bring nature to completion, rather than simply to "let nature be." In some ways Neo-Confucianism combines aspects of deep ecology and stewardship, and it avoids certain problematic tendencies in deep ecology such as a disconnection between human cultural activity and natural processes.

Before turning to the essays on Western religions, it is appropriate to highlight troublesome issues that Jordan Paper raises but, not surprisingly, does not completely resolve. Any consideration of a foreign religion such as Daoism that removes it from its cultural context distorts its character. But how can it be useful to us if we simply interpret it as inextricably part of a culture far removed from us? If we give Daoism or Neo-Confucianism a Western interpretation, will we not both falsify it and infect it with the very assumptions that have led to environmental catastrophe? If, however, we simply try to modify Western traditions from within, can we create the radical change that is necessary? How is Daoism or any other non-Western religion really useful in dealing with contemporary environmental problems, both practical and philosophical? These questions will continue to haunt comparative studies of deep ecology, but whatever one's view on them, the essays in this volume will help us clarify the issues and refine the debate.

Western religions do not show as many parallels with deep ecology as do indigenous and Asian religions, and as the following essays show, Judaism, Christianity, and Islam challenge deep ecology in productive ways. Eric Katz explores traditional Judaism, in particular the commands *tza'ar ba'alei chayim* ("the pain of living creatures") and *bal tashchit* ("do not destroy"). He finds parallels to deep ecology in a respect for nature, a recognition that the purposes and value of nature transcends human designs, a critique of a search for material affluence, and a sense of the limitations of our knowledge and control of the natural world. Differences emerge when we examine anthropocentrism. The constraints involved in the two commands (notably, "commands" and not "principles") focus on the human context, e.g., domestic animals and fruit trees. They do not demonstrate the kind of ecocentricism found in deep ecology and in Huayan Buddhism. In this, Judaism shares the combined concern for nature and human economic needs discussed by Chapple in relation to Hinduism. In addition, Judaism is theocentric, with absolute value placed in a transcendent realm and nature's value found in being God's creation. But Katz is troubled by such a theocentrism because, like Job, we are unable to grasp the Creator's designs, especially in response to massive evil such as the Holocaust. Our inability to understand and conform to the greater cosmic patterns seems opposite that of the anthropocosmology of Neo-Confucianism. However, Katz finds that we can come to understand and identify with the processes of Creation, becoming a "copartner" with nature. Such a view recalls not only Neo-Confucianism but also contemporary stewardship thinkers such as Wendell Berry. Deep ecology needs to consider seriously this stress on an activist participation in nature's processes.

John Carroll examines the Catholic tradition, noting that most contemporary Catholics are unaware of the ecological significance of its doctrines and practices. He begins by giving basic Catholic principles an ecological reading, but his main emphasis is on contemporary Catholic social teachings, not only from the Vatican but also (perhaps more importantly) from the pastorals of local bishops in this country. In addition, he discusses countercultural forms of ecospiritual praxis in rural communities such as Genesis farm and the group Sisters of the Earth. By providing lifepaths largely divorced from the consumer economy, they recall Hindu-based communities Chapple discusses and could be compared (with Paper's critique in mind) to Daoist ideals and also indigenous economies. Carroll also argues that Catholicism exhibits a historical trend toward greater valuing of the natural world, but whether this tradition can become truly ecocentric remains an open question. It seems likely that Catholicism, like Judaism and Protestantism, will remain fundamentally theocentric, however much it comes to affirm the sacramental dimension of creation.

Nawal Ammar's analysis of Islam centers on an interpretation of scriptures. There we find an emphasis on the sacrality and transcendence of God, who alone has ultimate spiritual value. Nature is neither sacred nor profane but reflects God's sacredness as Creation. Ammar thus points to a position that is, as in Katz's discussion of Judaism, theocentric. Humans have a special role in creation, with moral knowledge and thus responsibility to treat nature with care. The command to avoid evil and do good involves our relationship with the earth, which we must not use excessively or destructively. The natural world is for our use and fulfillment, but only when used kindly, sharing what we have and conserving what we can. This is not a mere environmental ethic but a call for devotional action that participates in Creation. Thus, Muslims might criticize deep ecology for attempting to separate humans from a supposedly pure wilderness. Deep ecologists, on the other hand, might well criticize such a stewardship view as retaining too much anthropocentrism. But the similarities are worth noting. Both Islam and deep ecology affirm that the natural world is an integrated whole (as Creation, for Muslims), with humans an inextricable part of that whole. Nature is not to be exploited but responded to with contemplation, appreciation, and protection.

John Cobb recounts his own movement toward an ecologically concerned theology within the Protestant context. Such a change, inspired in part by deep ecology, involved turning from a narrow focus on the salvation of the individual person. Like other process theologians, he came to reject the Kantian separation of nature and history, which relegated theology to the study of human history while placing nature in the province of science. The process ecotheology that Cobb presents rethinks some of the basic categories of Western thought and as such parallels the probing critique of its fundamental world view, characteristic of deep ecology in the sense of a methodological approach. Cobb also rejects certain forms of anthropocentrism, but he highlights his differences from deep ecology. He emphasizes social justice, starting with a concern for humans and expanding out to environmental issues. For Cobb, it is wrong and dangerous to consider humans as just one species among many; only by realizing our unique complexity and the dominance of our effects on nature can we develop the sense of responsibility needed. In part this recalls the Neo-Confucian view, but in this essay Cobb highlights a more "negative" responsibility of avoiding the destruction of nature rather than a call to participate in nature's process toward fullness. This view shares with Judaism, Catholicism, and Islam an understanding of the earth as sacramental but not sacred in itself, for only God as transcendent has absolute value. Like Neo-Confucianism, Cobb's process theology retains a hierarchy of value, although here his defense of this perspective is more pragmatic than ontological: a hierarchy is necessary to solve questions of conflicts of interest in environmental issues. He also tends to focus more on the welfare of individual animals than the environment as a whole, as do many ecofeminist critics of deep ecology.

Rosemary Radford Ruether, like Barnhill, considers the ecofeminist critique of deep ecology. For Ruether, deep ecology falsely locates the source of the problem in anthropocentrism, which shows deep ecology's neglect of androcentrism and the connection between the oppression of women and of nature. In doing so, she argues, deep ecology puts the blame on all humans, when in fact it is certain privileged groups, especially white males, that are guilty of most of the destruction. Ruether also examines the deep ecology critique of the Bible, responding that a positive theology can be drawn from it; like Cobb, she argues for a reinterpretation of traditional Christian theology. Ruether concludes with critical reflections on ecofeminism itself. She argues that essential ecofeminists, who uphold a special connection between women and the earth, reinforce false and dangerous gender associations. In addition, ecofeminism needs to be more concerned with issues such as poverty and class dominance. Moreover, she says, Western ecofeminism has much to learn from Third World ecofeminists who struggle with poverty and work to establish healthy alternative communities. Ruether thus echoes Chapple's discussion of a Third World critique of deep ecology and John Carroll's account of Catholic communities in this country.

In the last essay, Michael Zimmerman analyzes Ken Wilber, who represents a contemporary form of ecospirituality and a strong critique of deep ecology. Wilber agrees with spiritual deep ecology's criticisms of certain aspects of modernism, its assertion of the spiritual significance of the material world, and a transpersonal ideal of going beyond the ego. But contrary to many deep ecologists, and like Cobb, he affirms a transcendent dimension to reality. For Wilber, any metaphysical view that confines reality to the natural world (which would seem to include Huayan Buddhism) is one-dimensional. He also sees the universe evolving toward increasing complexity, an idea that informs Cobb's process theology. This sense of transcendence and evolution leads to a type of hierarchical view that places humans in the highest position, a perspective that recalls both Western religion and Neo-Confucianism but that deep ecologists tend to reject out of hand. Wilber chastises deep ecologists for splitting nature and culture and devaluing culture as "the original crime." In addition, he claims that deep ecology suffers from the "pre/trans fallacy": instead of working toward a truly transpersonal ideal, it regresses to a pre-conscious state of union with nature found in tribal cultures. Such a move, he says, will fail to stop the destruction of nature and will keep Americans from taking spiritual ecology seriously. Wilber and Zimmerman join Gottlieb in insisting that we need to retain certain positive aspects of modernism while criticizing other aspects. Zimmerman finds much of value in Wilber's view, but like most deep ecologists he lacks Wilber's confidence in the grand narrative of evolutionary advance and the related dismissal of tribal cultures.

These essays suggest the importance of deep ecology and the complexity of its relationship to religion. We cannot simply celebrate deep ecology's insights or point out parallels to world religions. As the methodological meaning of the term indicates, we need deep questioning—of deep ecology itself and of its religious significance. The severity of our situation calls for an increasingly subtle and comprehensive understanding on our part in order to formulate a vision, political activism, and way of life that embody a reverence for the sacred and vulnerable earth. This book is a small step in that direction.

NOTES

1. *Toward a Transpersonal Ecology* (Boston: Shambhala, 1990).

2. A "Deep Ecology Platform" was first proposed by Arne Naess and George Sessions in 1984.

3. There are currently two different systems of transliterating Chinese into English. In the older Wade-Giles system, we find Taoism, the *Tao-te-ching*, Chuang Tzu, and Hua-yen. The pinyin system established by the Chinese government is increasingly being used, in which we read of Daoism, the *Daode jing*, Zhuangzi, and Huayan.

I

Spiritual Deep Ecology and World Religions

A Shared Fate, a Shared Task

ROGER S. GOTTLIEB

D EEP ECOLOGY—THE PHRASE" originated recently as a stream of academic ethics stressing the intrinsic ethical value of the natural world. However, what we might call "deep ecology—the concept" is as old as the worship of the Earth Goddess, as widespread as any seven-year-old girl's fascination with frogs, as fundamental as the way any of us might have our breaths taken away by a brilliant tropical sunset or the startling clarity of a drab December landscape suddenly made white by the season's first snow. "Deep Ecology—the concept" is a sense of reverence and sacredness, insight and inspiration, that is found in (to use David Abram's felicitous phrase) the "more than human" world. Deep ecology in this sense is not a movement *outside* of world religions, which then might be juxtaposed to these related but essentially different forms of thought and practice. Rather, deep ecology occurs *within* the discursive, emotive, cognitive, and at times even institutional space of world religions themselves. As such, spiritual deep ecology shares something of the history, the tasks, and the dangers of the rest of the world's religious traditions.

THE "SPIRIT" IN SPIRITUAL DEEP ECOLOGY

By "religion" I mean organized and overlapping systems of belief, ritual, institutional life, spiritual aspiration, and ethical orientation which are premised on an understanding of human beings as other or more than simply their purely social or physical identities. Teachings can be marked as "religious" in the way they assert (as in Judaism, Christianity, and Islam) that humans are essentially connected to a Supreme Being whose author is distinct from earthly political and social powers; or by a suggestion (made by Buddhism) that we can achieve a state of consciousness that transcends the attachments, obsessions, and passions of our ordinary social ego; or in the Wiccan celebration of the sexual act as an embodiment of the life-giving force of the Goddess rather than as simply a grasping of moments of purely individual pleasure.

What is crucial is that religion serves as an alternative to understandings of the human identity that center on the social successes of money, fame, political power, career achievement, or community acceptance. Religious perspectives direct us toward what theologian Paul Tillich called "ultimate significance." They seek to orient us to that which is of compelling importance beyond, beneath, or within our day-to-day concerns with making money, getting famous, or having immediate pleasures. At the same time, however, religion also seeks to orient us to the familiar interpersonal world of family, community, and global connections, providing guidance that seeks to root everyday moral teachings in the ultimate nature or significance of a spiritual truth about who we really are. Religions necessarily direct us toward particular ways of living with other people and with the world.

Finally, religions provide rituals—acts of prayer, meditation, collective contrition, or celebration—whose goal is to awaken and reinforce an immediate and personal sense of our connection to the Sacred. These practices aim at a transformation of consciousness, to cultivate within the heart an impassioned clarity of connection to spiritual sensibility.

The celebration and awe for the natural world that are the hallmark of spiritual deep ecology match this conception of the essential features of religion. To begin, spiritual deep ecology challenges the (now) conventional notion that human beings are essentially different than, separate from, and superior to the natural world. Much of the world's religion, philosophy, law, education, commerce, and common sense have for some time[1] given human beings "dominion" (Genesis) over the earth. People have asserted that the distinctive human capacities for language, "reason," or property ownership signify that we alone have rights, or ultimate moral worth. By contrast, spiritual deep ecology prizes our connection to the natural world as vital to who we are. It makes much of our similarities, connections, and interrelations with earth and sky, flowers and fish. In this sense, deep ecology is not only a response to questions about whether or not nature has intrinsic value, it is also a distinct perspective about what people are. As other religions tell us that we are a spark of God or a pure awareness, so spiritual deep ecology tells us (or wants us to discover) that we are natural beings, tied hand, foot, and heart to a vast web of natural beings that are, in a way, sacred. "World as Lover, World as Self," proclaims Buddhist deep ecologist Joanna Macy, meaning that our essential connection to nature can combine love, identification, and intimacy. "We need wilderness," says Edward Abbey, "because we are wild animals." It is our sensuous connection to our surroundings, says Abram, that has allowed us to learn, and even to speak. Or, as in Paul Shepard's simple truth: "The Others have made us human."[2]

This sense of connection at times has been recognized in religions that are preponderantly anthropocentric. The Torah ruled that animals, and not just people, were to have the Sabbath for rest. The Buddhist sense of the interconnection of *all* beings was inscribed in children's stories in which the Buddha was reincarnated as an animal. Even in Christianity there were occasional voices that saw the face of God in nature. We might say, therefore, that deep ecology at times overlaps with other religious traditions. It expresses, as it were, a "natural" human tendency to respond to with care, love, and awe to nature. (E. O. Wilson dubbed this sentiment "biophilia" and argued that it possibly has genetic roots.)[3]

The vitality of our connection to nature is most obviously signalled by the constant realization of our dependence on it. Air, water, and food, the microbes in our gut, the nitrogen-fixing bacteria in the soil— without any of these our illusions of autonomy would crumble mighty fast. Yet there is a more precisely religious element in spiritual deep ecology. As Jews or Hindus see themselves as receiving The Truth from scriptures or direct encounters with God, the deep ecologist receives sacred truths from the natural world. The Native American sense that each person has a particular animal as a teacher of truths and virtues is thus a kind of "deep ecological" religious sensibility. This attitude appeared likewise when Aldo Leopold beheld a "fierce green fire" in the eyes of the wolf he himself had shot to make the world better for deer and deer hunters, and learned that from the point of view of the wolf, and the mountain it lived on, there were other and better ways to live in the world. Nature for the deep ecologist is not only a kind of

spontaneous mall, filled with things to meet our needs and give us pleasure ("And here, some food; there, materials for furniture; and, how
pleasant, now some lovely bird calls"). It is also a Sacred Teacher—a
Torah, Koran, or Gita. While anthropocentric religions have occasion-
ally celebrated the holiness of the natural world, usually as a manifestation of the holiness of its creator, it is only with the most extreme
rarity that they see it as a source of wisdom.

For deep ecology, further, the teachings of nature, like the Mitzvot
of Judaism or the ethical constraints of a traditional Buddhist teaching,
direct us back into the social world. Nature's revelations, it is believed,
have some very strong implications for social life. For one thing, the interdependence of different parts of an ecosystem, deep ecologists tell
us, teach us about the necessity to curb our personal and collective
greed, to exercise the kind of care we seem to have forgotten (or never
had), to treasure the multiplicity of species rather than cavalierly eliminate them. In this light, everything that lives is precious, just because it
is part of and contributes to, the precious, differentiated whole that is
the natural world. A realization of this truth is not simply a pleasant intellectual reflection, but a guide to moral behavior for individuals and
groups alike.

Further, an identification with nature can be the source of deep
pleasure and deeper calm. Just as people who hear the voice of God
may feel a little differently about a flat tire or being passed over for a
promotion, so a felt connection with a tree or a bird can soothe the anx-
ieties and relieve the sense of overwhelming pressure to achieve or possess in the social realm. Such a connection might even, if we let it, help
us learn not to be quite so (desperately, compulsively) busy. Experiencing ourselves as natural as well as social, part of a cosmos as well as a
community, we can find a remedy for the kinds of neuroses that typically are not part of the lives of ants, birches, or elks. Observing how vital all parts of an ecosystem are, we may learn to lessen our desires to
succeed at all costs, to triumph over others, or to achieve fame.[4] Seeing
how the birth and death of all beings takes places in a cycle of coming
forth and returning to the underlying matrix that makes life possible,
we can sense our own infinite future as part of what Rachel Carson
called a "material immortality."

These are just some of the spiritual lessons deep ecologists have
taken from nature. Interpreted through our multiple and varying social
contexts, deep ecologists in various historical and social settings have
made human sense of the more than human. As other religions have
struggled to interpret sacred texts, so those of us who find the divine in
the ordinary physical realities have had to decide what meanings they

have for our lives. The fact that interpretation has been necessary, that ocean and mountain do not carry transparent spiritual meanings, simply means that spiritual deep ecology is in the same situation as any other religious orientation toward Truth.

THE FATE OF RELIGION

One of the great surprises of the second half of the twentieth century is the worldwide resurgence of religion. How many people, after all, would have thought that Russian Christianity would outlive the Stalinist secret police, that some of the most powerful postcolonial regimes would define themselves in terms of their religious piety; or that in the last decade before the millennium perhaps the single most powerful unified ideological group in the United States (that bastion of science, democracy, progress, and research grants) would be the fundamentalist Christian Right?

What happened to the Enlightenment? (And, whatever happened, it is something that necessarily is happening to spiritual deep ecology as well as any other religious or spiritual outlook.)

Quite simply, too many of the promises of Enlightenment did not materialize. If we think of the secular enlightenment as based in the equation "science plus democracy plus the free market equals reason equals freedom plus happiness," we can sense some of the historical and psychological sources of our collective disappointment.

For a start, as the servant of government, business, and careerism, science and technology have proved a mixed blessing. Too many diseases seem impervious to a strictly detached, seemingly objective, medical expertise. "Scientific management" often proves to be an oxymoron. The nifty airplanes drop horrible bombs, the cooled-off cars cause skin cancer by eroding the ozone layer, the pesticide is transmuted into a gas to kill people. (Zyklon B, the gas used in concentration camps, was first noticed being used to eradicate insects from old buildings.) Later, we discover that pesticides kill people even when they are aimed at bugs.

As the early Western Marxist Georg Lukacs observed nearly eighty years ago, the modern age is marked by a combination of increasingly sophisticated parts integrated into an increasingly irrational whole.[5] One need only think of the technological prerequisites for—and the real life consequences of—ozone-depleting CFCs. Or traffic gridlock; or urban sprawl; or the way the overuse of antibiotics has bred new and virulent strains of bacteria.

On the level of social life, a collection of democratically connected individual producers and consumers seems, for many, to be a poor basis for community. We have the freedom to consume and pollute, to move and to get divorced, but all these seem to promote at least as much loneliness as they do fulfillment. Individually, a rather alarming percentage of the world's richest, most technologically oriented nation are addicted to alcohol, prescribed drugs, illegal drugs, work, sex, adrenaline, caffeine, nicotine, television, psychotherapy, or the Internet.

In the un (less) developed world, secular progress seems to go along with increased class stratification, the decimation of traditional culture, and the rape of the local economy by international corporate interests.

The point of these familiar observations is to locate the current resurgence of personal and collective religious life in a history of the failed promises of the Enlightenment. And, simultaneously, to point out that spiritual deep ecology *as anything like a widespread belief and sentiment* is in some ways a product of the same forces. Fundamentalist Christianity is in part a response to the availability of divorce and the presence of pornography. Jewish Renewal, Creation theology and other progressive/feminist/green/passionate forms of religious renewal are partly responses to the boring modernism of washed-out "reform" versions of Christianity and Judaism. Similarly, deep ecology is a response to the massive looming presence of the environmental crisis and the bland deadness of a universe presented as only the object of manipulative science and voracious productivism. In other words, deep ecology is a spiritual answer to the transformation of nature into environment—in which virtually all our earthly surroundings become stamped with a human mark, or threaten to become our pets, raw materials, or victims.

Simultaneously, as any religious movement worth its salt contains occasions for celebration as well as the capacity to warn us against sin, deep ecology offers delights not encapsulated by a vocabulary of individual rights, personal choices, and lots of trips to the mall. A resurgent Judaism advises us to recover the joys of the Sabbath and actually turn off our toys and jobs for twenty-five hours each week. Dorothy Day and the Catholic Worker movement advised us to recover the freedom of a freely chosen poverty. Spiritual deep ecology, besides warning us of our mistakes, is also a movement to return to delight in the simple beauties of land and air. It teaches us to find rapture in a brief staring contest with a weasel, or to marvel at the interdependence of plants and insects in a rainforest, or to celebrate the turning of the seasons. Deep ecology writing returns us to the magic time of childhood when at least some of the natural world was *fully* alive. It serves as a kind of magical regression to the wisdom of childhood. Consider Stephanie Kaza's simple evocation of

> Sycamores! Bright white trunks against the blue horizon! All this week I have been seeing you for a distance. Now I am lured closer for a conversation, for a chance to glimpse the world between your branches. Sweet billowy clouds dance above your arms in the piercing equinox light. The bright sun reflects off your tall trunks in the crisp, clear air.[6]

This childlike joy can be combined with, as David Barnhill puts it, the sage's sense that death is integral to life. Just because we see ourselves as deeply connected to a natural world that is not essentially defined by a conscious intelligence, the prospect of our own physical death is less daunting, and we are perhaps more likely to accept that birds, oak trees, mountains, and even the earth itself are subject to change. As religions cushion us against the fear of death by promising life in Another Realm, so spiritual deep ecology fulfills the same function by helping us see this one differently.

More familiar religious movements and spiritual deep ecology thus share a kindred origin. It is not surprising, then, that they can be seen as also sharing common dangers, tasks, and temptations.

RELIGIONS AND SPIRITUAL DEEP ECOLOGY

Like it or not, all resurgent religions, even the most hysterically fundamentalist, are post-Enlightenment religions. Unlike the religions before Galileo, Voltaire, Marx, and Freud, any religious tradition today knows that it exists in a social context marked by several new features.

First, there is the obvious growth of technical knowledge that, for all its faults, is essential to the daily personal and institutional lives of the religious devotees themselves. (Every fundamentalist, with the possible exception of the Amish, has his fax machine, Internet address, color TV, and long distance calling card! Or, at least, all of his leaders do.) *Second,* there remain aggressive and self-confident secular philosophies that have tried (with mixed results in practice to be sure—but then how much success has anyone had?) to offer fulfilling visions of human life in nonreligious terms. Secular philosophies and their adherents, despite the excesses of Stalin or Hitler, the *Wall Street Journal* or *Playboy,* still often feel themselves every bit the legitimate equal or superior to religious perspectives. Whatever the rise of religion in recent decades, these secular perspectives are not going to go away. Religions are thus in competition with other perspectives. They are not, and they know it, the only game in town. *Third*, the creation of a world community of language, publishing, travel, and scholarship means that any religion knows—in a way it never did before—that it lives in a world of virtually countless *other* religions as well. While this encourages some fundamentalists to claim, endlessly, that they alone have the Truth, in others it produces an uncharacteristic and refreshing modesty.

This modesty is even more essential to the *fourth* dimension, which is that of knowledge of religion's own past sins. If not particularly widespread among the fundamentalists, this awareness is essential to those progressive elements of the new religiosity, and therefore relevant to spiritual deep ecology. Progressive Christians tend to have some awareness of the shameful history of Christian antisemitism, of inquisitions and pogroms. Reform, Reconstructionist, and Jewish Renewal groups, even as they may be calling for more traditional forms of observance, take stands against the sexism of traditional Judaism.

One central effect of all these changes is that religion in *our* world lacks innocence of its own history, its own limits, and its own powers. For the new breed of fundamentalists, this means that there is always an Other to be opposed or suppressed. For people with any kind of progressive awareness, to have Religion after Enlightenment is to be faced with the choice of adopting a kind of pre-enlightenment fanaticism or learning how to combine a real religious identity with a kind of postmodern relativism, Kierkegaardian subjectivism, or open-minded ecumenism.

While deep ecology is a powerful critic of modernist scientific and economic reductionism, it is, as Michael Zimmerman has argued, always quite difficult to transcend the limitations of the Enlightenment while simultaneously keeping its accomplishments. We see the consequences of the rejection of those accomplishments in religious totalitarianism of all stripes. Political notions of individual rights and a spiritual understanding that mystical knowledge is essentially metaphorical are both foreign to any form of fundamentalism. The mullahs of whatever faith are sure they know what God wants; and they have the whips and chains to put that knowledge into practice. The problem for all contemporary religions is to maintain religious passion—without devolving into pre-Enlightenment tyranny.

What does this mean for spiritual deep ecology? Well, as a loose collection of spiritually oriented individuals and groups, the issue of collective power exercised over others is hardly applicable. Deep ecologists are unlikely to be party to inquisitions or schisms. However, deep ecology *is* capable of its own kind of fundamentalism, its own blindness to its own moral failings and the possibility of being one-sided, narrow, and dictatorial. In its passion for nature ("No compromise in defense of Mother Earth!" is the slogan of the radical, deep ecologically oriented Earth First!) and its frustration over the way our global civilization is destroying so much of what we need and (should) love, deep ecologists can forget the complexity of contemporary moral life and the dangers that inevitably arise when one identifies oneself as the sole source of value.

In this regard I remember an exchange I once had with a leading animal rights activist and writer. He had just appeared at a panel on animal rights issues at a large academic conference. Many in the audience had been less than sympathetic, raising rather tired complaints about the rights of hunters and whether or not cauliflowers felt as much pain as veal calves and thus ought not to be eaten either. The writer in question, livid at their responses, told me how "They" just "didn't get it." And it seemed, "they never would." In a rare compassionate mood, I was able to put away my own tendencies to self-righteousness and point out that while I disagreed with his critics, we *all* had our faults. For instance, the money we used to fly to this conference, stay at the convention hotel, and have dinners on our academic travel accounts, could have been used for countless other purposes: for instance, to aid animals, people, or ecosystems in distress all over the world. A blank look came over my friend's face, and he drifted away to discuss animal rights with someone else.

In a deeper political vein, *any* politically oriented movement in the late twentieth century, whether it has a spiritual orientation or not, must be deeply self-critical. As all religions now exist only after the Inquisition, so any political movement—that is, any movement one of whose goals is the a fundamental change in social policy and structure—exists "after Stalin." That is, all political aspirations exist after we have seen self-proclaimed revolutionaries who represented (or claimed to represent) the interests of society as a whole, devolve into brutal tyrants. While communists turned out to be no more hypocritical, inconsistent, or destructive than their counterparts in the world of capitalist politics, their rhetoric was much grander. They defined themselves as the servants of the downtrodden, and became, instead, their new masters.

Spiritual deep ecologists, then, must beware the way deep ecology can combine, however inconsistently, or uneasily, with "other" things that are not so pretty. We might remember in this regard Hitler's vegetarianism, and the way some leading members of the Nazi party espoused the inherent values of the natural world, criticized the endless industrial destruction of nature, and sought to protect areas of German wilderness. Sadly, this fascist deep ecology was rooted in a nationalistic account of the "special" German relation to "the soil," a relation that necessarily excluded non-Aryans. This Nazi love of nature, and for some Nazis it was quite genuine, combined with a virulent hatred of Jews.[7]

Closer to home, contemporary deep ecologist writers have at times manifested a rather simple-minded misanthropy, seeing population issues as the source of our problems with nature rather than as a complex consequence of poverty, imperialism, and patriarchy. Perhaps more important, deep ecologists have sometimes been blind to the social inequalities that make up the human-nature relationship. It is not—as many have already pointed out—simply a matter of an undifferentiated, and self-centered "humanity" wreaking havoc with other life forms. Humanity is divided up into vastly unequal groups: men and women, North and South, capitalist and worker, World Bank manager and dispossessed peasants, agribusiness and farm laborer. To forget this is to misconceive the forces that are centrally implicated in the destruction we seek to end.[8]

To confront these realities, spiritual deep ecology needs *social theory*. It needs systematic theoretical resources to explain, for instance, the expansion of commodity production, the effects of the world market, and the relation between the exploitation of nature and domination of women. The moral posture of spiritual deep ecology, without the focused knowledge of critical social theory, will be naive.

This same need arises, I believe, for the moral posture of any religious sensibility. Religions were invented, after all, at a time of comparatively simple, comparatively transparent, social relations. "Love thy neighbor" makes a kind of rough and ready sense when people generally live in tribes and villages. Yet in a world of acid rain and global warming, our neighborhood is the entire earth. Similarly, "Thou shall not kill" becomes a lot harder to follow when "automatically" withheld taxes support a military machine or a simple commute to work damages the world's climate.

On the more personal level, morally oriented religious sensibilities (which include deep ecology and all other religions) have need of something like modern psychological theory to help explain and understand "sin." That is, the simple assertion of right and wrong, which is characteristic of Western religions, or the simple appeals to ignorance or Karma, which tend to arise in Buddhism or Hinduism, need to be deepened by psychological accounts of early trauma, compulsion, addictions, and neurosis. The culture of therapy cannot substitute for moral language. But, for all its faults, excesses, and stupidities, that culture cannot be discarded either. To understand *why* people find it hard to stop consuming, for instance, spiritual deep ecology had better have some idea about how selfhood in a decentered, mass society is built on consumption. Just railing against our collective "greed" will not do. Social psychologies describing the nexus of personhood, sexuality, human relations, the media, and commodities need to be brought to bear. Similar issues arise when spiritual deep ecologists try to fathom the meaning of our collective powerlessness in the face of ecological madness. Answers (albeit depressing ones) to the despairing "Why can't we change the way we live?" do not arise from within the religious and spiritual traditions, but from accounts of nonviolently coercive mechanisms of social control. These accounts are found in, for instance, early Frankfurt School theory, neo-Marxist accounts of ideology, or feminist descriptions of the consequences of patriarchy. In other words, the moral subject matter that is essential for religious life needs to be supplemented by bodies of thought that are themselves not necessarily religious at all.

In short, contemporary religious sensibilities, including spiritual deep ecology, are bound by a radically new humility about their own past performance and have a central need to avail themselves of the accomplishments of social and psychological theory. If we are in some way to make a New World or repair this one—which is the dream of any religion that wants to bring the divine to the earth—we had better understand what we are facing.

THE DANGERS OF LIBERALISM

For all its newfound modesty and openness to other theories, it is nevertheless crucial that post-Enlightenment religions not sink into a mild-mannered, anything goes liberalism. Religion that cannot take a stand, that (a little like Bill Clinton) blows with any wind that happens to turn up, is no religion at all. While a newfound diffidence about *metaphysical assertions* is one of the hallmarks of progressive post-Enlightenment religion, such a diffidence cannot be extended into the realm of *morality*.

Of course this distinction may well be hotly contested at times. But struggling with it might be one of the hallmarks of a progressive, post-Enlightenment religion. Surrounded by competing religious and nonreligious perspectives, and knowing that it cannot "prove" its account of God or the Divine, such a religion seeks to combine a commitment to moral value with a strongly—but openly (relativistically, subjectively, etc.)—held view of religious metaphysics. On the one hand, we try to coherently assert that there are many paths to the Truth and many names for God. At the same time, however, we are quite dogmatic about our belief that these paths do not include sexism, exploitation, or selfish violence. To have any relation to the Divine that is not escapist and simply irrelevant to human relations, our image of divinity must commit us to certain moral values—*and thus to certain social relationships*—over others. Our accounts of "God" may be evocative poetry or performative exhortation, but our assertions about right and wrong, good and evil, have to be a little more straightforward.

Many of the particular positive values of spiritual ecology are easily read from its sense of the holy. Sustainability, respect for other species, conservation, celebration of wilderness, etc.,—that the deep ecologist is committed to these in the abstract is clear. However, the dangers of wishy-washy liberalism arise for the deep ecologist when the bland images of nature that sometimes emerge from its discussions distort what "nature" really is like. For example, our mystically based love of life may not extend to the AIDS virus; and our wariness at tampering with the sacred character of nature might be suspended when it comes to using genetic engineering to cure cystic fibrosis. Ghetto rats will probably escape the purview that holds all of life as sacred; as might the black flies that cause widespread blindness in Africa. Adopting a deep ecological perspective will not eliminate the hard choices we face—choices about how much to take for ourselves and how much to leave for others; how much to exercise the control we increase day by day, and how much to surrender. And it will not turn the real world into a PBS special on butterflies or dolphins. The love we feel for the more-than-human is not a love that can erase the realities of struggle, conquest, and death—of nature as one long and frequently quite painful food chain.

THE DIFFICULT COMBINATION

There is no easy way to describe the struggle of post-Enlightenment religions. Or, rather, this struggle can be stated fairly easily but its accomplishment is another matter! How are we to take a religious sensibility that includes within itself moral demands on both ourselves and the rest of social life and makes them socially relevant while at the same time avoiding the perils of dogmatism, sectarianism, and—if it comes to that—violence? The power of religious inspiration can be so overwhelming, yet all too often when it has been translated into social life it has become (in retrospect) so pernicious. On the other hand, the image of a do-nothing, know-nothing religious sensibility, keyed purely to an interior sense of virtue, has itself become dubious.

In fact, a good deal of post-Enlightenment religion, of whatever political persuasion, is socially activist. Just as spiritual life is necessarily affected by the successes—and failures—of modern science, so it has been affected by modern political ideas. Particularly, since the French Revolution there has arisen the notion of an organized, systematic, ideology-driven transformation of social life as a whole. Whatever the fate of political movements led by this idea, a part of it has become central to religious life: the notion that our moral commitments are not seriously held if we do not seek to have them reflected in social life as a whole. The "neighbor" of the golden rule is now the city, the nation, the world. Religion, necessarily concerned with morality, is now necessarily concerned with politics. Yet politics often seems to be a realm of purely strategic maneuvering, a ruthless quest for power, or bureaucratic blindness to the common good. Therefore, while religion is attracted to politics, it is also inevitably repelled.

One answer to the dilemmas of these tensions among religion, morality, and politics may be found in the movements led by King and Gandhi. The moral power of nonviolent civil disobedience appeals to the heart of the Other, and makes us vulnerable even while we are opposing evil. It seems to avoid the twin dangers of moral arrogance and moral passivity. Of course, interfering with the workings of the world might well be experienced *as* violence by people's whose jobs (or even toys!) are threatened. Any serious movement of noncooperation with industrial civilization would probably throw a few people out of work, or at least disrupt the morning commute. Yet there is at least *something* mitigating in the way those engaged in civil disobedience are sufficiently respectful of those they oppose to be willing to accept the civic penalties for their acts. This lessens, but hardly eliminates, the degree to which those who would reorient civil life to religious values are experienced as threatening or even assaultive.

Yet it should be remembered that the effects of the movements led by Gandhi and King were mixed. Indian independence was followed by a civil war that led to millions of deaths, and brought into existence two nations that hardly embodied the spiritual values Gandhi espoused. Although the U.S. civil rights movement integrated public facilities and the voting booth, it did not make the United States a color-blind society. Even the massive federal interventions on behalf of African Americans (the War on Poverty, AFDC, Affirmative Action) might be said to be a product of ghetto riots more than lunch counter sit-ins.

Further, we should recognize that the success of nonviolent politics in some settings does not guarantee its effectiveness in all settings. And in any case, we should be clear to what extent our endorsement of it as a political method is based on our sense that it works better than its competitors or that it contains a moral correctness that leads us to choose it regardless of the outcome. (Suppose we found out, somehow, that well-timed clandestine assassinations actually worked better than nonviolence—would we make the switch? Is our commitment to nonviolence subject to any kind of empirical test? Or is it just that we refuse to be violent *no matter what the outcome*?)

Perhaps most painfully, a spiritual deep ecologist might well wonder if the severity of ecological issues makes a peaceful, nonviolent, gradualist approach inappropriate to his or her concerns. Gandhi or King could trust that if the present generation of Indians or blacks did not get independence or civil equality, why then, the next one would. However: if what we are doing is defending threatened species, protecting at-risk ecosystems, preventing massive changes to the global climate, or trying to save the bottom of our common food chain, then the stakes are higher and (possibly) much more immediate. It may be that we are faced with critical problems that, if not dealt with now, preclude any chance that they can be made good "later." To take an extreme example: if, during the height of the Cold War folly, I knew that a launch of nuclear missiles was about to take place, I would not have hesitated to use violence to stop it. In such a case the usual nonviolent argument that "violence only provokes more violence" would carry no weight—for the absence of my violence in this case would simply preclude the possibility of any moral relevance in the future—since we'd pretty much all be dead! The long-term effects of environmental damage may not be as destructive as a nuclear war, but they may be tending (albeit much more slowly) in that direction.

Does this mean that spiritual deep ecologists might well express their values in violent action? That a utilitarian calculus of comparative happiness and pain might justify wrecking bulldozers, assassinating corporate polluters, or at least engaging in ecotage without offering oneself up for punishment? Does it mean that it is more important to try to stop the machine than to provide a moral example?

I do not know the answers to these questions, and in any case this volume is not the place to pursue them at length. I do know, however, that no simple answer about the dangers of "violence" will settle the matter. As the French philosopher Maurice Merleau-Ponty pointed out in response to Arthur Koestler's critique of communist politics in *Darkness at Noon*, the violence is there *already*. The question is not whether there will be violence, but what will we do about the violence that exists? And in the case of environmental violence, it is pervasive, ongoing, and involves us all. Just taking part in our society, even if we recycle and eat organic vegetables, inevitably leads us to be part of it. Each time we drive, pay our taxes, or switch on the electricity, we are contributing.

In any case, I believe it is a mistake to think that "violence" is everywhere and always one thing—and that we therefore can say that it is, or is not, without exception justified or unjustified. There is the violence of war, mass public slaughter initiated by impersonal governments. There are the quiet killings that are part of covert operations. There are back-alley muggings. There is domestic violence, brutality covered by a cloak of family life. There is the daily violence of racism, sexism, and homophobia. And there are all the different ways in which we can be assaulted by poisons in the environment.

Given this range (and surely many more examples could be offered), we can also think of all the different forms that legitimate, spiritually oriented resistance, might develop. There are nonviolent demonstrations against war, pacifist refusals to serve in armies, boycotts of chemicalized foods, individual women who strike back against abusive husbands, or indigenous tribes who try to protect themselves from hired thugs. We do have the shining examples of Gandhi and King—and also the shining examples of Jews who during the Holocaust killed guards in concentration camps and blew up Nazi troop trains.

The meaning, effect, and value of "violence" may be rather different in these different settings. And therefore I believe we must examine each one very carefully before we say, with anything like moral assurance: "These actions in the social world are somehow essentially compatible with the essence of a religious or spiritual approach; and these are not."

CONCLUSION

Spiritual deep ecology is at once the oldest and the newest of world religions. Certainly long before anyone prayed to the sky gods, chanted the *Sutras*, or followed a table of commandments, human beings knelt before the splendor of sky and water, and bowed to the mysteries of birth and death. And now that the sky and water bear our mark, and we seek to make ourselves masters of birth and death, it has returned. Spiritual deep ecology faces a divinity that is itself under siege. We are called not only to obey the teachings of the more than human, but to save it from ourselves. While in certain versions of Judaism God needed our help to repair or complete His creation, and in Christianity God suffers the flesh and its pains, surely for deep ecology the divine is at its most vulnerable. There is no teaching here of a guaranteed outcome, no messiah who will without doubt come riding over the hill at the last minute to stave off the enemy. For spiritual deep ecology that which is most dear is right before our eyes—most immediate, most dear, most fragile. (For those who take the Gaia hypothesis seriously, and see the earth as capable of a kind of self-corrective maintenance, human-caused ecological damage may soon be corrected by changes that will settle our hash quite nicely. Yet this readjustment will not bring back the slaughtered species or the human cancer victims, both of whose numbers are rising daily. And any cosmic view that "in the end it's all nature anyway" surely misses the point that individual people, beings, and places that we love are being poisoned and destroyed.)

Its task is to make its peace with fragility, and somehow communicate to the other religions of the world the deep truth of how we all share it. As a small sect, deep ecology necessarily fails, for all it holds dear will be ravished. It depends for success on our collective will to live (or what's left of that will)—and on the hope that buried in each of us (or enough of us) is that remembered kinship with the divine mystery of all those simple beings that we can touch and see, smell and hear and eat. If we can be brought back to our senses, there is a chance that our sense of the holy can be saved. If we ruin this Creation, I am not sure how any of us—deep ecologist or traditional religionists, secular or spiritual—will be able to look ourselves in the eye. And what will be left of religion, any religion, if that is the point to which we come?

NOTES

1. This period is variously construed as beginning with the fall of the female/nature gods some four to six thousand years ago, with the rise of monotheism three to four thousand years ago, or with the emergence of modern science and technology in the fifteenth to seventeenth centuries.

2. Of the vast literature that could be cited, here are four: David Abram, *The Spell of the Sensuous: Language and Perception in a More than Human World* (New York: Pantheon, 1997); Joanna Macy, *World as Lover, World as Self* (Berkeley: Parallax, 1994); Edward Abbey, *The Monkey Wrench Gang* (New York: Fawcett, 1974); Paul Shepard, *Nature and Madness* (San Francisco: Sierra Club, 1982).

3. Stephen R. Kellert and E. O. Wilson, eds., *The Biophilia Hypothesis* (Washington, DC: Island Press, 1993).

4. See Roger S. Gottlieb, *A Spirituality of Resistance: Finding a Peaceful Heart and Protecting the Earth* (New York: Crossroad: 1999).

5. Georg Lukacs, *History and Class Consciousness* (Cambridge, MA: MIT Press, 1971).

6. Stephanie Kaza, *The Attentive Heart: Conversations with Trees* (New York: Ballantine: 1993), 17.

7. See Michael Zimmerman, "Ecofascism: A Threat to American Environmentalism?" in *The Ecological Community*, ed. Roger S. Gottlieb (New York: Routledge, 1997).

8. I have developed this point at length in "Spiritual Deep Ecology and the Left," in *This Sacred Earth: Religion, Nature, Environment*, ed. Roger S. Gottlieb (New York: Routledge, 1996).

2

Indigenous Traditions
and Deep Ecology

John A. Grim

Kinship with all creatures of the earth, sky and water was a real and
active principle. For the animal and bird world there existed a
brotherly feeling that kept the Lakota safe among them. . . . The old
Lakota was wise. He knew that man's heart away from nature becomes hard; he knew that lack of respect for growing, living things
soon led to lack of respect for humans too. So he kept his youth
close to its softening influence.
—Luther Standing Bear, *Land of the Spotted Eagle*

Diversity enhances the potentialities of survival, the chances of
new modes of life, the richness of forms. And the so-called struggle of life and survival of the fittest, should be interpreted in the
sense of ability to co-exist and co-operate in complex relationships,
rather than ability to kill, exploit and suppress. . . . Ecologically-
inspired attitudes therefore favour diversity of human ways of life,
of cultures, of occupations, of economies. They support the fight
against economic and cultural, as much as military invasion and
domination, and they are opposed to the annihilation of seals and
whales as much as to that of human tribes or cultures.
—Arne Naess, "The Shallow and the Deep,
Long Range Ecology Movement"

THESE STATEMENTS by the Lakota writer, Luther Standing Bear, on
kinship, and by the father of deep ecology, Arne Naess, on diversity signal similarities and differences between these ways of

35

facing the world. In many instances the insights of indigenous peoples have been taken for granted as environmentally sensitive, but those appreciative often show little understanding of the thought and practice of indigenous communities. Recently, indigenous scholars have objected to an overly facile identification of environmentalism and traditional native life. These moments of discord present opportunities to consider the difference and resistance that indigenous peoples present to dominant societies.

Long known for their peaceful ways, the Hopi peoples of the Pueblo Southwest in the United States dismayed pacifists who had come to them expecting them to eagerly join their demonstrations. It seems the Hopi do not always agree that philosophical similarities necessarily lead to concerted actions.[1] Similar insights have occurred when environmental activists, who articulated philosophical positions associated with deep ecology, encountered native peoples who had their own ways of knowing and interacting with local regions. This lack of immediate collaboration has puzzled some environmentalists. Exploring both disjunctions and points of connection, this essay focuses on the relationships of *indigenous traditions* to *deep ecology*. Both communities of concern are alert to the diversity of local life, the interconnected character of the different orders of life, the ambiguities faced by the human in verbally expressing experiences of relatedness to life, and the depth of spiritual maturity acquired by intimacy with living things. So why are there occasional misunderstandings in this seemingly intrinsic alliance?

Three areas of comparative consideration will be discussed here, namely, *approaches, politics,* and *religions.* The term *comparative* is used here because such different entities, namely, the environmental thought systems broadly identified as deep ecology and those exceedingly diverse societies suggested by the phrase *indigenous traditions* are being imagined as creating a field for dialogue. Also, the author of this work is not himself a member of an indigenous society. The interpretive discussion is framed in an academic context and, as such, is a comparative project. Drawing largely from ethnography, this brief study discusses views of indigenous traditions that are taken from the written record. As such, this study is already removed from the experiential knowledge and communal contexts of understanding so basic to the peoples and traditions being discussed. Yet, the focus on experiential insights gained from contact with the living world, which is common to both indigenous traditions and deep ecology, may at times bridge that distance and align some misunderstandings.

These two topics, namely, indigenous traditions and deep ecology, are difficult to define since they have come to be used in so many different settings. Who are indigenous peoples? In a straightforward manner, "indigenous" refers to anything produced, growing, or living naturally in a particular region or environment. There are semantic and political difficulties involved in determining which peoples are indigenous. To a large extent these issues are beyond the scope of this discussion, but it is significant to note that the United Nations continues to grapple with these issues. The United Nations Declaration on the Rights of Indigenous Peoples, prepared for approval by the separate nation-states during the Decade of Indigenous Peoples (1994–2004), has posed this question largely within international law and human rights contexts.[2]

In these international forums, indigenous refers to ethnic groups with obvious cultural, linguistic, and kinship bonds who are often so marginalized by modern nation-states that their inherent dignity and coherence as societies are in danger of being lost. It is interesting to note that the stated goals of this "International Decade of the World's Indigenous Peoples" stress several issues such as human rights, social and economic justice, cultural diversity, and technical assistance—all of which are crucial. The central issue of homelands, however, seems carefully avoided, no doubt to gain the necessary signatories among the UN member states. Yet the issue of indigenous homelands and how they are understood both internationally and within nation-states having native populations is a critical item in any consideration of indigenous environmental thought.

The term *traditions* also deserves some comment as it may connote for some a fixed body of ceremonial and mythological lore slowly eroding in the acids of modernity. More pointedly, this negative view often sees any commitment to traditional life as a technological problem. Indigenous peoples are seen as caught in a less evolved cultural morass from which they need to be liberated through awareness and acceptance of modernity. That position is questioned here. For this essay, "traditions" refers to viable cultural wholes, or lifeways, that have continually been transforming themselves in ongoing encounters with other indigenous and non-indigenous peoples. They have, as well, been significantly altered of late by encounters with global economic forces and by industrialized modes of resource exploitation.

That indigenous cultures have survived demonstrates that they are capable of assimilating information from the non-native world, and of reinventing themselves through creative internal pathways closely related to what is commonly called "nature."[3] Indigenous terms for their local homelands typically do not separate out the ensemble of subsistence activities, ways of knowing, and ritual celebrations from the natural world. At present these thousands of remaining indigenous societies are under extreme pressures not only to adapt more mainstream economic lifestyles, but also to open their homelands for resource exploitation by multinational corporations and dominant nation-states.

Connections between indigenous traditions and deep ecology have been suggested since the phrase, deep ecology, was first introduced by the Norwegian philosopher Arne Naess, in 1973. It was nearly a decade before that original paper, "The Shallow and the Deep, Long-range Ecology Movements," received wider attention and articulation, for example, in Bill Devall and George Sessions's *Deep Ecology: Living As If Nature Mattered*. When that attention was given to deep ecology as a mode of environmental thought, indigenous traditions were identified as one of the "minority" traditions that reversed the oppressive, rapacious, hierarchical dimensions of the majority. These minority traditions were seen as rich with examples demonstrating the two key norms of deep ecology, namely, "self-realization" and "biocentric equality."

Labelled "primal," indigenous traditions were seen as embodying these norms in a manner that existed prior to modernity. This view of the diverse native traditions as manifesting a universal, environmentally sensitive humanity has been much criticized as culturally naïve. That is, indigenous communities are too diverse for such broad generalizations. Moreover, the devastating challenges facing native peoples cut across non-native philosophical views of these traditions and their subsistence relations with local bioregions. What might be more helpful are efforts to understand indigenous thought regarding: the diversity of indigenous lifeways, different community attitudes toward surrounding bioregions, the destructive pressures of globalization on indigenous homelands, and the right of indigenous peoples to express their own positions especially in public forums.

More recent works, related to but distinguished from deep ecology's radical environmentalism, such as the "land ethic" perspective of J. Baird Callicott, go a long way toward correcting the cultural limitations of earlier deep ecology views of indigenous peoples. Callicott comes to a postmodern affirmation of cultural diversity in the context of a reconstructive dialogue in which environmental ethics are plural, local, networked, and scientifically informed.[4] In this scenario indigenous traditions do not simply have a place at the table of deep ecological thought as a "minority," rather, these specific traditions have important roles in all their particularity, problems, and potential for understanding human-earth interactions. Seeking to expand this dialogue, the following section considers deep ecology and indigenous traditions in terms of their various approaches, or ways of knowing the earth.

APPROACHES

This section examines some of the conceptual foundations underlying both deep ecology and indigenous traditions. As an opening observation, it is appropriate to recall that deep ecology refers to a philosophical school with an activist agenda that demonstrates changes in the twenty years of its formulation.[5] Indigenous traditions refer to actual, dynamic societies whose identities are embedded in land, language, subsistence practices, kinship, narratives and time-honored customs.[6] This rich array of interrelated activities constitutes an indigenous lifeway. The indigenous conceptual approaches embedded in these lifeways were formerly dismissed by rational critics as superstitious, overly lax and immoral, or overly controlling and lacking the analytical distance required for rational thought.

What becomes obvious is that those misunderstandings failed to understand the complexity of indigenous concepts that constellate as a means of thinking about community relatedness to the earth. In a comparative context, deep ecology can be distinguished initially from a particular indigenous tradition's environmental knowledge as oriented more toward individuals than communities. "Communities" differ a great deal in indigenous contexts. For example, the concept of "person" extends into the natural world in Algonkian languages, and the consequent respect and regard given to individual persons is accorded in this indigenous thought system to the experience of some sites, lakes, stones, or winds.[7] Indigenous ways of knowing the world, then, were not expressed in abstract propositions, but in the symbolic language of visions and mythic narratives that are intimately connected to kinship, and ceremonials, place names, and sacred sites. As one native scholar says, "Over a long period of time tribes developed a general knowledge which linked together the most prominent sacred places. Some of these linkages evolved into ceremonial calendar years, instructing people when and where to hold ceremonies. Other combinations described hunting and fishing cycles and migrations."[8] Teaching a daughter how to gather grasses and weave a basket, or teaching a son the skills of hunting, trapping, and fishing draw on epistemologies of life lived close to a bioregion.

Deep ecology approaches the world as a call to a way of knowing that has philosophical, moral, and political implications for individuals. The key norms of deep ecology, namely, self-realization and biocentric equality, indicate a move beyond the Cartesian dualistic world view of the human as knowing subject and the natural world as simply objects known by the human.[9] In deep ecology the small "s," or individual self, is set within the capital "S," the larger Self of relatedness to all beings. Similarly, the Newtonian-Deist worldview of mechanistic science is rejected as a form of "shallow" ecology that addresses environmental problems from out of a techno-fix mentality. That is, mechanistic science is seen as an instrumentalist position that conceives all human and natural activity as capable of being altered, or "fixed," by human technological intervention. Arne Naess calls for a deeper, transformative vision that is cognizant of scientific insights when he writes:

> The central issue is that of transcending ecology as a science, looking for wisdom through the study of ecophilosophy, striving for an *ecosophy*—a total view inspired in part by the science of ecology and the activities of the deep ecology movement.[10]

The philosophical positions emphasized here are a "total view" and commitment to a radical investigation in which individuals question and explore larger, cosmological understandings of him or herself. There is both a Socratic and pre-Socratic character to this philosophical quest. One pointedly questions oneself about the gaps and blind forgettings in one's knowledge such as the deeper meanings of the material body and the sensual character of thought. Yet, there is also the search for the cosmological perspective of relatedness to the larger whole. This search for the "wisdom that men once knew" brings deep ecologists to see their formative sources as broad.[11] They include: "perennial philosophy, pastoral/naturalist literary tradition, science of ecology, 'new physics,' some Christian sources, feminism, philosophies of primal (or native) peoples, some Eastern spiritual traditions, and Gandhi's reflections on nonviolence and civil disobedience."[12]

Underlying the philosophical journey of the individual is an accompanying ethical call to action. In the following quote the deep ecology quest for self-realization and biocentric equality finds more local and regional focus:

> In addition to preserving species, an evolutionary and ecological ethic is concern with preserving natural processes and other biotic wholes. It is concerned with safeguarding genetic diversity and with preserving a substantial and widely distributed sample of the hierarchy of eco-systems—from ten-acre ponds and forty acre woodlots to vast moist tropical forests, deserts, temperate prairies, subarctic steppes, and arctic tundra. Its ultimate concern is to ensure the health and integrity of the biosphere as a whole. As Aldo Leopold expresses the summary moral maxim—the golden rule—

of the land ethic: "A thing is right when it tends to preserve the integrity, stability, and beauty of the biotic community. It is wrong when it tends otherwise."[13]

Here the larger "Self" of Naess's vision is framed within the "biosphere as a whole." Such an ethical turn helps to ground deep ecology and respond to charges that its cosmological move is actually a rationalizing and totalizing perspective that has political implications that may actually further marginalize indigenous peoples.[14] That is, moving from the environmental malaise to the cosmological gaze suggests that there is a univocal hyper-human perspective from which to understand relatedness to the world. Such a perspective is attributed to indigenous traditions. Callicott, however, avoids this type of cosmological distancing yet establishes relatedness to local life. Rather than evoking religion as a sleight of mind in which the human acquires a Brahmanic or transcendent God-like wisdom, recent efforts in deep ecology seek to understand cultural and religious modes for producing knowledge that engage the local bioregion as revelatory of life. With these perspectives and critiques of the approaches of deep ecology in mind, discussion of Maori perspectives provides entry into an indigenous approach to the world.

The Maori, native peoples of New Zealand, speak of themselves as *tangata whenua*, "people of the land." By grounding their identity as a people in their homeland, the Maori are not simply expressing a nationalistic patriotism, namely, that the land marks historic events that legitimate their coming to be a distinct ethnic group. Rather, *whenua* first and foremost evokes the Earth-mother herself, *Papa-tuanuku*, and, then, refers to the placenta.[15] Land is the connection both to larger mythologized cosmic forces as well as to the source of personal life. This approach is embedded in the traditional cosmogonic narratives that have been transmitted into the present by Maori individuals who have special ritual roles in their communities because of this knowledge.[16] Those myths describe how the Sky-father, *Ranginui*, is separated from the Earth-mother by their offspring, *Tane-mahuta*. This child, and the other children of *Rangi* and *Papa*, eventually give rise to all of creation. Thus, the mythic offspring bring about the primordial separation that introduces into creation such disparate, yet interconnected, forces as yearning, ambiguity, and fecundity.

Knowing, then, as an act of kinship and a way of dealing with primal forces is involved in all human relations with the natural world. Empirical observation in the Maori world view is accompanied by other modes of knowing. Interactions with the environment bring humans into contact with the *mana,* or inherent standing all of reality. That is, the existence of something carries within it, according to Maori thought, an inherent right to be where it is. The myths explain and affirm such different attitudes and actions associated with the hard *mana* of competition and aggression, as well as the soft *mana* of compassion and cooperation. All creatures possess *mana* suggesting that all reality has intrinsic worth, as well as a personal lifeforce, *maori.*

A proverb of the Maori presents a glimpse of this dynamic, interactive approach to the earth. The proverb reads: *Te toto o te tangata, he kai; te oranga o te tangata, he whenua,* which translates "The blood *(toto)* of humans *(tangata)* comes from food *(kai);* our welfare *(oranga)* comes from land *(whenua).*"[17] This Maori teaching links "blood," with the "food" that comes from the death of one's non-human kin, namely, animals and plants. The taking of life brings another set of inherent forces into the conceptual thought that undergirds Maori traditional environmental knowledge. In addition to *mana,* all food carries individual *tapu,* or sacredness. Subsistence practices involve treatment of our kin (the creatures) in ways that may be harmful to them but beneficial to ourselves. Inner life, or "blood," say the Maori depends upon correct spiritual relations with the creatures including ritual treatment of their *tapu.* "Welfare," or material prosperity, for the Maori flows from ethical relations with the land.

In effect, the ability of human individuals embedded within larger kin-groups to establish and maintain right relationships with the *mana, maori,* and *tapu* of creatures brings into being the *tangata whenua.* These knowledge-based processes establish the *maori,* or life force, of the people. *Maori,* moreover, can only be established by acting responsibly (*turangawaewae* "standing feet") or standing by the teachings. The traditional authority that Maori evoke to establish their claims to be *tangata whenua* in a particular local place in Aoteroa/New Zealand proceeds from an approach that takes the cosmological narratives seriously and responsibly. Indeed, the anthropologist Gregory Schrempp observed that, "the Maori appear to have maximally invested themselves in cosmology: they have adopted cosmology as the privileged idiom of their self-identification, sense of values, and political/social theory. If any society can be expected to have exhausted the possibilities of this concern, it would be this one."[18] The cosmological position establishes all the creatures, not simply the human, in a web of kinship that is also a conceptual schema. The ancestral prerogatives that come down to the present entail responsible approaches to the creatures and to the land in a way that is quite different from the conceptual positions of the ecological sciences that undergird deep ecology.

Politics

In April 1984 Arne Naess and George Sessions framed the deep ecology platform of eight "Basic Principles" of which numbers 6 and 8 have strong policy implications. They are: #6) "Politics must therefore be changed. These policies affect basic economic, technological, and ideological structures. The resulting state of affairs will be deeply different from the present"; and #8) "Those who subscribe to the foregoing points have an obligation directly or indirectly to try to implement the necessary changes."[19] The old order of politics that must be changed, according to this early presentation of deep ecology, is the complete subordination of any and all life to economic commodification and industrial exploitation.

Deep ecology critiques the dominant political agenda for implementing sustainable practices only for human welfare while other species continually lose habitat toward possible extinction. In opposing this commercialization beyond the commons, deep ecology focuses on wilderness as an ideal conservation ethic. This position echoes Henry David Thoreau's thought when he wrote:

> What I have been preparing to say is this, in wildness is the preservation of the world. . . . Life consists of wildness. The most alive is the wildest. Not yet subdued to man, its presence refreshes him. . . . When I would re-create myself, I seek the darkest wood, the thickest and most interminable and to the citizen, most dismal swamp. I enter as a sacred place, a *Sanctum sanctorum*. There is the strength, the marrow, of Nature. In short, all good things are wild and free.[20]

The shift from Thoreau's metaphysical term "wildness" to deep ecology's emphasis on "wilderness" suggests more than semantic differences. It orients the reader to a broad environmental activism transcending regional and national issues. The political views of deep ecology parallel, for example, the reform environmental politics of David Brower. He also objected to the treatment of undeveloped areas as potential outdoor recreation spaces or as subject to a "wise-use" conservation strategies of simply holding land for future human exploitation.

Almost unwittingly the spiritually nourishing view of "wilderness" became a perspective for critiquing the intrusive character of the modern human. In this sense, wilderness touted that place in which the human was absent as a space of spiritual solace and nourishment. Ironically, this imaging of wilderness as solace reverses an earlier American imaging of the savage wilderness of the pagan Indians into which the Puritans of

Massachusetts hoped to establish the city (New Jerusalem) as a beacon for the healing of the Old World. Deep ecology obviously draws on earlier Western philosophical and religious thought systems, but it transforms gnostic tendencies that interpreted material reality as simply degraded. Deep ecology has also held onto aspects of the prophetic call to accountability. Reversing perceived antagonisms to sacred land within Judaism and Christianity deep ecology calls for an ethos of reverence for the earth. Thus, deep ecology combines both an invitation to philosophical and ethical reflection as well as an appeal for environmental activism.

Expressions of the radical, or "deep," political and ethical implications of deep ecology, appear in the eco-defense practices of Greenpeace, Earth First!, and the Sea Shepherd Conservation Society. Seeing itself as the most militant group, Earth First! also attempts to model radical forms of social organization by being nonhierarchial, nonbureaucratic, maintaining no central headquarters, and avoiding wasteful practices that compromise the group's ecological vision.[21] Drawing on Gandhi's teachings regarding nonviolence, and deep ecology's articulation of the inherent dignity and worth of all creation, Earth First! members have carried on a campaign of militant environmentalism against overt ecological abuse, yet, even these militant practices have been revised when human life was endangered. Thus, earlier efforts to stop logging by placing metal spikes in trees have been curtailed when loggers and sawyers were endangered by this practice.

Alongside the visions of Thoreau and Gandhi, Earth First! members have explored their affinities with Native North American religions to the point of participating in, and adapting, a range of indigenous ritual practices.[22] Interestingly, even as Earth First! members adapt American Indian rituals in an effort to recover primal connections to the land, some Earth First! leaders have been critical of Native American subsistence practices and current land use policies.[23] Three policy issues emerge as points of tension and comparison between deep ecology and indigenous traditions, namely, the politicization of land as "wilderness," the charge of ecological abuse by indigenous peoples, and the adaptation of indigenous symbols and rituals into environmental religiosity.

From an indigenous perspective "wildness" and "wilderness," as areas in which the human is absent, are puzzling concepts. For example, Robert Jarvenpa reports of the Chipewyan and Han, Athapaskan peoples of the North American subarctic, that a number of relationships link humans to these open spaces. He writes:

> To the outsider, much of the subarctic landscape may appear "empty" or "unoccupied." This notion holds little meaning for

Athapaskans who see virtually all their surroundings as active, alive or occupied in some fashion. Almost any space, whether within or beyond the confines of currently inhabited settlements or camps, may have functioned previously as a culturally meaningful landscape where events transpired and activities occurred.

A fine-grained understanding of the landscape is symbolically codified in language. Athapaskan place name terminologies recognize a myriad of geographical features over extensive regions. Many of these are trenchant descriptions of environmental features and processes. The Chipewyan expression *ts'ankwi ttheba* ("old woman rapids") not only denotes a particularly turbulent section of the Mudjatik River but also evokes the circumstances of a tragic death at that location generations ago. In this way, conventional language and discourse continually situate the topographical landscape in terms of peoples' history and lore.[24]

From a Dene perspective, then, "wilderness" as the absence of the human is not a working concept. Rather, the traditional environmental knowledge (TEK) of open spaces is transmitted in a complex narrative, mnemonic system based on place names.[25] These place names may or may not refer to what outsiders call sacred sites.

Quite often an indigenous peoples' religious focus on a particular geographical site is seen by deep ecologists as an affirmation of "wilderness." That is, a natural site whose aesthetic, mythic, historic, or religious importance calls for special community protection and conservation. What is strikingly different between the two positions, however, is the understanding of how humans interact with that site. Typically, the indigenous sociopolitical commitment to homelands and sacred sites is characterized by a sense of space that has strong individual and communal biographical dimensions, a sense of ancestors placed in the land, and a traditional recognition of spiritual presences in selected sites. Thus, a site may be numinous and, as such, avoided, but the absence of humans does not confer spiritual value.

The Lakota lawyer and intellectual, Vine Deloria, saw a striking example of the confusion between indigenous use of homelands and environmental "wilderness" protection as that concept was used in the Supreme Court case *Lyng v. Northwest Indian Cemetery Protective Association*, 1988. Deloria wrote:

According to popular definitions of wilderness, its primary value is as an area in its pristine natural state, because this represents some intangible and difficult to define spiritual aspect of nature that has a superior value to commercial use of the land. In a sense we have a generalized secular use, albeit one that represents a recognition of intangible values no matter how shallow they might be emotionally, now holding a greater value than a specific religious use of the same region. The question here is whether the Indian argument is to be considered inferior to the wilderness argument because of a racial distinction.

Unfortunately, at the circuit court level and later with the Supreme Court, the close parallel in motive and perspective was neither recognized nor understood. This neglect should be a warning to Indians and non-Indians alike that the popular belief prevailing that non-Indians can somehow absorb the philosophical worldview of American Indians and inculcate "reverence" for the land into their intellectual and emotional perspectives is blatantly false. Inherent in the very definition of "wilderness" is contained the gulf between the understandings of the two cultures. Indians do not see the natural world as a wilderness. In contrast, Europeans and Euroamericans see a big difference between lands they have "settled" and lands they have left alone. As long as this difference is believed to be real by non-Indians, it will be impossible to close the perceptual gap, and the substance of the two views will remain in conflict.[26]

Deloria points out the ironies that Native American efforts to present a multiple-use argument was rejected in these legal proceedings by an argument based on "wilderness" preservation. That is, the native claim was turned back by a majority on the court saying that the indigenous minority argument threatened the preservation of the "wilderness" character of the region while a logging road did not. The indigenous argument would have prioritized the protection of native gravesites but not eliminated other non-native uses. Deloria sees the "wilderness" argument as a form of secular spiritualizing that is foreign to native perspectives. The "wilderness" conservation ethos suggests that the absence of humans and their intrusive work, marks the land as more meditative and spiritual. Indigenous lifeways emphasize the commingling of the spiritual and the material, and the covenantal character of working in and with the land.

Deloria's arguments mount a direct challenge to the deep ecology political position of preserving some environments by prohibiting and restricting human presence. Embedded in this exchange, of course, is the implicit agreement that indigenous lifestyles from Deloria's viewpoint, and "minority" traditions from a deep ecology perspective, do not degrade the landscape in the devastating manner of modern urban settlements and resource extraction. Two disagreements persist, however: first, the charge that some indigenous subsistence practices damage the environment and in the remote past actually extinguished species. Second, the critique of Native American scholars that radical environmentalists seeking self-realization openly exploit American Indian ritual life and thereby endanger the very indigenous peoples they emulate.

Without dwelling on the charge of environmental abuse by Paleolithic and more recent indigenous groups, it can be said that the arguments regarding the extinction of the megafauna in earlier geological periods are based on incomplete evidence.[27] Indigenous scholars respond, however, that the accusation of Paleolithic extinctions and more recent environmental abuse by indigenous peoples is simply a ploy to reduce indigenous lifeways to another example of human cultural fallibility. Indigenous spokespeople counter that such a charge suits the global development model of dominant societies that commodifies everything. Native scholars ask, is it not the case, "that Europeans found the Western Hemisphere to be a natural treasure house [which] indicates that misuse of the environment was not frequent or sustained over long periods of time."[28] More pertinent, suggest scholars of indigenous traditions, than the limited environmental damage of such indigenous practices as slash and burn agriculture is the appropriation of indigenous religiosity by environmentalists seeking "self-realization."

The projection after World War II of an ideal environmental model onto Native Americans by some conservationists has been seen as problematic. So also, the deep ecology movement may also have unwittingly intensified the appropriation of indigenous American Indian ritual life. Many environmental activists have looked to indigenous traditions for ways of cultivating environmental self-realization without grasping the politically sensitive character of religious lifeways. At times, adaptations of native symbols and practices by environmentalists have been guided by Native American teachers. Other American Indian leaders and scholars have criticized such sharing and borrowing as examples of ongoing colonial exploitation that undermines native cultures. George Tinker describes the borrowing of indigenous culture that has little or no understanding of the actual economic realities of native peoples. He writes:

> There are those in the world today who regularly espouse an environmental consciousness predicated on American Indian belief systems, summoning images of a simpler existence with a built-in

concern for the whole of creation. This common notion that American Indian peoples and other indigenous peoples have some
spiritual and mystical insight on environmental issues confronting the world today is usually an instinctive if unstudied
recognition of the differentness of those cultures. It thus tends to
be a relatively intuitive truth-claim based on little research and an
overabundance of romanticization. Even those who have had the
opportunity to witness the poverty of our poorest reservations,
evidenced by the rusting hulks of worn-out automobiles parked
in various states of abandonment around reservation homes, continue to recite their own facile version of Native concerns for the
environment.[29]

Some may say that Tinker is too hard on the rusted automobiles here,
but he lays down a striking challenge to those non-natives who admire
native thought without realizing that these communities struggle for a
just and moral survival. Others have suggested that the borrowing and
sharing is more complex with the possibilities for cultural respect and
religious innovation as likely as outright exploitation leading to the
degradation of native cultures.[30]

One critic of the environmentalists' appropriation of native ideas
and practices says: "Environmentalists are right to reach out to American Indians, and indeed original peoples throughout the world, for help
in discovering less destructive ecological ideas and practices. However,
we must not accept their aid and then cause their issues and their cultures to become the first causalities in our fight against environmental
responsibility."[31] What also remains to be clearly understood is the political role of current tribal governments in ecological assessment and
management. Tribal regulatory power on reservations requires that
these governing bodies, as well as federal and state environmental regulatory agencies, find ways to incorporate the values of indigenous ecological wisdom into environmental monitoring.[32]

RELIGIONS

In describing the norms of deep ecology, namely self-realization and
biocentric equality, Devall and Sessions make pointed connections with
religion. They write that these norms "are not in themselves derivable
from other principles or intuitions. They are arrived at by the deep
questioning process and reveal the importance of moving to the philosophical or religious level of wisdom."[33] Distinctions can be made
between the deep ecology movement associated with the platform prin-

ciples, Arne Naess's personal ecosophy, and the diversity of approaches to ecophilosophy. Not all of them have developed religious components, but Arne Naess laid down strong orientations toward religions. Naess is not particularly interested in institutional religions or even ethical systems in which many might look for texts supportive of environmental concern. Naess's concerns regarding religion are more experiential and intuitional. He writes:

> I'm not much interested in ethics or morals. I'm interested in how we experience the world. . . . Ethics follows from how we experience the world. If you experience the world so and so then you don't kill. If you articulate your experience then it can become a philosophy or religion.[34]

The Australian deep ecologist, John Seed, gives expression to the religious intuitions of Naess in a manner that is closer to indigenous perspectives than the South Asian Vedantic orientations that Naess himself acknowledges.[35] Seed wrote:

> As the implications of evolution and ecology are internalized . . . there is an identification with all life. . . . Alienation subsides. . . . "I am protecting the rain forest" develops to "I am part of the rain forest protecting myself. I am that part of the rain forest recently emerged into thinking."[36]

John Seed's mystical imaging of a deep ecology position is a powerful psychological performative that has elicited strong positive responses. It is also open to the critique of totalizing the anthropocentric position of the human as the ultimate observer and the essential link to all reality. One wonders who the "I" is in his moving statement and what relation that identity has to native peoples of the rain forest. Has there been sufficient reflection up to this point regarding the potential hegemonic character of scientific narratives, especially the story of evolution, in its relation to oral narrative traditions? Ethical questions surround this personal identification of the individual deep ecologist with the rain forest and other natural forms. This is especially the case if a deep mystical identification disregards the indigenous peoples who are being exterminated in those very rain forests.

When indigenous religions are considered in these intuitive journeys of self-realization, some of the following themes provide orientation for understanding the differences between indigenous religions and deep ecology, namely, *kinship*, and *spatial and biographical relations with place*. On the other hand, *traditional environmental knowledge*, and *cosmology* are themes that emphasize the shared concerns of indigenous communities and deep ecology.

As an example of these features of indigenous traditions and ecology consider the following description of the Temiar people of Malaysia. They speak of their quest to contact and transmit *kahyek* which they understand as a cool, healing liquid. *Kahyek* is the form taken by the upper soul of a spiritual being from the local Malayan rain forest. It can be imparted to human beings through dreams. The songs imparted in dreams enable selected humans to evoke and transmit this healing *kahyek*. The anthropologist, Marina Roseman, in her work *Healing Sounds from the Malaysian Rainforest*, wrote that:

> The Temiar locate themselves in social relations of kinship both with human and, through dream encounters, with the interactive spirits of their environment. These positions are reiterated each time they address one another, using terms such as "sister's husband" or "mother of [the dreamer]." In their dream they establish kinship relations with spirits who emerge, identify themselves, and give the gift of song. Receipt of a dream song from a spiritguide marks the pivotal moment in the development of mediums and healers. The song, sung during a ceremonial performance by the medium and an interactive female chorus, links medium, chorus, trance-dancers, and patient as they "follow the path" of the spiritguide. When the ceremony concludes, spirits and humans "return home" *(me am)* to their respective abodes.[37]

Such intimate relations with the landscape are often evident in the names given to specific places, trees, rocks, or rivers. Naming the landscape not only maps local spaces, but it can also express sacred regard for the environment by means of biographical memory of personal religious experiences at particular places. Naming marks abiding relations with place by means of kinship, and spatial relations. These modes of indigenous geographical linkage are completely different than rational markers of historical place. Indigenous relations with place might also express community identity, make present ancestors, and evoke oral narratives.[38] For example, the Dogon peoples of Mali in Africa are justifiably famous for their age-graded cosmologies which elaborate the close relationships that living Dogon share with their ancestors, their land, and the animals among whom the soon to be living reside.[39]

Along with kinship, spatial, and biographical relationships with places, another key feature of indigenous lifeways is traditional environmental knowledge. Just as individual Temiar of Malaysia demarcate their homelands as the resident spaces of significant memories, they also know the gifts of the spirits of herbs, roots, and other medicines capable of transforming human lives. Thus, the chronology of individual lives vested in named places in the environment is paralleled by the collective, empirical observations of the people regarding local flora and fauna.

Traditional indigenous environmental knowledge and deep ecology share a respect for animal and plant life though the conceptual basis for that respect is quite different. Perhaps one way to flag those differences is to focus on the giving act of animals and plants recognized by indigenous thought traditions. Plants and animals in the conceptual systems of many indigenous peoples willingly sacrifice their own lives for the human in need. Thus, indigenous traditions are distinguished by their consistent integration of religious attitudes in subsistence acts especially in accepting the gift of animal and plant lives. Deep ecology, furthermore, is identified with the perspective of biocentric equality, namely, the view that human needs are no more privileged than those of other species. Indigenous peoples generally regard species as unique in their own particularity, but not necessarily equal. That is, birds are better at flying and in being birds than fish. They are different, not equal. Even animals that come together to drink at the same waterhole, says an African Massai proverb, do not mate. They may share needs but they are not simply equals. This recognition of difference between "nations" of beings who nevertheless show respect and caution with one another is evident in the traditional environmental knowledge of indigenous peoples. The Salish-speaking Colville peoples on the Columbia River of eastern Washington, for example, weave ritual forms of knowing and proper approach into their sacred taxonomies of plants.[40]

Among the Yekuana peoples of Venezuela an ethics, constructed with mythological references, accompanies their traditional environmental knowledge. For example, the pragmatic use of plants and roots among the Yekuana as well as the location of grasses and roots for basket making are infused with religious dynamics of danger and allure, which also relate to personal and social accomplishment.[41] The Yekuana have developed a complex set of ethical teachings connecting the emergence of designs for baskets, the materials for making baskets, and limits on collecting those materials. Set within cosmological stories of the culture hero, Wanadi, these numinous webs of relationships are negotiated within the tense and ambiguous skein of the human condition. That is, the Yekuana participate in both the cosmic struggle of Odosha, Wanadi's troublesome offspring, as well as with the creative presence of Wanadi himself. These complex stories not only teach Yekuana traditional environmental ethics, they braid together cognitive and affective realms into a learned bodily practice of restraint. In effect, the weaving of baskets among the Yekuana is considered a finely developed aesthetic and contemplative act in which individuals mature in their self-realization of society and bioregion. This Yekuana ethics of limits with regard to natural consumption may not in itself appeal or apply to mainstream societies, but the emergence of an ethics of limits in relation to cosmological insights may hold significance for the current quest to develop viable limits to consumption.

Finally, what may be the most significant comparisons between deep ecology and indigenous religions are the felt experiences of interacting with the larger whole of reality. Cosmology is used here to suggest that context in which humans reflect upon their own bodies, the collective social order, and the understanding of how the world works. The Pueblo scholar, Gregory Cajete, speaks of the relational character of indigenous cosmological knowledge in this way:

> American Indians believe it is the breath that represents the most tangible expression of the spirit in all living things. Language is an expression of the spirit because it contains the power to move people and to express human thought and feeling. It is also the breath, along with water and thought, that connects all living things in direct relationship. The interrelationship of water, thought (wind), and breath personifies the elemental relationship emanating from "that place that the Indians talk about," that place of the Center where all things are created.[42]

For some Cajete may be seen as describing an essential, unreal "Indian," but Pueblo concepts arise from their myths of emergence in which breath, water and thought unite to bring forth life. These embodied concepts evoke the mutually reciprocal web of interrelationships centered on the ongoing creative act. This is creative self-realization. Creativity flows from the microcosm of the body in tension and in complementarity with the macrocosm of the local bioregion, the larger world.

CONCLUSION

Some in mainstream industrialized societies have begun to reflect upon the larger implications of evolution as a coherent story of great beauty, indeterminism, and creativity. Yet the possibility of an environmental ethics developing from that story remains a challenge. The thought of the French paleontologist, Teilhard de Chardin, provides a remarkable religious understanding of evolutionary science.[43] His efforts to integrate religion and science remain a significant challenge, even though three penetrating critiques of his religious thought have been raised, namely, his anthropocentric vision of the human as culminating evolution, his interpretation of the religious depth of different cultural thought systems, and his fixation on human technological capacities. More recently, Thomas Berry has reconstructed much of Teilhard's thought moving beyond human-centered concerns into an anthropocosmic position. In Berry's perspective the human undertakes the "great work" of recovering relatedness to all beings by environmental awareness and contemplation of the dynamics of the story of evolution.[44]

These thinkers are not identified as deep ecologists but they provide a reorientation for the work of self-realization and biocentric equality, so central to deep ecology. Berry also provides a bridge to indigenous traditions and deep ecology with his affirmation of cosmological concern in the worlds' religions, his critique of the relentless ethos of material plunder, and his regard for the moral vision of indigenous ways of knowing the local place. Much of the powerful insight of these thinkers is that they focus attention on evolution as sacred myth. In that mindfulness is the spadework needed to turn the compost of memory. As the historian Simon Schama observed:

> [T]hough it may sometimes seem that our impatient appetite for produce has ground the earth to thin and shifting dust, we need only poke below the subsoil of its surface to discover an obstinately rich loam of memory. It is not that we are any more virtuous or wiser than the most pessimistic environmentalist supposes. It is just that we are more retentive. The sum of our pasts, generation laid over generation, like the slow mold of the seasons, forms the compost of our future. We live off it.[45]

It is the local work, then, that remains the most important. That is, to examine our myth of emergence seriously without "becoming morally blinded by its poetic power."[46]

For the Dine/Navajo, the encounter with mystery is as evident as the wind that brought existence into being. One chanter described it this way:

> Wind existed first, as a person, and when the Earth began its existence Wind took care of it. We started existing where Darknesses, lying on one another, occurred. Here, the one that had lain on top became Dawn, whitening across. What used to be lying on one another back then, this is Wind. It was Darkness. That is why when

> Darkness settles over you at night it breezes beautifully. It is this, it
> is a person, they say. From there where it dawns, when it dawns
> beautifully becoming white-streaked through the Dawn, it usually
> breezes. Wind exists beautifully, they say. Back there in the under-
> worlds, this was a person it seems.[47]

Here the beauty of primordial existence is remembered and felt in the experience of Wind. This cosmology connects conscious thought and the
darkness of night as a reversal moment whose transformative energies
are still with the people. The tangible feel of breezes is the abiding beauty
of this ancient harmony. Ritual practices and oral narratives simultaneously connect these native peoples to a world that is pragmatic and problematic, meaningful and ambiguous, of ultimate concern and felt beauty.

For mainstream societies caught in the problematics of nuclear ar-
mament, surging populations, environmental degradation, and pollution, our darkness has yet to become a source of felt beauty. Indigenous
peoples certainly have no technological fix for these issues, nor is it just
and equitable to yearn for a panacea from oppressed peoples. What is
evident, however, is wherever indigenous peoples have endured, they
have maintained a loving experience of place, and an understanding
that spiritual forces capable of leading humans into understanding of
self and utilitarian need abide in all of these places.

NOTES

1. For a consideration of this position and similar observations see the essays by Vine Deloria Jr. "Religion and the Modern American Indian," and "Reflection and Revelation: Knowing Land, Places, and Ourselves," in *For This
Land: Writings on Religion in America* (New York: Routledge, 1999).

2. "Report of the Sub-Commission on Prevention of Discrimination and
Protection of Minorities on its Forty-Sixth Session," Geneva 1–26 August 1994
Draft United Nations Declaration on the Rights of Indigenous Peoples.

3. For a discussion of this concept from the perspective of a Native American scholar, see Jack D. Forbes, "Nature and Culture: Problematic Concepts for
Native Americans," in *Indigenous Traditions and Ecology* (Cambridge: Harvard
University Press for the Harvard University Center for the Study of World Religions, forthcoming).

4. J. Baird Callicott, *Earth's Insights A Multicultural Survey of Ecological
Ethics from the Mediterranean Basin to the Australian Outback* (Berkeley: University
of California Press, 1994). For short essays on this work see the journal *Worldviews: Environment, Culture, Religion* 1, no. 2 (August 1997).

5. See for example the continuities and changes in Arne Naess's thinking in his article "The Deep Ecological Movement: Some Philosophical Aspects," in *Environmental Philosophy*, ed. Michael Zimmerman et al. (Englewood Cliffs, NJ: Prentice-Hall, 1993), 193–212.

6. Compare, for example, the concerns of native scholars in *Defending Mother Earth: Native American Perspectives on Environmental Justice*, ed. Jace Weaver (Maryknoll, NY: Orbis, 1996), and a popular text on indigenous environmental wisdom by David Suzuki and Peter Knudtson, *Wisdom of the Elders: Sacred Native Stories of Nature* (New York: Bantam Books, 1992).

7. See Dennis McPherson and J. Douglas Rabb, *Indian from the Inside: A Study in Ethno-Metaphysics* (Thunder Bay, Ontario: Lakehead University, Centre for Northern Studies, 1993); and A. Irving Hallowell, "Ojibwa Ontology, Behavior and World View," in *Culture and History: Essays in Honor of Paul Radin*, ed. Stanley Diamond (New York: Columbia University Press, 1960), 207–244.

8. Vine Deloria Jr., "Out of Chaos," in *For This Land*, 260.

9. As Harold Glasser correctly points out, Arne Naess's deep ecology supports a wider diversity of norms than Naess's early formulations; see his article "On Warwick Fox's Assessment of Deep Ecology," *Environmental Ethics* 19.1 (spring 1997): 69–85.

10. Naess, *Ecology, Community, and Lifestyle: Outline of an Ecosophy*, trans. David Rothenberg (Cambridge: Cambridge University Press, 1989), 32.

11. Bill Devall and George Sessions, *Deep Ecology: Living as if Nature Mattered* (Salt Lake City: Gibbs Smith, 1985), 80.

12. Ibid.

13. Quote from J. Baird Callicott, *Earth's Insights*, 205; Aldo Leopold quote from, *A Sand County Almanac* (New York: Oxford University Press, 1949), 224–225.

14. For examples, see Jonathan Bordo, "Ecological Peril, Modern Technology, and the Postmodern Sublime," in *Shadow of Spirit: Postmodernism and Religion*, ed. P. Berry and A. Wernick (New York: Routledge, 1993); and Peter C. van Wyck, *Primitives in the Wilderness: Deep Ecology and the Missing Human Subject* (Albany: State University of New York Press, 1997).

15. Rangimarie Rose Pere, *Ako: Concepts and Learning in the Maori Tradition* (Hamilton, New Zealand: University of Waikato, 1982), 25; and Joan Metge, *New Growth from Old: The Whanau in the Modern World* (Wellington: Victoria University Press, 1995), 110–111.

16. See Antony Alpers, *Maori Myths and Tribal Legends* (Auckland: Longman Paul, 1964); and George Grey, *Nga Mahi o Nga Tupuna*, fourth edition (Wellington: A. H. and A. W. Reed, 1971).

17. Neil Grove, *Nga Pepeha a Nga Tupuna*, second edition (Wellington: Department of Maori Studies, Victoria University of Wellington, 1984), 140.

18. Gregory Schrempp, *Magical Arrows: The Maori, The Greeks, and the Folklore of the Universe* (Madison: University of Wisconsin Press, 1992), 143.

19. Devall and Sessions, *Deep Ecology*, 70.

20. From Thoreau's essay on "Walking" in *Thoreau's Vision: The Major Essays*, ed. Charles R. Anderson (Englewood Cliffs, NJ: Prentice-Hall, 1973); cited in Devall and Sessions, *Deep Ecology*, 109.

21. See Bron Taylor, "Earth First! and Global Narratives of Popular Ecological resistance," in *Ecological Resistance Movements: The Global Emergence of Radical and Popular Environmentalism* (Albany: State University of New York Press, 1995), 11–34.

22. See Bron Taylor, "Earth First!'s Religious Radicalism," in *Ecological Prospects: Scientific, Religious, and Aesthetic Perspectives*, ed. Christopher Chapple (Albany: State University of New York Press, 1994), 185–209; and "Earth First!: From Primal Spirituality to Ecological Resistance," in *This Sacred Earth*, ed. Roger Gottlieb (New York and London: Routledge, 1995).

23. See Dave Foreman, *Confessions of an Eco-Warrior* (New York: Harmony Books, 1992); and George Weurthner, "An Ecological View of the Indian," *Earth First!* 7, no. 7 (August 1987).

24. Robert Jarvenpa, *Northern Passage: Ethnography and Apprenticeship Among the Subartic Dene* (Prospect Heights, IL: Waveland Press, 1998), 8–9.

25. For a classic study see Kieth H. Basso, "'Stalking with Stories': Names, Places, and Moral Narratives among the Western Apache," in *Text, Play, and Story: The Construction and Reconstruction of Self and Society*, ed. Edward M. Brunner (Proceedings of the American Ethnological Society, 1983), 21–55; and his more recent work.

26. Vine Deloria Jr., "Trouble in High Places: Erosion of American Indian Rights to Religious Freedom in the United States," in *The State of Native America*, ed. M Annette Jaimes (Boston: South End Press, 1992), 280–281.

27. Compare, for example, Vine Deloria Jr., *Red Earth, White Lies: Native Americans and the Myth of Scientific Fact* (New York: Scribner, 1995) and Tim Flannery, *Future Eaters* (Sidney, Australia: Brazillier, 1994).

28. Donald A. Grinde and Bruce E. Johansen, *Ecocide of Native America: Environmental Destruction of Indian Lands and People* (Santa Fe, NM: Clear Light, 1995), 12.

29. George Tinker, "An American Indian Theological Response to Ecojustice," in *Defending Mother Earth*, 153–154.

30. See Bron Taylor, "Earthen Spirituality or Cultural Genocide? Radical Environmentalism's Appropriation of Native American Spirituality," *Religion* 27 (1997): 183–215.

31. David Waller, "Friendly Fire: When Environmentalists Dehumanize American Indians," *American Indian Culture and Research Journal* 20, no. 2 (1996): 124.

32. See Jeanette Wolfley, "Ecological Risk Assessment and Management: Their Failure to Value Indigenous Traditional Ecological Knowledge and Protect Tribal Homelands," *American Indian Culture and Research Journal* 22.2 (1998): 151–169.

33. Devall and Sessions, *Deep Ecology*, 66.

34. Naess quoted in Warwick Fox, *Toward a Transpersonal Ecology: Developing New Foundations for Environmentalism* (Boston: Shambala, 1990), 219.

35. Ibid.

36. John Seed, "Anthropocentrism," Appendix E in Devall and Sessions, *Deep Ecology*, 243.

37. Marina Roseman, *Healing Sounds from the Malaysian Rainforest: Temiar Music and Medicine* (Berkeley: University of California Press, 1993), 177.

38. See Keith Basso, "Stalking with Stories: Names, Places, and Moral Narratives Among the Western Apache," in *Text, Play, and Story: The Construction and Reconstruction of Self and Society*, ed. E. Brunner (Washington, DC: American Ethnological Society, 1984).

39. See Marcel Griaule, *Ogotemmeli* (New York: Oxford University Press, 1975), as well as the later works of his wife Gertrude Deterlin.

40. See Nancy Turner, Randy Bouchard, and Dorothy Kennedy, *Ethnobotany of the Okanagan-Colville Indians of British Columbia and Washington*, no. 21, Occasional Paper Series (British Columbia Provincial Museum, Victoria, 1980).

41. See David M. Guss, *To Weave and Sing: Art, Symbol, and Narrative in the South American Rain Forest* (Berkeley: University of California Press, 1989).

42. Gregory Cajete, *Look to the Mountains: An Ecology of Indigenous Education* (Durango, CO: Kivaki Press, 1994), 42.

43. See Teilhard de Chardin, *The Phenomenon of Man*, trans. Bernard Wall (New York: Harper & Row, 1959); and *The Heart of Matter*, trans. Rene Hague (New York: Harcourt Brace Jovanovich, 1979).

44. See Thomas Berry, *The Great Work* (New York: Bell Tower/Random House, 1999).

45. Simon Schama, *Landscape and Memory* (New York: Alfred A. Knopf, 1995), 574.

46. Ibid., 34.

47. James McNeley, *Holy Wind in Navajo Philosophy* (Tucson: University of Arizona Press, 1981).

3

Hinduism and Deep Ecology

CHRISTOPHER KEY CHAPPLE

> The grammar not only of language, but of culture and civilization itself, is of the same order as this mossy little forest creek, this desert cobble.
>
> —Gary Snyder, *The Practice of the Wild*

DEEP ECOLOGY SPEAKS of an intimacy with place, a sense of being in the world with immediacy, care, and frugality. Gary Snyder, drawing from an American tradition that stretches back to Thoreau, writes of how the wild enriches the human spirit and sacralizes the process of survival. Establishing oneself within in a sense of place gives meaning to one's existence; for a deep ecologist, this becomes a way of life, encompassing "an attempt to uncover the most profound level of human-nature relationships, stressing the need for personal realization as accomplished by integrating the self with nature."[1] Deep ecology also urges the examination of the underlying political and economic structures that work against intimacy with nature and thwart the development of a sustainable society.

Ecological thinkers in India proclaim the need for social change that includes the sustenance and uplift of the masses as integral to the process of environmental healing. They have been somewhat reluctant to embrace the concept of deep ecology as expressed through American authors, largely due to the particular situation of India's overwhelming population and suspicions that the deep ecology rhetoric smacks of neocolonialism, romanticism, and religion. The environmental movement on the part of India's intellectuals has been largely a secular movement; deep ecology moves into the realm of affectivity and a ritualization of life. Its near-religiosity would render deep ecology suspect for many contemporary Indian thinkers, for whom religion connotes fundamentalism, nationalism, and a return to a caste-bound past.[2]

In recent years, some scholars and activists within the Hindu tradition, inspired by industrial tragedies such as the Bhopal explosion, the depletion of forests, and the fouling of India's air and water, have started to reconsider traditional Hindu lifeways in terms of ecological values. In earlier writings, I have explored various modalities of environmental activism in India, including educational programs, the emphasis on social ecology by the post-Gandhians, and Brahminical and renouncer models for the development of an indigenous Indian environmentalism.[3] In this essay I will more fully explore how the Hindu tradition, broadly interpreted, might further its contribution to both a localized and a globalized sense of deep ecology.

DEFINING HINDU RELIGION

To look at deep ecology in light of Hindu religion, we must probe the term *Hinduism*. First of all, the term *Hindu* is inherently a non-Indian construct, first coined by Persians to describe those persons living on the other side of the Indus River. Another definition of Hinduism links the term to a cluster of religious faiths and theological schools that ascribe truth to the earliest of India's sacred texts, the Vedas, and the various texts and traditions stemming therefrom. Such persons might call themselves followers of Viu (*Vaiṣṇavas*), Śiva (*Śaivas*), or the Devī or Goddess (*Śakti*) or some other deity or of no deity in particular. This definition would include several million persons living outside India in such places as Sri Lanka, Singapore, Britain, and the United States. It would, in a sense, also include many persons of non-Indian descent who ascribe to the monistic Vedanta philosophy and to the many practitioners of Indian physical and spiritual disciplines such as Yoga.[4] The term Hindu could also refer in a general way to the people who live in the subcontinental region. This would include Jains, Buddhists, and Sikhs, as well as Indian Christians and Muslims, all of whom exhibit at least some common cultural traits associated with "Hindustan."

Hinduism does not operate in the manner of many traditional religions. It includes multiple doctrines, multiple deities, and many different types of people from various levels of society. Hence, rather than attempting to present a monolithic view of Hindusim and deep ecology, I prefer to suggest some ways in which I have discovered that

Hinduism, broadly defined, espouses a philosophy akin to the core sensibilities of deep ecology. Specifically, the following essay will begin with a discussion of the importance of the five elements in the Hindu world view and the relationship between meditative practices and the natural world. Ritual worship will be explored as providing a context for understanding the function of "embedded ecology" in Hindu life, with special reference to the Mannarassala Temple in Kerala. I will then turn to a discussion of sacred groves in India, with mention of some of the successes and difficulties encountered by those involved with tree planting in India. The essay will close with reflections on the challenge posed by contemporary consumer pressures in India and the suggestion that the meditative and ritual deep structures of India life and culture can help support an indigenous form of Hindu deep ecology.

THE FIVE ELEMENTS (PAÑCA-BHŪTA)

Hindu religious literature, from the Vedas to contemporary theorists, takes up a discussion of the natural world through a systematic approach to the five elements. This tradition provides an analysis of material reality in terms of its manifestation through earth (*pṛthivī*), water (*āp*), fire (*agni*), air (*vāyu*), and space (*ākāśā*). These elements find mention not only in the earliest of India's oral texts, the Ṛg Veda, but also play a prominent role in the later philosophical systems of Sāṃkhya, Vedānta, as well as the non-Hindu systems of Jainism and Buddhism. For instance, the *Vāmana Purāṇa* (12.26) states:

> Let all the great elements bless the dawning day:
> Earth with its smell, water with its taste,
> fire with its radiance, air with its touch,
> and sky with its sound.

These elements are not seen as abstractions or metaphors but literally compose the reality of the world and of one's own body. The *Mokṣadharmaparvan*, one of the books of the *Mahābhārata* epic, summarizes the relationship between body and cosmos first articulated in the Ṛg Veda and the Bṛhadāraṇyaka Upaniṣad:

> The Lord, the sustainer all beings, revealed the sky.
> From space came water and, from water, fire and the winds.
> From the mixture of the essence of fire and wind arose the earth.
> Mountains are his bones, earth his flesh, the ocean his blood.

The sky is his abdomen, air his breath, fire his heat, rivers his nerves.
The sun and moon, which are called Agni and Soma, are the eyes of Brahman.
The upper part of the sky is his head. The earth is his feet and the directions are
    his hands.[5]

This vision of the relationship between the body, divinity, and the order of the things becomes both descriptive and prescriptive in terms of the human relationship with nature in India. The world cannot be separated from the human body nor can the human body be separated from the world.

In the traditional Hindu view, the world exists as an extension of the body and mind; the body and mind reflect and contain the world. In describing the women of the Garwhal region of the Himalayas, Carol Lee Flinders notes that they "enjoy a connection with trees, rivers, mountains, livestock, and plants that is simultaneously their connection with divinity, and that connection is seen as absolutely reciprocal."[6] From the texts above, we can understand this continuity as an expression of what Vandana Shiva calls "embedded in nature" and Vijaya Nagarajan refers to as "embedded ecology." This notion of intimacy with the natural world, culturally supported by a anthropocosmic vision of the earth, instantiates a person in immediate and intimate contact with one's surroundings. Just as the Hymn of the Person in the Ṛg Veda identifies human physiology with the cosmos, correlating the feet with the earth and the head with the sky, so also a vision of deep ecology in the context of Hindu faith will seek to integrate and include its understanding of the human as inseparable from and reflective of nature.

MEDITATIVE MASTERY

Hinduism, while revering the five elements and venerating many gods and goddesses, places ultimate importance on the attainment of spiritual liberation (mokṣa). The path toward liberation requires a skillful reciprocity between spirit and materiality. Yogic practice (sādhana) cultivates an awareness of and intimacy with the realm of manifestation and materiality (prakṛti). Just as the Bṛhadāraṇyaka Upaniṣad proclaims a relationship between the body and the universe, so also the Yoga system urges one to gain mastery over how the body stands in relationship to the cosmos. The Yoga Sūtras of Patanjali state, "From concentration on significance and connection of the subtle [body] and the essence of gross manifestation, there is mastery over the elements."[7] This statement acknowledges a linkage between the realm of bodily sensation and the experience of the physical world. By concentrating on this relationship, one gains an intimacy with the elements that results in an understanding of one's embeddedness with one's environment.

The yogic accomplishment of mastery over the elements (*bhūta-jaya*) entails a detailed training that focuses on the elements over a period of several months. In this regimen, one begins with concentration on the earth, moving toward an appreciation of the special relationship between the sense of smell residing in the subtle body (*sūkṣma śarīra*) and the earth (*pṛthivī*). Moving up in subtlety, the practitioner then concentrates on the link between subtle taste (*rasa*) and water (*āp*); between visible form (*rūpa*) and light and heat (*tejas*); between touch (*sparśa*) and the wind (*vāyu*); and between sound (*śabda*) and space (*ākāśā*). Beginning with earth, the most gross aspect of manifestation, one progress to the lightest. This insight into the relationship between the senses and the elements leads to an ability to acknowledge and withhold the outflow of the senses (*prapñca*). Through this mastery, one gains freedom from compulsive attachment; this lightness (*sattva*) ultimately leads to liberation (*mokṣa*).

On the one hand, it might be argued that this process leads one away from intimacy to an introspective distancing from nature. On the other hand, it could also be stated that this meditative practice entails a greater rapport with nature, an entry into a purified, immediate state of perception freed from residues of past attachment. In the words of David Abram, "The recuperation of the incarnate, sensorial dimension of experience brings with it a recuperation of the living landscape in which we are corporeally embedded. As we return to our senses, we gradually discover our sensory perceptions to be simply our part of a vast, interpenetrating webwork. . . ."[8] By entering fully into a reflection on the workings of the senses through the practices of yogic meditation, one gains an intimacy with the foundational constructs of objects that transcends their specificity, leading one to a state of unity with the natural world.

RITUAL WORSHIP (PŪJĀ) AND ECOLOGY

Ritual worship performed by meditators and temple priests includes a veneration and internalization of the elements, a sanctification of the body that leads to identity with divine power. Anthropologist James Preston describes the experience of one temple priest at the Chandi Temple in Cuttack, Orissa:

One of the first steps in the *puja* is for the priest to transform his body into a microcosm of the universe. This is accomplished by combining the five elements represented within it. Kumar Panda explained the correspondences between nature and the human body: *earth* is equated with that part of the human body below the waist; *water* is symbolized by the stomach region; *fire* is represented by the heart; *wind* is equivalent to the throat, nose, and lungs; *sky* corresponds to the brain. As these elements are mixed together in symbolic rites, the priest is filled with divine power or *shakti*, which is the goddess herself. . . . Kumar Panda describes his inner vision during meditation: "After performing meditation and the ritual for two or three hours, lightning flashes before my eyes . . . I become the goddess. She who is *Ma* (Mother) is me . . . Water and the coldness of water, fire and the burning capacity of fire, the sun and the rays of the sun; there is no difference between all these things, just as there is no difference between myself and the goddess."[9]

This journey through the relationship between the body and the elements to the point of unity with the goddess bring the meditator to a point of visionary immersion, a form of profound and deep ecological awareness.

Within the context of celebrating the special relationship between the human person and nature, each region of India has developed an extensive ritual cycle. These festivals often coincide with times of harvest or renewal. For instance, the Pongal festival in South India takes place each January to acknowledge the rice harvest. Many Hindu rituals include reverence for sacred traditional plants such as the Tulsi tree; many explicitly invoke the elements as mentioned above and many celebrate the earth goddess or Bhū Devi. Vijaya Nagarajan has extensively described how the practice of the Kolam morning ritual establishes in Tamil women a sense of connectedness with their environment.[10] Madhu Khanna writes about how rituals practiced in the urban context maintain significant agricultural and hence ecological meanings. Ritual acknowledges and invokes one's position in the order of things and connects the worshipper directly with fecundity cycles.[11]

I would like to describe a fertility ritual in South India that provides a living example of embedded ecology in the state of Kerala. In 1997, I visited the Mannarassala Temple, between the cities of Cochin and Trivandrum. We spent many hours in the cool shade of this sylvan retreat and learned, through observation and friendly informants, of the mythic history and ritual cycles associated with this temple. My companion, Professor Surinder Datta, a retired biologist from the University of Wisconsin, Parkside, sought out this particular site because of its

renowned sacred grove. Adjacent to its buildings, behind a walled en-
closure, the temple maintains a fourteen acre preserve of forest. No one
is allowed to enter this towering woods except a small group of Brahman priests who enter once each year to gather medicinal herbs, to be
used in Ayurvedic treatments. The forest stretches as high as the eye can
see, a remarkable remnant of the tropical forests that once covered the
entire state of Kerala. Though not far from the main road, this compound stands in stark contrast to the densely populated and cultivated
surrounding landscape, which, though green and lush with rice pad-
dies and coconut groves, has been thoroughly domesticated by the
many people that live in Kerala. Similarly, even in the mountains, what
at first glance appears to be wild forest at a closer examination turns out
to be terraces of spice and coffee trees, creeping vines of black pepper,
and bushes of cardamon, all under cultivation.

According to the local tale, this particular temple arose on the spot
where Parasurama, an incarnation of Vishnu, met with the snake god
Nagaraja to obtain blessings to ensure the fertility of Kerala's soil. Years
prior, the mountains of Kerala were formed when Parasurama had
thrown his ax (parasu) into the ocean. The plain below the mountains,
though seemingly rich, was too salty to support life. Parasurama
pleaded with the snake king to purify the land. Now, in return, offerings
are made to the snake king to thank him for granting Parasurama's re-
quest and snakes, particularly in the wild areas, are protected. This story
divinizes the land of Kerala and offers a local rationale for preserving
both forest and wildlife in honor and respect for a viable ecosystem.

The Mannarassala Temple serves as a sacred place for human reproduction. Our visit to Mannarasalla Temple coincided with a fertility
thanksgiving in the form of a first name and first solid food ceremony
to bless several babies. For several decades, one woman, Valia Amma,
served as priestess of the temple. She was born in 1903 and, according
to our informants, she married a temple priest when she was thirteen or
fourteen years old. At the age of fifteen, in 1918, she renounced the car-
nal aspects of her marriage and dedicated her life to serving the temple.
She instituted *pūjā* or worship ceremonies at the temple that continue to
the present day, including weddings and the Kalasam tantric rite.[12]

During our visit, we witnessed a portion of the special rituals
known as the Choronu ceremony associated with the successful birth
and nurturance of babies. Young couples come to the temple priestess
for fertility blessings when they decide it is time to bear children. After
the birth of a child, the family returns when the baby reaches six
months, for the naming and first solid food ceremonies. The parents
first place the baby in a basket attached to a scale and fill the opposite

basket with grain. When the scale balances, the proper payment is accepted by the temple staff. Midst the smoke and light of the oil lamps and the blaring trumpets of a circumambulating band of musicians, we saw several children receive the name acknowledging their survival through the first six months of life. We also witnessed these babies being fed their first meal of cooked rice. A woman temple musician playing a one-stringed instrument held with her toe then sings a song in honor of the baby and then the family proceeds to receive *darshan* or blessing from the temple priestess, who greets people from the family quarter within the temple compound. Valia Amma died in 1993; we received blessings from her husband's brother's wife, who assumed the priestess duties upon her passing.

The ritual life of this temple complex exhibits the qualities of embedded ecology in its story of cosmic origins, its grounding in nature, and its function as promoting the good health and well-being of future generations.

SACRED GROVES

In her work on sacred groves, Frederique Apffel-Marglin describes such ritual centers as source of rejuvenation. She writes that "the network of sacred groves in such countries as India has since time immemorial been the locus and symbol of a way of life in which humans are embedded in nature. . . . It stands for the integration of the human community in nature. . . . The sacred grove, with its shrine to the local embodiment of the Great Goddess, is the permanent material sign of these periodic processes of regeneration."[13] Though Apffel-Marglin writes of her experiences in a sacred grove in northeast coastal Orissa, the grove parallels and mirrors that of Kerala, more than a thousand miles to the southwest. Both affirm the process of fertility. Both celebrate feminine powers of reproduction. Both serve as symbols of community and continuity, a place where, in Apffel-Marglin's words, "culture and society are embedded in nature, and the spiritual is embedded in the material."[14]

Ramachandra Guha notes that "sacred groves and sacred ponds . . . protection of keystone species . . . and the moderation of harvests from village wood-lots have persisted in Indian society over the historical period, sometimes to the present day."[15] He tells the story of the Bishnois sect, a group in the Rajasthan desert for whom the Khejadari tree became sacred. This tree, described as a "multi-purpose leguminous tree of great utility to the villagers" was never to be uprooted or killed.[16] In the 1650s a prince of Jodhpur attempted to cut a grove of Khejadari trees to fire a kiln to manufacture bricks for a new palace. The Bishnois revolted, laying down their lives to protect the sacred tree. Even today, the Khejadari serves as the backbone for desert subsistence; I have seen women in Rajasthan lopping its limbs to provide food for their goats; they also harvest its leaves and pods. Unlike the Joshua tree of the western United States which has lost its utility since the decimation of indigenous populations, the Khejadari reciprocally supports the people who sustain it through their protective customs.

WATER HARVESTING

Anil Agarwal and Sunita Narain have written of water catchment systems employed throughout India that have allowed human life to flourish in what otherwise would be arid wastelands. This system, like the prudent pruning of the Khejadari tree by desert women, works with the immediate available resources on a small scale. They note that "[a]ncient texts, inscriptions, local traditions and archaeological remains refer to a wide range of techniques—canals, huge tanks, embankments, wells and reservoirs—to harvest every possible form of water: rainwater, groundwater, stream water, river water and flood water."[17]

One of the tragic consequences of the British colonial period was a dismantling of many traditional water catchment systems. Before the British period, each village supported the workers who maintained the irrigation systems. The British, in an attempt to increase revenues, deemed these to be merely "religious and charitable allowances" and discontinued allocation for these functions. In time, the systems fell into disrepair, leading to "the disintegration of village society, its economy and its polity."[18]

Following independence from Britain, India initiated huge irrigation projects inspired by the example of the Soviet Union. Massive water projects have been and continue to be destructive to traditional life in India, disrupting indigenous ways of desert survival, as in the case of the Narmada Dam project in western India.[19] As the dry lands of Gujarat open to wetter styles of cultivation through the various planned irrigation channels, and as more desert dwellers and displaced tribals from the flooded valleys flock to the cities in search of employment in a cash-based economy, the age-old deep ecology based on a traditional economy of living within available means will disappear. Some have argued that progress is inevitable, that the benefits of wealth and increased nutrition outweigh clinging to an outdated lifestyle. However, from a religious point of view and from the perspectives of deep ecology, a sense of connectedness with the land becomes lost when large-scale development prevails. The World Bank has grappled with this issue and has put their funding of the Narmada Dam projects on hold.

NATURE AS ROMANCE?

Guha has argued against the romanticization of Western-style deep ecology, claiming that it merely extends the imperialism of a culture of abundance that can afford to set aside vast tracts of land in convenient preserves. Guha's position, unfortunately and probably unintentionally, can play into the hands of modern developers who would argue for "Wise Use," taking the position that progress is desirable and inevitable. However, for traditional India, Wise Use would entail protecting the sacred grove. For Nehruvian, progress-oriented contemporary India, Wise Use has led to the uprooting of people from their habitats, increased urbanization, and, ultimately, increased pollution.

In a probing analysis and critique of colonialism, Guha notes that British land use policies marginalized and impoverished the hunter-gatherers of India. The British usurped many common lands and required they be converted to food production and the production of cash crops for export such as indigo. Guha explains that the literate castes of India were able to move into clerical jobs and to operate as trading partners, but that "the others—hunter-gatherers, peasants, artisans, and pastoral and non-pastoral nomads—had all to squeeze into the already diminishing niche space for food production. And they, we have seen, suffered great impoverishment."[20] The emotional and material toll on great masses of the Indian population has been devastating. He writes:

> The consequence has been a scramble for resources and intense conflict, in the countryside and in the cities where people who have been driven out from elsewhere are flocking. . . . Endogamous caste groups remain cultural entities [in the cities], but have no common belief system to hold them together. No longer functional entities in the present scenario of shrinking niche space, castes and communities are set up against each other, with frighteningly high levels of communal and caste violence being the result.[21]

The cities of India teem with millions of street dwellers displaced from rural life who, having flocked to the cities without the benefit of education, perform menial tasks to eke out a survival living.

ESTABLISHING A NEW GROVE

Australian environmental activist John Seed paints a somewhat sobering picture of on-the-ground conservation in the Indian context. In 1987, Seed received a plea from Apeetha Aruna Giri, an Australian nun living near Arunachala mountain in Tiruvanamalai, Madras. She lived at Sri Ramana Ashram, a spiritual hermitage named after the famed Indian sage Ramana Maharshi, whose life energized spirituality in India during the first part of the twentieth century. She noticed that the surrounding areas had become stripped clean of vegetation due to local scavenging for firewood and fodder to feed the goats. Seed raised money for the development of a new NGO established by Apeetha: the Annamalai Reforestation Society. Through the efforts of this organization,

> The space between the inner and outer walls of the vast 23-acre temple complex has been transformed from a wasteland into the largest tree nursery in the south of India. Hundreds of people have received environmental education, and a 12-acre patch of semi-desert was donated to the project and transformed into a lush demonstration of permaculture and the miraculous recuperative powers of the earth. Hundreds of Tamil people have been trained in reforestation skills—tree identification, seed collection, nursery techniques, watershed management, erosion control, sustainable energy systems. Shiva's robes are slowly being rewoven.[22]

However, despite Seed's enthusiasm, this project has not been universally well received. Guards must be maintained to prevent local people from scavenging for fuel and fodder in the preserve, a practice that is enforced in various of India's national preserves and at other temple sites. Pilgrims to the sacred mountain complain that the trees block their view of the sunset. Clearly, the affection for trees in the Anglo-Australian love for nature movement does not necessarily work in the Indian context, where trees are seen as an economic resource necessary for human survival.

Seed himself speaks and writes of his own affirmation of the importance of this preservation work through a special quiet moment he experienced in the Arunachala forest with a troop of scores of monkeys:

> They groomed each other, they made love, mothers breast-fed their babies, children played and cavorted, utter unself-consciously living their everyday lives in my astonished and grateful presence. . . . I had never felt more accepted by the nonhuman world. I knew that Shiva had answered my prayer, had acknowledged my efforts, and was giving me his sign of approval.[23]

For Seed, this shamanic moment established a link between his work and the life of the mountain. For others, this fencing of the forest might be seen as an extension of colonialist attitudes that seek to ban Adivasi or aboriginal peoples from their source of livelihood, an example of "the colonials having saved the forests of South Asian from certain destruction by indigenous forest users."[24]

Recognizing the encroachment of desert lands in areas that were once forested and then under cultivation, the Indian government and several NGOs have promoted tree planting. Balbir Mathur, founder of Trees for Life, has planted thousands of trees in India.[25] Visheswar Saklani, recipient of the Vrikshamitra or Friend of Trees award bestowed by Indira Gandhi in 1987, has planted more than 200,000 trees.[26] Banwari, a contemporary environmentalist writer in India, attributes India's abundance and traditional economic strength to its magical forests, its sacred groves, and its medicinal trees. He writes of the care for forests and trees in India's ancient cities and towns and celebrates the forests that once stood in India as "the land of no war."[27] The tree and the grove provide a foundation through which some ideas akin to deep ecology might be appreciated or understood in the Indian context.

In my own travels to India over the past several years, I have been alarmed by the increase in air pollution, saddened by the lack of resolve to effectively clean India's rivers, and heartened by the extensive planting of trees on the northern plains. In 1980, one could gaze over lentil and vegetable fields for what seemed like miles, with no hedgerow, only a raised furrow to separate one field from another. Twenty years later, the same landscape vista now offers tall Asokha and Champa trees along the roadsides and throughout the fields. These new trees are not sheltered within sacred groves nor does one see them adorned or revered. Their quiet and pervasive presence nonetheless bears witness to a re-greening of the landscape.

THE CONTEMPORARY CHALLENGE

In this chapter, we have surveyed meditative and ritual practices, and the ancient tradition of preserving sacred groves, as possible models for deep ecology within Hinduism. However, just as we mentioned at the beginning of this essay that deep ecology might be a hard sell for secular intellectuals in India, so also it might be difficult to champion the old ways in light of the advent of modern consumerism. The automobile has arrived in full force in India. There has been a threefold increase in automobiles in the past ten years. Vehicles contribute more than 70 percent of India's urban air pollution. According to the Tata Institute, "air pollution in India caused an estimated 2.5 million premature deaths in 1997—equivalent to wiping out the entire population of Jamaica or Singapore."[28] Consumerism can be seen in all its splendor and allure. And with consumerism come the accompanying difficulties of waste disposal, air pollution, and water pollution. Can a deep ecological sensibility inspired by the Hindu tradition help counter these recent harmful developments? Most likely it will not for the urban peoples who have little touch with traditional ways and little interest in the meditative model presented by the wandering *sadhu* or renouncer.

The rising prevalence of urban life (and the imitation of urban life in rural areas) threatens to undermine the very embeddedness that has so characterized the underlying Hindu ecological sensibility. Vasudha Narayan laments that "a burgeoning middle class in India is now hungry for the consumer bon-bons of comfortable and luxurious living. . . . The rich in India can easily surpass the middle class and the rich of the industrialized nations in their opulent life-styles . . . unbridled greed reigns."[29] While visiting alumni and their families in India, I have noted that the number of electronic gadgets such as VCR players, TVs, and CD players in the average upper-middle-class Indian home far exceeds the modest accumulations in my own small American home.

Informants have told Vijaya Nagarajan that since inorganic substances (plastic, stone) are used in the Kolam (household threshold artistry) in place of rice paste,

> We do not know why we do the Kolam anymore. We have forgotten. If we had not, we would not make the kolam out of plastic or white stone powder. Now everything is modern, modern, modern. Before we would make it with rice . . . to feed a thousand souls . . . ants, birds, small worms, insects, maggots. . . . How ungenerous we are becoming![30]

Just as modernity moved the American masses from the countryside to the cities and suburbs, robbing its populace of operative barnyard metaphors and knowledge of basic pastoralism, the Indian urbanized population potentially will lose touch with some of its embedded relationship with nature. A woman from India, observing a fully lit football field at night, once commented that such uses of electricity "rob the sun of its power," a poignant statement laden with multiple meanings.

On a more optimistic note, environmental writer Bill McKibben has suggested the world consider the state of Kerala as a model for sustainable development. We have already discussed one ritual aspect of life in

Kerala that seems to indicate a living example of embedded ecology. Melinda Moore has written about how even the architectural design of a house in Kerala takes into account one's place in the cosmic scheme.[31] Along with maintaining ancient rituals, sacred places, and an integrated sense of the human's niche in nature, Kerala has developed a society that in quality of life equals that of most First World countries, but with a Third World economy. Specifically, of the twenty-nine million living in the state of Kerala, nearly 100 percent are literate, though the per capita income in Kerala ranges from $298 to $350 per year. The seventy-year life expectancy of the Keralese male nearly equals that of a North American male (seventy-two years), and during a recent visit one Kerala promoter boasted that home ownership in Kerala stands at over 90 percent. Essayist Bill McKibben, who has spent time in Kerala, writes:

> Kerala demonstrates that a low-level economy can create a decent life, abundant in things—health, education, community—that are most necessary for us all. . . . One recent calculation showed that for every American dollar spent or its equivalent spent anywhere on earth, half a liter of oil was consumed in producing, packaging, and shipping the goods. One-seventieth the income means one-seventieth the damage to the planet. So, on balance, if Kerala and the United States manage to achieve the same physical quality of life, Kerala is the vastly more successful society.[32]

Unlike most of the subcontinent, two monsoons visit Kerala each year, which allows for denser foliage than most of India. Consequently, women spend less time collecting fodder and firewood, allowing time for educational pursuits, a hallmark of Kerala's success. And its abundant spices have provided ready cash in the world economy for nearly three millenia. Nonetheless, the region's ability to maintain harmony with the land despite great population density, and to balance three powerful religions (Hinduism, Islam, and Christianity) stands as a beacon of hope for an operative, simple, deep ecology.

In India, the issues of social context, historical realities, and survival in a country with huge population pressures demand a different definition of deep ecology. Hundreds of millions of people in India live by subsistence, without certain access to clean water or adequate food. In some ways, this population lives according to the precepts of deep ecology. These people do not consume petroleum; their diet is largely grain and vegetable based; they own next to no consumer products or luxuries. India's middle class (of several hundred million), on the other hand, has developed an elaborate urban lifestyle replete with packaged foods, private scooters and automobiles, and numerous consumer luxuries. India's poor live in a deep ecology mandated by circumstance not design. The middle class has embraced all that America can offer; in the words of one Indian intellectual, "We want what we see on Star (satellite) TV"; many Indians have joined wholeheartedly the American consumerist model.

Between these two extremes of utter material poverty and material excess lies the possibility of a deep ecology that improves health, nutrition, and education for the poor and offers thoughtways, perhaps along the Gandhian model, to inspire restraint from overconsumption. Deep ecology in India must be linked to sustainable development with a focus on universal education (as in Kerala), adequate food supplies, and the development of appropriate technology and transportation systems.

People overpower the landscape, the place of India. Even in remote rural areas, stay still for a minute or two and a person will appear, off on a distant hill or in a hedgerow nearby. Ecologist Patricia C. Wright has commented that China and India have not willfully stumbled into pollution and overpopulation; they simply have been settled and civilized far longer than Europe or the Americas, which has led to a greater density of people. Consequently, any "nature policy" or sensitivity to the core values of deep ecology as outlined in this book must by necessity be instrumental. The human person will not disappear from the subcontinent, nor can one effectively escape from people into a pristine forest; even the sacred grove exists in reciprocity with human use. Gary Snyder has suggested that "[s]ome of us would hope to resume, reevaluate, re-create, and bring into line with complex science that old view that holds the whole phenomenal world to be our own being: multicentered, 'alive' in its own manner, and effortlessly self-organizing in its own chaotic way."[33] In a sense, India and the Hindu approach to environmental issues operates in a careening, inventive fashion, drawing from the tradition, yet recognizing the complexity of distinguishing between human need and human greed.

Conclusion

Deep ecology in the American context requires personal struggle to resist the temptations of overconsumption. For a middle-class American, a move toward an ecological lifestyle might include riding a bicycle to work and adopting a vegetarian diet. Such changes reduce harmful emissions into the air, improve one's health, and allow one to consume fewer natural resources by eating low on the food chain. One might also find inspiration in beautiful landscapes and in reading literature from the burgeoning field of nature writing.

In a Hindu context, deep ecology can be affirmed through reflection on traditional texts that proclaim a continuity between the human order and nature, through ritual activities, and through applying meditative techniques that foster a felt experience of one's relationship with the elements. Long ago, India developed yogic techniques for self-awareness, self-control, and the cultivation of inner peace. These techniques have been practiced by Hindus, Buddhists, Jainas, Sikhs, and Sufis throughout the world, and, as mentioned at the beginning of this chapter, have been embraced by many individuals in the Americas and Europe. The principles of abstemiousness and harmlessness associated with these meditative practices can help cultivate an awareness of one's place in the ecosystem and inspire one to live within the confines of a wholesome ritual simplicity.

These features of Indian thought can also inspire an environmental approach that acknowledges the significant needs of a large and growing population. Deep ecology in a Hindu context must take into account the harmful effects of urbanization due to pollution and use its insights to encourage earth-friendly attitudes in the villages and the cities.

NOTES

1. Mitchell Thomashow, *Ecological Identity: Becoming a Reflective Environmentalist* (Cambridge, MA: MIT Press, 1995), 58.

2. One reason for the underdevelopment of deep ecology in India lies in the absence of both religious and environmental studies as academic disciplines in the universities of South Asia. Religious instruction takes place in the observance of home rituals, story telling, and media presentations such as the literatalist television versions of the Ramayana, Mahabharata, and other religious tales. The rote and somewhat static nature of the conveyance of religion in South Asia has resulted in its rejection by many of the educated elite, who prefer to embrace secularism as their primary world view.

3. See Christopher Key Chapple, *Nonviolence to Animals, Earth, and Self in Asian Traditions* (Albany: State University of New York Press, 1993); "India's Earth Consciousness," in *The Soul of Nature: Visions of a Living Earth,* ed. Michael Tobias and Georgianne Cowan (New York: Continuum, 1994), 145–151; and "Toward an Indigenous Indian Environmentalism," in *Purifying the Earthly Body of God: Religion and Ecology in Hindu India,* ed. Lance E. Nelson (Albany: State University of New York Press, 1998), 13–38.

4. A. R. Victor Raj, *The Hindu Connection: Roots of the New Age* (Saint Louis: Concordia Publishing House, 1995), 62–119.

5. 182: 14–19, adapted from O. P. Dwivedi and B. N. Tiwari, *Environmental Crisis and Hindu Religion* (New Delhi: Gitanjali Publishing House, 1987), 126.

6. Carol Lee Flinders, *At the Root of This Longing: Reconciling a Spiritual Hunger and a Feminist Thirst* (San Francisco: Harper SanFrancisco, 1998), 260.

7. Christopher Key Chapple and Yogi Anand Viraj (Eugene P. Kelly Jr.), *The Yoga Sūtras of Patanjali: An Analysis of the Sanskrit with English Translation* (Delhi: Satguru Publications, 1990), 99.

8. David Abram, *The Spell of the Sensuous: Perception and Language in a More-Than-Human World* (New York: Pantheon Books, 1996), 65.

9. James J. Preston, *Cult of the Goddess: Social and Religious Change in a Hindu Temple* (Prospect Heights, IL: Waveland Press, 1985), 52, 53.

10. Vijaya Rettakudi Nagarajan, "The Earth as Goddess Bhu Devi: Toward a Theory of 'Embedded Ecologies' in Folk Hinduism," in *Purifying the Earthly Body of God: Religion and Ecology in Hindu India,* ed. Lance Nelson (Albany: State University of New York Press, 1998), 269–296.

11. Madhu Khanna, "The Ritual Capsule of Purgā Pūjā: An Ecological Perspective," in *Hinduism and Ecology: The Intersection of Earth, Sky, and Water,* ed. Christopher Key Chapple (Cambridge: Harvard University Center for the Study of World Religions, 2000).

12. Moozhikkulam Chandrasekharam Pillai, *Mannarassala: The Serpent Temple,* trans. Ayyappa Panikker (Harippad: Manasa Publication, 1991), 33.

13. Frederique Apffel-Marglin, "Sacred Groves: Regenerating the Body, the Land, the Community," in *Global Ecology: A New Arena of Political Conflict,* ed. Wolfgang Sachs (London: Zed Books, 1993), 198.

14. Ibid., 206.

15. Madhav Gadgil and Ramachandra Guha, *This Fissured Land: An Ecological History of India* (Delhi: Oxford University Press, 1992), 106.

16. Ibid., 108.

17. Anil Agawal and Sunita Narain, "Dying Wisdom: The Decline and Revival of Traditional Water Harvesting Systems in India," *Ecologist* 27, no. 3 (1997): 112.

18. Ibid., 115.

19. William F. Fisher, *Toward Sustainable Development: Struggling Over India's Narmada River* (Armonk, NY: M. E. Sharpe, 1995).

20. Gadgil and Guha, *This Fissured Land,* 243.

21. Ibid., 244.

22. John Seed, "Spirit of the Earth: A Battle-Weary Rainforest Activist Journeys to India to Renew His Soul," *Yoga Journal,* no. 138 (January/February 1998): 135.

23. Ibid., 136.

24. Mahesh Rangarajan, *Fencing the Forest: Conservation and Ecological Change in India's Central Provinces 1860–1914* (Delhi: Oxford University Press, 1961), 5.

25. Ranchor Prime, *Hinduism and Ecology: Seeds of Truth* (London: Cassell, 1992), 90.

26. Carolyn Emett, "The Tree Man," *Resurgence: An International Forum for Ecological and Spiritual Thinking*, no. 183 (July/August 1997): 42.

27. Banwari, *Pancavati: Indian Approach to Environment*, trans. Asha Vora (Delhi: Shri Vinayaka Publications, 1992).

28. Payal Sampat, "What Does India Want?" *World Watch* 11 (July/August 1998): 36.

29. Vasudha Narayanan, "One Tree Is Equal to Ten Sons: Hindu Responses to the Problems of Ecology, Population, and Consumption," *Journal of the American Academy of Religion* 65, no. 2 (January 1997): 321.

30. Narayan, "One Tree Is Equal to Ten Sons," 275.

31. Melinda A. Moore, "The Kerala House as a Hindu Cosmos," *India through Hindu Categories*, ed. McKim Marriott (New Delhi: Sage Publications, 1990), 169–202.

32. Bill McKibben, *Hope, Human and Wild: True Stories of Living Lightly on the Earth* (Saint Paul: Hungry Mind Press, 1995), 121, 163.

33. Gary Snyder, *A Place in Space: Ethics, Aesthetics, and Watersheds* (Washington, DC: Counterpoint, 1996), 241.

4

Relational Holism

Huayan Buddhism and Deep Ecology

David Landis Barnhill

> The widening and deepening of the individual selves *somehow*
> never makes them into one "mass." Or into an organism in which
> every cell is programmed so as to let the organism function as one
> single, integrated being. How to work out this in a fairly precise
> way I do not know. It is a meagre consolation that I do not find that
> others have been able to do this in their contemplation of the pair
> unity-plurality. "In unity diversity!," yes, but how?
> —Arne Naess, *Ecology, Community, and Lifestyle*

ENTRAL TO MOST PRESENTATIONS of deep ecology is an intuitive sense
of the whole of the natural world. Nature is not just a collection
of individual phenomena or even a community of related beings; in some sense there is a vast, encompassing totality that we can
connect to and that has unqualified value. Deep ecologists often discuss
this holistic perspective in terms of identification and an expanded
sense of the self. But as the above quotation by Arne Naess shows,
holism, the self, and the relationships among phenomena are complex
issues. It is easy to agree with Naess and feel his puzzlement and frustration: the urge to affirm both diversity and unity is strong, but preci-
sion in the conception of that combination is difficult to obtain.

Deep ecology's views concerning unity and diversity are a major
point of controversy, and ecofeminists in particular have criticized holistic views. These issues are also one of the principal points of overlap

between deep ecology and Buddhism. For more than two thousand years, Buddhism has offered radical views of the self and of the interrelatedness of the world. At various points it also has suggested at least some sense of holism, although as we will see the place of holism in Buddhism is contested. Partly because of this overlap, a number of deep ecologists have turned to Buddhism in their attempt to articulate and support their vision of the structure of reality, and my own approach to environmental philosophy began as a deep ecologist and a Buddhist. However, many of the criticisms of deep ecology have been persuasive, and what I seek is a broader deep ecology that learns from its critics. And although some have rejected the use of Buddhism in exploring ecological issues,[1] I will argue here that it can help us to clarify and refine deep ecology.

Many issues are involved here and much is at stake. How is reality constructed: atomistically as a collection of independent objects, relationally with distinct individuals in close interrelationship, holistically with individuals as parts of a single encompassing whole? Can one logically present a holistic view while also affirming the importance of relationships? What is the nature of the self and of its relationship to the transhuman world? These questions about reality are important in themselves, but they also point us to issues of value. Do only individuals have value, or do species, ecosystems, and nature as a whole? Does a claim of the existence and value of a "whole" inevitably devalue individuals and relationships? Such abstract questions are inextricably tied to more personal and political ones. Some deep ecologists would claim that only a holistic view allows full reverence of nature and enables us to avoid a focus on individuals that devalues those beings we are not close to.[2] For critics, on the other hand, holism weakens respect for individuals and can lead to ecofascism.

There is also the issue of the fundamental experience of nature. The philosophical views of deep ecologists are often grounded in an intuitive experience of nature as a unified totality that we can relate to and that in some sense we *are*. A sense of being part of a vast, inclusive whole can enable one to drop a confined view of the self, give a feeling of being fully a part of and at home in nature, and motivate environmental activism. However, some ecofeminist critics charge that such an experience is deluded and merely manifests masculinist tendencies to absorb the Other or to transcend the concrete world of individual phenomena—tendencies that have been principal causes of environmental degradation and social injustice. The authenticity and effectiveness of deep ecology's primary intuitive experience is at stake.

Unfortunately, something less substantial seems at times to be at stake: the supremacy of an ecophilosophical school of thought. A strident sectarianism is evident in some of the debates between deep ecology and ecofeminism, with these perspectives seen as mutually exclusive competitors. This, I believe, has blinded some to the ways in which each perspective can complement and even blend with the other.

Other questions concern Buddhism and its relationship to deep ecology. Is an experience of a unifying totality found in Buddhism? Does Buddhism support deep ecology's views of the self? Can Buddhism be used to enrich deep ecology's view, and can deep ecology critique or extend traditional Buddhist understandings of interrelationship? We can raise a more ambitious question: can a refined view of the self and holism, drawing on Buddhism, serve as a point of commonality between deep ecology and ecofeminism rather than a point of disagreement?

Given the controversial nature of these issues, it is appropriate to begin with criticisms of the deep ecology perspective, followed by a review of statements made by deep ecologists that seem to contradict those criticisms. After this introduction I will explore the view of self, relationship, and holism found in Huayan Buddhism, a philosophical school that is particularly relevant to this debate. Based on this Buddhist perspective, I will present a new typology of views concerning the self and relationship that includes a nondualistic approach. This approach, I believe, can help us to understand better deep ecology and the controversy surrounding holism.

CRITIQUES OF THE DEEP ECOLOGY VIEW
OF SELF AND HOLISM

Critics of deep ecology have often attacked its holistic views of self and cosmology. For some, holism is both distorted and dangerous because it fails to affirm the individuality of beings and to recognize the centrality of relations among individuals. Marti Kheel has argued that deep ecology involves "an identification not with individual beings but rather the larger biotic community or whole."[3] Jim Cheney frames the situation in a similarly "either-or" fashion: "Nor does ethical *holism* tend to place primary ethical emphasis on relations. It tends, rather, to locate worth in a kind of super individual: the ecosystem. We get a kind of atomism of one."[4]

Val Plumwood has refined this critique by proposing a threefold typology of deep ecology holism. "There seem to be at least three different accounts of self involved—indistinguishability, expansion of self, and transcendence of self—and practitioners appear to feel free to move among them at will."[5] (I will refer to these as monism, magnified egoism, and transcendental holism.) In her discussion of indistinguishability, Plumwood has suggested that we have two mutually exclusive options for opposing the traditional atomism characteristic of Western thought: deep ecology's holism and ecofeminism's relational view. "That people's interests are relational does not imply a holistic view of them—that they are merged or indistinguishable." In her view, "deep ecology proposes the obliteration of all distinction."[6]

The second account of the self involves a magnified male ego: "[T]his expanded self is not the result of a critique of egoism; rather, it is an enlargement and an extension of egoism." She relates this notion of the expanded ego to a lack of distinctions: "[T]he widening of interest is obtained at the expense of failing to recognize unambiguously the distinctness and independence of the other."[7] The criticism that deep ecology involves the aggrandizement of other selves has been common among ecofeminists.[8]

Critics also have characterized deep ecology as proposing a holism that transcends the concrete world of particulars and relationships. "This preference for identification with the larger 'whole' may reflect the familiar masculine urge to transcend the concrete world of particularity in preference for something more enduring and abstract."[9] Marti Kheel has argued that such transcendentalism is related to rationalism. "This treatment of particularity [by deep ecologists], the devaluation of an identity tied to particular parts of the natural world as opposed to an abstractly conceived whole, the cosmos, reflects the rationalistic preoccupation with the universal and its account of ethical life as oppositional to the particular."[10] In addition to transcending particulars and their relationships, such a view is seen as making the whole separate from and prior to the parts. "Deep ecologists have, in the main, given the idea of interconnectedness a holistic reading; they have taken it to mean that nature, as a metaphysical whole, is logically prior to its parts. . . ."[11] Summarizing Plumwood's critique of Warwick Fox on the "expanded self," Deborah Slicer argues that deep ecology "negates the identity and integrity of particular individuals and relationships by, in this case, abstractly transcending them."[12]

Critics of deep ecology seem to be making several arguments. The first is that there are three different types of holism presented by deep ecologists. The second is that all three are nonrelational, involving the denial or devaluation of individuals and their relationships. Third, nonrelational holism is an essential characteristic of deep ecology, rather than one kind of holism that some deep ecologists present. Fourth, critics claim that there are two, mutually exclusive options: a relational view and a holistic view.[13]

DEEP ECOLOGY ACCOUNTS OF HOLISM AND RELATIONALITY

There is a striking difference between the prevalence and persistence of these criticisms and some statements made by deep ecologists. In his analysis of transpersonal identification, Warwick Fox does clearly emphasize holism (for which he has been the subject of repeated criticism). In fact, one of his principal concerns is that individualism or personalism may lead to an exaggerated and destructive sense of autonomy. Yet his holism is combined with an affirmation of particularity and relationality in two ways. First, his "cosmological transpersonalism" explicitly rejects monistic indistinguishability or transcendental holism, seen most clearly when he discusses various images for the transpersonal self. In offering metaphors for the structure of the cosmos, Fox approvingly cites David Bohm's image of ripples on an ocean of energy and the image of knots in a cosmological net because they combine both the whole and the individual. However, he finds them insufficiently relational. Instead, he prefers the image of a tree with many leaves on it. One of the reasons he favors this image is because, "although it clearly suggests that all entities (all leaves) are interconnected (by virtue of the fact that they are all part of the same tree), it also gives due recognition to the relative autonomy of different entities (different leaves). In contrast, some of the other images (especially that of drops in the ocean) can easily suggest the loss of individuality." In addition, while Fox stresses cosmological identification with all particulars, he notes that such identification is a matrix for realizing individual and contextual identifications: "[C]osmologically based identification proceeds from a sense of the cosmos (such as that provided by the image of the tree of life) and works inward to each particular individual's sense of commonality with other entities."[14] Here at least, Fox is clearly affirming that an identification with the whole and with individual phenomena can coexist.

Deep ecologist Andrew McLaughlin makes a similar claim. He praises the holism that Freya Mathews presents in her book *The Ecological Self*. For McLaughlin, her view is valuable because it "amounts to a deep way to discern, define, and respect individuals within a holistic perspective. The crux of such an argument lies in granting some sort of intrinsic value to systems that take themselves as an end. Such a conception of the status of individuals within a larger holism is an effective counter to the charge of fascism against holistic theories."[15]

Matthews is, in fact, quite explicit that her holism does not disregard or devalue individuals. Consider the various organisms that fill the niches in an ecosystem. An ecosystem is a functional unity but it implies, indeed requires, the distinctness and integrity of species, organisms, and niches. Similarly, organisms exist as individuals, but they exist only within and *as* a self-realizing, self-maintaining ecosystem. In this way holism and individuality entail each other. Matthews puts this in terms of a functional unity that involves relative ontological individuality.[16]

Arne Naess, too, recognizes that the extremes of monism and individualism must be avoided. At some points, Naess speaks of the expanded self as Atman, a Hindu term that can imply an undifferentiated whole that transcends concrete particulars. However, at other times he observes that "the expression 'drops in the stream of life' may be misleading if it implies that individuality of the drops is lost in the stream. Here is a difficult ridge to walk: To the left we have the ocean of organic and mystic views, to the right the abyss of atomic individualism." His term "Self-realization," rather than involving monistic indistinguishability, a magnified ego, or a transcendental Self, encompasses various levels, from the personal to the cosmological. Self-realization "thus includes personal and community self-realization, but is conceived also to refer to an unfolding of reality as a totality."[17] He explicitly has rejected the idea of an eternal, universal, absolute Self abstracted from the concrete world of process and relationship.[18] And as the quotation at the opening of this article shows, Naess is committed to uncovering a way of affirming both unity and plurality. Indeed, despite references to Atman, Naess's writings are filled with criticisms of indistinguishability, magnified ego, and abstract transcendentalism.

How can we reconcile such statements with the criticisms of deep ecology we saw in the previous section? Deep ecologists might respond by saying that their critics have misrepresented their views, either because of simple misunderstanding or as a rhetorical move to portray deep ecology in a way that is most incriminating and accentuates the differences rather than the similarities between them and, say, ecofeminism. Given the academic sectarianism that has plagued some of the debate, such a response might have some merit. But certainly some statements made by deep ecologists do reflect indistinguishability, magnified egoism, or abstract transcendentalism. In certain cases, such statements seem to reflect the fact that some deep ecologists hold such views. In other cases, however, the source of the discrepancies may be (as some critics have suggested) a lack of clarity as deep ecologists move back and forth between relational and monistic discourses. While such an ambiguity could be dismissed as fuzzy thinking, it also may suggest that (as in the quotation that began this article) some deep ecologists are struggling toward a view that encompasses both relationality and holism.

I think we can bring greater clarity to this discussion by avoiding attacks and countercharges and pursuing instead a more constructive course. Some of the discrepancies and disputes, I believe, are due to the inadequacy of our vocabulary and typologies concerning self and holism. To a great extent, both deep ecologists and their critics are still limited by Western dualistic thinking that leads us to speak in terms of *either* holism *or* relationality and individuality. We do not yet have precise enough terminology to suggest a truly nondualistic view. I would argue that a wide range of ecophilosophers have in fact pointed toward a combination of holism and individualism,[19] yet even here there is a strong tendency to end up emphasizing one end of the continuum and criticizing those who emphasize the other. If we can clarify a truly nondualistic view, we may not only make our philosophical discussions and our experience of nature more precise. We also may find that there is far more agreement among deep ecologists and ecofeminists, as well as social ecologists, than we have believed. Buddhism, in the Huayan[20] school, can help us move in that direction.

THE HUAYAN BUDDHIST EXPERIENCE
OF INTERCONNECTEDNESS

Huayan is a school of Chinese Mahayana Buddhism that developed the traditional Buddhist idea of interrelatedness into a sophisticated philosophy. Because the Huayan view is complex and radically different from traditional Western views, I cannot offer a thorough explication here.[21] Nor can I consider many of the problems and tensions involved in such a view. But a brief discussion can help us to see that there is a "middle path" between a monistic holism and an anti-holistic relationalism. After this discussion, we will consider in the next section the significance of Huayan for ecological issues.

Huayan expanded on the idea of "emptiness" (Sanskrit: *sunyata*) that had been used since the earliest Mahayana Buddhist writings. The Indian Buddhist Nagarjuna (second or third century) had emphasized the epistemological aspect of emptiness and given a "negative" interpretation of the term: because phenomena are interrelated and impermanent, no philosophy (including a philosophy of emptiness) can capture the nature of reality. Thus, Nagarjuna's approach was largely deconstructive.[22] Although his basic position became accepted in Mahayana thought, later Buddhists (especially in East Asia) felt the need for a more positive account of the interrelated character of reality. Huayan has provided the fullest Buddhist philosophy of nature, in part because it analyzed in detail two kinds of relationships: the interrelatedness of individual phenomena with reality as a whole (the part-whole relation) and the interconnections among phenomena (the part-part relation).

We can take two approaches to understanding its view of the relationship between phenomena and the whole. First, we can consider it in terms of the interconnection between the *absolute reality* and *phenomena* (*li* and *shi* in Chinese). The nature of this relationship was a major issue for Buddhism, for there was the possibility of viewing ultimate reality as separate from the world of phenomena, with the absolute as an unconditioned realm free from the forms, changes, and conditions of our world. With few exceptions, Buddhism has consistently denied such a transcendental view, seen perhaps best in the famous phrase from the Heart Sutra: "form is emptiness, emptiness is form." Huayan, too, insists that there is in actuality no difference between the absolute and phenomena. Ultimate reality is not some transcendental One but this very world, and phenomena are themselves the absolute.[23]

The Huayan master Fazang (643–712) attempted to explain this aspect of reality to the Chinese Empress Wu with his analogy of the golden lion.[24] Gold represents the absolute, while the shape of the lion represents phenomena. Complex relationships pertain between gold and the lion shape. We can intellectually distinguish the lion shape from the gold, but in actuality there can be no such shape without the gold that is shaped. Similarly, gold always has a shape, whether it is a lion, a temple, or a blob. So too, the phenomenal world is the ever-shifting form of the absolute. Phenomena and the absolute cannot exist separately from each other. The absolute is not a metaphysical reality behind or beyond or underneath the world of rocks and raccoons. The concrete, shifting world of mountains and rivers—and sewers—are not emanations from a deeper ultimate reality, they are ultimate reality. Huayan thus offers a fully nondualistic view of the relationship between the absolute and phenomena.

Another way to consider the Huayan experience of the relationship between the individual and the whole is to think in terms of the whole and the parts. Huayan rejected the commonsense view that there is a whole separate from the parts. In such a conventional view, there can be a whole (let's say a barn) separate from the parts (rafters, paneling, etc.). From this perspective, there are pieces of wood, nails, etc., and then there is a barn. In addition, one can replace one piece of wood and still have the "same" barn. Huayan, however, says that there is no whole separate from the particular parts. Indeed, each part *is* the whole. A rafter is the barn.[25]

As Francis Cook has noted,[26] the human body can be used to clarify this identification of the part and the whole. Let's say someone from a strange land is trying to figure out what "my body" is. She points at my ear questioningly. "No," I say, "that is my ear, not my body." She then points to my elbow, and I reply in like fashion. After pointing all around, the stranger would no doubt grow frustrated and leave, shaking her head. Not very enlightened of me. My ear, of course, is a *part* of my body, just as my elbow is. But it also *is* my body. There is no body separate from my parts. Should I cut off my ear in a fit of passion, it is no longer my body, and no longer a part of my body. In fact, it is no longer a "part" at all. Indeed, it is no longer an "ear," in the functional sense of an instrument for hearing. It is merely a rather ugly hunk of flesh. So a part is itself the whole; a grain of sand is the universe. But, common sense might reply, while my ear may no longer be my body, my body remains, and thus it is not the same as the parts. Huayan disagrees. The body that once existed is no more. Another body exists, with this new whole identical with its own particular set of parts. The whole is the parts; the universe is inseparable from the stardust and smokestacks that constitute it.

Another image used to explain this point is waves on an ocean. In the conventional view, waves are independent, self-existent things. From the perspective of emptiness, however, the waves are recognized as lacking independent existence: they are water in a distinct and temporary form, yet the waves are not separate from the ocean, they *are* the ocean. They are the form the ocean takes at any given moment, the activity of the ocean. Ocean and wave, whole and part, may be abstractly distinguishable, but they are not different.

Thus Huayan spoke of *li shi wu ai*: the mutual noninterference of the absolute and phenomena. One might complain that this disagreement concerning the whole and parts is just semantics, merely a different way of using words. But for Huayan, it points to a radically different way of experiencing reality that affects deeply how we relate to the world. Some of these effects will be considered in the next section.

Huayan is most famous for its views of the other type of interrelationship, the relationships among phenomena.[27] While the details of Huayan's view tax our conventional way of understanding, its simultaneous emphasis on both the distinctness of all things and their radical interrelatedness is critical to refining our discussions of self and relationality. The Chinese term that summarizes the Huayan view is *shi-shi wu-ai*, the mutual "non-interference" among all things.[28] There are two aspects of this relationship. The first concerns function: *integration* and *differentiation*. All phenomena are functionally integrated by being the "sole and total cause" of the whole and thus of all the others. All are differentiated because they play different roles. An image we can use to illustrate this quality is the tripod.[29] The tripod, of course, is made of three legs. What happens when you take away one of the legs? The tripod as a whole and each leg collapses. This is what Huayan means by sole and total cause. It does not mean that *only* this particular part is the cause for the whole. Instead, each single leg *by itself* is necessary for the whole to exist. If one leg is missing, than the whole cannot exist. Thus it is the "sole" cause. Similarly, each part *causes the entire whole*—it is the "total" cause—because without that part, the whole cannot exist. So all parts, all trees, rocks, and squirrels, are the same in that they function as sole and total causes of the whole.

The tripod image also gives us another perspective on the nondualistic relationship between whole and the parts. If the tripod (the whole) collapses, so do the legs (the parts), and vice versa. In fact, if it should collapse, the tripod would no longer exist as a tripod. And very importantly, nor would the legs: they would now be sticks of wood. Their identity as legs comes from their function in the tripod. As a result, each leg is a sole and total cause not only of the tripod (the whole) but also of every other leg (the parts).

So the legs are fully *integrated* in the sense of mutually conditioning each other and the whole. But this can occur only if they are *distinct* from each other. If all three legs leaned in the same direction, they could not stand up. Each one has to play its unique part for the tripod to stand up and for each leg to be a leg for the tripod. They have to lean into each other at different angles in order to be integrated. So too the phenomenal world. Every single thing in the world is different and plays a unique role in the universe. Each thing is the universe and makes the universe what it is. Without that grain of sand, it is a different universe. Everything exists in differentiated integration.

The radical interrelationship among phenomena has another double quality: *identity* and *difference*. The classic image used to represent these characteristics is Indra's net, which is described in the *Gandavyuha Sutra*.[30] In this image, the universe is considered to be a vast web of many-sided and highly polished jewels, each one acting as a multiple mirror. In one sense each jewel is a single entity. But when we look at a jewel, we see the reflections of other jewels, each of which contains the reflections of other jewels, and so on in an endless system of mirroring.

Thus, in each jewel is the image of all other jewels as well as the entire net as whole. The jewels interpenetrate each other and, in Huayan's sense of the term, they share the same identity. Yet each one contains the others in its own unique way in its distinctive position, and so they are different. This type of identity does not imply being identical or involve merging into an undifferentiated One.

Huayan uses the word "include" to suggest this identity. Each thing "includes" the others in the sense of "requires and works in conjunction with." The basic point here is that while each part (e.g., a tripod leg) can be said to be the sole and total cause, it requires the presence of the other parts (the other tripod legs) to make up the whole. We can understand this notion of "including" by returning to the image of the waves and viewing it from the mutual interpenetration of phenomena. The waves are seen as acting in interdependent harmony, each one affected by and affecting all the others, each one an integral part of the whole ocean. In fact, each wave *is* the ocean. But in order for a single wave to be the ocean, each wave "includes" (works in conjunction with) all the other waves.

Given the criticisms of deep ecology's holism, it is important to highlight that in discussing *shi* and *li*, Huayan thinkers made use of notions of part and whole and of identification. The Chinese Huayan master Tu Shun stated that "*Shih* is completely identical, and not partially identical, with *li*. Therefore, without causing the slightest damage to itself, an atom can embrace the whole universe." In this identification, there is an affirmation of both particularity and the whole. "The *shih* remains as it is and yet embraces all."[31] Commenting on Tu-shun's view, Steve Odin points out that "Tu-shun asserts that although each unsubstantial event (*shih*) fully interfuses with the totality (*li*) as well as every other event (*shih*), there is yet no violation of its own ontological integrity; for it both contains and permeates the whole cosmos while still retaining its unique structural identity and individual pattern."[32]

The Korean Huayan master Uisang wrote a verse characterizing the nondual dialectic of the one and the many.

> In One is All,
> In Many is One,
> One is identical to All,
> Many is identical to One.
> In one particle of dust,
> Is contained the ten directions.

For Uisang, phenomena "Are mutually identical. / Yet are not confused or mixed, / But function separately."[33]

The Chinese Huayan thinker Fazang also emphasized the mutual affirmation of the one and the many: "[T]he one and the many establish each other. Only when one is completely the many can it be called the one, and only when the many can be completely called the one can it be called the many. There is not a separate one outside the many, for we clearly know that it is one within the many."[34] Note that the one is not transcendental or abstract; it is fully within the plurality and concreteness of the phenomenal world.

One way to consider this type of holism is with the analogy of field theory. An electromagnetic field is an unbroken continuity. There are no real borders or edges to electromagnetic charges (though clearly there is a diminishing of power and effect with distance). Each location in the field is unique, but it is continuous with the entire field as it affects and is affected by all other places.[35] Similarly, a gravitational field is a single but differentiated continuum. A more prosaic analogy is a trampoline. If you add a weight to one end, the entire trampoline is immediately affected. Add a weight to the opposite end, and again the whole is affected, with the stretching at the location of one weight affecting and affected by the stretching at the location of the other. The cosmos is like a trampoline with all phenomena functioning as "weights" that mutually condition each other and the trampoline/cosmos as a whole. It is of course true that the affect may be extremely small. We can say that the gravitational pull of my own body is part of the gravitational field of the solar system, but its affect on that field is negligible. Huayan is not overstating the importance of each phenomenon. It is, however, insisting that we see the whole as a single field of being with every place and thing unique but wholly continuous with and interrelated to all others.

Cleary, Huayan is using language in an unconventional way. Terms such as *identity, include, sole and total cause* have different meanings and associations than we initially expect. This is not mere playing with language. Huayan would say that our conventional language is inextricably tied to our tendency to isolate phenomena from each other and to our dualistic view of whole and parts. As long as we see identity as complete sameness, as long as we think that inclusion implies the denial of difference, as long as we think of causation in a linear way, we will remain trapped in our traditional view of nature. Desires, anxiety, alienation, and the exploitation of nature will continue unless we transform our language and way of thinking.

If we see phenomena as independent from each other and from ourselves, we experience the world as an aggregation of separate things from which we are essentially divided. The world is, in a sense, broken, and we are not fully integrated into it. We could insist that phenomena exist communally, but still the sense of relationship is partial and there is no experience of being a part of an encompassing whole. Without a view of the radical interpenetration of phenomena and of the integration of the individual into the whole, the world remains discontinuous and we are not fully a part of the cosmos. For Buddhism, this opens the door to craving, aversion, and anxiety. They arise only when we feel ourselves in any sense separate from the world and lacking anything. And if we fail to experience phenomena as part of a continuous whole, we can treat them as mere things. Only by seeing the world as an unbroken but differentiated continuum can we leave behind desire, anger, and distress.

Along with this sense of interrelationship, the Huayan experience involves a radical sense of impermanence. One of the limitations of images such as the jewel net and the tripod, as well as of some of the terms used to explain the Huayan view of relationship, is that they seem to imply a static universe. But for Huayan, as for any school of Buddhism, the world is characterized by constant change. Interrelationship is characterized by ongoing *interdependent co-arising*. Every moment the universe is changing, with each phenomenon conditioning the arising and passing away of all other phenomena. This results in an extreme sense of impermanence. If each phenomenon is the sole and total cause of the whole and all other phenomena, then at every single change—thus at every single moment—the universe passes away and arises anew.

What is the significance of a view that experiences the world as a differentiated whole of interdependent co-arising phenomena, all things new each moment? For Huayan, each phenomenon takes on an unqualified value: on it depends the entire universe; indeed it *is* the universe as a whole and all other phenomena. As Francis Cook has said,

> In the Hua-yen universe, where everything interpenetrates in identity and interdependence, where everything needs everything else, what is there which is not valuable? To throw away even a single chopstick as worthless is to set up a hierarchy of values which in the end kills us in a way in which no bullet can. In the Hua-yen universe, everything counts.[36]

In addition, the world is experienced as "fresh" each moment, for it is a universe that has just come into being. It also partakes of the heightened value of the ephemeral, for the universe is also about to pass away forever. In a profoundly spiritual way, there is never a dull moment.

The result is an experience of a vast, continuous whole; of the uniqueness but interrelatedness of all things; of the unqualified value both of each thing and of the cosmos as a whole. Involved also is an experience of our full integration into that reality. We are part of that interdependent co-arising with all other phenomena; we are part of the universe's coming-into-being and passing-away.

What is most important for our purposes is Huayan's combined holistic and particularistic focus. The basic experience is of the oneness of this phenomenal world, a oneness that is characterized by radical relationality. Things are experienced as unique, but they so interpenetrate and depend on each other that one feels an unbroken wholeness. This sense of the "one" does not point to a transcendent reality; it arises from the fundamental quality of this concrete world of distinctions and flux. Zen master Suzuki Shunryu has captured the complexity and dialectical character of this point well:

> Strictly speaking, there are no separate individual existences. There are just many names for one existence. Sometimes people put stress on oneness, but this is not our understanding. We do not emphasize any point in particular, even oneness. Oneness is valuable, but variety is also wonderful. Ignoring variety, people emphasize the one absolute existence, but this is a one-sided understanding. In this understanding there is a gap between variety and oneness. But oneness and variety are the same thing, so oneness should be appreciated in each existence.[37]

As Sallie King has noted, this statement describes well the Buddhist notion of "thusness." When delusions are removed, we see the thing "as it is" in its nonduality as both individual and fully interpenetrating with other phenomena and with the whole.[38]

King, like critics of deep ecology, emphasizes the rejection of monism or a transcendental One. "There is no One to which phenomena could be reduced. . . . The perspective of Thusness is the very opposite of monism insofar as the immediate givenness of the plenitude of phenomena is the locus of Thusness."[39] But in this discussion we need to retain the dialectical nature of Buddhism's "Middle Way." While phenomena cannot be reduced to a One, the totality of phenomenal world cannot be "reduced to" merely the sum of many individual relationships. There is also Oneness. We can put this dialectic in a different way by referring to a famous (or for some critics of holism, infamous) poem by Robinson Jeffers, "The Answer."

> . . . Integrity is wholeness, the greatest beauty is
> Organic wholeness, the wholeness of life and things, the divine
> beauty of the universe. Love that, not man
> Apart from that. . . .[40]

A Huayan Buddhist might well respond, "Yes, but also love individual phenomena, not the whole apart from them, for when you love both the whole and the individual in its relationships you embrace the thusness of things, which is truly the greatest beauty."

THE ECOLOGICAL SIGNIFICANCE OF HUAYAN'S VIEW

Much of environmentalism is a response to a fundamental realization: something is very wrong with how we usually conceive of and treat the natural world. But what is the exact problem with our view of nature and our attitudes, and what would constitute an authentic intimacy with the natural world and an effective concern for the earth? There is always the danger that an environmental philosophy, however sophisticated, will miss the primary substance of the problem. Indeed, the ideal we establish may not only fail to help significantly, it may in fact compound the problem or create new ones.

Thus, some deep ecologists fear that if we stay limited to a concern with individual relationships, we will fail to realize a sense of the larger totality that integrates all of nature. Besides missing the spiritual depth of such an experience, we can remain trapped in an individualism or personalism[41] that lies at the base of our alienation from the earth and our ongoing destructiveness. Only a realization of an encompassing whole can give us a full sense of our connectedness with the natural world and of the intrinsic value of all things that participate in the life of the planet. Some critics, however, contend that a belief in a larger whole actually removes us from the concrete reality of our interrelationships and reinforces the inclinations to absorb the Other or to transcend the particulars of life—tendencies that have led to estrangement from nature, environmental destruction, and social oppression. Holism, in this view, takes us away from a true connectedness with nature and is, at root, inauthentic.

Huayan offers an alternative to these two opposing views: a mode of experiencing that affirms the concreteness of phenomena and the particularity of their relationships yet also involves a strong sense of a wider and integrating whole. We can isolate five distinct but interrelated aspects of this affirmation of both individuality and totality. First, there is an emphasis on experiencing reality as a whole and not just a collection of parts, however interrelated. The whole is real and has unqualified value. Second, the whole is not some transcendental realm but is concrete and ever-changing: the absolute is nothing other than phenomenal world. Third, the whole is not separable from, prior to, or more important than the parts. Each part is not only necessary for the whole to exist, it *is* the whole. To value the whole is to value the part, and vice versa. Fourth, despite the holism involved, each part remains distinct. Like the leg of a tripod or my ear, the uniqueness of each part is essential in its role of being a cause for—and being—the whole. Fifth, while Huayan presents a holistic view of reality, relationships are accentuated: the whole is single field of differentiated integration. Huayan's holism thus differs substantially from monistic indistinguishability, magnified egoism, or abstract transcendentalism.

These aspects of the Huayan view analysis help us to evaluate statements made about the significance of Buddhism for environmental philosophy and its relationship to deep ecology. John McLellan, for instance, has emphasized nonduality in the Buddhist ideal of saving all sentient beings.

> I've sometimes thought the greatest single clarification that could be brought to this subject might be to drop the *s* from "beings." The project suddenly becomes the vaster and simpler one of saving Sentient Being. . . . Simply drop the bothersome *s*, and Sentient Being itself looms up, vast, inconceivable, glowing and humming, in all ages and all spaces—indestructible, beyond confusing particulars. The vast Presence of aliveness, of sentient Isness, filling the time-space cosmos . . . is inexhaustible, self-sufficient, needing nothing, wanting nothing.[42]

The denial of individuality ("not beings but Being") suggests the abstract transcendentalism that some critics claim characterizes deep ecology, and there is a clear danger in characterizing beings as confusing and bothersome. In addition, McLellan's language of self-sufficiency recalls ecofeminist critiques of an expanded masculine ego.

It would be a mistake, however, to identify Buddhism with such a view. True, there is an aspect of self-sufficiency in the Buddhist view of reality, but there is equally strong element of vast suffering, boundless compassion, and the need for liberation. The suggestion of a single Sentient Being may be helpful in understanding Buddhism and developing an ecophilosophy, but only if it is presented in a dialectical view that also affirms the reality and importance of "beings." From a Huayan perspective, it misleading to talk about a Sentient Being "beyond particulars." Sentient Being is made of beings, each distinct and of unqualified value. The suffering of individuals is fully real and worthy of our earnest attention, an attitude that McLellan's statement seems to undercut. Here both ecofeminism and Huayan steer us from an unhelpful holism.

It also would be a mistake to identify deep ecology in general with such transcendentalism and expanded egoism. Huayan helps us see that the holism prized by deep ecologists can be combined with the relationality emphasized by ecofeminists. One way of seeing this is to consider the notion of identification. This term is often used to describe deep ecology's fundamental intuition of connectedness with nature, but it is an idea that is often criticized by ecofeminists for signalling the denial of difference and relationality. A Huayan perspective on identification can refine deep ecology's view in a way that brings it in line with some of the major concerns of ecofeminism.

Part of the problem is that both deep ecologists and especially their critics seem at times to impose Western substantialist assumptions on the notion of identification. Substantialism as I use it here involves seeing phenomena as consisting primarily of a discrete essence or an inherent substance distinct from the substances of all other phenomena. It is this assumption, I suggest, rather than holism per se, that has led to much of the dissonance in ecophilosophical debates. For instance, if we think of phenomena as substantial things with (to use a Buddhist phrase) "own-being," identification with other individuals easily comes to imply absorption of phenomena into the self, with difference and relationality being lost. Similarly, in a substantialist framework identification with the whole comes to mean unity with some single "thing," and thus there is an "atomism of one," to use Cheney's phrase.

But a Buddhist, especially Huayan, approach to identification is quite different. We can speak of two types of Buddhist identification. At the level of individual phenomena, identification is with individuals, each of which are a distinctive sets of relationships in unique positions. The individuality of each phenomenon is found not in a discrete substance but in its particular set of relationships with the rest of the world, like the uniqueness of a jewel in Indra's net. From a Buddhist standpoint, it is a delusion to identify with something as a "thing." Phenomena are particular and momentary conjunctions of relationships, mutually conditioning and conditioned by all other phenomena, rather than discrete and enduring entities. To identify with them is to identify with their various specific relationalities. Buddhism, then, would agree with criticisms of indistinguishability, magnified ego, and abstract transcendentalism. But it would disagree with any suggestion that identification necessarily has one or more of these characteristics. One can, in fact, identify with something in a way that affirms uniqueness and relationality. In fact, for Buddhism, this is the only way to truly identify with something.

Put differently, identification is not with the *being* of another phenomenon but with its *interbeing*. Identification involves the experiential recognition that I and that squirrel and that mountain are ontologically continuous and functionally interwoven. Yet such an experience recognizes at the same time that the interbeing of the squirrel is different from the interbeing of the mountain, and mine is different from theirs.

The second type of Buddhist identification concerns the whole. The Huayan ideal involves an identification with the entire field of interbeing, a whole that includes an infinite number of unique interbeings. Indeed, ultimately the interbeing of one phenomenon *is* the entire field of relationships—and that field *is* the interbeing of each phenomenon. There is one, boundless field made of distinctive sets of interrelationships. Such a way of experiencing reality is both holistic and relational.

As with the notion of identification, we can recognize Western assumptions at work in discussions of holism. In critiquing the deep ecology view of the whole, Dean Curtin makes three assumptions that may, in fact, be true in Western holistic views, but are not necessarily true of all holisms or of deep ecology. They certainly are not true of Huayan's view of the whole. First he makes the claim we have seen before, that a whole is inherently nonrelational: "Naess and others are in danger of defining the Self nonrelationally. The whole *cannot* relate to anything else just because it is the whole." Curtin's interpretation thus echoes Cheney's notion of an "atomism of one." Such a view leads him to a dualistic view of relationality and holism as mutually exclusive options: "[T]he relational self cannot be expressed in terms of parts and wholes."[43] But from a Huayan perspective, we *can* express relationality in terms of parts and wholes because the whole does in fact relate to something else: it relates to its parts. One can see a simple parallel in the body. The body is a whole, but as a whole system it is related to the functioning and health of its parts.

Second, Curtin claims that a whole is necessarily abstract, separate from concrete particulars. He cites the Japanese Zen master Dōgen as an embodiment a relational view rather than a nonrelational holistic view Curtin assigns to deep ecology. "Dōgen's relational self resists the abstractionist language of 'the whole' by highlighting the provisional, contextual borders of the self in relation to other things: *this* pine tree, and *this* meal."[44] But holistic language is abstractionist only if one makes Western assumptions. Indra's net is precisely this pine tree and this meal. To return to the analogy of the body, the body is a whole but it is also quite concrete, and by affirming the wholeness of the body we are not being abstract or transcending the concrete particularities of the organs. Just because Western thought may have ignored both the body and the possibility of a concrete whole does not mean we must, or that we should impose that assumption on deep ecology.

Third, Curtin seems to imply that holism involves immutability. In commenting on the views of Naess and Mathews, Curtin claims that "[i]t would appear that *this* version of the deep ecological Self is still conceptually tied to the old hierarchical project whose goal is to find an entity that is whole, 'permanent,' 'unsmeared by change.'"[45] Again, it may be true that in the West (starting with Plato) the whole has tended to be seen as unchanging, but one can have a whole that undergoes constant flux, whether it is the body or Indra's net.

We can get a better sense of the possibility of a truly nonsubstantialist, nontranscendent, nonmonistic experience of the whole by making use of a traditional Buddhist image. In East Asia, the term used to translate the Sanskrit word for emptiness is "sky" (Chinese: *kong;* Japanese: *kū*). In itself the boundless sky is empty in the sense that it is not a thing, nor is it the collection of all things. It is, rather, the field in which all things have their interexistence. Even (or especially) here we need to be careful of allowing substantialist and dualistic assumptions to distort this perspective. In the Buddhist view, the sky is not a container that includes but is separate from the things in it. It is rather a field within which all things arise and shift in their manifold interrelationships. The co-arising and interdependent shifting of these interrelationships *is* the sky.

We can think of the sky of emptiness and interrelationship in at least three ways. It is the *totality* of that field, which cannot be separated from the phenomena that make it up. Second, the sky is the *mode of existence:* the mutual co-arising of phenomena. Empty is, in this sense, more like an adverb than an adjective. The clouds come into being and change and go out of being intricately interdependent with all other clouds and conditions. Third, the sky is also a *quality* that allows this co-arising, a quality of openness and a sense of letting-be. The sky does not force the clouds into existence, it does not cling to them, it does not push them away. It is an unobstructed emptiness in which all things can arise and flourish and pass away.

While my discussion has focused more on what we might call the ontological aspect of interdependence, the psychological dimension is also relevant both to the question of relational holism and the imagery of the sky. Some aspects of Tibetan Buddhism can help us see that linkage.[46] Certain Tibetan texts refer to a Sky Woman, who represents the unbounded vastness of the experience of wisdom. The spaciousness is sometimes referred to as a "single sphere." Anne Carolyn Klein cites a Tibetan text that refers to the traditional equivalence of samsara (the phenomenal world of suffering and rebirth) and nirvana, but does so in a way that demonstrates the nonduality of holism and plurality: "[A]ll of samsara and nirvana is . . . the single sphere *because there are many contradictory perspectives.*" She emphasizes that

> Far from undermining variety, the concept of the single sphere finds in the inevitable contradictions of the world proof for its own existence. Put another way, it is precisely being rife with pluralism that validates it as an all-pervasive expanse, and in this sense as single. The single sphere, like mindfulness and concentration, models a nontotalizing, nonmastering form of subjective coherence. Its coherence comes from a certain style of awareness, not from any uniformity among the many perspectives or phenomena that participate in it. Indeed, its very plurality demonstrates its singularity. To feel that one's mind both is and participates in a single sphere means that there is no one feeling, thought, or identity that wholly defines it, and yet it is whole.[47]

To the enlightened mind, the interpenetrating world is experienced as a single whole that is characterized by multiplicity. Here, too, Buddhism presents an alternative to a nonrelational holism and a non-holistic relationality.

The Huayan experience of the interwoven character of the world has social significance beyond what traditional Buddhism has recognized. We can see this by considering a potential criticism. A deconstructionist could argue that Huayan is making universalistic claims that involve an imperialistic denial of difference. Huayan's view is, in fact, universalistic, but we need to clarify in what ways it is and is not. First, metaphysically, Huayan proposes that emptiness and nondualistic interdependence are the fundamental characteristics of reality. To the extent Buddhism proposes a philosophy of nature, emptiness and interrelatedness are presented as universal metaphysical truths.[48] Second, psychologically, Huayan claims that interrelatedness is the fundamental characteristic of our consciousness of the world. Our inherent Buddha mind, by virtue of its profound interrelatedness with reality, experiences things in their "thusness," in their emptiness and interrelatedness.[49] However, our delusion covers and distorts that primary experience, so that we actually experience separateness and alienation, craving and suffering. Thus, Huayan argues that nondual interrelatedness is universally true ontologically and essentially true phenomenologically.

However, this view does not deny difference. Enlightened or not, all people occupy a different social and political position and thus experience reality in their own way. Some are priveleged; some are exposed to more pollution than others; some are considered subversives and tortured by governments. These social differences and the suffering involved remain in the experience of Indra's net. As Anne Carolyn Klein has argued in terms of Tibetan Buddhism and mindfulness, the nonduality of Buddhist views and the experience of enlightenment do not dissolve the socially constructed positionality of the self. "Ontological nondualism" is her term for experiencing simultaneously "the constructed and non-constructed, the conditioned and unconditioned aspects of the self. . . . The Tibetan Buddhist view of personhood affirms both the lack of substantial or permanent self [its unconditioned emptiness] and also one's particular place in the social network [its conditioned construction]."[50] Indeed, Huayan especially underscores positionality, as each jewel has its uniqueness in its distinctive place in Indra's net.

There is, however, a crucial difference between Huayan's traditional metaphysics of co-arising and the interrelatedness of social structure. The interbeing of social structure is not an ontological given. It is historically and politically created, and it can be changed.[51] This point does not undercut Huayan's view; instead, it gives it two new functions. The notion of radical interdependence can be adapted as an approach that helps us to analyze critically the particular psychological and social interbeing of a society and the social dynamics and power structures that created it. It also can help us imagine a different psychological and social interbeing, one that causes less suffering and is less based on greed, hatred, and delusion. Speaking of the social construction of the self, Klein has observed that the Buddhist notion of nonself does not "elaborate how the psychological self is constructed through very specific kinds of interactions, and in dependence on various political, historical, racial, and gendered causes. Such elaborations, however, can certainly be seen as an expansion of the meaning of dependent arising."[52]

Christopher Ives has argued that Buddhist wisdom

> not only provides an insight into human entanglement in dualistic subjectivity as a fundamental cause of social problems, but also provides a mode of experience that promotes discernment of the complex interactions of socio-historical factors constituting the secondary cause of social problems.

He notes, however, that for Buddhist wisdom to function in these ways, it must become an "informed wisdom," engaging in social analysis and developing a "social *upāya*" (skillful means in solving problems).[53] Gary Snyder's complex political critique is an example of a Huayan-influenced ontology of interbeing that leads to a critical analysis of different forms of the interrelatedness involved in various social structures, East and West. "The mercy of the West has been social revolution; the mercy of the East has been individual insight into the basic self/void. We need both."[54] Buddhism's holistic but relational vision provides a creative base for both the analytical and constructive aspects of a political application of interrelatedness.

A New Typology: Relational Holism

The Huayan perspective clarifies that holism and relationality are not necessarily mutually exclusive. Curtin provides an effective summary of the conventional interpretation that they are inherently opposed to each other:

> The problem is that the deep ecology literature has endorsed *both* a holist and nonholist, a nonrelational and relational, understanding of Self. There has not been clear, univocal recognition that there are (despite Mathews) *three* competing models of self: the Cartesian atomic self, the Spinozist, holist Self expanded to the supreme whole, and Dōgen's relational self.[55]

Curtin's primary intent here is to argue that there has been ambiguity and inconsistency in the writings of deep ecologists. It is easy to agree that there has been. But Curtin also is making two other statements that need to be reconsidered. First, that holism is essentially and necessarily nonrelational; and second, that the only options are atomism, nonrelational holism, and a nonholistic relational view. Huayan shows that the situation is more complex.

By considering Huayan metaphysics as well as some of the statements made by deep ecologists, we can supplement Plumwood's distinction between indistinguishability, magnified ego, and abstract transcendentalism by adding another alternative: *relational holism*. An expanded typology could be articulated as shown in table 4.1.

Atomism is particularistic in its exclusive focus on individuals, which are seen as isolated selves lacking fundamental relationality. *Communalism* is my term for what is espoused by Plumwood, Cheney, and other critics of deep ecology, especially ecofeminst ones. Like atomism, the focus of communalism is particularistic, that is, on individuals. But unlike atomism, the emphasis is upon relationality. There are many selves, which are distinct but inherently interrelated, and our goal is to realize fully that relatedness of self-with-selves. *Relational holism* high-

TABLE 4.1   Approaches to the Self

Approach	View of Relationships	Focus	View of the Self
Atomism	Atomistic	Particularistic	Isolated ego
Communalism	Relational	Particularistic	Self-with-selves
Relational holism	Relational	Holistic and Particularistic	Self-with-selves-in-Self-as-selves
Magnified egoism	Nonrelational	Holistic	Cosmic Ego
Transcendental holism	Transrelational	Holistic	Transcendental Self
Indistinguishability	Monistic	Holistic	Atman

lights relationship not only between particulars but also between each particular and the entire field of relationships. In this sense it is *more* relational than communalism. The whole is not separate from or transcending the parts, and it does not subsume the parts. It is the interworking of the parts as a single, unified system. Thus, its view of the self could be stated, with some humor, as self with other selves within a Self that is the field of selves.

Magnified egoism is holistic in a different way than relational holism, because individuality is absorbed in a single cosmic ego, an aggrandizing self that includes all phenomena. The focus here is not ontological indistinguishability (there continues to be some distinction between "me" and the "rain forest"), but the experience of multiple identities and relationality is lost in an unbounded sense of "I" ("I am the rainforest"). *Transcendental holism* is characterized by transcending the world of particularity. I term it "transrelational" because rather than dissolving relationships, it ignores them in its affirmation of an abstract whole beyond individual relationships in concrete contexts. *Indistinguishability* involves a merger of all things in which ontological difference is denied. We can call this "monistic" because there are no individual phenomena to be related. There is only an undifferentiated one: Atman.

Like all typologies, this one is a simplification, but it helps to clarify that there is an alternative to non-holistic relationalism and nonrelational holism. A key to the typology is the distinction between *views of relationship* and what I call *focus*. The notion of holism concerns the focus, not the issue of relationality. Holism is the affirmation of and focus on the whole or wholes. It may or may not include relationality. *Relational* holism, such as found in Huayan Buddhism, affirms and focuses on individuals as well as the whole, and upholds the integrity and importance of relationships.

Some advocates of communalism, in their insistence on relationality, have rejected holism, assuming that the holistic affirmation of the whole involves a denial of relationship—confusing the two distinct issues of relationality and focus. In a similar way, advocates of holism, in underscoring the importance of a sense of the whole, have at times used language that is nonrelational. Some deep ecologists, in fact, may hold views that belong to the last three, nonrelational categories. But others, I believe, at times slip into nonrelational language in order to emphasize holism, even though they affirm relationality. Perhaps a recognition of the option of a relational holism can clarify the debate.

CONCLUSION: RELATIONAL HOLISM IN DEEP ECOLOGY, ECOFEMINISM, AND SOCIAL ECOLOGY

I suggest that deep ecology is neither essentially characterized by nor limited to monistic indistinguishability, magnified egoism, or transcendental holism, although such views are certainly possible within this perspective. Relational holism is fully in line with deep ecology, and that term seems to me to be a more accurate way to interpret the views of Naess, Fox, and several other deep ecologists. The discussions of deep ecologists at times suggest the more extreme forms of holism while at other times implying a relational holism, but the inconsistency can be explained at least in part by the difficulty in overcoming Western dualistic assumptions of holism versus relationality.

Of course relational holism is not "essentially" a deep ecology view. It can also be seen in the writings of ecofeminists and social ecologists. Charlene Spretnak's "ecological postmodernism," for instance, suggests relational holism. She calls for an ecofeminism characterized by a radical nonduality that, like Huayan, recognizes "a dynamic system of relations wherein any particular manifestation functions simultaneously as a distinct part and the unbroken whole. The parts are not derivative of the whole, nor vice versa. Each aspect constitutes the other." Like many ecofeminists, she affirms both the importance of particularity and also the role of social construction in the experience of the self. But she also argues for the need to recognize "an inherent and continuous systemicity within the unfolding universe, a constitutive unity that exists *along with*, not instead of, manifestations of particularity and subjectivity."[56]

Social ecologist John Clark has presented another formulation of relational holism in terms of "dialectical holism." He speaks of a "unity-in-difference" that avoids the extremes of monism and individualism. Individual things are not simply parts of a single whole but are "holons," both parts of a larger whole and wholes in relation to their own parts. Such a view fits with the multiple and multilevelled wholes involved in the notion of ecosystem: my back woods is an ecosystem in itself, with parts that are themselves an ecosystem (e.g., a squirrel's fur) while at another level the woods is a part of the larger ecosystem of the central Piedmont. Cook notes that this view is found also in Huayan: "[W]ithin the Great Immensity there are many other wholes which also have parts. . . ."[57] Also found in Huayan Buddhism is Clark's emphasis that things are both centers within a surrounding environment and part of the environment of other centers.[58] The Chinese master Fazang discussed this point in terms of the interchangeability and interpenetration of "principal" and "satellites": each thing is both principal and satellite depending on one's perspective at that time, and principal and satellite reflect and include each other.[59] Similarly, Huayan emphasizes that each phenomenon has an active and passive aspect, "having power" in the sense of conditioning everything else, "lacking power" in being conditioned by everything else.[60] This dialectical view of phenomena, including both a "vertical" holonic relationality as well as the "horizontal" mutual co-arising (to use a Buddhist term), leads to a simultaneous emphasis on individuals in their relations and the unifying web of interdependency, i.e., a differentiated integration. Clark thus rejects any necessary association between holism and monism or an abstract transcendentalism:

> Critics of holism sometimes identify it with an extreme organicism that denies the significance, reality, or value of the parts. It is important, therefore, to understand that "holism" does not refer exclusively to a view in which the whole is ontologically prior to the part, more metaphysically real than the part, or deserving of more moral consideration than the part. In fact, a dialectical holism rejects the idea that the being, reality, or value of the parts can be distinguished from that of the whole in the manner presupposed by such a critique.[61]

I do not mean to suggest that the nondualistic holisms of Spretnak, Clark, and some deep ecologists are exactly the same. However, it seems accurate to classify these various thinkers as relational holists because they affirm the full integrity of both the whole and the parts, and also the importance of both unity and relationality. Nor do I want to suggest that relational holism is essentially or necessarily a Buddhist view. It could take various forms and be cast in a variety of metaphysical and spiritual frameworks. However, Huayan presents a long-standing and sophisticated view that helps us see that we need not choose between holism and relationality, and it can serve as a counterpoint for clarifying different but related views.

The notion of relational holism helps to clarify the nature of an intuition of the relatedness and unity of reality. Such an experience can be used to solve some central metaphysical issues in environmental philosophy, and in doing so resolve some of the acrimonious debate in our current academic sectarianism. It also helps us realize that we can value both individuals in their concrete relationships as well as the total field of relationships of which we are a part—we needn't choose one or the other. Indeed, in this way of experiencing the world, to value the individual is to value the whole, and vice versa. And relational holism can help in the ever-present concern with motivation. Ultimately, the value of environmental philosophy is in cultivating a deeper sensitivity to the beauty and the devastation of nature, leading us to a stronger commitment to work for its well-being. The approach of relational holism, and images such as Indra's net, are effective in emphasizing our full responsibility to one and to all.

Notes

1. See, for instance, Val Plumwood, "Ecosocial Feminism as a General Theory of Oppression," in *Ecology*, ed. Carolyn Merchant (Atlantic Highlands, NJ: Humanities Press, 1994), 216.

2. Warwick Fox makes this latter argument in his *Toward a Transpersonal Ecology* (Boston: Shambhala, 1990).

3. Kheel, "Ecofeminism and Deep Ecology," in *Reweaving the World*, ed. Irene Diamond and Gloria Feman Ornstein (San Francisco: Sierra Club, 1990), 135.

4. Cheney, "Ecofeminism and Deep Ecology," *Environmental Ethics* 9, no. 2 (1987): 130.

5. Plumwood, "Nature, Self, and Gender," in *Environmental Philosophy: From Animal Rights to Radical Ecology*, second edition, ed. Michael E. Zimmerman et al. (Upper Saddle River, NJ: Prentice-Hall, 1998), 299–300. It is in fact unclear whether these are necessarily three different accounts. The second, which is sometimes described as the aggrandizement of the male ego to include all others and the whole of nature, could take the form of monistic indistinguishability or transcendental holism. However, the distinctions remain helpful in pointing to different emphases. See my typology later in the article.

6. Plumwood, "Nature, Self, and Gender," 307, 301. For similar arguments, see Deborah Slicer, "Is there an Ecofeminism-Deep Ecology 'De-

bate'?" *Environmental Ethics* 17, no. 2 (summer 1995): 168, where she argues that deep ecology involves an "indistinguishable merger of the selves in relation." Even Freya Mathews, whose metaphysics are quite holistic, has stated that in ecofeminism, "We are urged to respect the otherness, the distinct individuality of these beings, rather than [in deep ecology] seeking to merge with them, in pursuit of an undifferentiated oneness" ("Ecofeminism and Deep Ecology," in *Ecology,* ed. Carolyn Merchant [Atlantic Highlands, NJ: Humanities Press, 1994], 243). From a different perspective, Peter C. van Wyck also has charged that deep ecology has an ideal of undifferentiability, a "complete breakdown of the distinction between self and other" in which the self "fades and dissolves into the world" (*Primitives in the Wilderness: Deep Ecology and the Missing Human Subject* [Albany: State University of New York Press, 1997], 41).

7. Plumwood, "Nature, Self, and Gender," 302.

8. Cheney, for example, has discussed the inauthenticity of deep ecology's attempt to counter the sense of alienation implicit in the traditional Western view: "[A]lienation is not overcome in good faith by eliminating the other, even if it is elimination by incorporation of the other or by expansion of the self to include the other"(Cheney, 128).

9. Kheel, "Ecofeminism and Deep Ecology," 136.

10. Plumwood, "Nature, Self, and Gender," 303.

11. Mathews, "Ecofeminism and Deep Ecology," 239.

12. Slicer, "Is there an Ecofeminism-Deep Ecology 'Debate'?" 168.

13. Mathews, in "Ecofeminism and Deep Ecology," argues that we need both a relational and a holistic view. However, she treats them as distinct approaches that should be held jointly, while I will argue that Huayan actually combines the two views.

14. Fox, *Toward a Transpersonal Ecology* (Albany: State University of New York Press, 1995), 258, 262–263.

15. McLaughlin, *Regarding Nature* (Albany: State University of New York Press, 1993), 159.

16. Matthews, "Conservation and Self-Realization," *Environmental Ethics* 10, no. 4 (1988): 350.

17. Arne Naess, *Ecology, Community, and Lifestyle* (Cambridge: Cambridge University Press, 1989), 84, 165.

18. Naess, "Gestalt Thinking and Buddhism," 1983, 12–13, 16–17. Quoted in Fox, 113.

19. At the end of this essay I will briefly discuss an ecofeminist and a social ecologist who have expressed this fusion of holism and relationality.

20. In this article I use the modern pinyin system of romanizing Chinese. In the older Wade-Giles system this school is called Hua-yen.

21. For overviews of Huayan thought, see Francis Cook, *Hua-yen Buddhism* (University Park: Pennsylvania State University Press, 1977) and Thomas Cleary, *Entry Into the Inconceivable* (Honolulu: University of Hawaii Press, 1983).

22. For a comparison between Nagarjuna and deconstruction, see Robert Magliola, *Derrida on the Mend* (West Lafayette, IN: Purdue University Press, 1984).

23. For a subtle exposition that highlights the paradoxical character of this idea, see "Mirror of the Mysteries of the Universe of the Hua-yen," by Tu Shun and Cheng-kuan, in Cleary, 69–124.

24. For one of the many translations of this famous essay, see Garma C. C. Chang, *The Buddhist Teaching of Totality: The Philosophy of Hwa Yen Buddhism* (University Park: Pennsylvania State University Press, 1971), 224–230.

25. For an extensive analysis of this Huayan image, see the chapter "The Part and the Whole," in Cook, 75–89.

26. Ibid., 9–10.

27. In other words, the part-part relation. However, as we will see, the interrelatedness of part and part reinforces and further clarifies the relations between part and whole.

28. "Non-interference" refers to the fact that the interrelatedness among things (indeed their "identity" in Huayan's sense of the term) does not interfere with their distinctness, and the individuality of things does not interfere with their interpenetration.

29. Cook develops this image in *Hua-yen Buddhism*, 13–14.

30. For a translation, see Thomas Cleary, *Entry Into the Realm of Reality: The Text* (Boulder: Shambhala, 1987), especially pages 365–372 on Indra's net. This book is the final section of the larger *Avatamsaka Sutra*.

31. Cited in Steve Odin, *Process Metaphysics and Hua-yen Buddhism* (Albany: State University of New York Press, 1982), 24. As noted in the Introduction, there are two systems of romanizing Chinese currently in use. In the older Wade-Giles system we find Hua-yen, *shih*, and Fa-tsang; in the pinyin system established by the Chinese government we find Huayan, *shi*, and Fazang.

32. Ibid., 24.

33. Ibid., xix–xx.

34. Ibid., 25.

35. Cook notes that "Faraday, over a hundred years ago, made the startling remark that an electric charge must be considered to exist everywhere" (Cook, 17).

36. *Hua-yen Buddhism*, 19. Cook's statement obviously raises questions about a nondualistic approach to value. Does toxic waste have absolute value? After all, it is the sole and total cause of the universe. Some of the problems involved are discussed in terms of "Buddha Nature" in John McClellan's "Nondual Ecology" (*Tricycle: The Buddhist Review* 3, no. 2 [winter 1993]). Ian Harris, among others, dismisses the relevance of Huayan to environmental ethics because of this. See his "Getting To Grips With Buddhist Environmentalism: A

Provisional Typology," *Journal of Buddhist Ethics* 2 (1995): 177. I believe such a dismissal is premature, but to develop a defense of Huayan axiology would take an entire essay.

37. Suzuki Shunryu, *Zen Mind, Beginner's Mind* (New York: Weatherhill, 1970), 83. Zen has been heavily influenced by Huayan thought.

38. King, *Buddha Nature* (Albany: State University of New York Press, 1991), 164.

39. Ibid., 107.

40. *The Selected Poetry of Robinson Jeffers* (New York: Random House, 1938), 594.

41. Fox claims that a personally based identification "*inevitably* leads one to identify most with those entities with which one is most involved" (262, his emphasis) and that such gradation is a cause of greed, war, and ecological destruction. It seems easier to defend the claim that this is a tendency rather than an inevitability. In struggling with the tension between a personally based, graduated identification and a holistic identification, we can look not only to Buddhism for insight but to Neo-Confucianism as well. For an excellent study of this issue in the context of Neo-Confucianism, see Donald Munro, *Images of Human Nature: A Sung Portrait* (Princeton: Princeton University Press, 1988).

42. McClellan, 63–64. The statement that the cosmos needs or wants nothing is, of course, problematic in an environmental context. If this is true, why worry about environmental destruction? While McClellan emphasizes the self-sufficiency of nature for most of the article, he states at the end (without sufficient explanation) that one should care and be involved. A more thorough discussion is needed, but we cannot pursue it here.

43. Dean Curtin, "Dōgen, Deep Ecology, and the Ecological Self," *Environmental Ethics* 16, no. 2 (1994): 205, 206.

44. Ibid., 210.

45. Ibid., 205.

46. Tibetan Buddhism shares a number of the characteristics found in Huayan, but it has tended to delve more deeply into the psychological significance of Buddhist teachings. The psychological views discussed here are, I believe, in concert with Huayan.

47. Klein, *Meeting the Great Bliss Queen* (Boston: Beacon Press, 1995), 163–164. Her emphasis in the translation. The psychological dimension is actually implied in all of Huayan writings because of the belief that all of reality is Mind. However, a discussion of the relationship between mind and reality cannot be pursued here.

48. Buddhism, especially with the notion of emptiness, questions any philosophy of nature that purports to accurately and fully describe reality. However, a Buddhist view of nature is a "provisional truth" that (according to Buddhism) best approximates the character of reality and helps the practitioner toward enlightenment.

49. Klein notes that the "universal" nature of this experience does not reflect a rationalistic or abstract withdrawal from particulars that concerns Plumwood (see note 13). In Buddhism, "The subtle knowing of emptiness is thus the innermost and most 'personal' experience possible; in another sense, however, because all emptinesses are the same, it is universal experience" (Klein, 140).

50. Klein, 21, 40. She further analyzes how the unconditioned emptiness of the self and its conditioned social construction are compatible, noting that Buddhism would criticize postmodernism for a one-sided focus on the conditioned or "dependent arising" of the socially constructed self without attending to the unconditioned emptiness of the self, which allows the possibility of experiencing the world in an unconditioned way (136–137).

51. Gary Snyder has criticized Buddhism's neglect of social critique and political engagement. See, for instance, *The Real Work* (New York: New Directions, 1980), 101.

52. Klein, *Meeting the Great Bliss Queen*, 133.

53. Ives, *Zen Awakening and Society* (Honolulu: University of Hawaii Press, 1992), 102–103. Obviously I cannot here develop a Buddhist social critique or ideal, but Ives's book serves as an excellent first step in that direction.

54. "Buddhism and the Coming Revolution," *Earth House Hold* (New York: New Directions, 1969), 92. For studies of Snyder's Huayan Buddhist view of ecology, see my "Great Earth *Sangha*: Gary Snyder's View of Nature as Community," in *Buddhism and Ecology: The Interconnection of Dharma and Deeds*, ed. Mary Evelyn Tucker and Duncan Ryūkan Williams (Cambridge: Harvard University Center of the Study of World Religions, 1997), 187–218, and "Indra's Net as Food Chain: Gary Snyder's Ecological Vision," *Ten Directions* 11, no. 1 (1990): 20–28. I am not aware of any discussions of Huayan by traditional masters or contemporary scholars that apply its view to social distinctions and political interrelations.

55. Curtin, "Dōgen, Deep Ecology," 206.

56. Charlene Spretnak, "Radical Nonduality in Ecofeminist Philosophy," in *Ecofeminism: Women, Culture, Nature*, ed. Karen J. Warren (Bloomington: Indiana University Press, 1997), 427, 429.

57. Cook, *Hua-yen Buddhism*, 75.

58. Clark, "A Social Ecology," in *Environmental Philosophy: From Animal Rights to Radical Ecology*, second edition, ed. Michael E. Zimmerman et al. (Upper Saddle River, NJ: Prentice-Hall, 1998), 421.

59. "Cultivation of Contemplation of the Inner Meaning of the Hua-yen," in Cleary, *Entry Into the Inconceivable*, 168.

60. On this point, see Cook, 69. The dialectical character of this perspective radically undercuts anything like a magnified egoism, which implies the ego is the only principal and all other things are merely satellites.

61. Clark, "A Social Ecology," 421, 422–423.

5

Chinese Religion, "Daoism," and Deep Ecology

JORDAN PAPER

PROLOGUE

SINCE THE INCEPTION of a doctoral program in the Faculty of Environmental Studies at York University a half decade ago, I have served as either the thesis supervisor or on the dissertation committee of those graduate students interested in religion. This introduced me to deep ecology and its use of Asian and Native American traditions, or, more precisely, what were assumed to be such traditions. In this essay, I will critically review the most frequently quoted deep ecology formulations pertinent to Daoism, compare them with the most often cited relevant studies by philosophers familiar with the Chinese materials, relate both sets of studies to skeptical ones, and conclude with an exposition of reasonable possibilities.[1]

Having participated in a number of conferences on ecology,[2] however, I am well aware that a sanguine response is preferred: from a religious tradition, one is expected to advance a solution to the environmental crisis. But if any aspect of Chinese tradition has had a major effect on me, it is that aspect which is the antithesis of Western intellectualizing. Chinese theorizing proceeds from real problems by developing means for resolving those specific problems. To the contrary,

An earlier version of this paper was published with the title, "'Daoism' and 'Deep Ecology': Fantasy and Potentiality," in *Taoism and Ecology* (Cambridge: Harvard University Press, forthcoming).

Western theorizing tends to proceed from ad hoc premises to create theories only tangentially related to the problems to which they may be applied. Hence, Western intellectuals and Western-influenced Chinese intellectuals tend to derive theories from Chinese texts that have little if any relationship to Chinese modes of thinking. Similarly, Chinese religion, as virtually all non-Western religions, focuses on religious experience, whether it be personal ecstatic experiences, experiences from participating in rituals, or experiencing superhuman beings via possessed spirit mediums or the work of shamans. Again in contrast, Western religions tend to proceed from belief in religious principles, dogma, theological formulations, etc., although there are always subgroups that focus on religious experience.

A second pattern of behavior I have learned from Chinese culture is to criticize perceived errors in understanding and reacting to problems. Traditional Chinese government early institutionalized such criticism in a Board of Censors, and my doctoral thesis, from so long ago that it now seems to me a previous incarnation, focused on the literary remnants of such an official.[3] Accordingly, I hope that if not forgiven, there will at least be a degree of understanding in my taking more of a critical than an enthusiastic note with regard to this volume. I consider the imminent destruction of this planet for human habitation through the predation of humans so immediate and momentous that I have become rather immoderate in my impatience toward the assumption that donning the rose-colored glasses of romantic interpretations of other cultures will save the world.

To write that Chinese religion is poorly understood in the West would be a considerable understatement. It has become a scholarly dogma that there are three religions in China. This concept was created in the late sixteenth century by Matteo Ricci, a Jesuit missionary in China, who had accepted a post in the Chinese government. Accordingly, he had to take part in state rituals, behavior that led to his execution under the Inquisition. Hence, he presented a reading of Chinese religion that deliberately ignored virtually all of Chinese normative religious rituals. Dominican and Franciscan missionaries to China, who later worked among the people and knew better, opposed this interpretation, which led to the Rites Controversy in the Vatican that the Jesuits eventually lost in the eighteenth century.[4]

Chinese religion is actually the oldest continuing tradition for which we have relatively complete literary records; the rituals can be traced back for at least 3,500 years, and suggestive archaeological evidence would add at least more than one thousand years to that time depth. The religion focuses on family in and of itself, including the dead of the family and those yet to be born. The rituals center on offering food and wine, as well as other understood necessities, to the family dead which is then shared by the living members. For the last thousand years, Chinese deities have been modelled on the dead of the family, as they are dead human beings willing to assist persons who are not members of their own family. For the last two thousand years, most religious rituals, whether family, clan, or state, are modelled on the above summarized ritual. Over time, subsidiary religious developments added to rather than replaced the essential aspect of Chinese religion. These would include sinified forms of Buddhism and institutional Daoism (daojiao).[5]

As with Chinese religion in general, Daoism is grossly misunderstood in the West. The only Daoists per se, from a Chinese perspective, are hereditary, initiated priests or monks-nuns.[6] With regard to Daoism as a philosophical orientation (daojia), we are essentially speaking of two enigmatic texts: the Zhuangzi and the Laozi / Daode jing. The earliest strata of the former proceed from those of the aristocracy who had no need to be productive members of society and focused on individual ecstatic experience. The latter, in the received version (i.e., excluding a recently excavated variant version), seems to have initially functioned as an ideological justification for a ruthless, totalitarian government. Both then came to be perceived as relevant to the search for the extension of life by the elite, and the latter written by a divinity. Only with the developed civil service system,[7] as part of the elite ideology complementary to the more pragmatically oriented aspects of rujia thought (the ideology of the Civil Service System commonly but mistakenly translated as Confucianism), do we find modes of thought that might be realistically relevant to the environmental crisis. Again, except for the nuns and monks of the Quanzhen order, modelled on Buddhism, Daoist religious rituals function together with the normative religious rituals and concerns of Chinese religion. It is difficult to understand how artificially separating out either actual Daoist thought or Daoist religious practices from their ideological or religious context, according to the Western rather than the Chinese understanding, can contribute anything meaningful to resolving our urgent environmental problems.

Recent usages of the term Daoism have further confused the situation. There are now sectarian attempts in Taiwan to claim the term for normative Chinese religion in general.[8] This in turn is leading some new religions to wrest the term for themselves to the consternation if not indignation of the Daoist priests. On the mainland, the Chinese government is attempting to enfold all of indigenous Chinese religion within the Quanzhen order of Daoism as a means to control an otherwise amorphous, noninstitutional religion, since the order itself is under a government ministry. Unfortunately, a half millennium of the Western insistence on a trinitarian concept of distinctly separate religions in China, while ignoring normative Chinese religion, has led to this new use of the term Daoism for indigenous Chinese religion as a whole. This convention but replaces the unfortunate mistranslation of "Confucianism" for *rujia* as a term for normative Chinese religious practices, practices that long preceded the time of Kungfuzi (Confucius), let alone *daojiao*. Finally, I have noticed in the Toronto area, at least, that Westerners who run commercial teaching institutions based on Chinese practices, such as *taiji*, or who are involved with various forms of healing practices based on Chinese modes, such as *qigung*, tend to preface these institutions or practices with the term "Daoist," while those from China with similar involvements do not.

Although several scholars of Chinese religion have long attempted to point to Chinese religion as a singular, complex religious construct (e.g., Thompson), this has not as yet caught on, although we comfortably use the term Judaism to refer to the religion of the Jews or Hinduism to refer to the religion of Hindus, the Western term for the majority of South Asians who do not identify themselves with a specific term. It would now be most confusing to use one term of the ersatz trinity of Chinese religions for the whole.

Nonetheless, if we can bring to an end the romanticism of deep ecology with regard to their construction of "Daoism," deep ecology could then proceed in more viable directions, particularly by trying to work within and modifying Western traditions through being informed by a more realistic understanding of Daoism. Secondly, by looking at Chinese ideology holistically from a Chinese perspective, while fully acknowledging that environmental degradation is already mentioned in virtually the earliest extant texts and contemporary China is an environmental basket case, I do believe we can bring forward articulated attitudes of long standing, beginning with the *Mengzi (Mencius)* rather than the *Zhuangzi*, and also reflected in *jiao* (renewal) rituals, that may, indeed, be useful in reconceptualizing attitudes toward the environment both here and in China.

DEEP ECOLOGY

Deep ecology can be traced at least as far back as a seminal article, published three decades ago, by Lynn White Jr., "The Historical Roots of Our Ecological Crisis," in which he pointed to Western philosophical and religious traditions as the basis of our present plight: "Human ecology is deeply conditioned by beliefs about our nature and destiny. . ." (1205). But White is also dubious about the application of non-Western traditions to the Western experience, in contrast to the later deep ecologists. The term itself seems first to have been used by the Norwegian philosopher, Arne Naess, in 1973.[9] The term was intended to distinguish between "environmentalism," the practical side of environmental concerns, and "ecosophy" or philosophical ecology, which brings in not only Western thinkers but Native American thought, as well as Daoism and Zen Buddhism, to address fundamental ways of understanding the environment.

According to my graduate students, the most influential works with regard to deep ecology's use of Daoism, verified by the deteriorated condition of these books in my university library are Clark, although it does not address the term directly; Devall and Sessions; and LaChapelle. These works find the Western religious paradigms to be the root of the ecological crisis and virtually irremedial. Instead, they turn to non-Western religious traditions—of which Daoism, as they understand it, is preeminent—for a new foundation for understanding life and the world, in order to solve the environmental ills. Before turning to these and related depictions of Daoism, for purposes of comparison, we might quickly review writings on these topics by those who have spent their scholarly lives studying Chinese texts in the original language.

SINOLOGIST PHILOSOPHERS AND THEIR FRIENDS

The best known writings by philosophers, who are not environmental specialists, on Daoism and ecology are found in two volumes, both published in the late 1980s; these scholars are either associated with the University of Hawaii or each other. Volume 8 (1986) of *Environmental Ethics* contained articles by Ames and Cheng.

Ames provides a thorough and reasonable analysis of the topic and provides a crucial admonition, one that tends to be ignored by those environmentalists espousing deep ecology who have read the article:

> Taoism's [Daoism's] concreteness returns us to our own particularity as the beginning point of the natural order. We cannot play the theoretician and derive an environmental ethic by appeal to universal principles, but must apply ourselves to the aesthetic task of cultivating an environmental *ethos* in our own place and time, and

recommending this project to others by our participation in the environment.[10]

My sole caveat to this point, relevant to the concluding discussion, is that I find nothing specifically Daoist here but rather the nature of traditional Chinese thought as a whole (see Nakamura).

With an erudite discourse on Chinese terms that are not in and of themselves exclusively Daoist, Cheng formulates a position that could "eventually lead to a maturity of the environmental ethics of the *Tao* [*dao*] and *Ch'i* [*qi*], and it is in terms of this mature form . . . that we will be able to speak of the embodiment of a new reason in the mind of man."[11] Of course, by then humans may already have rendered themselves extinct due to environmental degradation.

An anthology, edited by Callicott and Ames, contains three articles relating to Daoism, the article by Ames above, retitled, and articles by Parkes and Hall. From the "Introduction: The Asian Traditions as a Conceptual Resource for Environmental Philosophy," it is apparent that the editors intended the anthology for an audience of deep ecologists. They note that recasting "environmental philosophy may not go far enough. A deeper break with traditional Western philosophical commitments may be required."[12] But they also note that

> There has been a general assumption that Eastern traditions of thought could provide important conceptual resources for this project, and there has been a lot of loose talk about how they might. But with the exception of a handful of essays, no direct and extensive work by experts in Eastern thought has been undertaken of the environmental philosophy problematic.[13]

This was the inspiration for the volume.
  Parkes finds that,

> Since there is no evidence that Nietzsche knew anything about Taoism, the number of his ideas about nature which correspond to Taoist views suggests that there may be further, hitherto unexplored philosophical (re)sources in the Western tradition which may prove helpful to consider in our current predicament.[14]

Hall elaborates aspects of "the Taoism of classical China" in its "cultural matrix" pertinent to developing an "altered sense of human nature and of nature per se." He seems not to concern himself as to why it had not done so within its own "cultural matrix."

DEEP ECOLOGY AND FANTASIES OF DAOISM

For want of some order, the more popular deep ecology texts will be addressed by date of publication. Clark has but a single chapter on non-Western phenomena and that is exclusively on Daoism, beginning with the sentence: "The *Lao Tzu* is one of the great anarchist classics."[15] Indeed, he understands it to be the preeminent work on the topic, "East or West." Clark is aware of the major translations of the work at the time his book was written and quotes from the Wing-tsit Chan version, refers to relevant articles by Roger Ames and David Hall, points to the works of Ursula Le Guin, whom he considers "perhaps the most widely read contemporary anarchist writer, and also a Taoist."[16] Among the reasons for Clark's conclusion, I will list but the most dubious ones, for in the text he finds both compassion and the rejection of coercion. Perhaps he missed such key passages as "the sage governs the people by emptying their minds and filling their bellies, and by weakening their aspirations and strengthening their bones," and he dismisses the reference to treating people as straw-dogs (*Laozi*, chapters 3 and 5). Perhaps Clark is reading the text from a Mahayana Buddhist perspective. He also writes of "a Taoist community" as if it actually exists (aside from religious communities) and "the Taoist ruler-sage" as more than a hypothetical figure.[17] Certainly, this is a *Laozi* that radically diverges from the sinological perspective, at least that common interpretation that finds the extant text, reinforced by the 2,000-year-old library excavated at Mawangdui, compiled to provide an ideological basis to *fajia* totalitarianism.[18]

Devall and Sessions, among "Eastern sources," find the *Laozi* and the writings of Dōgen particularly inspiring for their purpose.[19] They are familiar with Clark's work, for they have a virtually identical, unattributed sentence: "[T]he Taoist way of life is based on compassion, respect, and love for all things."[20] There is oblique reference to *ziran* (self-actualization/spontaneity/nature-natural), which I would agree is most *apropos*: "One metaphor for what we are talking about is found in the Eastern Taoist image, the *organic self*. Taoism tells us there is a way of unfolding which is inherent in all things."[21] *Deep Ecology* contains no sustained argument, but rather bits and pieces of poetry, rituals, etc., considered relevant to the theme of the work. There are several poem-translations from the *Laozi* by Tom Early[22] and a detailed plan for an "Autumn Equinox Taoist Celebration," seemingly held at Dolores LaChapelle's center in Silverton, Colorado.

LaChapelle's extended rhapsody centers on Daoism; the chapter entitled "Taoism" "constitutes the deep core of this work."[23] Her interest began several decades ago on reading Volume 2 of Joseph Needham's *Science and Civilization in China*, and developed through studying *taiji* for decades and subsequently teaching the subject:

> Now after all these years of gradual, deepening understanding of the Taoist way, I can state categorically that all these frantic last-minute efforts of our Western world to latch on to some "new idea" for saving the earth are unnecessary. It's been done for us already—thousands of years ago—by the Taoists. We can drop all that frantic effort and begin following the way of Lao Tzu [Laozi] and Chuang Tzu [Zhuangzi].[24]

LaChapelle understands that Western thinkers dismissed Daoism because they confused it with the practices of "superstitious village priests."[25] Certainly she holds no truck with religious Daoism, although she readily creates "Taoist" religious rituals of her own. Written in a New Age style, the book presents an exposition of a Daoism based on personal living and selected, extensive reading, ready to be adopted by those of her readers who choose to do so.

The above three works are the primary sources on Daoism for environmental studies students, as well as others, who come to the topic through writings by environmentalists. There is another work from the same period written from the same romantic standpoint that is frequently referred to in the environmental literature. Ip is oft quoted as representative of the indigenous Chinese scholarly perspective—according to the statement provided in the anthology where the article is found, the author is a secretary at Lingnan College in Hong Kong. Depicting Western philosophy as "patently anti-environmentalistic," Ip argues that Daoist philosophy is able to fulfill all that is needed to transcend the human predicament, and, at the same time, is "compatible with science and is thus capable of providing a minimally coherent ethics." By "Taoism," Ip means the *Laozi* and excerpts from the *Zhuangzi* found in Wing-tsit Chan's source book on Chinese philosophy, as well as Joseph Needham's references to the *Huainanzi*—there are no references to or mention of the texts in the original Chinese. Ip understands Daoism to be uncontaminated by religion. For example, Ip notes that *Tien* (Sky) "was a highly naturalistic notion which has no strong religious connotation."[26] Apparently, he was unaware that *Tien* was so sacred that for anyone other than the Imperial couple to sacrifice to *Tien* and *Ti* (Earth) was ipso facto treason.

The most recent work in this grouping is the book by Marshall, the first chapter being on "Taoism: The Way of Nature." Confused with regard to Chinese literary chronology by two centuries, Marshall, referring to the *Zhuangzi*, finds that

> The first clear expression of ecological thinking appears in ancient China from about the sixth century B.C. . . . The Taoists . . . offered the most profound and eloquent philosophy of nature ever elaborated and the first stirrings of ecological sensibility.[27]

His references are to the most common translations utilized by those in environmental studies: the Gia-Fu Feng and Jane English free rendering of the *Laozi*, the dated Herbert Giles translation of the *Zhuangzi*, and the Victorian, James Legge translation of the *Yi*. Like many of these authors, Marshall is pleased that Daoism has but a minimal relation to religion, terming it a pure philosophy, and finds that it models the most desirable form of government:

> Although containing elements of mysticism, the Taoists' receptive approach to nature encouraged an experimental method and a democratic attitude. . . . [Taoism] provides the philosophical foundations for a genuinely ecological society and a way to resolve the ancient antagonism between humanity and nature which continues to bedevil the world.[28]

While most sympathetic with many of the views expressed by the writings of deep ecology and tangential works, I find the Daoism expressed simplistic to the point of absurdity: it is ahistorical; the authors have no understanding that the interpretation of the texts continually changed over time, as did Chinese culture, according to changing needs and values; they assume a philosophy can be based on two enigmatic, early texts, one containing contradictory parts developed over several centuries, and the second probably edited from diverse sources; they presume that there were single authors for both works; they provide contemporary Western interpretations of the texts, which is acceptable only if they recognized what they were doing; and, strangest of all, they celebrate an assumed antimystical, antireligious orientation in texts clearly related to both mysticism and religion in China, especially since these authors critique the coldness and distance of Western post-Enlightenment philosophy. Given that the deep ecologists are seeking a fundamental transformation of culture, their attitude toward religion is puzzling: philosophies do not transform cultures, religions do.[29]

The romanticized translations tend to be read literally, with little understanding of metaphor. The descriptions of an ideal rustic life of small villages separated by virgin forests already reflected an idealized antiquity in these last Zhou (fourth to third centuries B.C.E.) texts. In any case, the texts were written for the literate aristocracy, not peasants. Even the epitome of the aristocratic Daoist "dropout", Tao Qian, of more than a half millennium later, had servants[30] and played at farming, when he was not drinking with his wealthy, aristocratic friends or writing poetry. To assume that reversion to a simple rusticity could be applied to the billion and a quarter people of grossly overpopulated China, when it could not at a time the population was less than 10 percent of the present day, to be blunt, is asinine.

In summary, the Daoism of the deep ecologists is utterly a modern Western one. That a Western Daoism can solve a crisis assumed to be brought on by and unredeemable through Western thinking implies a logical contradiction.

THE SKEPTICS

As early as 1968, Yi-Fu Tuan, a geographer, published an article that remains as cogent and definitive today as when it was written. He exemplifies the pragmatism of Chinese thinking in pointing out the obvious:

> The history of environmental ideas, however, has been pursued as an academic discipline largely in detachment from the question of how—if at all—these ideas guide the course of action, or how they arise out of it.[31]

Tuan notes the environmentalists' references to the *Laozi*, etc., but points to actually stated environmental concerns in the *Mengzi* (*Mencius*, the most important *rujia* text for the last thousand years), early offices for inspecting forests, and memorials to the throne. Tuan briefly lays out the evidence for early environmental destruction in China. He ends by comparing the European formal garden and the Chinese naturalistic garden, suggesting "that these human achievements probably required *comparable* amounts of nature modification."[32]

Anyone who has travelled through China other than in tour groups, I trust, would have a difficult time in understanding how Chinese traditions can be lauded for ideal environmental attitudes.

While environmental destruction has enormously accelerated in the twentieth century, the degradation is longstanding. Vast areas of forests were denuded and many waters became highly polluted, etc., well over a millennium ago. For those who are but aware of China vicariously, Smil's *China's Environmental Crisis* should serve as a necessary corrective.[33]

More recently, Rolston presented an argument similar to Tuan's, but from the perspective of philosophy. This article is popular among students, leading one to wonder, as university professors often do, whether students actually read to the end of an essay. Rolston begins with the question of his title, "Can the East Help the West to Value Nature?" Pointing to the test of the ability of these traditions to resolve environmental problems in Eastern nations (he incorrectly assumes that these problems did not exist in premodern times), he concludes: "My own judgement is that the East needs considerable reformulation of its sources before it can preach much to the West."[34]

POSSIBILITIES

Aside from the fanciful, simplistic interpretations of "Daoism" by the deep ecologists, all of the above discussed interpretations, including some by sinologists, disturb me in two regards. First is the separating out of Daoist thought, let alone two particular texts, from Chinese thought as a whole. This ignores the intellectual context, as well as the actual applications, of this aspect of Chinese thought, especially on the subject of environmental concerns. Yi-Fu Tuan, who is aware of the wealth of relevant material points this out, but so, indirectly, does J. Baird Callicott, the philosopher who has probably published more on religion and ecology than anyone else.

In a chapter entitled "Traditional East Asian Deep Ecology" in *Earth's Insights*, Callicott has sections on "Taoism," where he notes that Western environmental ethicists "have been drawn chiefly to Taoism," and "Confucianism," where he posits that "[b]y transposing the Confucian social model from the human to the biotic community, the ecological holist is encouraged to add a fourth dimension to the web of life."[35] Actually this already took place centuries ago.

As Chinese religion evolved, *xiao* ("filial piety"), the fundamental aspect of social relationships of the *rujia* tradition based on natural, nuclear-family ties, was stretched to the realm beyond humans. Wang Yangming, the early sixteenth-century *rujia* theorist—a *rujia* that incorporated aspects of *daojia* as well as a sinified Buddhism—who so influenced literati ideology, wrote:

> Everything from ruler, minister, husband, wife, and friends to mountains, rivers, spiritual beings, birds, animals, and plants should be truly loved in order to realize my humanity that forms one body with them, and then my clear character will be completely manifested, and I will really form one body with Heaven [Sky], Earth, and the myriad things.[36]

For Wang Yangming, family not only included the state, it included the natural world, a realization undoubtedly arising from the ecstatic religious experience of union with the entire environment. What blocks this understanding is simply greed, the contemporary global ethic rapidly spreading around the planet from its Western, capitalistic roots:

> Thus the learning of the great man [person][37] consists entirely in getting rid of the obscuration of selfish desires in order by his[/her] own efforts to make manifest his[/her] clear character, so as to restore the condition of forming one body with Heaven [Sky], Earth, and the myriad things, a condition that is originally so, that is all.[38]

In the concluding section of *Earth's Insights*, Callicott finds value not in separating the strands of Chinese thought but in their actual gestalt:

> The potential for the development of an explicit indigenous Chinese environmental ethic based on classical Chinese thought is tremendous. And the potential contribution of classical Chinese thought to deep ecology, ecofeminism,[39] and, more generally, to a global consciousness and conscience is equally great.[40]

It is only when the Western deconstruction of Chinese thought is disregarded, as well as the focus on "classics" while ignoring the history of their interpretation and development, that we can find much of relevant value in the tradition as a whole.

My second concern in the above discussed interpretations of Daoism is the continuation of the Christian missionary dismissal of Chinese religion as ignorant superstition. I have not yet been able to wrap my mind around the conundrum of viewing Chinese religion negatively while positively valuing the writings of not only those who were a part of it and whose thinking was formed by it—particularly since Chinese religion and family are coterminous—but who, as government officials, were priests in the state rituals as well as their clan and family sacrifices.

Certainly, the two texts that are at the basis of deep ecology, the *Laozi* and the *Zhuangzi*, are essentially religious texts, and it is their religious understanding, as well as the developments that later took place in Daoism as an institutional religion *(daojiao)*—ignored by all the deep ecologists—that offers the must useful possibilities for saving the planet.[41]

Ruminations on the mystic experience (the ecstasy of absolute self-loss/union)[42] are transmitted by but a few cultures: those that are socially stratified (for nonproductive ecstacies to be valued) and literate (for transmission to those of other cultures or other times)—the monotheistic, South Asian and East Asian traditions. These ruminations may have existed in the Central American civilizations, but due to the thoroughness of the Spanish friars' destruction of their libraries, we may never know. The South Asian traditions tend to understand the experience of the void *(śūnyatā)* as the escape *(moksha, nirvāna)* from ceaseless existence *(samsāra)*, the world understood as illusion *(māyā)*. The monotheistic traditions, in positing a disjunction between a single creator and the created, tend to understand the experience of loss of self as merging with the creator or an aspect of it, of transcending the created world.

In China, life was understood by the educated elite to be singular; that is, this life is the only one we have and death is terminal, albeit a natural concomitant of being born. There is no continuity of any sort after death. This is why the equivalent of an orientation toward eternal life after death, the essence of Christianity, is paralleled in China with a search for longevity, for an extension of this life. Of the many practices to this end, *taiji*, well known in the West, illustrates the gymnastic aspect.[43] As there is but a single existence, it is to be enjoyed rather than avoided or denied. Hence, in China, the mystic experience, contrary to South Asian and Western religious traditions, enhanced the importance of this world, at least until one died and one's body was recycled.

The mystic experience, or rather the coming out of it, led to the understanding that we constantly create not only the world around us, but ourselves. This is the essential meaning of the central term in Daoist *(daojia)* thought: *ziran. Ziran* literally means arising from itself; accordingly it can be translated as "spontaneity," but is also means "nature." The Chinese artist, Hong Shiqing, in a letter to me discussing his Daoist-oriented aesthetics with regard to his rock art, wrote (in Chinese), that he "used *ziran* (spontaneity) to beautify *ziran* (nature)" and that "[m]y artistic creations must become a single entity with great nature/spontaneity *(ziran).*"[44]

Ziran is based on the actual experience of coming out of the mystic experience. In doing so, we literally experience moving from nothingness *(wu* = the mystic experience) to a somethingness *(yu)*, initially a singleness (the *dao*), and that singleness, as we begin to distinguish things and ourselves, splitting into two *(tiendi* [Sky-Earth] and/or *yinyang),* three, and quickly, all the myriad things. The *daojia* summation of cosmogony reflects and arose from the real experience of awakening from the mystic experience.

Hence, this world that each of us continually creates/recreates may in its essence be *wu,* but it is all we have, and we might as well enjoy it as it is, that is, naturally *(ziran).* By extension, we cannot enjoy it unless the environment for human life survives, requiring active involvement in environmental protection when the environment is threatened. For well over a millennium, this experience was articulated through the Three Incomparables *(sanjue):* poetry, calligraphy, and painting, especially of landscapes *(shanshui:* mountains-waters), which specifically stands for the numinous Earth. This mode of communication is perhaps best epitomized in Su Shi's well-known "Red Cliff *Fu* (prose-poem) #1."

> ". . . Moreover, each thing between Sky and Earth has its owner; even a single hair which is not mine can never be a part of me. Only the cool breeze on the river and the full moon over the mountains caught by the ear becomes sound and encountered by the eye becomes color. No one can prevent us from having them, and there is no limit to our use of it. These are the limitless reserves of all that is created, and you and I can share in the joy of it."

> My friend smiled, consoled. We washed the cups and poured more wine. When the food was all gone and the wine cups and dishes lay scattered about, we lounged against each other in the boat, and did not even notice the sky turning white in the east.[45]

This viewpoint, of course, is anthropocentric. The metaphorical Chinese cosmos consists of three layers: the masculine Sky, the feminine Earth, and in between, produced from the creative interaction of male and female productive energies, are humans, as well as the myriad creature, and the realm they inhabit. Being pragmatists, the Chinese may understand the cosmos in spiritual terms, but they do not romanticize it. Humans, at the top of the biotic chain, live on plant and animal life. As early as the *rujia* text, the *Mengzi* (Mencius) of 2,400 years ago, it was understood that the sensitive, empathetic person could well feel discomfort as animals were led by to be sacrificed to feed the spirit realm and humans, but the slaughter still took place and the meat was still first offered and then eaten, indeed enjoyed. Enjoying life involves living off of other life, especially the grains of the plant community.[46]

Since we are social beings, we must enjoy life within our environment with other humans. Contrary to Western eremitic inclinations, the Chinese group-over-individual value extends into religio-philosophical lifestyles. Eremitism in China means not to live alone but rather, for the elite, not to hold office. The famous fourth-century aristocratic poet, Tao Qian (Tao Yuan-ming) avoided office, but "opened three paths" for his friends to come visit and drink with him. The middle-class poet of a millennium ago, Han Shan (Cold Mountain), quit his post, most likely as a government clerk, but longed for a companion to enjoy the solitude in the mountains with him.

Daojia and rujia thought were not separate. Those inclined toward daojia still had a rujia education, and those more inclined toward rujia were invariably familiar with the primary daojia texts listed above. Some of the major figures in Chinese intellectual history from both persuasions, such as Su Shi mentioned above, have left us both rujia writings relating to their holding government office and daojia writings from those times when they were not holding office.

It is in regard to the understanding that we must enjoy the world/ nature with others that daojia thought works in conjunction with rujia thought. For we can only enjoy it with others through understanding fundamental relationships that involve duties and responsibilities. These relationships, given an understanding of the essential falseness of distinctions learned through the mystic experience, include not only humans, but everything that exists. Moreover, we cannot enjoy it through unnecessary, wasteful consumption, due to meaningless greed—the bête noire of many rujia theorists and practitioners for two and a half millennia. We must be exceedingly careful in dealing with problems arising from nature, however, or we may exacerbate, rather than ameliorate, the problems.

While such cogitation arose from a few and, more often than not, fell on deaf ears, others were creating ritual ceremonies (jiao) that celebrated cosmic renewal and ritual behaviors that reinforced the connections between human and the spirit realm, including Earth, Waters, and Sky, which are thoroughly divinized in the Chinese understanding. These rituals combined with those continuing from the inception of horticulture, the offering of gifts and gratitude to the soil itself for the food on which our lives depend, as well as to the dead of the family, on whom our family's well-being depends. Such rituals are not just of the distant past, for they continue to today and are constantly being renewed, particularly in the most industrialized of Chinese cultures: Taiwan, Singapore, and Hong Kong. In spite of a half-century of suppression as unscientific superstition due to Marxist influence, shrines to

Grandmother and Grandfather Earth are reappearing in mainland China's agricultural fields.[47]

The rigid, in that they have been fixed for many centuries, *daojiao jiao* (cosmic renewal) rituals are, to a degree, being supplanted in Taiwan by the spontaneous (that is, based on continual inspiration from the deities through spirit-possession) *fahui* (the Chinese Buddhist term being borrowed) renewal rituals of the contemporary society of mediums.[48] It is these rituals in particular that have the potential to forcefully articulate through the voices of the deities (via possessed mediums) the growing environmental awareness to be found there. For when the deities speak, they may not be ignored.[49]

A brief example from normative Chinese religion may suggest the rich possibilities in these regards.[50] Chinese religion, like virtually all non-monotheistic traditions, has always celebrated and understood Earth and its produce as female numinous beings (e.g., grain goddesses in early European culture). In traditional times, the imperial couple sacrificed to Sky and Earth; regional governors, as well as the emperor, sacrificed at altars to Soil and Grain; and farming families continue to sacrifice at small shrines in the farm fields to Grandmother and Grandfather Earth (the names varying according to local usages), as well as their images on the family altars in farmers' homes. Understanding the earth to be not only numinous but capable of denying humans food mitigates against deliberate abuse. To the contrary, both agribusinesses and the previous massive agricultural communes in China and the former Soviet Union desacralized Earth, allowing it to be raped at will.

None of this can be directly meaningful in Western culture. But indirectly, it can suggest means for reinterpreting Western traditions to reverse rapid environmental degradation. As liberation theology, inspired by the continuation of Native American lifestyles and understandings in Central America, clashed with invested power, including that of the Vatican, with regard to destructive political and economic domination, similar theologies could, and are starting to, speak to the global destruction of human habitation. Only awareness of the realities of Chinese thought—pragmatic thought—and rituals as a whole can suggest viable responses for Christians. Those seeking to create alternatives to the dominant Western traditions are not likely to find a firm basis in fantasies of a Daoism that never existed. They too need to understand the realities, both positive and negative, of Chinese culture for models alternative to Western ones that will stand some chance of surviving the rapidly changing fashions of New Age religion.

We do not need to create wholesale new rituals based on romanticized fantasy. An examination of North and South Native American rituals and understandings, plus those of East, South, and West Asia, and Africa, as well as those of pre-Christian and Islamic Mediterranean areas and northern Europe, indicate a human commonality in the perception of humankind's relationship, celebrated and maintained in rituals, to Earth and Sky, as well as the animals and plants with which we share the surface of this planet and on whom we depend.[51] We do not need to invent religious rituals based on wild imaginings; they already exist, waiting to be modified to accord with any particular culture's religio-ecological niche and religious foundations.

NOTES

1. Appreciation is due to Adrian Ivankiv and Sherry Rowley for providing lists of deep ecology texts pertinent to Daoism.

2. E.g., Jordan Paper and Li Chuang Paper, "Chinese Religions, Population, and the Environment," in *Population, Consumption, and the Environment: Religious and Secular Responses,* ed. Harold Coward, 173–191 (Albany: State University of New York Press, 1995).

3. Paper, *The Fu-tzu: A Post-Han Confucian Text* (Leiden: E. J. Brill, 1987 [1971]).

4. See Jordan Paper, *The Spirits are Drunk: Comparative Approaches to Chinese Religion* (Albany: State University of New York Press, 1995), 4–12.

5. See Paper, *Spirits,* 23–50.

6. Kristopher Schipper, *The Taoist Body* (Berkeley: University of California Press, 1993), 3.

7. The "civil service system" is the term used to designate the sociopolitical structure that determined membership in the aristocracy. Beginning two thousand years ago and reaching its full development approximately one thousand years ago, the system designates a series of written examinations, based on a set of classical texts, the passing of which led to government office, the only means of both prestige and wealth in China to 1911.

8. For example, the title of Saso's excellent encapsulation of normative Chinese religious practices, especially in Taiwan, as well as the thrust of Schipper.

9. Peter Marshall, *Nature's Web: Rethinking Our Place on Earth* (New York: Paragon House), 413.

10. "Taoism and the Nature of Nature," *Environmental Ethics* 8 (1986): 348.

11. Ibid., 370.

12. In *Nature in Asian Traditions of Thought: Essays in Environmental Philosophy* (Albany: State University of New York Press, 1989), 3.

13. Ibid., 11–12.

14. "Human/Nature in Nietzsche and Taoism," in *Nature in Asian Traditions of Thought: Essays in Environmental Philosophy,* ed. J. Baird Callicott and Roger T. Ames (Albany: State University of New York Press), 80.

15. *The Anarchist Movement: Reflections on Culture, Nature, and Power* (Montréal: Black Rose Books, 1984), 165.

16. Ibid., 188.

17. Ibid., 180, 185.

18. Recently excavated fragmentary texts suggest that some early versions that did not continue may have had different foci.

19. *Deep Ecology* (Salt Lake City: Peregrine Smith Books, 1985), 100.

20. Ibid., 11; compare to Clark, 176.

21. Ibid., 11.

22. I could not find a bibliographic reference.

23. *Sacred Land Sacred Sex—Rapture of the Deep: Concerning Deep Ecology and Celebrating Life* (Silverton, CO: Finn Hill Arts, 1988), 340.

24. Ibid., 90.

25. Ibid., 91.

26. "Taoism and the Foundation of Environmental Ethics," *Religion and the Environmental Crisis,* ed. Eugene C. Hargrove (Athens: University of Georgia Press, 1986), 94–106, 102–105.

27. Marshall, *Nature's Web,* 9.

28. Ibid., 23.

29. "Philosophy" is understood to refer to theorizing about the nature of knowledge by intellectuals for intellectuals. "Religion" does not necessarily mean formal institutions but concerns the expression of that which is central to both a cultural and an individual understanding of life itself, including the notions of cosmos, time, continuity, disruption, identity, reality, etc., and particularly all those activities that pertain to it; that is, those behaviors that create and connote significance and meaning among those who take part.

30. The fragment of a letter by Tao Qian retained in his official biography mentions his sending one of his servants to care for his son.

31. "Discrepancies between Environmental Attitude and Behaviour: Examples from Europe and China," in *Ecology and Religion in History,* ed. David Spring and Eileen Spring (New York: Harper Torchbooks, 1974), 91.

32. Ibid., 111–112, emphasis added.

33. Smil's *China's Environmental Crisis* (1993) is a follow-up on Smil's *The Bad Earth* (1983), which was reviewed in many major journals, was translated into Chinese (1988), and was available to the formative deep ecology writers.

34. In Callicott and Ames, *Nature in Asian Traditions of Thought*, 189.

35. *Earth's Insights: A Survey of Ecological Ethics from the Mediterranean Basin to the Australian Outback* (Berkeley: University of California Press, 1994) 67, 84–85.

36. "Inquiry on the *Great Learning*," *Instructions for Practical Living and Other Neo-Confucian Writings by Wang Yang-ming*, trans. Wing-tsit Chan (New York: Columbia University Press, 1963), 273.

37. Chinese language does not indicate gender except where its indication is essential to meaning; hence, the many androcentric translations reflect the viewpoint and English language usage of the translator rather than the Chinese original.

38. Ibid.

39. There are more possibilities in this regard than generally realized, see the chapters pertaining to China in my *Through the Earth Darkly: Female Spirituality in Comparative Perspective* (New York: Continuum, 1997).

40. *Earth's Insights*, 85.

41. Saving China itself requires a reconceptualization of family from a patrilineal basis to a bilateral one in order for the policies to stabilize the population to succeed, given that the primary obligation in Chinese religion is to continue the family. For an exposition of this point, see Paper and Paper.

42. This experience has been termed the "zero-experience" by an anthropologist and the "void-experience" by a psychologist. Both terms coincide with Chinese expressions found in the *Zhuangzi*: *"wu sang wo"* (I have lost myself) and *"tso wang"* (sitting in forgetfulness)—it is the experience of *wu* (absolute nothingness).

43. This understanding is seemingly contradictory to normative Chinese religion, which assumes that the souls (China is one of many multi-soul cultures) continue after physical death. But for the intelligentsia, the sacrificial rituals were primarily valued for the positive effects they have on the family and society as a whole, as well as participating individuals.

44. For more see, Paper, *Spirits*, 191–193.

45. For translation of complete text, see Jordan Paper and Lawrence G. Thompson, eds., *The Chinese Way in Religion* (Belmont, CA: Wadsworth Publishing, 1998), 194–196.

46. Certain *taojiao* practices involve avoiding both meat and grain, but these are very specific practices, often limited in duration, for precise purposes.

47. For illustrations of the above, see Paper, *Chinese Religion Illustrated* (CD-ROM) (Belmont, CA: Wadsworth Publishing, 1998).

48. See Jordan Paper, "Mediums and Modernity: The Institutionalization of Ecstatic Religious Functionaries in Taiwan," *Journal of Chinese Religion* 24 (1996): 105–130.

49. Faith is not a component of Chinese religion, since, as in all medium-istic religious traditions, we directly encounter the deities and other spirits via possessed mediums.

50. Negative aspects have already been treated in Paper and Paper.

51. A study of these rituals, as well as female roles in these regards, will be found in Paper, *Through the Earth Darkly*.

6

Confucianism and Deep Ecology

Mary Evelyn Tucker

IN DRAWING UPON the great religious traditions of the past for new ecological orientation in the present it is clear that the traditions of East
Asia have much to offer. Indeed, Confucianism, Taoism, Buddhism,
and Shinto all have significant insights into the interrelatedness of nature and the need for humans to be in harmony with nature. While the
latter three are often recognized as having ecological dimensions, Confucianism is not so readily considered in such discussions.[1] Yet within
the Confucian tradition, there are rich resources for understanding how
other cultures have viewed nature and the role of the human in nature.
From the early integration of the human into the great triad with
heaven and earth, to the dynamic interactions of nature as expressed in
the *Book of Changes (I Ching)*, to the more complex metaphysical discussions of the relationship of principle *(li)* and material force *(ch'i)* the
Confucian world view provides a wealth of suggestive resources for rethinking our contemporary ecological situation.

Tu Weiming has spoken of the Confucian tradition as one that is
based on an anthropocosmic vision of the dynamic interaction of
heaven, earth, and human.[2] He describes this as a "continuity of being"
with no radical split between a transcendent divine person or principle
and the world of humans. Tu emphasizes that the continuity and
wholeness of Chinese cosmological thinking is also accompanied by a
vitality and dynamism. He writes: "While Chinese thinkers are critically aware of the inertia in human culture which may eventually lead
to stagnation, they perceive the 'course of heaven' *(t'ien-hsing)* as 'vig-
orous' *(chien)* and instruct people to model themselves on the ceaseless
vitality of the cosmic process."[3] This does not imply, however, that there

is not frequently a gap between such theories of nature and practices toward nature in both premodern and contemporary East Asian societies.[4] It is thus with the awareness of our own positionality within a modern Western framework and against the background of a looming environmental crisis that we undertake this examination of Confucianism and its relation to deep ecology.

It might be said from the outset that the broad question concerning to what extend Confucianism has ecological elements clearly needs further discussion. This idea was examined in some detail at a conference held at Harvard's Center for the Study of World Religions in June 1996. The papers from this conference are now published in a volume on *Confucianism and Ecology: The Interrelation of Heaven, Earth, and Humans.*[5] The general conclusion of the conference and the volume is that there are significant ecological dimensions to Confucian thought. This discussion needs to be deepened and expanded, especially in relation to particular ecological philosophies such as deep ecology.

While we recognize the disjunction of comparing and contrasting Confucianism and deep ecology, it is, nevertheless, a fruitful exercise. The disjunction arises because of the different cultural contexts in which these two systems arose. Confucianism is profoundly linked to the premodern history of East Asia, especially in China and by extension Korea, Japan, and Vietnam. Deep ecology comes out of a modern Western context and is indebted to various philosophical sources including Spinoza and Heidegger.[6] In addition, it draws on certain Asian and indigenous religions, as well as key nature writers and poets. Nonetheless, there are grounds for bracketing these substantial differences of cultural origin to examine in what ways Confucianism might be seen as deeply ecological. The answer is quite mixed, as one might expect.

First, it is appropriate to establish some general criteria of comparison. At the risk of oversimplification of more complex ideas and nuances, one might say that deep ecology, in general, would embrace a world view characterized by the following principles:

1. Nature is primary; humans are secondary.
2. Nature has inherent value; hierarchy results in dominance.
3. What fosters nature is valuable; what destroys nature is problematic.
4. Harmony with nature is essential; human self-realization is achieved in relation to and in harmony with nature.

Using these general principles, which are descriptive but not exhaustive, let us then examine the Confucian tradition.

On the one hand, Confucianism has conventionally been described as a humanistic tradition focusing on the roles and responsibilities of humans to family, society, and government. Thus, Confucianism is identified primarily as an ethical or political system of thought with an anthropocentric focus. However, upon further examination and as more translations become available in Western languages, this narrow perspective needs to be reexamined. The work of many contemporary Confucian scholars in both Asia and the West has been crucial to expanding our understanding of Confucianism. In East Asia we have profited from the work of Fung Yu-Lan and others on the mainland, as well as the New Confucians in Hong Kong and Taiwan such as T'ang Chun-i, Ch'ien Mu, Hsu Fu-kuan, and Mou Tsung-san. In the west we have had the comprehensive work of Wm. Theodore de Bary, Julia Ching, Tu Weiming, Rodney Taylor, John Berthrong, and Robert Neville.

Some of the most important results of this reexamination are the insights that have emerged in seeing Confucianism as not simply an ethical, political, or ideological system. Rather, Confucianism is being appreciated as a profoundly religious tradition in ways that are different from Western traditions. This may eventually result in expanding the idea of "religion" itself to include more than criteria adopted from Western traditions such as notions of God, salvation, and redemption. Moreover, Confucianism is being recognized for its affirmation of relationality not only between and among humans but also with humans and the natural world. This may help to reconfigure humans as not simply individualistic entities but as communitarian beings.

It is this emerging understanding of the religious, relational, and ecological dynamics of Confucianism that has particular relevance for our topic here. In short, by its traditional description in the West, Confucianism would not be perceived as being compatible with deep ecology. However, with this emerging broadened view of Confucianism, there are a number of aspects that are quite compatible. Indeed, we may even identify ways that Confucianism might contribute to the expansion of deep ecological thought itself. Let us examine Confucianism, then, with regard to our earlier definition of key principles characteristic of deep ecology.

With regard to the first principle, *nature is primary; humans are secondary,* Confucianism might not go as far as deep ecology in this direction. However, the tradition can be described, thanks to the writing of Tu Weiming, as "anthropocosmic," not simply anthropocentric. In other words, the human is understood to be embedded in nature not dominant over nature. In this sense nature has a particular primacy. The Confucian world view might be described as a series of concentric circles where the human is the center, not as an isolated individual but as embedded in rings of family, society, and government. This is especially clear in the text of the *Great Learning*.[7] All of these circles are contained within the vast cosmos itself. Thus, the ultimate context for the human is the "10,000 things," nature in all its remarkable variety and abundance.

From the classical texts to the later Neo-Confucian writings there is a strong sense of nature as a relational whole in which human life and society flourishes. Indeed, for Confucians there is a recognition that it is the rhythms of nature that sustain life in both its biological needs and sociocultural expressions. For the Confucians the biological dimensions of life are dependent on nature as a wholistic, organic continuum. Everything in nature is interdependent and interrelated. Most importantly, for the Confucians nature is seen as dynamic and transformational. These ideas are seen as early as the *Book of Changes* and are expressed in the *Four Books,* especially in *Mencius,* the *Doctrine of the Mean,* and the *Great Learning.* They come to full flowering in the Neo-Confucian tradition of the Sung and Ming periods. Nature in this context has an inherent unity, namely, it has a primary ontological source (*T'ai chi*). It has patterned processes of transformation (yin/yang) and it is interrelated in the interaction of the five elements and the 10,000 things. It is dynamic through the movements of material force (*ch'i*).

Within this world view of nature, human culture is created and expressed in harmony with the vast movements of nature. Thus, there developed the great Han period synthesis of all the elements, directions, colors, seasons, and virtues.[8] This need to consciously connect the patterns of nature with the rhythms of human society is very ancient in Confucian culture. It is at the basis of the anthropocosmic world view where humans are seen as working together with heaven and earth in correlative relationships to create harmonious societies. The mutually related resonances between self, society, and nature are constantly being described in the Confucian texts. In this context, nature *is* primary and humans realize themselves by forming a triad with nature.

With regard to the second principle, *nature has inherent value; hierarchy results in dominance,* Confucians would agree to the first part while not subscribing fully to the second. For Confucians, nature is not only inherently valuable, it is morally good. Nature, thus, embodies the normative standard for all things; it is not judged from an anthropocentric perspective. There is not a fact/value division in the Confucian world view, for nature is seen as the source of all value. In particular, value lies in the ongoing transformation and productivity of nature. A term repeated frequently in Neo-Confucian sources is *sheng sheng,* reflecting the ever-renewing fecundity of life itself. In this sense, the dynamic transformation of life is seen as emerging in recurring cycles of growth, fruition, harvesting, and abundance. This reflects the natural processes of growth and decay in nature, human life, and human society. Change is thus seen as a dynamic force with which humans should harmonize and interact, rather than withdraw from.

In this context, the Confucians do not view hierarchy as leading inevitably to domination. Rather, they see that value rests in each thing, but not in each thing equally. Everything has its appropriate role and place and thus should be treated accordingly. The use of nature for human ends must recognize the intrinsic value of each element of nature, but also its value in relation to the larger context of the environment. Each entity is considered not simply equal to every other; rather, each interrelated part of nature has a particular value according to its nature and function. Thus, there is a differentiated sense of appropriate roles for humans and for all other species. For Confucians hierarchy is seen as a necessary way for each being to fulfill its function. In this context, then, no individual being has exclusive privileged status. The processes of nature and its ongoing logic of transformation (yin/yang) is the standard norm that takes priority.

With regard to the third principle, *what fosters nature is valuable; what destroys nature is problematic,* Confucians would ascribe to this in principle if not always in practice. Confucians were mindful that nature was the basis of a stable society and that without tending nature carefully imbalance would result. There are numerous passages in *Mencius* advocating humane government based on appropriate management of natural resources and family practices. Moreover, there are various passages in Confucian texts urging humans not to wantonly cut down trees or needlessly kill animals. Thus, like deep ecologists Confucians would wish (at least in theory) to nurture and protect the great variety and abundance of life forms.

However, the establishment of humane society, government, and culture inevitably results in the use of nature for creating housing, means of production, and governance. In this sense, Confucians might be seen as more pragmatic social ecologists who recognize the necessity of forming human institutions and means of governance. Nonetheless, it is clear for Confucians that human cultural values and practices are grounded in nature and part of its structure, dependent on its beneficence. In addition, the agricultural base of Confucian societies has always been recognized as essential to the political and social well-being of the country. Humans prosper by living within nature's boundaries and are refreshed by its beauty, restored by its seasons, and fulfilled by its rhythms. Human flourishing is thus dependent on fostering nature in its variety and abundance; going against nature's processes is self-destructive. Human moral growth means cultivating one's desires not to interfere with nature but to be in accord with the great Tao of Nature. Thus the "human mind" expands in relation to the "Mind of the Way."

The final principle is: *harmony with nature is essential; human self-realization is achieved in relation to and in harmony with nature.* Confucianism subscribed fully to these ideas. In fact, the great triad of Confucianism, namely, heaven, earth, and humans, signifies this understanding that humans can only attain their full humanity in relationship to both heaven and earth. This became a foundation for a cosmological ethical system of relationality applicable to spheres of family, society, politics, and nature. The individual was always seen in *relationship* to others. In particular, the person was grounded in a reciprocal relationship with nature. This resonance with nature and with other humans is described as "correlative thinking" and is at the heart of the Confucian world view.[9] There is no self-realization apart from nature in this world view system.

Nature functions in this world view as great parents to humans, providing sustenance, nurturing, intelligibility, and guidance. In return, nature requires respect and care from humans. Human self-realization is achieved by fulfilling this role of filial children to beneficent parents who have sustained life for humans. Humans participate in the vast processes of nature by cultivating themselves in relation to nature, by caring for the land appropriately, by creating benevolent government, and by developing human culture and society in relation to nature's seasons and transformations. This process of cultivation will be described more fully in the following section on cosmology and cultivation.

Human self-realization implies understanding the continuities of nature in its daily rhythms and seasonal cycles. Yet humans also recognize that these orderly patterns contain within them the dynamic transformations engendering creativity, spontaneity, and openness. This is the challenge for humans within a Confucian context. How to live within nature's continuities and yet be open to its spontaneities. Thus, while nature has an intelligible structure and patterns, it also operates in ways to produce and encourage novelty.

With regard to establishing human culture and maintaining institutions, the same great dynamic tension applies within the Confucian tradition. How to be faithful to the past—the continuity of the tradition—and yet be open to the change and innovation necessary for the ongoing life of the tradition. Achieving self-realization for the Confucians required a creative balancing of these two elements of tradition and innovation against the background of nature's continuities and changes. To illustrate this dynamic interaction we will explore how Confucianism encouraged the cultivation of the self in relation to nature. This fundamental idea for Confucianism may have suggestive resonances for deep ecology as it develops its own blend of personal philosophy, group rituals, and individual and collective activism.

COSMOLOGY AND CULTIVATION: NATURE AND THE SELF

In the Confucian tradition, as in deep ecological thinking, there exist underlying patterns of cosmological orientation and connectedness of self and the universe. Indeed, one might say that Confucianism as a religious tradition is distinguished by a concern for both personal groundedness and cosmological relatedness amidst the myriad changes in the universe. The desire for appropriate orientation toward nature and connection to other humans is a perduring impetus in Confucianism. Indeed, this need to recognize and cultivate such relatedness is the primary task of the Confucian practitioner in attaining authentic personhood. Such relationality is often expressed as correlative thinking, which reached one of its most developed expressions in the Han period as A. C. Graham has suggested.

> It is through a cosmology rooted in Yin and Yang and the Five Processes, which by correlating moral with physical categories incorporates human morality into the cosmic order, that the threatening gulf between Heaven and man was closed in China before man had time to rethink himself as a solitary exception in a morally neutral universe.[10]

This relatedness takes many forms, and variations of it constitute one of the means of identifying different periods and thinkers in the tradition. In China, from the classical period of the *Book of Changes*, to the Han system of correspondences and the Neo-Confucian metaphysics of the *Diagram of the Great Ultimate*, concerns for cosmology and cultivation have been dominant in Confucian thought. In Korea one of the most enduring expressions of this was the four-seven debates, which linked the metaphysics of principle *(li)* and material force *(ch'i)* to issues of cultivating virtue and controlling the emotions. These debates continued in Japan, although without the same intensity and political consequences. Instead, in Japan the effort to link particular virtues to the cosmos became important, as did the expression of cultivation in the arts, in literature, and in practical learning. In this manner one's cultivation was shared for the benefit of the society in both aesthetic and practical matters.

In these varied forms of East Asian Confucianism, the human is viewed as a microcosm in relation to the macrocosm of the universe. This is expressed most succinctly in the metaphor of humans as forming a triad with heaven and earth. This is not intended simply to describe a vague mystical unity with the "all." Rather, the Confucians situate the human within concentric circles of embeddedness. The individual is never viewed in isolation but is seen as part of these interlocking circles, which touch each other like ripples in a pond. The family is at the center and the circles move outward toward friends and the larger society, they connect to the political order, and inevitably unite with the cosmos itself. This is the anthropocosmic world view of Confucianism.

These circles are distinguished by patterns of reciprocity and resonance that are culturally learned and biologically grounded. In other words, each collective human sphere (family, society, politics) has its patterns of appropriate behavior and interaction expressed in rituals. All of this is contained within the sphere of the cosmos itself. Thus, ritual patterns of relatedness are seen as embedded in analogous biological processes that consciously or unconsciously ground human life and social organization. These are most fully expressed in the images in the *Book of Changes*.[11]

At the same time, the virtues one cultivates frequently have both human import and natural analogues. One of the key Confucian virtues, for example, is filiality *(hsiao)*, by which one is said to have devotion to one's parents, to one's ancestors, and to heaven and earth as the great parents of all life. Thus, filiality is a virtue with both personal and cosmological components. Tu Weiming has described it as "a meta-ethical principle underlying the anthropocosmic worldview."[12]

The effort at relational resonance, namely at increasing the "sympathetic presence of things to each other,"[13] is at the heart of the dynamic relationship of cosmology and cultivation in the Confucian tradition. Thus, the terms *cosmology* and *cultivation* are essentially metaphors for the various macrocosm-microcosm relations, namely the interpenetration of humans and nature, self and society, individual and body politic. As Benjamin Schwartz observed many years ago, these are the mutually implicit polarities of Confucian thought.[14]

While we can describe these polarities as coexisting dialectics, it may be interesting to note that the triad of heaven, earth, and human may require a different kind of understanding of the nature of inter-

penetration. It also demands a rethinking of the categories of immanence and transcendence. These may not be fully adequate categories in
a context described as "a continuity of being" rather than a dualism of
humans and divine as in the Western tradition. This is particularly true
because the Confucian tradition is not simply concerned with the relationship between heaven and humans, but with the mutual presence of
heaven, earth, and humans. While earth in this triad clearly means
something different than it does in the present period, there can be no
doubt as to the presence of natural, biological, and botanical imagery in
many of the key Confucian texts. Ultimately it is an anthropocosmic
world view of continuity that has a deeply cosmological basis.

Thus, for the Confucians to be rooted in a world of meaningful relationships suggests being grounded in nature, situated in the body,
and reciprocal with all life forms. Cultivation implies evoking and establishing resonances between the human and the natural worlds. To be
fully human means to locate oneself in patterned relationships to the
changes in the cosmos, to the fluctuation of the seasons, to the rhythms
of the agricultural cycles, and to the varied demands of human life.
Thus, the natural world is not simply "background" or even "landscape." It is both the container and the context for human action. An ef-
ficacious social order and a functional political system relies on a
productive agriculture system. On both a practical and a spiritual level
human life and sustenance depend on relatedness to the land. How to
nurture this in a sustainable social/political order was ultimately linked
with fostering moral practice in the human order. Furthermore, human
health and the health of the society were seen as closely connected. The
human body, civil society, body politic, and the cosmic order were interrelated. In a fundamental sense, then, cultivating the land and cultivating oneself became analogous means of creating harmonious
Confucian societies and thus fulfilling heaven's mandate.

NATURALISTIC IMAGERY OF CONFUCIAN RELIGIOSITY

Self-cultivation in this context is seen as essential to develop or to recover one's innate authenticity and one's connection to the cosmos. It
is a process filled with naturalistic imagery of planting, nurturing,
growth, and harvesting. It is in this sense that one might describe the religious ethos of Confucianism as a dynamic naturalism aimed at personal and societal transformation. This means that the imagery used to
described Confucian religious practice is frequently drawn from nature,
especially in its botanical, agricultural, and seasonal modes.[15] Thus to

become fully human one must nurture *(yang)* and preserve *(ts'un)*, namely cultivate, the heavenly principle of one's mind and heart. These key terms may refer to such activities as nurturing the seeds of goodness that Mencius identifies and preserving emotional harmony, mentioned in the *Doctrine of the Mean (Chung-yung)*.

In *Mencius* there is a recognition of the fundamental sensitivity of humans to the suffering of others (IIA:6). This is demonstrated through the example of a child about to fall into a well being rescued though activating the instinctive compassion of an observer, not by eliciting any extraneous rewards. Indeed, to be human for Mencius means to have a heart with the seeds (or germs) of compassion, shame, courtesy and modesty, right and wrong. When cultivated these will become the virtues of humaneness, righteousness, propriety, and wisdom. When they are developed in a person they will flourish, "like a fire starting up or a spring coming through" (IIA:6). Thus, the incipient tendencies in the human are like sprouts or seeds that, as they grow, lean toward becoming fully cultivated virtues. The goal of Mencian cultivation, then, is to encourage these natural spontaneities before calculating or self-serving motives arise. This begins the art of discerning between the Way mind *(Tao hsin)* and the human mind *(jen hsin)*.[16]

In a similar manner the *Doctrine of the Mean* speaks of differentiating between the state of centrality or equilibrium before the emotions (pleasure, anger, sorrow, joy) are aroused and the state of harmony after the emotions are aroused. This balancing between the ground of existence (centrality) and its unfolding process of self-expression (harmony) is part of achieving an authentic mode of human existence. To attain this authenticity *(ch'eng)* means not only that one has come into harmony with oneself but also that one has achieved a unity with heaven and earth. Thus, the identification of the moral order and the cosmic order is realized in the process of human cultivation. Self-authenticity is realized against the backdrop of the sincerity of the universe. This results in participation in the "transforming and nourishing processes of heaven and earth." As the *Doctrine of the Mean* states:

> Equilibrium is the great foundation of the world, and harmony its universal path. When equilibrium and harmony are realized to the highest degree, heaven and earth will attain their proper order and all things will flourish.

> Only those who are absolutely sincere can order and adjust the great relations of mankind, establish the great foundations of humanity, and know the transforming and nourishing operations of heaven and earth.[17]

In *Mencius* that self-cultivation is seen as analogous to the natural task of tending seeds and is thus enriched by agricultural and botanical imagery. Moreover, in the *Doctrine of the Mean* this cultivation is understood within the context of a cosmological order that is pervasive, structured, and meaningful. The human is charged to cultivate oneself and in this process to bring the transformations of the cosmos to their fulfillment. It is thus possible to speak of early Confucianism as having religious dimensions characterized by naturalistic analogies of cultivation within a context of cosmological processes of transformation.

All of this, then, involves a religiosity of analogies between the human and the natural world. In the Han period this religiosity based on intricate correspondences of the microcosm (human) to the macrocosm (nature) becomes further developed. The patterns in the universe are seen as corresponding to patterns in human affairs. Just as in the *Book of Changes*, harmonizing with these patterns was the heart of self-cultivation. Religiosity meant establishing sympathetic resonances with other humans and with nature itself. To be out of harmony was to cause a rupture in this dynamic, organic, continuity of being. This is true in both the political and the personal realms.[18]

The *Book of Changes* was again a major source of inspiration for spiritual practice and cosmological orientation for the Neo-Confucians.[19] This was seen amidst the transformations of the universe celebrated as production and reproduction *(sheng, sheng)*. For the Neo-Confucians it was clear that many of the virtues that a person cultivated had a cosmological component. For example, humaneness *(jen)* in humans was seen as analogous to origination *(yüan)* in nature. Thus, the growth of this virtue in humans had its counterpart in the fecundity of nature itself. To cultivate *(han yang)* one needed to practice both inner awareness and outer attention, namely, abiding in reverence within and investigating principle without. This required quiet sitting *(ching tso)* and extending knowledge through investigating things *(ko wu chih chih)*. To be reverent has been compared to the notion of recollection *(shou lien)* which means literally to collect together or to gather a harvest.[20]

THE JAPANESE CONTEXT:
TOKUGAWA NEO-CONFUCIAN COSMOLOGY

In turning to the Japanese context, then, it is clear that these same patterns of cosmology and cultivation were pervasive especially in the flourishing of Neo-Confucianism in the Tokugawa period (1603–1868). The *Book of Changes* continued to play an important role[21] and issues of self-cultivation in relation to principle *(li)* and material force *(ch'i)* were intensely debated. Moreover, the key relationships of self, society, and nature were mediated through symbolic structures of correspondences many of which can be traced back to Han Confucianism.[22] While in certain circumstances such symbolic structures were, no doubt, used in East Asia for political control or ideological hegemony,[23] it is also evident that numerous individuals were inspired by concerns for both personal cultivation and common social good. More than enhancing their status, many Japanese were attracted to Confucianism for a variety of reasons, not the least of which was to promote benevolent government to ensure peace and practical learning that would enhance prosperity.[24]

We will discuss two such individuals in premodern Japan who utilized various dimensions of Confucian thought and practice. This is not to suggest that they were uniform in their acceptance of Confucian philosophy. On the contrary, they struggled with doubts and disagreements within Confucianism, they questioned Confucianism's relevance to the Japanese context, and they debated the merits of Confucianism vis-à-vis Buddhism and Shinto. In other words, they wrestled with how to adopt and adapt Confucianism to the Japanese context. As Kate Nakai notes,[25] what becomes particularly interesting in this process of naturalization of Confucianism is why Confucianism had such an appeal to the Japanese. Further exploration of this topic needs to be undertaken.

Our project here, however, is to highlight aspects of their thought with regard to nature that might be seen as fruitful in relation to contemporary discussions on ecology in general and deep ecology in particular.[26] Once again, we realize the problems involved in such an effort and we proceed with advised caution. We are making no claims to an idealized view of nature that existed in the Japanese context nor to a pristine ideology of harmony with nature in the Confucian tradition. We are simply using the lens of human-Earth relations to explore perspectives in the Confucian tradition in the Japanese context. The study is limited to two seventeenth- and eighteenth-century figures and makes no claims to be exhaustive or definitive. Rather, we hope to suggest grounds for future work in this field.

In this spirit we will discuss Kaibara Ekken's naturalistic philosophy of material force (Ch. *ch'i;* Jp. *ki*) and his ecological doctrine of filiality (Ch. *hsiao;* Jp. *kō*). We will explore Miura Baien's notion of *jōri*. The influence of both philosophical concerns and practical leaning (Ch. *shih hsüeh;* Jp. *jitsugaku*) in these thinkers is clear.[27] The implications for deep ecologoical thinking are suggestive.

The practical learning movement which originated in China had adherents across East Asia and was embraced by many Japanese Confucians in the Tokugawa period (1603–1868). Essentially practical learning *(jitsugaku)* implied "real" or "true" learning in contrast to "false" or "empty" learning *(kyogaku)*. For the Confucians the term *false learning* was often applied to Buddhism or Taoism as these traditions were seen as not connected to or less concerned with the "real world" of social and political affairs. The contrast between engagement in the world and detachment from the world was central to these distinctions.

As Chu Hsi described it:

> At the beginning of this book, it speaks of one principle, and towards the middle it speaks of this principle dispersing and becoming the myriad things, and near the end, it speaks of their in turn reuniting to become one principle. Release it, and it expands to fill the entire universe; recall it, and it is contained within one's innermost being. Its savor is endless. It is all real learning *(jitsugaku)*.

He elaborates on this term in the following manner:

> [Since the death of Mencius], ordinary Confucians have devoted even greater effort to textual studies than [is required by] the *Elementary Learning,* and yet their efforts have been useless *(wu-yung).* The heterodox schools have espoused doctrines of emptiness and quietude which are loftier than those of the *Great Learning* and yet their doctrines are impractical *(wu-shih).*[28]

Chu Hsi's concern for real learning emphasized the importance of moral cultivation and human relatedness as at the heart of his teachings. Thus, moral practice was central as opposed to abstract philosophical speculation or flowery exegesis and commentaries on texts. Withdrawal from contemporary concerns was looked down on by Confucians who were deeply engaged with educational issues as well as social and political problems.[29]

In a similar manner, practical learning was a primary concern for all of the figures being discussed here. The concern, however, is of particular interest in this context because *jitsugaku* was inevitably connected to the relation of humans to nature either philosophically or practically.

KAIBARA EKKEN

Biography and Intellectual Development

Kaibara Ekken (1630–1714) was born in Chikuzen on the island of Kyushu.[30] His father was a physician to Lord Kuroda and his own study of medicine began at home. Although he appreciated Buddhism as a

youth, at the age of fourteen his interest in the Chinese classics grew under the tutelage of his elder brothers. At the age of twenty-six he left for
Tokyo to become a physician, a common path for Confucian scholars.

Two years later he went to Kyoto to study Confucianism in greater
detail. Here he studied with some of the leading Confucian scholars
and immersed himself in the thought of Chu Hsi, the great Sung Neo-
Confucian synthesizer. As his respect for Chu Hsi deepened and his desire to spread his ideas grew, he published selections of Chu's works
with punctuation so they could be read by ordinary Japanese. He also
wrote the first Japanese commentary on Chu's principal compilation,
Reflections on Things at Hand (Chin-Ssu Lu).

By the time he was forty he had read widely in the Chinese sources
and became especially influenced by the Ming Confucian, Lo Ch'in-
shun (1465–1547), and eventually adopted his monism of *ch'i*. Like Lo,
Ekken came to have certain reservations about Chu Hsi's thought.
He felt it relied too heavily on Buddhist and Taoist sources (for example, the *Diagram of the Great Ultimate*) and that its emphasis on self-
cultivation tended to be too quietistic. Ekken set forth these reservations
in his treatise *Grave Doubts (Taigiroku)*. It was clearly difficult for Ekken
to disagree with Chu Hsi or to make a complete break with Chu's
thought. Thus, Ekken might be best understood as being a reformed
Chu Hsi thinker[31] who derived much of his sensitivity toward nature
from Chu Hsi and other Sung thinkers.[32] This reverence toward nature
became the primary motivating force in the development of his own
type of "useful learning" *(jitsugaku)*.

Practical Learning: Content and Methods

Ekken's *jitsugaku* was of a broad and comprehensive nature spanning
both the humanities and the natural sciences with an end toward moral
cultivation and alleviation of social problems. His scholarly interests
were wide ranging, encompassing the fields of "ethics, manners, institutions, linguistics, medicine, botany, zoology, agriculture, production,
taxonomy, food sanitation, law, mathematics (computation), music, and
military tactics."[33] He was inspired by Chu Hsi's directive to investigate
things and explore their principle.

Yet Ekken was not interested in simply collecting data or in becoming a specialist or a technician of knowledge. He wanted to be able to
bridge the gaps between the humanistic studies and the study of nature
and between specialized research and popular education. Perhaps
Ekken's greatest achievement along these lines was his attempt to develop the investigation of nature as part of his religious world view

rather than as something completely distinct from it. While his success may be debated by later generations the significance of his inquiry can hardly be lost on the modern reader, especially those interested in deep ecology. To encourage an investigation of nature that did not simply objectify nature as something apart from the human was one of Ekken's major contributions to the history of Tokugawa thought.

The Ethical and the "Empirical" Paths: Bridging the Humanities and the "Sciences"

Like many Confucians before him Ekken warned against the limitations of methods used by both the humanist scholar and the "objective" researcher.[34] For him *Tao hsüeh* as an essentially ethical path must be distinguished from the textual studies or technical skills as becoming ends in themselves. He urged scholars to maintain a reflective and contemplative posture when reading the classics so as not to fall into the traps of linguistic analysis and empty exegesis. Similarly, he rebuked the scholarly specialists who were interested only in personal recognition and the technicians who were obsessed with manipulative processes. As Okada Takehiko points out, Ekken felt that "[t]o forget about the cultivation of the moral sense *(giri)* within one's own heart and to seek after worldly success was the way of a specialist, and that to attempt to discover techniques to penetrate into the principle underlying all things was the work of the technician."[35]

Yet in terms of the content of education he sought to bring together both the humanities and the natural sciences. Thus, he advocated a practical learning that would foster self-cultivation while also assisting others. He urged that learning should be "preserved in the heart and carried out in action."[36] Both traditional humanistic values and specifically technical skills should be used for the benefit of self and society. In this way the scholar would be assisting in the traditional Confucian aspiration to participate in the transformative processes of heaven and earth.

To bring together "humanistic" and "scientific" concerns Ekken felt that a physician should practice humaneness while helping to "nourish life." His skills could not be dispensed without an understanding of his larger ethical role. Similarly, to study horticultural techniques or to cultivate plants only because of their beauty was to trivialize their larger role in the natural world. By being concerned with manipulative processes of cultivation a person could fall into the danger of "trifling with things and losing one's sense of purpose."[37] Rather, horticulture and agriculture ought to be undertaken with an understanding of "the proclivity of nature to give birth to living things."[38] An appreciation of nature's mysterious fecundity as the source of life was essential to Ekken's practical learning.

Finally, at the heart of this attempt to bridge the humanistic and scientific modes of learning was his understanding of the unity of principle and the diversity of its particularizations (Ch. *li-i fen shu;* Jp. *riichi bunshu*). An important extension of this idea is his belief in both the constancy of principle along with its transformations. Thus, while principle is a unified and constant source of value in human society, it is similarly the source of order in the natural world. Yet at the same time and without contradiction, principle is manifested in a diversity of forms and in a myriad of transformations. Thus, both continuity and change are embraced by principle. The elucidation of this idea became a motivating force of his own form of practical learning.

Because Ekken, following Lo Chin-shun, collapsed the distinction between principle and material force, his *jitsugaku* was directed toward finding principle within the transformations of material force itself. In terms of moral cultivation this meant a rejection of the distinction between one's original heavenly nature and one's physical nature. He saw them as essentially the same and therefore one's original nature or principle was to be sought within one's own mind or within itself *(ch'i)*. This same monism could be applied to the natural world to undertake empirical studies uncovering the principle within material force.

The Creative Principles of Filiality and Jen

Ekken's practical learning was inspired not only by his monism of *ch'i* but also by his doctrine of *jen* and filial piety as extended to the natural world. From Chang Tsai's doctrine of forming one body with all things Ekken elaborated his unique understanding of assisting in the transforming and nourishing powers of heaven and earth. While other Confucians, such as Nakae Tōju (1608–1648), saw filiality as having a counterpart in the human and natural worlds, Ekken took this understanding a step farther by stressing the need of the human to activate a filial reverence for the natural world.

A primary motive in this activation of filiality was a sense of the debt of humans to heaven and earth as the parents of us all. Ekken recognized the importance of loyalty and reverence to one's parents as the sources of life and he carried this feeling of respect to the whole cosmic order. He maintained that since nature is the source and sustainer of life one should respond to it as to one's parents, with care, reverence, and consideration. Indeed, humans must serve nature as they would their parents in order to repay their debt for the gift of life. He urged humans to cherish living things and avoid wantonly killing plants or animals.

This care for nature is a motivating force behind his own investigation of things, for he saw it as connected with filiality.

Central to his doctrine of a cosmic filial relationship is an all-embracing humaneness, which is characterized by a sense of sympathy within which brings blessings to humans and all things. His scientific and spiritual pursuits are further linked by his understanding of a direct correspondence between humaneness in persons and the origination principle in nature termed "the heart of nature" *(tenchi no kokoro).*[39] Just as birth and origination are the supreme attributes of the natural world, so is benevolence the supreme attribute of the human. Thus, birth or origination is the counterpart in nature of *jen* or humaneness in persons.

The creative dynamics of the universe find their richest expression in the creative reciprocity of human beings. The fecundity of nature and the wellsprings of the human heart are seen as two aspects of the all-embracing process of change and transformation in the universe. He said that humans have a harmonious energy granted by nature and this principle governs the lives of humans. "Just as plants and trees continue to sprout without ceasing, so too the 'life force' thrives within us and the heart is made eternally glad—this is happiness."[40] And when extended to others this is the creative virtue of humaneness.

For Ekken, then, the human is the "soul of the universe" and thus has both great privileges and awesome responsibilities in the hierarchy of the natural world. One can live up to these responsibilities by studying the classics, investigating principle, and activating humaneness. He also added the significant directive to "follow the example of nature" in achieving inner wisdom and contentment. With great detail he describes the seasonal changes with which one should harmonize one's own moods and activities. He saw this as participating in the process of transformation which for the human is the key to both knowledge and moral practice.

Briefly stated, then, these are some of the central ideas in Ekken's thought, namely that filial piety should be extended to the whole cosmic order, humaneness is the principle of creativity corresponding to origination in nature, and humans are the soul of the universe and participate through great substance and total functioning in the transformative processes of heaven and earth.

MIURA BAIEN

Miura Baien (1723–1789) might be viewed as one who carried on Kaibara Ekken's explorations of the natural world. As we have seen, one of Ekken's primary motives in his investigation of nature was his strong religious belief in the familial connection between the human and heaven and earth. Studies of nature became a means of expressing one's filial duty and of activating the creative virtue of *jen* in the human.

Baien, while being less overtly religious, nonetheless maintained strongly Confucian values at the root of his study of nature. Indeed, his central impetus in his research was to "benefit the people" and thus to contribute to the advancement of human relationships.[41] Furthermore, like Ekken, he recognized the debt of humans to heaven and hoped to provide a means of cooperating with the transformative powers of heaven and earth. He wrote: "In order not to impair things given by heaven one has to aim at helping along the creativity of nature according to each one's status and ability. Doing so they would not go against the great virtue of heaven and earth."[42]

One of Baien's most significant contributions was his adamant insistence that while the human can only be understood in relation to nature, we must see nature in its own terms and not simply project anthropomorphic ideas onto it. Wishing to make a clear break with more mythical and animistic ways of representing nature, he wanted to describe nature's own inherent dynamics. For Baien this became a lifelong pursuit taking the form of an epistemological method that he felt provided a "key for opening the gates of Heaven."[43]

Biography and Intellectual Development

Miura Baien was born, like Ekken, the son of a physician in Kyushu. From the time he was fifteen until he was nineteen he studied at a local provincial school with a prominent Confucianist scholar, Ayabe Keisai (1676–1750) who had been a student of the leading Confucians, Ito Togai and Muro Kyuso. At the age of twenty-three he visited Nagasaki where he made his first contacts with the Dutch scholars of his day. It is important to note that Western science, especially through Dutch Learning coming in at Nagasaki, was making an impact in Japan during the eighteenth century. Indeed, several of Baien's colleagues and followers studied Western science at the Kaitokudo in Osaka. It is also true that Baien, like Fang I Chih in seventeenth-century China, lamented the lack of interest in science by many of the Confucians and the overconcern of Western scholars with pragmatic details while ignoring moral concerns.

Baien's practical interests extended to the political and economic spheres and he has been compared to Adam Smith for his economic theories. In 1756 he drew up the regulations for a credit union to assist the local peasants. It was sustained by small, regular contributions from which the farmers could obtain a loan when in need. While he had strong words for those who were poor due to laziness, he had great sympathy for those who were in difficulty because of natural disasters, sickness, old age, or lack of heirs to assist them. It is said that many thousands of people benefited from this association, the results of which have lasted until recent times.[44]

The Creativity of Nature: Continuities and Discontinuities in Baien's Thought

Miura Baien saw his study of nature simultaneously as a means of understanding the universe and of knowing the will of heaven.[45] While his thought is considered unique and original, it was nonetheless motivated by some of the most enduring concerns of Confucians in China, Korea, and Japan.

Like the Sung Neo-Confucians, he was preoccupied with the nature of change in the universe, seeing it as real and not insubstantial as had the Buddhists. He realized that change is the source of the creative forces of nature and sought to explore this as a way of understanding how the human can assist this creative process. He was deeply influenced by the *Book of Changes* and by the ideas of the circularity of movement and the fusion of opposites found there.[46] Like the Sung masters before him he spoke of the "creativity of nature *(zōka)* which makes flowers bloom, children to be born and produces fish and birds."[47] This he felt is what should cause both wonder and doubt in the human as regards our own role. He celebrated the creativity of heaven as its great virtue which "generates things ceaselessly."[48]

The challenge of the human is to see oneself as assisting in this transformative process: "In order not to impair things given by heaven one has to aim at helping along the creativity of nature according to each one's status and ability. Doing so they would not go against the great virtue of heaven and earth."[49] Baien broke with Chu Hsi's dualism of principle *(li)* and material force *(ch'i)*. Like Ekken, he adopted a monism of *ch'i* more in line with Chang Tsai's thought on the creativity of *ch'i*. Also like Ekken, Baien spent many of his early years in a state of doubt until at the age of thirty he had a breakthrough where he "first recognized that heaven and earth is *ch'i.*"[50]

Baien's significant restatement of an appropriate method of studying nature began with an urgent call to view the natural world objectively in its own terms. He felt nature is our only teacher and that book learning is an important but limited road to the truth. Indeed, he said repeatedly, "Heaven-and-earth [nature] is the teacher."[51] We must therefore cast aside all tendencies to project our habitual ways and past knowledge on to the natural world. Indeed, he felt that habits were "enslavements of the minds,"[52] which prevented one from seeing the world as it really was. This he considered was a major obstacle to a discovery of the "logic of things," *jōri*. He also realized that these habitual perspectives fostered a lack of intellectual curiosity about one's surroundings.

One of the continuing habits of humans was their tendency to anthropomorphize the natural world. Baien wished to break free of this mythical way of perceiving the forces and elements of nature. He felt that humans must not set themselves above or apart from nature and then project their ways onto nature's movements.

Baien combined a reverence for the creative processes of nature with a perspective that aimed at objectivity in investigation. To know the will of heaven and to assist the transformation of things remained significant motivation behind his observational studies. He struggled to demonstrate that humans need to understand both their connection to the cosmos while appreciating the workings of the natural world on its own terms. Thus, an intimacy and a distance, an identity and a differentiation was needed for authentic investigation of nature. Humans ought to understand the larger context in which they undertake such studies while not losing the objectivity necessary for accurate research. In doing this, Baien repossessed and expanded two central concepts in the Neo-Confucian tradition, namely, the appreciation of the fecundity of the natural world along with an understanding of the principle or order that lies within things.

Jōri as Objective Method and Patterned Structure

Baien enlarged the concepts of principle and the investigation of things to include both an objective method and a patterned structure. He advocated careful scrutiny of everything in nature and within ourselves. He called for an examination of our sense powers and our ways of knowing. As an epistemological method of inquiry, Baien described the three essential aspects of the logic of things *(jōri)*:

1. It is essentially dialectical in structure, positing a thesis, an antithesis, and a synthesis.
2. It calls for eliminating all bias and prejudice.
3. It demands empirical verification.[53]

Through this method of inquiry and investigation he felt one would begin to discover the external and internal structure of things.

As an ontological structure *jōri* is essentially "botanical in conception"[54] with *jō* referring to the branch and *ri* referring to principle or to the grain in wood. As Wm. Theodore de Bary has noted, *jōri* was a means of describing the external harmony of the natural world and its inner ordering quality.[55] Just as the branches of a tree reflect an external pattern, so does the grain of wood describe its internal structure. While the branches continue to grow and develop, so do the inner rings of the tree reflect a patterned counterpart of that growth. Thus, there is an essential identity between external diversity and inner unity.

Minamoto Ryoen has suggested Baien is writing from the view of an "independent empirical rationalism,"[56] while Rosemary Mercer describes his perspective as one of "scientific realism."[57] Shimada Kenji, however, notes that: "It is my opinion that his philosophy is not, as is commonly said, to be judged as the prenatal stirrings of the concepts of modern science, rather it should be described as the highest culmination of late Confucian natural philosophy."[58] This refers to the Sung Neo-Confucian interest in the investigation of things.

The fascination of Baien's thought is his attempt to respond to the stirrings in Japan of an interest in Western science both as a cosmology for ordering the self in the universe and as a methodology for studying the universe. Baien's cosmological views were revised some twenty-three times in the *Genkiron* over the same number of years. In its simplest form he described the universe as being filled with the primal *ch'i*: "The one primal *ch'i* fills the universe, the tip of the finest hair does not escape it. Dividing and combining, it generates and destroys without cease. The enfolding heaven is outermost and the earth rests with it."[59]

Baien said there is no room for void because *ch'i* penetrates everything in the universe. Moreover, it supports life through *ch'i* in the air, soil, food, blood, etc. The *ch'i* of heaven and earth refers to image and shape while the *ch'i* of yin and yang refers to going and coming. Heaven turns endlessly while earth is held motionless in the center. The *ch'i* of yang is warm and light while the *ch'i* of yin is cold and dark. Yin and yang are the fundamental opposites that make up the universe. Baien described key opposites in the universe such as heat and cold and water and fire. Furthermore, Baien noted that all objects have their own *ch'i* and no object can exist without *ch'i*. He accounted for the movement of the one primal *ch'i* as the "motive power." This generates yin and yang which in turn give rise to shapes with characteristics of soft and hard, large and small, and so on.

CONCLUSION

A century after Baien's death the Meiji restoration had occurred and the modernization process in Japan was well underway. The charged debates between technology and tradition, between "Western science" and "Eastern morality" became central to Japan's mode of entry into the twentieth century. The tensions of tradition and modernity were deeply felt and have both caused polarization and compromise for many decades. Indeed, many of the ambiguities of contemporary Japan still find their expression in these complex ambiguities.

While thinkers such as Ekken and Baien could not have fully anticipated the rapid pace with which Japan entered the technological age, some of the problems they raised remain as pressing now as when they first articulated them to their own contemporaries: How can humans assist in the transforming and nourishing processes of nature through both understanding and investigating nature as well as through respecting and caring for nature?

Ekken's answers to these questions tended to emphasize the moral, namely, the activation of humaneness *(jen)* in the individual in relation to nature, while Baien's answers lay more in the investigative, namely, the discovery of principle *(li)* in all things. Yet neither individual was willing to eliminate the ethical engagement or the reflective distance required by their studies. Both of them were fascinated by the dynamic processes of nature unfolding in *ch'i*.

It is in our own times that the gap appears to be widening between moral and religious issues and the scientific study of nature with still unforeseen consequences. It is, then, not inappropriate that we should now be raising the same questions that preoccupied these Tokugawa Neo-Confucians. Their concerns, far from being outdated, are as significant now as then. They reach across cultural boundaries to examine the very dynamizing energies of the human venture in relation to the vast processes of nature.

These two thinkers challenge our views regarding the nature of ecological thinking in general and deep ecology in particular. While many people would argue that Confucianism, as traditionally understood, is anthropocentric and thus incompatible with deep ecology, on further examination it has a profound regard for the primacy of nature which might be seen as remarkably compatible with deep ecological thinking. While relationality and interdependence are valued in both Confucianism and deep ecology, the principal difference between the two is the value of distinctive hierarchical relations and roles which Confucianism embraces. Finally, Confucianism is probably more proactive in terms of creating and maintaining social and political institutions. In this sense, it is quite compatible with aspects of social ecology. In terms of self-cultivation and realization of the individual, Confucianism has worked out a remarkable system of correlative thinking in relation to nature Moreover, as we can see in the life and thought of Ekken and Baien the study of nature did not require such a distance that manipulation or exploitation of nature resulted. Rather, it evoked a profound respect for nature's dynamic rhythms. In these aspects, then, perhaps even deep ecological thinking may be thus broadened by a further exploration of Confucian thought and practice as it unfolded in East Asia.

NOTES

1. See, for example, the series on world religions and ecology published by the World Wide Fund for Nature 1992 which included Hinduism, Buddhism, Judaism, Christianity, and Islam. An exception to this is the book edited by J. Baird Callicott and Roger Ames, *Nature in Asian Traditions of Thought* (Albany: State University of New York Press, 1989) with Tu Weiming's article on Confucianism.

2. See Tu's development of this term in "The Anthropocosmic Vision," *Centrality and Commonality* (Albany: State University of New York Press, 1989), 102–107.

3. "The Continuity of Being" in *Nature in Asian Traditions of Thought*, 70.

4. Vaclav Smil, *The Bad Earth* (Armonk, NY: M. E. Sharpe, 1984).

5. Ed. by Mary Evelyn Tucker and John Berthrong (Cambridge: Center for the Study of World Religions and Harvard University Press, 1997).

6. Two of the leading deep ecologists, Arne Naess and George Sessions, especially acknowledge the influence of Spinoza. Michael Zimmerman helped make the links to Heidegger but later distanced himself from that connection. See Bill Devall and George Sessions, *Deep Ecology: Living as if Nature Mattered* (Salt Lake City: Peregrine Smith Books, 1985) and Michael Zimmerman, *Contesting Earth's Future: Radical Ecology and Postmodernity* (Berkeley: University of California Press, 1994).

7. See Wm. Theodore de Bary and Irene Bloom, eds., *Sources of Chinese Tradition*, Vol. 1 (New York: Columbia University Press, 1999).

8. Ibid.

9. This term is used by A. C. Graham in *Disputers of the Tao* (La Salle, IL: Open Court, 1989).

10. Ibid., 313.

11. Chung-ying Cheng underscores the importance of the *I Ching* in Confucian and Neo-Confucian thought. See, for example, "Chinese Philosophy and Symbolic Reference" in *New Dimensions of Confucian and Neo-Confucian Thought* (Albany: State University of New York Press, 1991).

12. *Centrality and Commonality* (Albany: State University of New York Press, 1989), 106.

13. This phrase is used by Thomas Berry in an unpublished article titled "Authenticity in Confucian Spirituality."

14. "Some Polarities in Confucian Thought," in *Confucianism and Chinese Civilization*, ed. Arthur Wright (Stanford: Stanford University Press, 1964).

15. From a philosophical perspective Anne Birdwhistell maintains that "[t]he dominant paradigmatic example of Confucian thought may be termed 'living entity', which in turn is characterized by order and organization. . . . This theoretical frame entailed a generative or biological metaphor, in that it was based on ideas of birth, growth, patterned development, change, activity, decline, and death." *Li Yong (1627–1705) and Epistemological Dimensions of Confucian Philosophy* (Stanford: Stanford University Press, 1996), 13.

16. For further discussion of this process of discernment, see my book *Moral and Spiritual Cultivation in Japanese Neo-Confuciansm: The Life and Thought of Kaibara Ekken 1630–1714* (Albany: State University of New York Press, 1989).

17. "The Doctrine of the Mean" in Wing-tsit Chan, trans., *A Source Book in Chinese Philosophy* (Princeton: Princeton University Press, 1963), 98, 112.

18. See, for example, John Major, *Heaven and Earth in Early Han Thought*; chapters 3, 4, and 5 of the *Huainan zi* (Albany: State University of New York Press, 1993); and Charles Le Blanc, *Huai-Nan Tzu and Philosophical Synthesis in Early Han Thought* (Hong Kong: Hong Kong University Press, 1983).

19. See Kidder Smith, Peter Bol, Joseph Adler, and Don Wyatt, *Sung Dynasty Use of the I Ching* (Princeton: Princeton University Press, 1990).

20. See Julia Ching, "What is Confucian Spirituality?" in *Confucianism: The Dynamics of Tradition*, ed. Irene Eber (New York: Macmillan, 1986). I am indebted to Julia Ching's suggestive comments in this article on "The Language of Growth" in Confucian spirituality.

21. See, for example, Benjamin Wai-ming Ng, "Quantitative Notes on *I Ching* Scholarship in Tokugawa Japan," *The Japan Foundation Newsletter* 23.5 (Feb. 1996) and his "Study and Uses of the *I Ching* in Tokugawa Japan," *Sino-Japanese Studies* 9.2 (April 1997).

22. Toshinobu Yasunaga, *Andō Shōeki: Social and Ecological Philosopher of Eighteenth-Century Japan* (New York: Weatherhill, 1992).

23. Aihe Wang, "Cosmology and the Transformation of Political Culture in Early China," Ph.D. Thesis, Harvard University, Cambridge, MA, 1995.

24. Indeed, Wm. Theodore de Bary has made numerous efforts to describe the reformist efforts of Confucianism *(The Unfolding of Confucianism, Principle and Practicality, The Liberal Tradition in China)* as well as to note its problematic dimensions *(The Trouble With Confucianism)*.

25. Kate Nakai, "The Naturalization of Confucianism in Tokugawa Japan: The Problem of Sinocentrisim," *Harvard Journal of Asiatic Studies* 40 (1980): 157–199.

26. David Shaner and Shannon Duval, "Conservation Ethics and the Japanese Intellectual Tradition," *Environmental Ethics* 11 (1989): 197–214.

27. See Wm. Theodore de Bary, Introduction, *Principle and Practicality* (New York: Columbia University Press, 1979).

28. Ibid.

29. It is fair to say that most deep ecologists are also keen to be seen as engaged with issues of contemporary import and are not simply theorists but are also activists.

30. This material on Ekken is adapted from my book on him and has appeared in other versions in several other articles. See *Moral and Spiritual Cultivation in Japanese Neo-Confuciansm: The Life and Thought of Kaibara Ekken 1630–1714* (Albany: State University of New York Press, 1989).

31. Okada Takehiko, "Yamazaki Ansai and Kaibara Ekken" in *Principle and Practicality,* ed. de Bary and Bloom (New York: Columbia University Press, 1979), 290.

32. Ibid., 267.

33. Ibid., 268.

34. I am not using science here in the sense of modern experimental science, but rather in the genre of studies of natural history and categorization that had a long precedent in Chinese thought. The term *empirical* also reflects this study of nature that is observation rather than experimental.

35. Ibid., 276.

36. Ibid., 279.

37. Ibid., 277.

38. Ibid.

39. Ibid., 284.

40. Ibid., 259.

41. Miura Baien, "An Answer to Taka Bokkyo," trans. Gino K. Piovesana, S.M., *Monumenta Nipponica* 20:3–4 (1965): 442.

42. Ibid., 442.

43. Bary and Bloom, *Sources of Japanese Tradition,* 483.

44. Gino Piovesana, "Miura Baien: 1723–1789," *Monumenta Nipponica* 20:3–4 (1965): 393.

45. Ibid., 443.

46. *Deep Words, Miura Baien's System of Natural Philosphy,* translation and philosophical commentary by Rosemary Mercer (Leiden: E. J. Britt, 1991), 5.

47. Baien, "An Answer to Taka Bokkyo," 423.

48. Ibid., 440.

49. Ibid., 442.

50. Mercer, *Deep Words,* 4.

51. Ibid., 158.

52. Baien, "An Answer to Taka Bokkyo," 422.

53. Ibid., 427. See also Bary and Bloom, *Sources of Japanese Tradition,* 482.

54. Bary and Bloom, *Sources of Japanese Tradition*, 483.

55. Bary and Bloom, *Sources of Japanese Tradition*. The next few lines rely on Professor de Bary's interpretation in the *Sources* (483) and Baien's discussion of *ri* in "Answer to Taka Bokkyo," in *Monumenta Nipponica*, 428–429.

56. Wm. Theodore de Bary and Irene Bloom, eds., *Principle and Practicality* (New York: Columbia University Press, 1979), 451.

57. Mercer, *Deep Words*, 18.

58. Ibid., 196.

59. Ibid., 19.

7

Faith, God, and Nature

Judaism and Deep Ecology

Eric Katz

God's Answer

In the book of Job we find some of the most troubling verses in the Hebrew Bible. Near the end of the book, Job is able to question God about the misfortunes that have befallen him, and God answers him out of the whirlwind:

> Where wast thou when I laid the foundations of the earth? Declare, if thou hast understanding.
>
> Who hath laid the measures thereof, if thou knowest? or who hath stretched the line upon it?
>
> . . . Who hath divided a watercourse for the overflowing of waters, or a way for the lightning of thunder;
>
> To cause it to rain on the earth, where no man is; on the wilderness, wherein there is no man;
>
> To satisfy the desolate and waste ground; and to cause the bud of the tender herb to spring forth? (Job 38:4–5; 25–27)

The meaning of these verses is chilling. Job seeks an explanation of his troubles, and instead God delivers a lecture about the creation and the operation of the natural world. Although the Lord's tirade goes on for four chapters (a total of 129 verses), these five verses are especially important. The Lord is reminding Job that humanity was not present when God created the universe. The world was not created *for* humanity. The events of the natural world—rain, for example—do not take place for the benefit of humanity. Rain falls on the wilderness where no man is; it is thus a mistake to see the rain as God's contribution to human agriculture and livestock.[1]

These verses are disturbing because they question the idea that human purpose, human good, and human reason lie at the heart of divine activity. Human beings are finite; we are not omniscient. We want to believe that although God may act in mysterious ways, these actions are for a purpose and a good that do not lie outside of human interests. We want to believe that everything that happens in the world is for the best. We have a faith that the universe is rational, ordered, and essentially benign, ruled by a caring omnipotent God. God's answer to Job undermines that faith. Although the universe may be rationally ordered, this rational order may not at all be connected to human interests and concerns.

These lines from the Book of Job, I believe, provide a framework for a comparison of a Jewish response to the meaning of the environmental crisis and the philosophy of deep ecology. The key idea expressed here in Job is non-anthropocentrism, the removal of human interests from the center of value in our understanding of the operation of the natural world. Over the last twenty-five years, much of environmental philosophy has emphasized the need for, and the possibility of, a non-anthropocentric revolution in our thought toward the natural world. An adequate environmental ethic, it has been argued, will only be possible from a perspective of non-anthropocentrism.[2] But does the non-anthropocentrism expressed in these lines from the book of Job represent the basic perspective of Judaism? What are the non-anthropocentric elements in the Jewish philosophy of the ethics of nature? And can the non-anthropocentric themes in Jewish thought be seen as similar to the central ideas in the philosophy of deep ecology? I must admit that I am skeptical: I have profound misgivings that traditional Judaism can be understood as an ally of deep ecology, that Jewish ideas about the nonhuman natural world can be seen as an expression of deep ecological principles. This essay is an attempt to confront my skepticism: here I offer my personal reflections on the problem of reconciling a Jewish philosophy of nature with the philosophy of deep ecology.

Two Principles of Jewish Ethics

First, consider two central commands in the environmental ethics of Judaism: *tza'ar ba'alei chayim* ["the pain of living creatures"] and *bal tashchit* ["do not destroy"]. Anyone searching for a basic non-anthropocentrism in Jewish thought will find these two principles a useful starting point.[3] *Tza'ar ba'alei chayim* is perhaps the most important principle in Judaism concerning the human relationship with animals: it requires an attitude of compassion for all animal life. In particular, humans have a special obligation to care for and consider the pain of the domesticated animals that live within the larger human community. Thus, the fourth commandment concerning the Sabbath requires rest for one's livestock as well as for humanity (Exodus 20:10 and Deuteronomy 5:14). There is also the law forbidding the yoking together of animals of unequal strength (Deuteronomy 22:10), for this would cause pain to the weaker animal. And one is not permitted to muzzle an ox during the threshing of the grain (Deuteronomy 25:4). All of these commandments are based on a compassion for animal suffering, and thus demonstrate that Judaism extends the realm of moral consideration beyond the limits of the human community, at least into the realm of domesticated animal life.

Judaism, of course, does not advocate an absolute reverence for all life, nor does it require vegetarianism. Genesis 1:29 *does* prohibit meat-eating—"And God said, Behold, I have given you every herb bearing seed, which is upon the face of all the earth, and every tree, in which is the fruit of a tree yielding seed; to you it shall be for meat"—but this prohibition was rescinded for Noah and his descendants after the flood—"Every thing that liveth shall be meat for you; even as the green herb have I given you all things" (Genesis 9:3). And yet the freedom to eat meat comes with an obligation to treat the animal food source with a certain amount of respect, for the next verse places a limit on the methods and kind of meat to be eaten: "But the flesh with the life thereof, which is the blood thereof, shall ye not eat" (Genesis 9:4). This limitation on the eating of blood, the eating of life itself, became the basis for the laws of kosher slaughtering, laws designed to minimize the pain of the animals being killed. Although eating meat was thought essential for human survival, it did not nullify an obligation for compassion for all living animals.

The principle of *bal tashchit* concerns the prohibition against the wanton destruction of natural entities, living beings (plants and animals) and even human artifacts. Its source is a passage from Deuteronomy 20:19–20:

> When you besiege a city for a long time . . . you shall not destroy its trees by wielding an ax against them. You may eat of them, but you

> may not cut them down. Are the trees in the field men that they
> should be besieged by you? Only the trees which you know are not
> trees for food you may destroy and cut down, that you may build
> siege-works against the city . . .

The point here appears to be that the trees may be destroyed only if they are not food-producing and only if their destruction will be useful for the war effort. To destroy trees that produce food will ultimately be harmful to all humans; similarly, to destroy trees for no useful purpose is pointless and counter-productive.

Bal tashchit becomes, in Jewish thought, a general principle against vandalism. For example, in the *Sefer Hahinukh* (529) it is written this comment on *bal tashchit:* "In addition [to the cutting down of trees] we include the negative commandment that we should not destroy anything, such as burning or tearing clothes, or breaking a utensil—without purpose." But this raises the fundamental issue of what constitutes a good or justifiable purpose for the destruction of something, and in particular, for the destruction of a natural entity, such as a tree. Judaism does not exclude the consideration of economic motives. In the Talmud (*Baba Kama* 91b–92a) there is an extended discussion on the permissibility of cutting down trees based on their economic worth: a fruit-bearing tree may be destroyed if the value of its crop is less than the value of the lumber the tree would produce; moreover, the tree may be destroyed if the land is needed for the construction of a house, or if there are more productive trees in the same area. These exceptions to *bal tashchit* are not permitted for purely aesthetic reasons, such as landscaping.[4] Thus, the commentator Eric G. Freudenstein concludes: "[T]he standards of bal tashchit are relative rather than absolute. The law is interpreted in the Talmud as limited to purposeless destruction and does not prohibit destruction for the sake of economic gain."[5]

Although this analysis is far from complete, it is clear that *bal tashchit* requires some consideration of the social implications of actions that harm nonhuman entities. It concerns, in part, the proper human response to the nonhuman environment. Similarly, *tza'ar ba'alei chayim* concerns the proper human response to animal life and animal suffering. But do these principles express what contemporary environmental philosophers would call non-anthropocentric values? Can they be the basis of a robust non-anthropocentric environmental ethic? Are these principles similar to basic ideas in the philosophy of deep ecology? To answer these questions, we need to look closely at the fundamental principles of deep ecology.

DEEP ECOLOGY

What is the philosophy of deep ecology? This is a difficult question to answer, because there are a large number of different positions that are called deep ecology, and many other environmental philosophies that are deep ecological even though they do not use the label. So what is the *real* deep ecology? Does it make sense to ask this question?

In an essay of this limited scope, I cannot pretend to give a full account of the meaning of deep ecology as an environmental philosophy. Instead, I will present what I consider to be the most important features of deep ecological thought as a general world view, i.e., as a philosophical system regarding the environment. As is now well known, the terminology was introduced in a rough outline by the Norwegian philosopher Arne Naess in 1972 where he contrasted the political and social movement of "deep ecology" from that of "shallow ecology."[6] Naess claimed that shallow ecology developed policies that merely reformed human practices regarding the environment—such as pollution abatement or energy conservation—and that mainly affected the well-being of those people in the more affluent nations. Deep ecology, in contrast, was concerned with re-thinking the fundamental human relationship with the natural world. Deep ecology was truly a *philosophical* outlook on the environmental crisis, for it asked us to develop, not environmental policies per se, but rather basic principles about the meaning of human life.

In this initial formulation, deep ecology is essentially an approach, a strategy—a *methodology*—for thinking about the human relationship with the natural world and the environmental crisis. But the merely methodological framework of questioning basic principles soon developed a substantive content of its own. These substantive ideas perhaps can be traced to the Platform of Deep Ecology, written down in 1984 by Naess and the American philosopher George Sessions. It must be emphasized that the platform expresses the basic ideas of the deep ecology *movement*, not the basic ideas of the *philosophy* of deep ecology. Nevertheless, Andrew McLaughlin has called the platform "the heart of deep ecology,"[7] and thus it is a useful place to begin to tease out its central philosophical ideas. Here is the platform as it appears in Naess's *Ecology, Community, and Lifestyle:*

1. The flourishing of human and non-human life on Earth has intrinsic value. The value of non-human life forms is independent of the usefulness these may have for narrow human purposes.

2. Richness and diversity of life forms are values in themselves and contribute to the flourishing of human and non-human life on Earth.

3. Humans have no right to reduce this richness and diversity except to satisfy vital needs.

4. Present human interference with the non-human world is excessive, and the situation is rapidly worsening.

5. The flourishing of human life and cultures is compatible with a substantial decrease of the human population. The flourishing of non-human life requires such a decrease.

6. Significant change of life conditions for the better requires change in policies. These affect basic economic, technological, and ideological structures.

7. The ideological change is mainly that of appreciating *life quality* (dwelling in situations of intrinsic value) rather than adhering to a high standard of living. There will be a profound awareness of the difference between big and great.

8. Those who subscribe to the forgoing points have an obligation directly or indirectly to participate in the attempt to implement the necessary changes.[8]

From the perspective of a philosophical system, what is most important about this platform is the emphasis on nonhuman intrinsic or inherent value. Nonhuman life must flourish even if this reduces human affluence or human population. In addition, the ideas of richness and diversity play a significant role here, not only as a value-principle for the evaluation of the natural environment as a whole, but also as a guiding principle in the evaluation and reexamination of the ends of human life. In many ways, deep ecology is a philosophy as old as Western civilization, for it reinforces a critique of the single-minded pursuit of material abundance. Human activity, in and of itself, and in relation to the natural environment, will be guided by a respect for all life forms, noninterference in natural processes, and a resistance to the homogenization and simplification of both natural and human systems.

The ideas of the platform are expressed quite broadly, so as not to exclude any potential sympathizers to the political and social movement of deep ecology. But two specific philosophical ideas have been omitted from the platform, even though almost all versions of deep ecology include them in some fashion—these are the ideas of identification and Self-realization.[9] By identification, the philosophy of deep ecology means that each human individual identifies with all other entities in the natural world. This is not an identification of actual personal identity—I do not believe that I am literally the tree in my garden. It is an identification of *interests*. A human being who identifies with the entities of the natural world considers the interests of all other living beings as closely connected to his or her own interests. This identification leads directly into the notion of Self-realization as the ultimate goal of the philosophy of deep ecology, where the upper case "S" in Self implies that there is a larger, more comprehensive, Self than the self (with a lower case "s") of the individual ego. Because I identify with the rest of the natural world, I care for the rest of creation. I expand myself outward to include an interest in the value and flourishing of the entire natural environment. I come to understand that I can only fully realize myself through the flourishing—the Self-realization—of the entire natural universe.

In sum, the basic principles of the philosophy of deep ecology include: a respect for and identification with all natural entities, a de-emphasis on human interests as the focal point of moral evaluation, and the understanding that the maximization of good involves the fullest realization of all forms of life. These philosophical ideals lead to practical principles of action: a policy of noninterference in nature (or at least a policy of minimal intervention) and a desire to restructure human society to be more in harmony with natural processes. Two philosophers of deep ecology, David Rothenberg and George Sessions, have summarized this philosophical position with the term ecocentrism—i.e., the idea that the ecological system or the ecosphere is the center of value. Rothenberg comments: "The whole designation 'ecocentrism' is closer to an equivalent for what Naess means by 'deep ecology': centering on the ecosphere."[10] And Sessions sees ecocentrism as the essential point of the platform: "The philosophy of the Deep Ecology movement is characterized essentially by ecocentrism, as outlined in the 1984 Deep Ecology platform."[11] Deep ecology values the ecosphere—the ecological systems and the natural entities that comprise the living and developing natural world. Deep ecology values the ecosphere in itself, not merely for human purposes. Its chief practical concern is for the ecosphere to continue to develop and flourish with a minimal amount of human interference, degradation, and destruction. To accomplish this task, human social institutions must be reoriented so that they can exist in harmony with the processes and life forms of the natural world.

THE MATTER OF ANTHROPOCENTRISM

At this point in the exposition, it should be easy to compare the philosophy of deep ecology with those principles of Jewish environmental thought that were examined above, *tza'ar ba'alei chayim* and *bal tashchit*, for both Jewish ideas stress that humans should be concerned for entities and life forms that are nonhuman. *Tza'ar ba'alei chayim* and *bal tashchit,* may be expressions of a kind of non-anthropocentric thought in the Jewish tradition. If so, there would be at least a prima facie similarity between the central ideas of deep ecology and important principles of Judaism regarding the nonhuman natural world, even if there were differences in practical activity and policy.

Yet I hesitate to make this facile comparison. Two problems appear significant. First, in my desire to find resonances of non-anthropocentrism in Jewish thought, I may have overemphasized Judaism's concern for the nonhuman. *Tza'ar ba'alei chayim* and *bal tashchit* may not be fundamentally non-anthropocentric ethical principles. Second, questions can be raised about the standard interpretation of deep ecology that I have outlined above. It may be that deep ecology itself is fundamentally an anthropocentric point of view. These problems, as we will see below, reintroduce a consideration of the lessons from the book of Job with which I began this essay.

First, we must reexamine the non-anthropocentrism of *tza'ar ba'alei chayim* and *bal tashchit.* Does *tza'ar ba'alei chayim* really demonstrate a universal moral concern for the pain of all living creatures? Notice that virtually all of the examples used to demonstrate the human concern for animal suffering involve domesticated animals, livestock—animals that exist in a community with human beings. There is one possible exception to this, one place where the suffering of a wild creature is considered: in Deuteronomy 22:6–7 one is warned not to take a mother bird along with the eggs from its nest, but to let the mother fly away. But the passage actually makes no mention of the suffering of the mother bird, and whether or not the suffering of the mother is the main reason for the divine command is a controversial issue in the intellectual history of the passage.[12] In general, Judaism does not prescribe principles of action regarding wild nature, the environment outside of human institutions and community. Wild nature, as we discover in God's answer to Job, is beyond human comprehension and human influence. The beings of the wild are quite different from the domesticated animals that are part of the broader human community. By virtue of the human power over domesticated animals, we have ethical obligations to them—thus, we must consider animal pain as stated in *tza'ar ba'alei chayim.* But the human power over wild nature is much more limited, and so it is possible to see that *tza'ar ba'alei chayim* does not extend to wild creatures. *Tza'ar ba'alei chayim,* in sum, does not seem to be primarily a non-anthropocentric principle of moral evaluation—it is best understood as an ethical precept regarding the organization and treatment of animal life within the human community.

What of *bal tashchit*? Here the case for non-anthropocentrism is even more problematic, for the ban on destroying fruit trees appears to be tied directly to the future potential use of the trees for human good. Human interests and human value are the basis of the ethical command. Thus, the expansion of the prohibition to create a ban on wanton destruction is also connected to artifacts of use to humans. Maimonides is explicit on the importance of human interests. He first notes that one is permitted to cut down non-fruit bearing trees, "even if one does not need" the tree for any purpose. Moreover, the commandment of *bal tashchit* applies, in Maimonides's list, to household goods, clothing, food, buildings, and a spring—all objects of human utility.[13] A later commentator, Baruch Halevi Epstein, supports Maimonides's view: "[O]ne is permitted to destroy both trees or other things when there is bodily need for them . . . [i.e.,] whenever a person's need is fulfilled through this destruction."[14] Thus, *bal tashchit* prohibits purposeless destruction, but purpose is dependent on human needs and human good.

In a recent survey of the literature on *bal tashchit*, Eilon Schwartz demonstrates that Jewish thought concerning this commandment has developed in two opposing traditions. In the minimalist tradition, "human needs and wants take precedence over the rest of creation"—as in the passage by Maimonides cited above. In the maximalist tradition, human wants are "counterbalanced with the legitimate claims of the natural world," primarily in the sense that destruction is not permitted merely for the sake of human *luxury* goods.[15] But Schwartz concludes that neither the minimalist nor the maximalist position can be understood as endorsing contemporary ideas about non-anthropocentrism in environmental ethics. The Jewish tradition explicitly denies a holistic ecocentrism, a concern for the extensive system of nature outside of the human realm. *Bal tashchit's* "concern was domesticated nature, nature in contact with day-to-day living,"[16] just as we saw in *tza'ar ba'alei chayim*. Even more problematic for a comparison with deep ecology, Judaism is opposed to a neoromantic notion that humans can reconnect with a truer, more natural reality by increasing their respect and care for the natural environment. As Schwartz concludes, there is "a strong preference in Jewish ethical philosophy to see morality as transcendent of the natural world and not immanent within it."[17] *Bal tashchit*, in short, is not a step on the path to the deep ecological identification with nature and human Self-realization. Neither *bal tashchit* nor *tza'ar ba'alei chayim* appear to be primarily non-anthropocentric.

The second problem concerns the interpretation of deep ecology. Perhaps the philosophy of deep ecology is itself an anthropocentric view.[18] Consider the interconnected goal of Self-realization and the process of identification, two central ideas in the deep ecology position. On closer examination, both appear to be fundamentally anthropocentric—i.e., they both acquire meaning through their connection to human ideals, human thought, and human value. According to the philosophy of deep ecology, human individuals will only realize themselves, achieve the highest levels of satisfaction and fulfillment, by the complementary realization of all other living and natural beings. The realization of the individual ego, self-realization with a lower case "s," is only possible through Self-realization, the fulfillment, actualization, and flourishing of the larger non-egoistic Self, all living beings in the world (or ecosphere). Each individual human is to conceive of himself or herself as part of the more comprehensive Self that comprises the whole world. We achieve this Self-realization, in the main, through the process of identification: we identify the interests of the nonhuman natural world with our own human interests. We come to see that we and all other living things share a commonality of interests. In practice, then, we will work to preserve the flourishing of the natural world because in doing so, we act to preserve ourselves—human individuals—and our own flourishing. In harming the interests of the natural world, we harm ourselves. The focus of the preservation of natural processes is the maximization of human interests.

It seems clear, as Richard Sylvan points out in his criticism of deep ecology, that we should be wary of the entire notion of self-realization, for it has an anthropocentric history and pedigree.[19] The goal of self-realization "emerges direct from the humanistic Enlightenment; it is linked to the modern celebration of the individual human, freed from service to higher demands, and also typically from ecological constraints." Sylvan reminds us that the concept involves the maximization of egos, individual selves, or, at best, the privileged class of human-like selves. Even the attempt to escape egoism, with the notion of a capital "S" Self as a holistically extended super-self, only succeeds because we are identifying ourselves with the universe through an anthropocentric notion, a comparison to ourselves as individual human beings.

The anthropocentric character of the idea of self-realization is actually only one version of a more general problem in the methodology of environmental ethics, a problem originally discussed by John Rodman but elaborated by Sylvan.[20] In the attempt to ascribe value to entities in the universe, we human evaluators select features of these entities, and generalize these features as the standard or the criterion for possessing value, or being in the class of morally considerable entities. But "no simple species or subspecies, such as humans or superhumans, no single feature, such as sentience or life, serves as a reference benchmark, a base class, for determining moral relevance and other ethical dimensions." Any such feature we select is "arbitrary" and "loaded"—i.e., it is inherently biased toward characteristics possessed by the elite human class. A truly unbiased environmental ethic must be based on a notion of "eco-impartiality" in which none of the characteristics of any particular class of entities is used as the sole determining factor of moral value.[21] Deep ecology, with its emphasis on self-realization—and to a lesser extent, the goal of all living entities to flourish and blossom—fails this test.[22] Deep ecology selects as a fundamental value the fulfillment, flourishing, and realization of the Self—but this realization-value is based on characteristics of human life and human experience. Thus, the processes of identification and Self-realization are clearly anthropocentric in character, structure, and goal.

It is in considering the problems inherent in the deep ecological ideas of identification and self-realization that we once again encounter the challenge of the book of Job. Quite simply, the challenge is this: can we *identify* with the processes of nature? God's speech to Job suggests that we cannot, for God tells Job that the operations of the divinely created natural world are beyond the understanding of the individual human mind. "Where wast thou when I laid the foundations of the earth? Declare if thou has understanding" (Job 38:4). God causes it to rain where no humans will benefit (Job 38:26). He brings into existence wild beasts such as the behemoth and the leviathan whose power dwarfs that of humankind (Job 40:15 and 41:1). How is it possible for humans to identify with a natural, wild, and inhuman world such as this? Does the deep ecological principle of identifying with the interests of the nonhuman world make any sense in a universe that lies beyond the comprehension of humanity? And if we are unable to understand or to identify the interests of the natural world, and feel their compatibility with our own interests, then what sense is there to the idea of Self-realization? How can my fulfillment be based on the flourishing of nonhuman entities whose interests and goals, ordained by God, are beyond my limited understanding? How do I become fully realized by protecting the wild natural processes of the ecosphere, when only God understands these processes?

Perhaps the answer lies in accepting God's understanding of the natural order, without imposing a human framework—human categories—

on the divine creation. As E. L. Allen wrote about the Book of Job fifty years ago, long before there was an ecological crisis to consider: "The untamed world beyond the frontiers of human society is fraught with the numinous, it is a constant reminder that man is not master in the world but only a privileged and therefore responsible inhabitant of it."[23] God's message to Job is that the universe does not exist for human benefit. It is God's world, a theocentric universe, and at best humans will be fulfilled if they accede to the interests and demands of God.

Judaism offers us a theocentric universe, a world that is fundamentally divine because it is literally God's world: it belongs to God. "The earth is the Lord's, and the fullness thereof; the world, and they that dwell therein" (Psalms 24:1). Once we acknowledge that the world belongs to God, the ambiguities and complexities of *tza'ar ba'alei chayim* and *bal tashchit* tend to resolved. The point of *tza'ar ba'alei chayim* is to care for the living creatures that are part of the divine creation, that belong to no one but God. The principle emphasizes domesticated animals that are part of the human community because those are the animals that are most clearly affected by human action. The pain of wild animals is of little concern to humans—at least during the time the Hebrew Bible was composed—because the lives of wild animals were so removed from the daily lives of humans. The basis of *bal tashchit* also now becomes obvious. The prohibition against wanton or purposeless destruction does not revolve around the presence or absence of merely human goods—it concerns the destruction of worldly entities that belong to God. Humans must care and preserve all that exists in the universe, for all that exists is divine—it was created by God and it belongs to God.

The essential tension between the philosophy of deep ecology and the Jewish tradition regarding the natural world is now apparent. Deep ecology is, at best, an attempt to blend the anthropocentric self-interest of humans with the ecocentric interests of entities in the natural order. Deep ecology encourages individual humans to identify their interests with the interests of natural entities, and thus to protect the natural environment because it is in their wider interest to do so. Deep ecology is a type of ecocentric world view in which human individuals and human institutions are understood as part of the totality of the ecosphere. But Judaism is not an ecocentric view—it is a theocentric view. In Judaism, value, purpose, and meaning all emerge from God and his divine creative activity. The world exists because God has created it thus. The value of natural processes lies not in their usefulness for humanity but in their existence as part of the divine plan. This is the message of Job: do not believe that the rain falls for you.

POSTSCRIPT

Perhaps this discussion of Judaism and deep ecology should end here. But permit me a few personal reflections, a concluding un-religious postscript. I am uncomfortable with the uncompromising theocentrism that has concluded the previous section. I lack the faith.

In the autumn of 1995, I travelled to Eastern Europe to witness first-hand the sites of the Holocaust, the planned extermination by Nazi Germany of European Jewry. I do not know if every Jew should make this trip, but I knew that it was necessary for me, in order to come to terms with my history and the history of my people.

One of my stops was the Jewish cemetery in Warsaw, across the street from the downtown area that once was the Warsaw Ghetto. The Jewish cemetery is a remarkably beautiful and serene place. Because of neglect for decades after World War II the cemetery has been over-whelmed by the growth of trees and unchecked plant life. I visited the cemetery on a rainy day, and through the mist and fog it was difficult to see the tombstones, for the trees and underbrush have grown almost everywhere. A path led to a clearing, a clearing of grave stones, not trees. Here was the mass grave of the Jews who died in the Warsaw Ghetto before the deportations to Treblinka began in July 1942. The mass grave appeared as a meadow under a canopy of tree branches. Dozens of memorial candles were flickering there, remaining lit despite the light rain. The beauty of this mass grave surprised and shocked me. It is a monument to human evil, but it nevertheless demonstrates the power of nature to create beauty and peace in the universe.[24]

The Holocaust, of course, is the defining event for Jews in the twentieth century, and it surely represents the supreme crisis of faith for any individual Jew. When we view the destruction and evil of the Holocaust, are we like Job seeking a reason from God for his suffering? Can there be a rational explanation for the extent of the evil that surrounds us? Or must we accept the answer from the whirlwind, as Job did, that God alone can comprehend the meaning of events in a universe that God created. Is the explanation for the Holocaust only understandable to God?

The theocentrism of the book of Job leaves me with nothing but despair. It is impossible for me to accept an incomprehensible divinity as a guide to human action. The eminent Jewish scholar, Robert Gordis, in discussing the Jewish response to the environmental crisis, argued that humans need to do more than merely preserve the natural environment. Humanity is the "copartner of God in the work of creation" and thus we have a duty to enhance and improve the world.[25] But how can we be a partner with a divine being that we do not understand?

The processes of nature, however, I can understand. I can see in the Warsaw cemetery that nature heals the remnants of one of the most absolute evils of human history. God offers me no explanation, but I have faith in the healing presence of natural processes. That faith is the foundation of my abiding belief in ecocentrism. I can be a partner with nature, and work for the preservation and flourishing of all the natural entities of the universe.[26]

NOTES

1. I was initially inspired to think seriously about Job by reading Bill McKibben's discussion in his book, *The End of Nature* (New York: Random House, 1989), 75–80.

2. Most environmental philosophers trace the position of non-anthropocentrism from Aldo Leopold's "The Land Ethic," in *A Sand County Almanac* (New York: Oxford University Press, 1949). Other major texts that espouse a non-anthropocentric environmental ethic are: J. Baird Callicott, *In Defense of the Land Ethic: Essays in Environmental Philosophy* (Albany: State University of New York Press, 1989); Holmes Rolston III, *Environmental Ethics: Duties To and Values in the Natural World* (Philadelphia: Temple University Press, 1988); Paul Taylor, *Respect for Nature: A Theory of Environmental Ethics* (Princeton: Princeton University Press, 1986); and Andrew Brennan, *Thinking About Nature: An Investigation of Nature, Value, and Ecology* (Athens: University of Georgia Press, 1988). My own work also examines and defends a non-anthropocentric environmental ethic. See Eric Katz, *Nature as Subject: Human Obligation and Natural Community* (Lanham, MD: Rowman and Littlefield, 1997).

3. The discussion of these two principles is taken from my essay, "Judaism and the Ecological Crisis," in *Nature as Subject*, 205–220.

4. See Norman Lamm, "Ecology and Jewish Law and Theology," in *Faith and Doubt* (New York: KTAV, 1971), 170, and Eilon Schwartz, "Bal Tashchit: A Jewish Environmental Precept," *Environmental Ethics* 19 (1997): 360.

5. Eric G. Freudenstein, "Ecology and the Jewish Tradition," *Judaism* 19 (1970): 411.

6. Arne Naess, "The Shallow and the Deep, Long-Range Ecology Movement. A Summary," *Inquiry* 16 (1973): 95–100.

7. Andrew McLaughlin, "The Heart of Deep Ecology," in *Deep Ecology for the Twenty-first Century*, ed. George Sessions (Boston: Shambhala), 95.

8. Arne Naess, *Ecology, Community, and Lifestyle*, translated and edited by David Rothenberg (Cambridge: Cambridge University Press, 1989), 29.

9. These two ideas are most closely identified with Naess and his personal version of deep ecology, what he calls Ecosophy T. See *Ecology, Community, and Lifestyle*, 63–212.

10. Rothenberg, "Introduction," in *Ecology, Community, and Lifestyle,* 15.

11. Sessions, *Twenty-first Century,* xiii.

12. Maimonides, for example, does think the main issue is the pain of the mother (*Guide for the Perplexed* 3:48), while Nachmanides (Commentary on Deuteronomy 22:6) does not.

13. Maimonides, *Mishnah Torah,* "The Book of Judges," Kings 6:9–10.

14. Baruch Halevi Epstein *Torah Temimah* to Deuteronomy 20:19. I wish to thank Rabbi David Kraemer of the Jewish Theological Seminary for this reference.

15. Schwartz, "*Bal Tashchit:* A Jewish Environmental Precept," 371. A detailed explanation of two positions can be found on pages 365–371.

16. Ibid., 372.

17. Ibid.

18. See my essay, "Against the Inevitability of Anthropocentrism," in Eric Katz, Andrew Light, and David Rothenberg, eds., *Beneath the Surface: Critical Essays in the Philosophy of Deep Ecology* (Cambridge, MA: MIT Press, 2000).

19. Richard Sylvan and David Bennett, *The Greening of Ethics* (Tucson: University of Arizona Press, 1994), 154. Although this volume is coauthored, it is clear that most of the criticisms of deep ecology derive from the work of Sylvan. Most of the arguments critical of deep ecology in this book are taken from Sylvan's 1985 essay "A Critique of Deep Ecology," published in two parts in *Radical Philosophy* 40 (summer 1985): 2–11 and *Radical Philosophy* 41 (autumn 1985): 10–22. With apologies to David Bennett, I will refer only to Sylvan. Another important criticism of deep ecology can be found in William Grey, "Anthropocentrism and Deep Ecology," *Australasian Journal of Philosophy* 71:4 (December 1993): 463–473.

20. See John Rodman, "The Liberation of Nature?" *Inquiry* 20 (1977): 83–131, and Sylvan and Bennett, *Greening,* 140 ff.

21. Sylvan and Bennett, *Greening,* 142.

22. For more, see Sylvan's criticism of biocentrism in "A Critique" Part I, 8–10.

23. E. L. Allen, "The Hebrew View of Nature," *Journal of Jewish Studies* 2, no. 2 (1951): 103.

24. For a more complete discussion of my experiences with Holocaust sites, see Eric Katz, "Nature's Presence: Reflections on Healing and Domination," in *Nature as Subject,* 189–201.

25. Robert Gordis, "Judaism and the Environment," *Congress Monthly* 57, no. 6 (September/October 1990): 10. Gordis cites *Talmud B. Shabbat* 10a.

26. I owe a great deal of thanks to Rabbi Steven Shaw of the Jewish Theological Seminary. Without his inspiration and advice, I would never have begun an examination of the Jewish philosophical tradition regarding the natural environment.

8

Catholicism and Deep Ecology

JOHN E. CARROLL

A T A MEETING ON ECOLOGY and religion some years ago, participants, gathered in a circle, reflected on and spoke about the many contributions of various Christian denominations, of Eastern philosophies and of indigenous peoples' often ecologically based spiritualities to the dialogue on the ecology—religion relationship. A Catholic priest, a Jesuit, stood up and expressed some degree of shame and embarrassment that Catholicism had seemingly contributed so little to this dialogue. Immediately, Jewish, Protestant, indigenous peoples, and representatives of other religions retorted, "Was not St. Francis of Assisi Catholic? Was not Teilhard de Chardin Catholic? Was not Thomas Merton Catholic?" The list went on. Not only had Catholicism been found to have contributed a significant share to the dialogue, but it immediately became apparent that Catholics themselves were not prone to think of these and other significant contributors from Catholicism as being particularly ecological. And yet it is Francis of Assisi, "patron saint of ecology," St. Benedict of monastic stewardship fame, Thomas Merton of modern-day monasticism with a strong ecological and ecumenical conscience, scientist-theologian Teilhard de Chardin, the medieval mystic and religious, Hildegard of Bingen, along with her contemporaries Julian of Norwich and Meister Eckhart, Thomas Berry, cultural historian and "geologian" and godfather of contemporary ecological thought, Catholics all, and all of whom have been among the giant thinkers and voices of ecological thought. The lack of understanding or appreciation of that fact within Catholicism itself is testament to how far the culture of Catholicism has separated itself from the earth, from nature, from the key theological doctrine of immanence, of the Creator in the created, of God in all.

A second experience also comes to mind. This writer has attended Catholic liturgy (Mass) in a monastic environment in which, early in the morning with the birds starting to sing, the service was temporarily interrupted out of acknowledgment of a command from the Creator to listen to, to enjoy, to take pleasure in the wonders of God's creation, the singing of birds. This was done in an atmosphere where it was felt to be clearly wrong not to do so, not to so honor the Creator and respect the creation. How many Catholics would resonate with this, or would ever have heard of such a thing? Practically none, another indication of the divorce of contemporary Catholicism from nature around us and from the awe that God's creation can and should inspire.

"Deep ecology," as used here, incorporates the principles of ecology in thought and practice; a sense of the sacred in nature, in the creation; the intrinsic value of nature, of the creation; ecocentrism, as fully inclusive of humanity; and the integrity of creation, in process and evolution, as an unfinished work.

"Catholic" means universal. As the largest, broadest, and probably most diverse portion of the Judaeo-Christian historical and cultural tradition, Catholicism cannot be readily explained or represented in a modest or simple manner. However, it is the intent of this chapter to give the reader a sense of Catholic thought and tradition, especially in the Roman Catholic context in the United States. Attention will be devoted to core theological teaching, to Catholic social teaching, and to the activities of various known Catholic individuals and Catholic institutions relative to ecology and environment, to ecological thought and values.

When one thinks of Catholicism institutionally, one often thinks of a very established, ordered, and hierarchical church institution: of the Vatican in Rome, of a Pope, of cardinals, archbishops, and bishops, of men's and women's religious orders, and of various localized institutions (parish churches, schools, hospitals, etc.). There is no attempt in this chapter to officially represent any of these institutions in the text, though reference will be made to various of them. It is intended, however, that a bit of the idea of Catholicism, the culture of Catholicism in the modern world, in its many forms, be communicated, so as to clarify and locate Catholicism within the broader spectrum of Christianity and other world religions.

FUNDAMENTAL CATHOLIC PRINCIPLES

Catholicism constitutes a major portion of that world religion known as Christianity. Catholics, by definition as Christians, must claim to be and attempt to be followers of Christ, followers of a very specific set of principles known as the teachings of Jesus Christ, stemming from the Gospels. Of course, the Catholic and the entire Christian heritage derives from Judaism, has its roots set in that older tradition, and cannot be viewed as fully separate.

Within Christianity there are obviously somewhat differing interpretations of Christ's teaching and a range of belief on the subject. But virtually all who claim to be Christian or who study Christianity, virtually all who know the story of Jesus Christ, including all Catholics, would assent to the following teachings as among the central tenets of Christ's gospel: the command to love thy God, and to love thy neighbor as thyself; to avoid worship of false gods; to live simply; and to avoid the sin of pride.

Loving thy God, given the theological principle of immanence, of God in all, of the Creator in the created, and of the consequent sacrality of all of creation, is a command to love and, indeed, to reverence the sacrality of all creation.

Loving thy neighbor, given that not all human beings have been accepted as neighbor in the past; and, given what we know, in ecology, of the interrelationship of all things, that all life is interrelated, that all creation is interrelated, that all creation is neighbor; we must, therefore, love God's creation, both for God's presence within, and for its role as neighbor.

Avoiding the worship of false gods, of false idols, of attributing God-like qualities to things, is a perennial problem within humanity, from the gods of the sun, fire, lightning, etc. of the past to gods of money, of wealth accumulation, of celebrity, of materialism, of self-image, of power, of science, of technology, of growthism, of economism today—we have indeed no fewer gods today than did the ancients, and the problem and the challenge of this command continues, with enormous ecological consequences. The Franciscan priest Richard Rohr has said, "If I had to summarize the social teaching of Jesus in one phrase, it's the doctrine of non-idolatry. Don't idolize anything. Serve God's world, but worship nothing."[1]

Living simply appears to be a significant and consistent teaching of Jesus Christ, carried down through the centuries by many, Christian and non-Christian alike. The connectedness of simple living (i.e., non-consumptive lifestyle) and basic ecological thought, ecological impact, should be obvious to anyone, and appears to be basic Catholic doctrine, a doctrine that teaches that less is more.

Avoiding the sin of pride is equally basic, to the formation of our belief system and our lifestyle relative to the ecosystem, to the cosmos, and to basic Christian practice. It is false pride, excess pride, that enables our arrogance, our hubris, our domination over nature and over one another, which is one of the most central sins that we are capable of committing. Christ's gospel is very clear on the question of pride as a serious sin, and the connection of pride to the destruction of creation and one another is quite explicit.

If these, among others, are the basic teachings of Christ, then Jesus Christ has had to have been an ecologist, a practitioner of ecological thought. If Catholics and other Christians claim to be followers of Christ and of Christ's gospel, then they must at heart be ecologists, be ecologically minded and ecologically sensitive.

Finally, Catholics affirm the Sermon on the Mount as the heart of the teaching of the historical Jesus. And the Sermon, which raises basic questions of greed, powerlessness, nonviolence, noncontrol, and simplicity, is a strong ecological document, as basic a set of ecological principles as could be found.

In summing Christ's teaching, it's interesting to note, as the Franciscan priest Richard Rohr tells us, "He doesn't quote Scripture; that's why his authority is not like the authority of the scribes and the Pharisees. He doesn't quote 'paper encyclicals.' He most often uses nature as an authority. He points to clouds, sunsets, sparrows, lilies, corn in the field, leaves unfolding, several kinds of seeds, oxen in a ditch! Nature instructs us everywhere. Look and learn how to see. Look and see the rhythm, the seasons, the life and death of things. That's your teaching, that's creation's plan in front of you . . ."[2]

During Christianity's first three hundred years, up until the time of the rule of the Emperor Constantine (the period of "early Christianity"), Catholicism, the only form of Christianity in existence at the time, was separated from and at odds with power and wealth. It was recognized for the subversion it was, as a threat to the concentration of power and wealth, a threat to the state, and dealt with accordingly, as one would expect. It was put down and kept down ruthlessly and relentlessly. Around 300 A.D., when Constantine designated Christianity as the state religion, all of that changed, setting a role for Christianity that has lasted for seventeen hundred years. During this long era, much of Christianity, including Catholicism, has been comfortable with wealth and power, a seeming distortion of the very idea of Christianity and of the cross, a seeming fundamental rejection of Christ's teaching. Various reform movements notwithstanding, and there have been many, Christianity and Catholicism fell prey, as humans and as human institutions, to the very human sin, as Richard Rohr tells us, of power, pride, and possessions. Such an open and accepting linkage of these three human temptations is not only antithetical to the idea of Christianity but also to the idea of ecology, fundamentally denying the basic principles of ecological thought.[3]

Thus, central Christian and Catholic teaching can be demonstrated to be ecological, while basic human temptation, to wealth and power and pride, lead fundamentally to the opposite of both Christian/Catholic thought and ecological thought.

Catholicism in North America, somewhat unlike Catholicism in Europe, has been dominated in its culture by an urban and immigrant focus that has historically been removed from the land, removed from nature. There are exceptions in the rural farm population of Catholics in the Midwest, largely of German parentage, and in the traditional Spanish and Chicano populations of New Mexico, both of which are land and nature oriented in many respects. But it is the great waves of Irish, Italian, and Eastern European immigrants settling in the large cities that have largely charted the course of development for the Catholic Church in the United States. And, though not necessarily removed from nature and the land in their European homelands, large numbers of these Catholics in America charted a very urban future and a life far removed from ecological realities. The average Catholic priest or bishop today, and likewise the average Catholic institution, thus is far removed from any feeling of connection to the ecosystem, to nature, or to the mystical (and nature-related) sense of Christianity that could still be found in Europe. The hierarchical and authoritative character of the Catholic Church in the United States assured both the spreading and the dominance of this rather mechanistic culture, abetted by an open embrace of and identification with the Protestant work ethic and the conviction of the anthropocentric dominance of the human over all. It is for this reason, for example, that so many American Catholics embrace recycling as a civic duty, the command to be a good citizen, and are much more skeptical of attaching spiritual, religious, or liturgical significance or role to this behavior. It is hardly surprising that many Catholics, therefore, feel very distant and removed from ecological concern as a religious or spiritual or Christian issue—it is simply too removed, not from their theology but from their culture.

Removed or not, however, no Christian, no Catholic, can deny the ecological validity of Christ's central teachings, not the least being one of the most important sets of principles to arise from those teachings, the Sermon on the Mount. That Sermon, which all Catholics and Christians claim adherence to, in its call to and praise of humility, is as fundamental an ecological statement as one could find.

Catholics, like all Christians, believe in the theological doctrines of both transcendence and immanence. But, as with the rest of Christianity,

Catholicism, both in theory and in actual practice, has emphasized transcendence, the notion of a creator God who is above and beyond humanity in both time and space, and thus separated from humanity. This emphasis (some would say overemphasis) has occurred at the expense of the equal theological doctrine of immanence, the notion of God in all, the Creator in the created. This, of course, inevitably means that all is sacred, since all is the creation of the Creator and contains the Creator. Our surroundings thus are not available for us to abuse or use unwisely, and our surroundings, as for all fellow human beings, command our respect and our reverence. This includes the birds of the air (all animal life), the lilies of the field (all plant life), and, as well, the stones and rocks, the mountains and rivers and oceans, the planet itself. It is not in any sense limited to just human beings. (Today we generally accept, as a minimum, all fellow human beings as our neighbor, which Christians are commanded by God to love, but it was not too long ago when only a portion of humanity, those who are "like us," was included—Christianity was quite exclusive rather than inclusive, the Sermon on the Mount notwithstanding, and to some extent is so still.)

American Catholics have long been guided in their religious teaching and education by a book called a catechism. A new revision has recently come into use, one that is somewhat sensitive to ecological concern, identifying ecological harm as a sin proscribed by the Fifth Commandment, "Thou shalt not steal" (including from future generations). However, the catechism in use by American Catholics for more than a century has been the very traditional and conservative Baltimore Catechism, named after the city of its origin. One need go no further than page one of the children's edition of this catechism to receive profound ecological wisdom and insight. For on that page the question is asked, "Where is God?" And the answer is given: "God is everywhere." This is a testament to the importance of the theological doctrine of immanence to Catholic thought and practice. Such is not to say that very many Catholics behaved as if they believed this answer, though all would likely give it lip service. But it is to say the belief, as a most basic religious and theological belief, was most clearly expressed. The implication is, of course, that all nature is sacred, is God's creation, not that of humans, that it contains God, and that it requires, nay compels, not only respect but, more importantly, reverence. If we behaved as if we believed in that necessity for reverence, that command from what we claim to be our religious belief, our faith, or if we even tried to do so, our world, our global ecosystem, would be a very different place.

Catholicism appears to be moving toward an increasingly ecocentric and therefore deep ecological stance, based upon documents (bishops' pastorals, U.S. Conference of Catholic Bishops documents, Papal encyclicals, and various Vatican statements) and upon behavior (especially that of Catholic women religious and some evidence from monastic communities). Catholic Christianity has somewhat more of a base for this evolution than does Protestant Christianity, given the former's stronger tradition of mysticism and ritual and the dual reliance on faith and reasoning, as evidenced in the most recent Papal encyclical, "Fides et Ratio" (Faith and Reason). (Orthodox Christianity shares in the tradition of mystical and ritual heritage and, although initially slow to respond publicly to ecological concern, has now developed a strong stance, including designation of anti-ecological behavior—pollution, etc.—as sin within its moral theological teaching.) Roman Catholic thought is somewhat ahead of official Church response, as is usually the case, as the two-thousand-year-old institution of the Catholic Church generally carefully considers new issues over a long period of time before acting in a more official capacity. But it is the mystical, ritualistic, and faith-based nature of Catholic Christianity that enables thinking of the type we see from Fr. Thomas Berry, a Catholic priest and moral ethicist who, while a brilliant intellectual and student of cultural history and Asian philosophy and religion, still ultimately relies on matters of the heart, of the spirit, far more than the life of the intellect. He would appear to be a perfect image of Pope John Paul II's admonition that Catholics must observe and rely on a combination of both faith and reason, always maintaining a respect for and a balance between the two. Protestant Christians, at least those in the mainstream, have historically relied more on reason than Catholics and have been more subject to Cartesian and Newtonian scientific rationality and the work ethic deriving therefrom, both of which have been identified as part of the problem. To a significant extent Catholics have bought into this reliance on Enlightenment rationality creating the cultural problem of distance between their ordinary lives and ecocentric or deep ecological ecological thought. But all continues on its evolutionary path, a path that is open to alliance with creation-based views affirming the intrinsic value of nature.

CATHOLIC SOCIAL TEACHING

In addition to that to which all Christians would claim adherence, there is, within Catholicism, that which is called "Catholic social teaching." This includes Papal encyclicals and much more that is local, pastoral letters of bishops of dioceses' worldwide, among other pronouncements.

Many such teachings of the past century, and particularly of the last two to three decades, have contained significant ecological direction.

It is unfortunate, however, that many practicing Catholics remain oblivious to most of these teachings. They get very little attention in church services, the principle arena of contact between the church and its members, and most local pastors and priests have very limited knowledge of their existence. They do, nevertheless, represent the official view of the Catholic Church, a church that is becoming increasingly sensitive to the existence of an ecological challenge. (The Church's official, i.e., Vatican., teaching on artificial birth control is, however, in the minds of most people, highly unecological. The Church compensates somewhat in its social position, which recognizes the ecological and social destruction of the high per capita consumption and atmosphere of consumerism that pervades all Western industrial countries, especially the United States. This is recognition of the magnitude of the problem which most peoples of "developed" nations, and particularly North Americans, do not wish to see or discuss, focusing, as they would prefer, on net population numbers rather than on per capita consumption.)

Catholic religious, in the United States as elsewhere, are often members of particular orders adhering to particular charisms. This is true of all women religious (nuns or sisters) and of many, though not all, men religious (priests and brothers). Other male clerics are not members of orders but are members of and employed by a diocese, a basic Catholic organizational subdivision of a geographical nature, and such men are answerable to the clerical head of the diocese, a bishop or archbishop, rather than the superior of an order, of which each has its own history and character.

Statements issued and positions taken by the Vatican are obviously of importance to Catholics, and especially in these times to those who adhere to a more traditional and/or conservative bent. The current Papal regime, that of John Paul II, is known to Americans as very conservative theologically. What is very little known to Americans, Catholic or otherwise, as a result of significant underreporting in the American mass media, is the very liberal direction of the Papacy on questions of social justice and related questions of distribution of wealth. In his encyclicals and other pronouncements, Pope John Paul II has been exceedingly harsh on the consumption habits of the industrialized nations, on their acquisitiveness and greed, most particularly the excesses of North Americans in this regard. Government policy, "free trade," banking and finance policy, the adamence of banks regarding Third World debt repayment, have all been sharply criticized and roundly and unambiguously condemned by this Pope who sees many of the modern-day trends toward globalization as disastrous to both nature and humanity. The ecological implications of this sharp Vatican critique are clearer even than the Vatican's more direct and explicit ecological pronouncements.

All of this stands in seeming contrast to the clear and well-known Vatican position on artificial birth control, a position that has significant implications for the planet's population growth, and one that appears to be fundamentally anti-ecological in its results. In the eyes of the world, therefore, the Vatican environmental position might be regarded as ambiguous. The Vatican's social ethics position leaves no doubt, however, that the high per capita consumption of the West is roundly condemned, a key element in any ecological assessment of the Vatican, and one that would be surprising to many American Catholics if they were better informed.

The Bishops Speak: Ecological Pastorals

Another area of official Catholic pronouncement and one even less well known to most Catholics is that of the pastoral letters of bishops to the Catholics of their dioceses. Recent years have seen a profusion of these letters in the subject area of this book, ecology and environment, as well as many in closely related areas, such as agriculture, land use, and the food system, economic development, and, as well, social justice concerns directly linked to environment and to the environment of specific regions and ecosystems. Increasingly these pastorals have been issued and signed by bishops of multiple dioceses covering a broader region, such as Appalachia which contains numerous dioceses spread across multiple states, or New Mexico, which contains three dioceses and thus three bishops. Both of these pastorals, covering Appalachia and New Mexico, are known for their clarity, their directness, their depth on matters ecological, and the consequence of those pastorals to Catholics in their respective geographical areas.

The New Mexico bishops' pastoral, "Reclaiming the Vocation to Care for the Earth," was published by the Church on 11 June 1998 and was signed by Archbishop Sheehan of Santa Fe and Bishops Ramirez of Las Cruces and Pelotte of Gallup, representing the entirety of the Catholic community of that state. Although a short statement in length, the pastoral clearly recognizes the moral nature of the ecological challenge, affirms a sacramental dimension to the universe (coming close to affirming the intrinsic value of nature, of the Creation), and calls for activism in this area in the name of Catholic social justice teaching. That activism calls for a reclaiming of our vocation as God's stewards of all creation, specifically through:

- examin(ing) our behaviors, practices, and policies as individuals, as families, as parishes and institutions to see where we might take steps to cease the destruction of our planetary home and contribute to its restoration and flourishing;

- teach(ing) . . . children how to love and respect the earth, to take delight in nature, and to build values which look at long-range consequences . . . ;

- invit(ing) . . . celebrants and liturgists to incorporate in their prayers and themes our confessions of exploitation;

- invit(ing) our parish leaders to become better informed about environmental ethics so that religious education and parish policies will contain opportunities for teaching these values;

- invit(ing) our public policy-makers and public officials . . . to eradicate actions and policies which perpetuate various forms of environmental racism and to work for an economy which focuses more on equitable sustainability rather than unbridled consumption of natural resources and acquisition of goods.[4]

An equally direct but much lengthier pastoral has come from the twenty-five Catholic bishops and archbishops of Appalachia covering a region stretching from New York to Georgia and west to Kentucky and Tennessee. "At Home in the Web of Life: A Pastoral Message on Sustainable Communities in Appalachia" was issued on the twentieth anniversary of an earlier Appalachian pastoral with significant but less directly defined environmental values entitled "This Land Is Home to Me." Placing very heavy emphasis on the question of human and ecological sustainability across the much exploited Appalachian region, this lengthy pastoral contains strong ecological language and contains sections on natural and social ecology, on the gift of the Appalachian ecosystem, on the revelatory nature of the region's mountains and its forests, on the serious social justice and economic concerns prevalent in the culture of death (i.e., anti-ecological culture), which has heretofore been so powerful in the region, and strong emphases on sustainable forestry and sustainable agriculture, sustainable (i.e., small-scale) technologies, and sustainable (i.e., local) ownership. Tied throughout are the link between ecological justice and social justice, as in, "If we fail to care for our precious Earth and for the poor, then creation itself will rebel against us." And, "[T]o undermine nature and the poor is to reject the word of God in creation." The detail and depth of ecological sensitivity in this lengthy statement, signed on to by so many church prelates, is no small matter in attempting to understand the question of Catholicism and ecology.

The linkage of eco- and social justice has been given earlier reinforcement in the widely publicized 1993 statement of Bishop John Malone of Youngstown, Ohio, in his pastoral, "Environmental Degradation and Social Justice." Bishop Malone himself receives strength from the Catholic Bishops' of Florida's earlier (1991) pastoral statement on the dangers of overconsumption, the responsibilities of ecological stewardship, and the necessity for humans of a caring cooperation in nature. Bishop James T. McHugh of Camden's early pastoral, "Stewards of Life, Stewards of Nature," carries many similar themes. Bishop Malone elevates long-expressed notions of the "common good" in the human and societal sense to a new and, for this discussion, a most important plateau: "Now our awareness of threats to planetary ecology provokes another transformation in the idea of the common good, namely, that we need to think and act in response to the planetary good or what we might call the 'good of creation,'" a further step toward affirming intrinsic value in the Creation.

Foundational in a way to all of these Bishops' pastorals, and especially important for its breadth of representation as a document that represents all the Catholic bishops in the United States (effectively the Catholic Church in America in an "official" context) was the 1991 U.S. Bishops document "Renewing the Earth: An Invitation to Reflection and Action on the Environment in Light of Catholic Social Teaching." This is a detailed statement containing many basic themes, including:

- the ethical dimensions of the environmental crisis;
- the ecology–poverty–development linkage;
- eco-justice and the ecological suffering of the poor;
- the need for serious attention to sustainability;
- the role of religion and the Church in environmental questions.

The Bishops recognized that "[a]rrogance and acquisitiveness . . . led time and again to our growing alienation from nature"; that "[s]afeguarding creation requires us to live responsibly within it rather than manage creation as though we are outside it"; and that "Christian love forbids choosing between people and the planet." There is great detail in the document, including a number of ecological case studies and examples; detailed relevance to Scripture and the Gospel message; a direct linkage between respect for human life and respect for all creation; the link of Catholic social teaching and environmental ethics; a reinforcement of the idea that the universe is sacramental and thus requires reverence; a critique of consumption in the West; the co-creative role of human beings with God; a reinforcement of the ecologically significant theological principle of immanence (God in all, the Creator in the created); an acknowledgment of life as a web (ecology); and a very specific call for new actions for all categories of individuals, the professions, and institutions. Powerfully, the Bishops conclude that "[a] just and sustainable society and world is not an optional ideal, but a moral and practical necessity." This remarkable ecological statement is perhaps best summed up philosophically by the remark, "Nature is not, in Catholic teaching, merely a field to exploit at will or a museum piece to be preserved at all costs. We are not gods, but stewards of the earth."

Vatican Statements

Although the Bishops explicitly state in the famous ecological pastoral of 1991 that an ordered love for creation is ecological without being eco-centric, they now accept as a principle of Catholic social teaching the principle of the integrity of creation. This principle does not limit the common good to humans alone but extends to all of creation, a creation existing in a web of life that has value beyond what human beings might use it for, i.e., an intrinsic value to nature. The idea of "God" as verb rather than as noun, the idea of God as process, is an increasingly important element of Catholic thought.

The strength and breadth of "Renewing the Earth," an American statement, perhaps owes much to a famous Vatican pronouncement of just one year earlier, Pope John Paul II's famous "Peace with God the Creator, Peace with All of Creation," the Pope's message for the celebration of the World Day of Peace, 1 January 1990. This address is regarded by many as the Vatican's strongest and clearest commentary on the ecological challenge of our times. And it has been warmly applauded by environmentalists across the globe.

The document, too, presents the inherent "goodness" of the planetary ecosystem, a goodness given by God, not by humanity, by the Creator to the created, and thus constitutes some movement in the direction of the affirmation of intrinsic value to the planet, to nature. The ecological crisis clearly is identified within as a moral problem, therefore, as a religious problem and a church problem. The integrity of creation, a most fundamental ecological principle, is prominently expounded upon in this document. The Pope identifies an urgent moral

need for a new solidarity to address ecological issues and states categorically that no solution to the ecological problem can be found unless
modern society takes a serious look at its lifestyle. (The latter has been a
constant theme of and critique by John Paul II for many years, a fact little known to American Catholics since this aspect of the current Vatican
regime receives almost no attention in American media. The message
does not likely sit well with American concentrations of wealth, including the corporations owning and controlling the media.) The Pope also
calls specifically for education in ecological responsibility, and for the
responsibility of everyone in this matter. He includes in this call the development of a strong appreciation for the aesthetic value of creation. In
his closing words, John Paul placed very heavy emphasis on the model
of St. Francis of Assisi as the patron saint of ecology, an action the Holy
Father had earlier taken in 1979. No purer ecological model could be
found anywhere.

The 1990 New Year's Day address is indeed a strong statement, and
the clearest by the Vatican up to that time or since that directly relates to
ecology. However, even Catholics may need reminding that it is
grounded in a host of Papal encyclicals on social justice stretching from
the closing decades of the nineteenth century to the present, and constitutes not a departure from but a further evolution of past teachings. It
did not come from nowhere and should not be viewed simply as a necessary response to an atmosphere of "political correctness" or "political
necessity." Pope Leo XIII's 1891 social encyclical *Rerum Novarum* (On the
Condition of the Working Class), Pope Pius XI's *Quadragesimo Anno* of
the 1930s, Pope John XXIII's 1961 *Pacem in Terris*, the Second Vatican
Council's *Gaudium et Spes* (Pastoral Constitution on the Church in the
Modern World), Pope Paul VI's 1967 encyclical, *Populorum Progressio*,
and his 1971 Apostolic Letter *Octogesima Adveniens*, and the 1971 Vatican
document *Justice in the World*, John Paul II's *Laborem exercens* and *Re-
demptor hominis* all provide foundation for the developments of the 1990s
discussed above. And they represent a progressive evolution increasing
toward attribution of intrinsic value to nature (an ecocentric approach),
although it must be clearly stated that Catholic dogma has not yet arrived at that point. And the heavy emphasis of these documents, not
only on social justice concerns, but also on labor, work, and the economy,
inherently strengthen the development of an ecological viewpoint, without ever (for the most part) directly mentioning ecology. Out of this base
comes both the "Catholic Framework for Economic Life," a ten-point
policy document issued by the U.S. Conference of Catholic Bishops, and,
as well, the ecologically important concept of subsidiarity. Subsidiarity,
developed by socially conscious nineteenth-century European Catholics

and the Vatican of the time, teaches a principle that is at one and the same time Christian, Buddhist, and ecological. "Subsidiarity stands for the proposition that action to accomplish a legitimate government objective should . . . be taken at the lowest level of government effectively capable of addressing the problem." (Pope Pius XI, *Quadragesimo Anno*, 79, 1931) Subsidiarity is analogous to the Buddhist principle that one's basic needs should be fulfilled by the nearest possible source, enabling an ability to accept moral responsibility for our actions through the knowledge gathered by the nearness of the impacts of our decisions, impacts on fellow humans, on the ecosystem, and on future generations. The implications for ecology are enormous.

Further example of "official" Catholic Church involvement in matters ecological is a Vatican document, *Ex Corde Ecclesiae*, promulgated by Pope John Paul II in 1990. This document is an apostolic constitution for Catholic colleges and universities which, in its implementation by American Catholic bishops, calls for programs in "defense of nature." The document states, "In its service to society a Catholic university will relate especially to the academic, cultural and scientific world of the region in which it is located. Original forms of dialogue and collaboration are to be encouraged between the Catholic universities and other universities of a nation on behalf of development, of understanding between cultures, *and of the defense of nature in accordance with an awareness of the international ecological situation.*"[5]

Praxis: National Catholic Rural Life Conference

The important principle of subsidiarity and a number of other principles of Catholic social teaching of strong ecological significance are being brought to the fore today by a national Catholic organization known as the National Catholic Rural Life Conference (NCRLC), based in Des Moines, Iowa. NCRLC molds ecological and environmental protection, sustainable agriculture (including community-supported and congregation-supported agriculture, farmers markets, low chemical and organic forms of agriculture, all of direct ecological significance), and strong campaigns against concentration in agriculture (livestock concentration, factory farming, absentee ownership, corporate for profit ownership, all of which are inherently anti-ecological) in an attempt to protect the threatened interests of agricultural and other rural ecosystems, of farms, of farmers, and of farm and rural communities. All of their extensive work is done as an official arm of the Catholic Church in America. Their active leadership involves bishops (generally from rural dioceses), men and women religious and laity, and the governance and operational philosophy of this organization is very much in the direction of the themes raised throughout this chapter. In operating under the direct guidance of Catholic social teaching, NCRLC is not only accomplishing much of ecological value for rural America, but it constitutes a living demonstration of Catholic social teaching and practice, contributing to interpreting that teaching in a far more ecological vein than has heretofore been the case. NCRLC derives its guidance from, among other sources, the Vatican itself, and particularly Pope John Paul II's 1987 encyclical, *Solicitudo Rei Socialis*, in which he posited three considerations:

> First, development must recognize the nature of each being and its mutual connection with everything else in an ordered world. Animals, for example, should not be used simply for economic gain. They have their own place in the cosmos and, as the Catholic Catechism says, "deserve respect and dignity."
>
> Second, natural resources are limited. We have a responsibility to our own and future generations to care for them in a responsible stewardship.
>
> Third, local peoples deserve respect and a healthy, wholesome quality of life.

NCRLC accepts these premises, puts them to work, and in turn helps formulate a practical application of Catholic social teaching and sets the stage for how Catholics (and Catholic institutions) are to behave. The existence, the mission, and the actual work of this organization is a testament to a deep ecological belief system within American Catholicism.

Praxis: Sisters of Earth

NCRLC is one institutional and national area of praxis in this arena. Another important but rather little-known area of ecological praxis of a very high order is the nationwide movement of Catholic women's religious orders toward ecological thought, ecological teaching, ecological demonstration and practice. This is perhaps the closest example in practice of organized Catholicism moving toward deep ecology and an ecocentric viewpoint. Perhaps no greater voice has inspired this movement nationally than that of Fr. Thomas Berry. But it is the women, almost exclusively, who have taken the opportunity and have put it into practice. Led perhaps by Dominican Sisters Miriam Therese McGillis of Genesis Farm in New Jersey and Miriam Brown of Sinsinawa in Wisconsin, this movement has spread across numerous Dominican communities in the

United States from Massachusetts to Kansas. From these, and in some cases simultaneously, the ball has been picked up by the Franciscans, the Sisters of St. Joseph, the Sisters of Loretto, the Sisters of Notre Dame, the Sisters of Charity, the Benedictines, and by a number of other orders. Taking their inspiration from the Christian mystical tradition of the tenth century's Hildegard of Bingen and Julian of Norwich, strongly inspired by Thomas Berry and an expanding circle of like-minded thinkers and writers, men and women, religious and lay, Catholic and some non-Catholic, these Catholic women religious have formed a loose new and non-hierarchical organization called Sisters of Earth, and gather annually under that name. Formed in 1994, they have embraced the earth as their ministry and live the spirit of Hildegard's theology of greening: "We are greening with life, we bear our fruit for all creation, limitless love, from the depths to the stars, flooding all, loving all." What do they do? On their plots of land they run eco-theologically oriented retreat centers; conduct all forms of ecological education for children and adults; conduct community-supported agriculture projects; conduct college-level earth literacy graduate programs; plant and tend extensive and certified organic gardens (which are labor intensive); produce art, greeting cards, stationery on recycled paper with ecological themes; organize local community recycling programs; establish inner city gardens in poor neighborhoods; provide environmental and nature education outreach to the poor; serve as paralegals and helpers in eco-justice questions; build buildings modelling sustainability, energy conservation, and ecological concern, with specific accessibility to the low income and poor (including strawbale structures that are very accessible to low income people), solar, wind, and other renewable energy sources and ecological design; manage their land ecologically, including forests and woodlands, pastures and prairie, crop land and ponds; grow crops, harvest forest products, manage livestock, manage orchards; and assist the start-up and maintenance of ecologically oriented farms and numerous kinds of small businesses.

The national development of these Sisters of Earth efforts probably represents the highest form of "walking the talk" to be found anywhere in the nation, in Catholic or in non-Catholic circles. They also represent a significant inclusion of a social justice element into American environmentalism, the latter being a movement that has seen very little of that kind of content in its practice or in its theory. Without doubt, Sisters of Earth is one of the most important, perhaps the single most important, entity in the institutional Roman Catholic Church that is currently addressing environmental issues. As Carondelet St. Joseph Sister Mary Southard, a founding member of Sisters of Earth, has said, "In the

Church, women religious are more attuned to the environment as a spiritual issue than any other religious group. . . . (W)omen religious have always jumped in when no one else would. We started hospitals, schools, and went into social work when none of them were institutional things yet." Given their noninstitutional and non-hierarchical ecological philosophy, the work of Sisters of Earth will never likely lead to large visible institutions, but rather to a proliferation of very small "institutions" or communities and lands in many different places, spread widely across the landscape and operating at the very grass roots level. And given the propensity of these strong-willed and determined American women religious who believe in doing, not talking, who believe in action, not words, we are not likely to hear too much about these extraordinarily pure ecological communities unless we get out there and see for ourselves. Where we will, however, see the product of their work is in the individual lives they affect, and in the depth of that effect. It would not be surprising if the Sisters begin to develop individuals as strong, as committed and as dedicated as they themselves are. As Sister of Charity Paula Gonzalez has said, "'Thy will be done' has to be looked at in a new way: namely, that we maintain ecological community. In the end ecological kinship is the only valid way in which to pay homage to our Creator."

MONASTICISM

Ecology is countercultural and, given its insistence on a first principle that all things are connected to all other things, it is subversive as well. Indeed, ecology has been called the "subversive science" because it subverts the dominant paradigm both in our society and in all other sciences (with the likely exception of quantum physics/quantum mechanics and chaos theory in mathematics). Monasticism is countercultural, too (so, too, all Christianity, if practiced properly, but that's another story). Christian monasticism has had a very long rich tradition and has been a part of Christianity almost from the beginning. Since Protestant Christianity does not include monasticism, it is up to Orthodox and Catholic Christianity to carry on the tradition. In the United States, Catholic monasticism is best known, and, for a number of reasons, contains some direct linkage to ecological thought. First, Benedictine monasticism, the largest single category, maintains two related principles given under the Rule of Benedict that are highly relevant to ecology: the concept of stewardship which pertains directly to the land, to nature, to the creation; and the related idea that the secular utensils or tools, made by humans or nature, are to be treated the same as utensils of the altar, i.e., they are equally sacred. This is a reinforcement of the theological notion of immanence, of the Creator in the created, and thus of the sacrality of all. These provide firm ground for the cultural development of an ecological ethic.

Second, the "otherness" of monasticism, the basic rejection of routine life in the world and the establishment of what is most often a very alternative lifestyle, opens up the mind and heart to other alternative life possibilities and the real rejection of a materialistic consumer culture, which "garden variety" Christianity, including Catholicism, seems to have become quite comfortable with. The cultural acceptance of consumerism and growthism by Christians, including Catholics, is surprisingly very, very pervasive, and monasticism is one of the few potential areas of true questioning of this rather blind acceptance. Monasticism is thus, at least potentially, far more open to a truly ecological lifestyle. And, in keeping with the sensitivity of women religious to matters ecological, women's monastic communities show even greater potential in this area.

Third, the connection between Christian monasticism and Buddhist and other non-Christian Eastern forms of monasticism exists and they have much in common. Thanks to the pioneering work of Trappist monk Fr. Thomas Merton and Camaldolese Benedictine monk Fr. Bede Griffiths, much progress has been made, and it is not unusual to find earth-friendly Zen Buddhist practice and approaches in Catholic monasteries. Such opens up a whole realm of possibilities for ecological thought and for ecological practice.

None of the above represents a guarantee that a given monastic community will function with ecological sensitivity (and certainly not all do), but it certainly provides a head start. Monasticism's inherent connectivity to stability, to self-sufficiency and to the development of a sense of place makes it an ecological element representing enormous potential to influence through its modelling much of the rest of the Church in America, and, in some ways, the broader society as well.

THE REALITY IN PRACTICE

Interestingly, the level of interest in Catholic monasticism, and in the work of the Sisters of Earth as well, is probably stronger among non-Catholics than among Catholics, many of whom tend to be very ill-informed about the tradition of monasticism and, as well, about Sisters of Earth and similar movements. Indeed, much has been said in these pages about the extraordinarily clear and explicit linkage of ecology and Catholicism, both in the official Church fora (Vatican documents, bishops' pastoral letters, the work and pronouncements of the U.S. Conference of Catholic Bishops) and from a host of highly regarded Catholic thinkers with significant training in Catholic theology and in Catholic religious practice. One would think from this that the Catholic Church and/or American Catholicism was some sort of an icon of ecological thought. But this is far from the truth, for a number of reasons:

1. The aforementioned cultural divide between the typical Catholic priest, seminarian, nun, or active lay Church-goer for that matter, and ecological thought or the natural world. That is a formidable gap, to be sure.

2. The fact that the Catholic Church, albeit more reluctantly than Protestant churches, bought into the same mechanistic anti-ecological Cartesian–Newtonian–Baconian philosophical paradigm as did the rest of the European peoples and those they influenced, the Church thus becoming part of the dominant culture of power, pride, possessions, and to maintenance of the established order at all costs, in spite of the Sermon on the Mount and other basic teachings.

3. The strong tendency for most Catholics to have a very undeveloped and immature understanding of the basic Catholic faith and theology in which they have been baptized and of which they claim to be a part—this includes nearly wholesale ignorance of Catholic social teaching in any of its aspects.

4. More mundanely, the reality that the only way that Catholic teaching is brought to most practicing Catholics is through the pulpit on Sunday morning, and this venue is almost never used to address Catholic social teaching, to address ecological responsibilities of Catholics, to address the existence of bishops' pastorals, or any other goings on in the Church or its institutions. This reluctance in the pulpit is occasioned by the need to address other matters, such as the day's Scriptural readings, and to do so sparingly lest the service become objectionably long; by the lack of qualification and/or interest of the preacher; by the fear of controversy that would necessarily result, as social justice and eco-justice questions, as with any questioning of wealth or power, are controversial, and, therefore, uncomfortable for too many (and especially, of course, for those with wealth or power).

The non-Catholic reader of this chapter can hence rest assured that only very few Catholics know much about the foregoing. This situation is a bit analogous to the European university student anticipating learning more about the United States from the American exchange students in their midst, only to learn that the American exchange student often has less knowledge or insight about America than does the European student viewing America from afar.

For all of these reasons, American Catholicism today in practice is no more a paragon of ecological thought than is most of the rest of society, and Catholics are as well represented as anyone else in the ranks of those who wantonly abuse and destroy the Creation, their religious faith or claimed values notwithstanding.

Official documentation of the Catholic Church, i.e., statements and publications of the Vatican and the bishops and bishops' conferences indicate that Catholicism has not embraced an ecocentric approach or deep ecology approach to the creation, that is, an approach that sees human beings as embedded in but not in any way separate from, or dominant over, the rest of nature. However, a clear trend in this direction is evident in these documents, a trend toward recognition of nature as having intrinsic and not simply extrinsic or utilitarian value. The increased usage of the phrase and concept of the "integrity of creation" is one sign of this trend.

It is without doubt, however, that there is a very considerable amount of ecocentrism within Catholic thought and among Catholic thinkers, clergy, women religious, monastics of various religious orders, and lay Catholics, including Catholic theologians. Some of this has been present for centuries within Catholic mysticism, which has been oriented this way. The magnitude and diversity of this thought will undoubtedly ultimately have influence over the hierarchy of the "official" church. Much of unofficial but serious Catholic thought does at this time approach or encompass deep ecology and ecocentrism, with a not inconsiderable influence from the work of Thomas Berry.

To the extent that Catholicism is a culture as well as a religion, a theology, a spirituality, it is and has been subject to the cultural temptations toward compromise with power and wealth. Given that natural human temptation, Catholicism will have to continue to strive to know its roots, its origins, its essence, and to understand itself in the context of the creation in which it is embedded, a creation that, according to Catholics and, indeed, all Christians, has been celebrated by the very centerpiece of Christianity, the incarnation, of Christ on earth, no less human than divine. Such reality provides all Catholics the ultimate rationale for the sacrality of nature, the sacrality of God's creation. Such reality speaks directly, well, to deep ecology as a basis for a Catholic approach.

NOTES

1. Rohr, Richard, O.F.M., *Simplicity: The Art of Living* (New York: Crossroad, 1992).

2. Ibid., 36–37.

3. See Rohr, "Christianity and the Creation: A Franciscan Speaks to Franciscans," in *Embracing Earth*, ed. LaChance and Carroll (New York: Orbis Books, 1994) for further insight.

4. New Mexico Bishops, "Reclaiming the Vocation to Care for the Earth," in *Origins: CNS Documentary News Service*, 28, no. 4 (June 11, 1998).

5. "*Ex Corde Ecclesiae:* A Rural Life Update," *Rural Landscapes* 4, no. 6 (June, 1997). Emphasis added.

AN ABBREVIATED BIBLIOGRAPHY OF CATHOLICISM AND ECOLOGY

Documents that constitute official pronouncements of the institutional Roman Catholic Church bear an asterisk (*). The latter include official publications of the Church and those carrying a formal endorsement of approval by the Church itself. Those entries without an asterisk (*) represent Catholic thought that has not been submitted to the Church for its approval and has been published independent of the institutional church.

Berry, Thomas, C.P., with Thomas Clarke, S.J. *Befriending the Earth: A Theology of Reconciliation Between Humans and the Earth*. Mystic, CT: Twenty-Third Publications, 1992.

*Bishop James Malone, Diocese of Camden. "Environmental Degradation and Social Injustice." *Origins: CNS Documentary News Service* 22, no. 40, 18 March 1993.

Carroll, John E., Paul Brockelman, and Mary Westfall. *The Greening of Faith: God, the Environment and the Good Life*. Hanover, NH: University Press of New England, 1997.

Carroll, John E., and Keith Warner, O.F.M. *Ecology and Religion: Scientists Speak*. Quincy, IL: Franciscan Press, 1998.

*Catholic Bishops of Appalachia. *At Home in the Web of Life: A Pastoral Message on Sustainable Communities in Appalachia*. Webster Springs, WV: Catholic Committee of Appalachia, 1996.

*Christiansen, Drew, S.J., and Walter Grazer. "*And God Saw That it Was Good*": Catholic Theology and the Environment. Washington, DC: United States Catholic Conference, 1996.

Cummings, Charles, O.C.S.O. *Eco-Spirituality: Toward a Reverent Life*. New York: Paulist Press, 1991.

Edwards, Denis. *Jesus the Wisdom of God: An Ecological Theology.* New York: Orbis Books, 1995.

Evans, Bernard F., and Gregory D. Cusack, eds. *Theology of the Land.* Collegeville, MN: Liturgical Press, 1987.

Fragomeni, Richard N., and John T. Pawlikowski, O.S.M., eds. *The Ecological Challenge: Ethical, Liturgical and Spiritual Responses.* Collegeville, MN: Liturgical Press, 1994.

Fritsch, Albert J., S.J. *Environmental Ethics.* New York: Anchor/Doubleday, 1980.

———. *Appalachia: A Meditation.* Chicago: Loyola University Press, 1986.

———. *Renew the Face of the Earth.* Chicago: Loyola University Press, 1987.

———. *Eco-Church.* San Jose: Resource Publications, Inc., 1991.

———. *Down to Earth Spirituality.* Kansas City: Sheed and Ward, 1992.

Haught, John F. *The Promise of Nature: Ecology and Cosmic Purpose.* New York: Paulist Press, 1993.

Hill, Brennan R. *Christian Faith and the Environment: Making Vital Connections.* New York: Orbis Books, 1998.

Irwin, Kevin. *Preserving the Creation: Environmental Theology and Ethics.* Washington, DC: Georgetown University Press, 1994.

Kavanaugh, John F. *Still Following Christ in a Consumer Society.* New York: Orbis Books, 1995.

LaChance, Albert, and John E. Carroll. *Embracing Earth: Catholic Approaches to Ecology.* New York: Orbis Books, 1994.

Lonergan, Anne, and Caroline Richards, eds. *Thomas Berry and the New Cosmology.* Mystic, CT: Twenty-Third Publications, 1987.

McCarthy, Rev. Scott. *Celebrating the Earth: An Earth-Centered Theology of Worship with Blessings, Prayers, and Rituals.* San Jose: Resource Publications, Inc., 1991.

McDonagh, Sean. *To Care for the Earth: A Call for a New Theology.* London: Geoffrey Chapman, 1986.

———. *The Greening of the Church.* New York: Orbis Books, 1990.

———. *Passion for the Earth: The Christian Vocation to Promote Justice, Peace, and the Integrity of Creation.* New York: Orbis Books, 1994.

Murphy, Msgr. Charles. *At Home on the Earth: Foundations for a Catholic Ethic of the Environment.* New York: Crossroad, 1989.

*New Mexico Bishops. "Reclaiming the Vocation to Care for the Earth: Pastoral Letter of Archbishop Michael Sheehan of Santa Fe, Bishop Ricardo Ramirez of Las Cruces, and Bishop Donald Pelotte of Gallup." *Origins: CNS Documentary News Service* 28, no. 4, 11 June 1998.

*North Dakota Bishops. "Giving Thanks through Action: A Statement by the Roman Catholic Bishops of North Dakota on the Crisis in Rural Life." Bismark, ND: North Dakota Catholic Conference, 1998.

Rohr, Richard, O.F.M. *Simplicity: The Art of Living.* New York: Crossroad, 1992.

Scharper, Stephen B., and Hilary Cunningham. *The Green Bible.* New York: Orbis Books, 1993.

Scharper, Stephen B. *Redeeming the Time: A Political Theology of the Environment.* New York: Continuum, 1997.

*United States Bishops' Statement. "Renewing the Earth: An Invitation to Reflection and Action on the Environment in Light of Catholic Social Teaching" *Origins: CNS Documentary News Service* 21: 425–432.

*United States Catholic Conference, *Renewing the Face of the Earth: A Resource for Parishes.* Washington, DC: Department of Social Development and World Peace, U.S. Catholic Conference, 1994.

In addition to individual articles and books by Catholics, there are now a number of newer periodicals entirely devoted to this subject. They include "Canticle of Creation: A Franciscan Environmental Networking Newsletter" (Franciscan); "Loretto Earth Network News" (Sisters of Loretto); "EC News" (Earth Connection—Sisters of Charity); "Rural Landscape" (National Catholic Rural Life Conference); "Catholic Rural Life" (National Catholic Rural Life Conference); "The Sextant" (Centre for Ecology and Spirituality, Port Burwell, Ontario, Canada); "Renewing the Earth: A Catholic Response to Environmental Justice" (United States Catholic Conference, Washington, DC); "Appalachian Alternatives" (Appalachia: Science in the Public Interest [Jesuit]); "SpiritEarth" (Newsletter of the Center for Spirituality, Saugerties, New York); "The Promised Land" (Rural Life Ministry, Diocese of Amarillo, Texas).

9

Islam and Deep Ecology

NAWAL AMMAR

INTRODUCTION

IN THE LAST DECADE of the twentieth century my conversations with colleagues about Islam and ecology often resulted in suggestions about a need for a new theology or a reformation of the religion to provide a vision of a new earth.[1] With more than half of the forty armed conflicts in the world taking place in Islamic countries, the crude birth rate of Muslim countries being one percent higher than that of the developing world as a whole, and Cairo, the Islamic capital with one thousand minarets, being the second most polluted city in the world, the anxiety about the role of Muslims in protecting the environment is reasonable.[2]

Islam, however, like all religions and ideologies, can be misconceived and misinterpreted, and hence, instead of a new theology we need to retrieve the fundamentals of Islam, and in so doing seek the spirit of the progressive theological elements that the Prophet Muhammad brought to Arabia in the seventh century. In a progressive Islam the connection and linkage between nature and other creations of God lie at the center of the theology and social existence. Nature in Islam, notes al Faruqi, is not "an enemy. It is not a demonic force challenging and inciting humanity to conquer and subdue it. . . . Nature is a perfectly fitted theater where humanity is to do good deeds."[3] This connection is based on three premises: everything on earth is created by God, every thing that God creates reflects His sacredness, and that every thing on earth worships the same God.[4] As such humans have to respect and protect nature not because it is sacred, but because it is a reflection of God's glory, power, and might. Many verses in the Qur'an speak of respecting and reflecting on God's glory in His creations (for example see 50:6–8; 21:30; 13:2; 6:73).[5] One verse of the Qur'an clearly states God's supremacy over creation: " Don't you know that to God belongs the skies and the earth; Without him you have neither a patron nor a supporter" (2:107).[6]

In Islam the central concept of *Tawhid*, Oneness of God as a creator, links His creation to His sacredness, but does not make creation sacred in and of itself. *Tawhid* requires a dependency on the one source of life, God, and links His creation together in an ephemeral relationship of interdependency and respect.

In this chapter I examine Islam's teachings about *Tawhid* and how they translate into an ecological ethic and action that are "deep" and not "shallow." Islam has a complex view of humans, the universe, and their relationship to God. At one level such a relationship may be viewed as "shallow" ecology in that Islam is not an aesthetic religion: it does not view nature as sacred. In the Islamic vision, "(Hu)man(s) are a distinct part of the universe and have a special position among the other parts of the universe." Nature is seen as being of use for human fulfillment and utilization. Yet at another level, humans are part of this universe, "whose elements are complementary to one another in an integrated whole."[7] Hence, if Islam's view of nature is examined from one perspective it can be misconstrued. It is, therefore, important to understand the Islamic view in its totality and complexity, especially the *Tawhid* perspective, in order to understand how as a religion it respects the universe and nature, and in turn how this reflects a deep relational perspective on natural and social ecology.

In Islam the relationship between humans and nature is one of use as well as contemplation, worship, appreciation of beauty, moral responsibility toward protection, prohibition of destruction and revival. This relationship is a moral destiny; if fulfilled it will lead humans to their desired Gardens in Heaven.

It is worth noting, however, that the one vision presented here in this chapter will have both supporters and opponents. As it is well known, there are more than one billion Muslims in the world today who live in more than 83 countries, and I make no claims to speak on behalf of all of them. Yet, "at any point of history each individual Muslim wishing to respond to his/her awareness of God's guidance may do so"[8] and not until Judgement Day can its appropriateness be evaluated.

Tawhid (Oneness) and Deep Ecology in Islam

The Creator and the Created: The Duality of Holism

Tawhid refers to the belief in the absolute oneness of God, Lord and Master of all things. In the *Shahadah*, the first pillar of Islam, Muslims are to declare that there is no God but Allah and that Muhammad is the Prophet of God, *la ilaha illa Allah wa Muhammad Rasul Allah*. This oneness of God is the essence of Islamic civilization and religion.[9] *Tawhid* is a belief that sees God as one who stands in a dual relationship with what He creates. It is an article of faith that connects and diverts every thing created to the divinity of God; it also binds the parameters of responsibility for God's creation to humans.[10]

> al Faruqi and al Faruqi note about *Tawhid* that the duality in Islam is of, God and non-God; Creator and creature. The first order has but one member, Allah the Absolute and Almighty. He alone is God, eternal, Creator, transcendent. Nothing like unto Him; He remains forever absolutely unique and devoid of partners or associates. The second is the order of space-time, of experience, of creation. It includes all creatures, the world of things, plants and animals, humans, jinn and angles, heaven and earth, paradise and hell and all their becoming since they came into beings. The two orders of creator and creation are utterly and absolutely disparate. . . . Neither can the Creator be ontologically transformed so as to become the creature, nor can the creature transcend and transfigure itself so as to become in any way or sense Creator.[11]

The *Tawhid* perspective, which creates a duality between God and the creatures, renders all created equal and alike. At the same time, however, none of the created are sacred except in their relationship to God and in fulfilling the purpose of God's creation. It is at this level that the Islamic vision may be mistaken for a naturalistic one. It is essential to underscore the issue that in Islam to consider nature or other creatures as sacred is in direct opposition of the *Tawhid* perspective, which views only God as sacred and only Allah to be worthy of worship. The created are considered equal in their relationship to God. This relationship is one of obedience, worship of, reverence to, and dependence on God. It is a relationship that makes the created subservient to and followers of God's commands. The Prophet repeatedly stated that all God's creation is dependent and supported by God and, "He loveth the most, those who are beneficent to His family."[12]

The Unity of the Created within a *Tawhid* Perspective

The *Tawhid* perspective in Islam renders nature a creation of God by a sheer commandment, for God's creation is not a generative act. As such the Qur'anic verse notes, "Say: He is Allah, the One and Only. Allah, the Eternal, Absolute; He begetteth not, nor is He begotten; and there is none unto Him" (112:1–4); "He just has to say to it 'Be' and it evolves into 'Being'" (2:117). Nature itself is not sacred. It is sacred insofar as it is a reflection of the will of God. Hence the Qur'anic verse, "To Him belongs what is in the heavens and on earth and all between, and all beneath the soil" (20:6); "Do they not look at the Camels how they are created?, and the Sky how it is raised high, and the Mountains how they are fixed firm and the earth how it is spread" (88: 17–20). Islam has a transcendental view of nature. To attribute sacredness to nature is to associate other beings with God and that is against *Tawhid* and the Oneness of God, *shirk*. This transcendental vision, however, does not relegate nature to the secular or profane. It is not a duality of separate domains of God the creator as sacred and the creation as profane. It is rather a totality, a dependency where nature reflects the glory of sacredness but is not itself sacred. Such a unified vision renders the deep ecologists' call for "the sacredness of nature/creation" an impossible task for Muslims. At the same time, however, it coincides with the deep ecologists' call for respect and glorification of nature.

Islam postulates that God owns all the universe (*al mulk lilah*), and nature is a blessed gift of God, granted to humans to do good deeds. The Qur'anic verse says, "It is God who created heaven and earth . . . that you may distinguish yourselves by your better deeds" (11:7).

The duality of the Creator and created renders the latter in Islam (e.g., nature, animals, humans and other creatures) a unified class of God's creation. The Prophet in regard to God's creation said, "[A]ll creatures are God's dependents and the most beloved to God among them is the one that does good to God's dependents." These dependents, though diverse, still have many characteristics in common. First, all creation is a reflection of God's sacredness, glory, and power. The Qur'anic verse notes about such creation, "Whithersoever you turn there is the Face of God" (11:115). Second, God's creation is orderly, has purpose, and exists with function. The Qur'anic verses say, "And the earth we have spread out; set therein mountains firm and immovable; and produced therein all kinds of things in due balance" (15:19); and "Verily, all things have been created with measure" (59:49).

Third, the created category is all actualized to worship and obey God. Hence, the Qur'anic verse states, "Sees thou not that to Allah bow down in worship all things that are in the heavens and earth, the sun, the moon, the stars; the hills, the trees, the animals; and a great number among humankind" (22:18).

Fourth, the created have all been created from the same element, water.[13] The Qur'anic verse states, "We made from water every living thing" (12:30), and continues in another verse by stating, "And God has created every animal from water of them there are some that creep on their bellies; some that walk on two legs; and some that walk on four. . . . It is he who has created humans from water" (24:45).

Fifth, the unity of God's creation as a category is also exemplified in Islam in terms of the social structure.[14] The Qur'an states that all that God created He created in communities by stating, "There is not an animal (that lives) on earth. Nor a being that flies on its wings, but (forms a part) of a community like you" (6:38).

The likeness and unity of all creatures created by God is also exemplified in certain *Hadiths* and *Sunnah*, Prophet's Sayings and tradition. The Prophet spent his early days of contemplation in a cave where he saw himself close to nature. It is also reported that the Prophet said about the mountain Uhud, close to Mecca: "It is a mountain that loves us and we love it," and he also spoke to this mountain after an earthquake saying: "Be calm, Uhud."[15]

Islam, in considering all God's creation as having common characteristics and divine reflections, echoes views of deep ecology. The whole universe is one single system created and united by Allah. Looking at the universe with such a perspective where all creatures are connected reveals common principles in Islam and deep ecology. Humans and other creations here have a relationship with each other and the universe reflecting kinship, admiration, respect, contemplation, adoration, and consideration, but not sacredness.

This unity of God's creation and the relationship of its components, however, becomes more complicated at the level of using and protecting nature as well as the role of humans in such endeavors. Although Islam's final teachings parallel the objectives of deep ecology, it nevertheless approaches the details of such objectives differently because the *Tawhid* perspective views the various components of nature as engaged in an order of interdependence for the final objective of glorification of God. As such the respect for nature is an outcome of mutual respect among the elements in nature, not because nature is sacred or because nature should be respected by itself, but because of its link to the One God, creator of all.

Tawhid, the Human Responsibility, and the Ecology:
A Devotional-Moral Dimension

Tawhid views only God, the Creator, as having the special quality of in-dependence, while the created as being interdependent on each other and dependent on God. In this relationship of interdependence among the created, Islam places the keeping of the earth and heavens under the hands of humans, as the *Khalifah* (vice-regents) on earth. The Qur'anic verse states, "I am setting on the earth a vice-regent" (2:30). The *Khalifah* is a manager not a proprietor, a keeper for all generations. The Qur'anic verse (2:22) stating, "Who has made the earth your couch and the heav-ens your canopy and sent rains from the heavens, and brought forth-with fruits for your sustenance, *then set not up rivals unto Allah when you know,*" clearly ends with a plural "you," carrying the message that the universe is not for one generation but for every generation past, pres-ent, and future.

Humans were given the responsibility for managing the earth be-cause they possess special qualities, and not because they have better qualities. Raisail II notes,

> All creatures are alike. . . . Plants are superior to minerals in being able to absorb nourishment, to grow and feed, animals in addition to these powers have one or more of the five senses, and (hu)man(s), while of the animal kingdom in other respects and pos-sessing all senses, also speaks and reasons.[16]

These special qualities attributed to humans, notes Izzi Dien (1992:27–28), include their ability to speak and know the names of the creation, an independent will to know good from evil, and their ability to prevent evil. The Qur'anic verses state,

> *And He taught Adam all the names; (2:31)*
> *By the Soul, and the proportion and order given to it, and its*
> *enlightenment as to its wrong and its right. (91:7–8)*

Additionally, humans are the managers of earth because in His search, God found that only humans agreed to take on the responsibil-ity. The Qur'anic verse notes, "God offered his trust to heaven and earth and mountain, but they shied away in fear and rejected it, Humans only carried it" (33:72). For these reasons the universe is given to humans as a "trust," *ammanah,* which they accepted when they bore witness to God in their covenant of *Tawhid.* There is no God but *Allah.* According to the Qur'an this covenant was renewed throughout the years (7: 65,69, 87;

10:73; 11:56,61) until it reached Muslims in verses such as "Generations before you we destroyed when they did wrong"(10:13); "Then we made you heirs in the land after them to see how ye would behave" (10:14).

The role of humans as *Khalifah*, vice-regent, on earth is to better it and improve it and not to spread evil and destruction. The Qur'an is full of injunctions concerning such behaviors and states clearly that this responsibility of improving the earth will be checked by God to see how it has been accomplished, "And follow not the bidding of those who are extravagant" (26:152); "O my people! Serve Allah, and fear the Last day: nor commit evil on the earth, with intent to do mischief" (29:36); "But they strive to make mischief on earth and Allah loveth not those who do mischief" (5:64); "And look for his Creation for any discrepancy! And look again! Do you find any gap in its system? Look again! Your sight, having found none, will return to you humbled" (67:3–4); "He it is who created the heavens and the earth. . . . That He might try you, which of you is best in conduct" (11:7); "That which is on earth we have made but as a glittering show for the earth in order that we may test them as to which of them are best in conduct" (18:7).

Scholars of Islam[17] note that God created humankind for the purpose of protecting the universe. Purpose, as al Faruqi and al Faruqi put it, "pervades the whole creation without exception."[18] Humans are an integral part of this purpose, hence, note the Qur'anic verses, "We have not created heaven and earth and all that stands between them in sport . . . we have created them in righteousness . . . for the purpose of confuting evil and error with truth and value" (44:38; 21:16). God did not create earth in vain, but as a test for humans to do good. It is the purpose and the moral duty of humans to act on the responsibility placed in their hands. al Faruqi notes this protection is human destiny (purpose) to show their moral and devotional abilities and if they fail in fulfilling it they displease God the creator.[19]

Muslims, however, are left with another duty, namely to enjoy and use the bounties of the earth. Humans in Islam have a dual relationship with nature/earth/universe. On the one hand they are their manager, but they are also their user. The Qur'anic verse notes, "Do you not see that Allah has subjected to your (use) all things on the heavens and on earth, and has made his bounties flow to you in exceeding measure, both seen and unseen" (31:20); "It is He who made the earth manageable for you, so traverse ye through its tracts and enjoy of the sustenance which he furnishes" (67:15). Islam has a clear view that encourages the use of the bounties of earth, and the engagement in other human pleasures. The Qur'anic verse states, "Wealth and children are *zinat* (beauty, decoration) of this worldly life." Islam does not tolerate abstinence, thus the absence of priests and nuns in the mainstream religious hierarchy. One of the sayings, *Hadiths*, of the Prophet reports that three believers came to his home to declare their piety and belief in and love of God. One of the believers said, "I want to show my belief in God that I will abstain from food." The second one said, "I will show my belief in God by not sleeping nights." The third one said, "I will show my belief in God by not touching my wife." The Prophet stopped them and recommended, "that God does not tolerate the extremes of abstentions and that moderation is the best path to piety."

This dual role of the *Khalifah*, vice-regent, creature of God and user of earth, poses the theological test for Muslims. Central to reaching the Gardens of Heaven is the issue of keeping the equilibrium between having been charged with managing the earth and bettering it, while at the same time using its bounties for their fulfillment. The Qur'anic verse states, "Thus we have made of you an Ummah (a community) justly balanced" (2:143). The Qur'an speaks of God's trust in human ability to maintain the balance and do well, "Behold God said to the angels I will create a viceregent on earth. They said will You place one who will make mischief and shed blood? While we celebrate your praises and glorify your holiness, He said, I know what you know not?" (2:30). The Qur'an warns Muslims throughout of the consequences of doing mischief (not fulfilling their role as vice-regents who maintain justly balance):

> When he turns his back his aim everywhere is to spread mischief through out the earth and destroy crops and populations; (2:205)
>
> And Allah loveth not those who do mischief; (5:60)
>
> Fear Allah and obey me and follow not the bidding of those who are extravagant who make mischief in the land and mend not their ways. (26:150–152)

Islam recommends a clear path to achieving the equilibrium between use and protection, namely action. The balance of this chapter discusses some of the actions taken by Muslims to maintain the balance, and also explores the contemporary ecological crisis in light of such action.

TAWHID, DEEP ECOLOGY, AND DEVOTIONAL ACTION

Islam is often defined as the total submission to God, and portrayed as the religion of predestination. As such the role of humans is often relegated to little free will and choice. The discussion of free will and predestination in Islam is a long, protracted, unresolved, and highly volatile issue.[20] Islam, however, has prescribed rationalism and the ability of humans to know right from wrong, hence the Qur'an notes, "Say (unto them Muhammad): Are those who know equal to those who know not?" In terms of action to better life and to attain the moral purpose, Islam clearly sees a place for human action and good deeds. As such the Qur'an states, "Let there be among you a group of people who order good, *al-maruf* and prohibit evil, *almunkar*" (3:104). This ordering of good and prohibition of evil in Islam is an important form of action and it includes various verbal and other components, hence the Prophet's saying, "Any one who witnesses evil should remonstrate upon it by his hand, his mouth or his heart, the last is the weakest of faith." This order of *maruf* and prohibition of *munkar* does not differentiate between actions toward humans or other creatures of God. Within the perspective of *Tawhid* it is all good deeds performed by the created to please the Creator. As such a saying of the Prophet notes, "A good deed done to a beast is as good as doing good to a human being; while an act of cruelty to a beast is as bad as an act of cruelty to a human being."[21] The ordering of good and prohibition of evil according to Islam is not only done for the Day of Judgment, but should be done for the here and now. Hence, the Prophet enjoined Muslims to "work in this world as though you are living forever and work for the hereafter as though you are dying tomorrow." The commandment of *maruf* and prohibition of *munkar* in Islam is an essential part of the continuity of life. In the Qur'an Muslims are warned that if they do not perform good deeds and act against evil they will perish: "Generations before you were destroyed when they did wrong" (10:13).

There is ample evidence both in the Qur'an and in tradition about how action (both in negating evil and performing good deeds) is required for Muslims to maintain the equilibirum of use and protection. The Qur'anic verse says, "Do no mischief on the Earth after it has been set in order" (7:85). This call, however, is not of a hands-off approach but rather of engagement, and those who do not act or engage will be at a loss, according to the Qur'anic verse, "Verily humans are at a loss, except those who have faith, and *do righteous deeds* and (together they join) *in the mutual teaching of truth*" (103:1–2, my emphasis).

The Prophet's tradition and sayings also reveal action toward performing good deeds and averting evil, with more particular reference to nature and earth. Many of the Prophet's sayings speak of acting to improve and protect nature (including animals, and resources). In relation to plants the Prophet has said,

> if any one plants a tree or sows a field and humans, beasts or birds
> eat from it, he should consider it a charity on his part;

Whoever plants a tree and looks after it with care until it matures
and becomes productive, will be rewarded in the hereafter.

The Prophet has also claimed the need to protect animals (including
humans). The Prophet has said, "[W]hoever is kind to the creatures of
God is kind to himself." The Prophet has forbidden the beating of animals on the face, and prohibited the throwing of stones at animals. He
has recommended that every care should be taken when slaughtering
animals. It is forbidden to make animals the object of human sports or
entertainment. The Prophet asks humans to feel within their souls the
pain animals feel and avoid all practices that torture and frighten living
beings. The Prophet says about using animals in game, "A sparrow that
was used just for entertainment would on the day of judgement complain to [God] against the person who did so just for fun."[22]
     There is evidence throughout the early history of Islam that action
toward protecting the environment by doing good deeds and averting
evil continued. Hence, it is reported that the first Muslim Caliph ordered his army "not to cut down trees, not to abuse a river, not to harm
animals and be always kind and gentle to God's creation, even to your
enemies." It is reported that the fourth Caliph and the cousin of the
Prophet said to a man digging a canal and reclaiming a land, "[P]artake
of it with joy, so long as you are a benefactor, not a corrupter, a cultiva-
tor not a destroyer."[23]
     Performing good deeds and averting evil as devotional actions in
Islam toward attaining equilibrium between use and protection of the
earth have taken many forms throughout Islamic history. I will discuss
two of them, namely, legal and educational actions.

Legal Forms to Protect the Environment

Muslims throughout history have to strive to fulfill their moral obligation to God toward being protectors and users of earth. As such they
have developed rules and regulations that protect nature. Such rules
can be subsumed under five general regulations:

1. Use nature and its resources in a balanced, not excessive manner;
2. Treat nature and its resources with kindness;
3. Do not damage, abuse or distort nature in any way;
4. Share natural resources;
5. Conserve.[24]

To many, the above rules sound like a World Bank report for a sustainable development project and in many ways they could. It is, however, the Islamic sense of theology in its devotional morality and action that underlies these rules and that differentiates them from sustainable development. Themes mentioned above such as the likeness of all creatures, the accountability of humans to God, and the subservience of nature as part of God's will render these regulations the essence of life on earth and the afterlife in Heaven. Muslims ought to tremble in fear from the catastrophic consequences of pollution, ozone depletion, famines, extinction of species, disease and epidemics, since such signs indicate *fasad*, corruption on earth, which they will be held responsible for during Judgment Day.[25] As such, acting on rules and regulations that reduce the corruption of the earth has a theological and spiritual resonance imposed and, unlike the effect of those that come from development and aid institutions such as the World Bank, emanates from within to serve the higher authority, the Creator, God.

Additionally, the points of departure of Islamic regulations are different from those of sustainable development. As mentioned above, humans are not here to make nature or resources subservient to their needs and utilization. Nature has already been made subservient by God and not by humans or other creatures. The aim is not to use nature by controlling it, but rather to use it by managing it for devotional purposes, i.e., to attain the Garden of Heaven in the hereafter.

Islamic Regulations and the Notion of Use

The issue of use here is an important one to underscore. Islam provides a basis for an economic system of use, ownership, exchange, and production. The general system has been set in the Qur'an, and legal scholars have worked its details.[26] The rules revolve around three principles. The reduction of waste, exchange, or consumption through use value and partnership in use.[27] All these principles work to reduce overconsumption by humans, one important source of corruption of and harm to nature.

Reduction of Waste

The reduction of waste is a very clear principle in the Islamic economic system. The rule that defines waste is one that states, "the merit of utilization in the benefit it yields, in proportion to its harm." If the harm in use exceeds the benefit then it is wasteful. The Qur'anic verse clearly admonishes against waste by stating, "Eat and drink but waste not in indulging in excess, surely God does not approve" (7:31). The Prophet's *hadiths*, sayings, also show Islamic concern about waste and hence, overconsumption. It is reported that the Prophet said to someone who was using water in excess while performing *wudu'*, ablution, to pray, "do not waste." He was then asked if there can be waste of water during a sacred ritual such as ablution. He replied, "[T]here can be waste in anything."

Use Value

Islamic exchange is based on the transfer of goods and services for another equivalent in value, and exchange determined by other forces such as supply/demand is considered usury. Usury is seen as unjust exchange that exploits resources (both human and natural). The Qur'an warns, "That which you lay out for increase through the property of [other] people, will have no increase with God: but that which you lay out for charity seeking the countenance of God, [will increase], it is these who will get a recompense multiplied" (30:39).

Partnership

Islam sees partnership as the essence of use. The Prophet has said, "people are partners in water, pasture land and fire." Partnership implies permission in using the elements as well as equality in the distribution of use patterns. For one group to use resources without permission or to use more than its share implies transgression and could result in losing its right of use completely. The Qur'an for example says regarding water, "And tell them the water is to be divided amongst them" (54:86).

EDUCATION AND ECOLOGY IN ISLAM

Muslims have consistently been engaged in action to perform good deeds and avoid evil ones in nature and the universe through education. We can find in Islamic history scientists who were concerned with nature, such as vegetal pharmacologist Ibn Bytar (who lived in the middle thirteenth century c.e.) who translated and added to the works from Persia, India, and the Mediterranean about plants and medicine.[28] Ibn Bytar mentioned in his books more than 1,400 natural medicinal drugs to cure humans and animals.[29] The medical botanist al Razi (who lived in the ninth century c.e.) used to collect flowers, leaves, and roots from nature and mix them to prepare medicines. Jabir Ibn Hayyan, the father of chemistry, was concerned about pollution and its effects on humans and the rest of the environment. The Arab Muslim thinker, al-Jahiz wrote in the eighth century C.E. of the effects of environmental changes on animal behavior. Al-Izz bin 'abd al-Salam who lived in the thirteenth century C.E. wrote about the rights of animals.[30]

In other parts of the Islamic world there are many names that are associated with teaching and learning about the linkage between humans and nature and its preservation. In Saudi Arabia, the Kingdom's Meteorology and Environmental Protection Administration (MEPA) has funded good research about Islamic principles and the environment.[31] There is also an Islamic environmental organization in the U.K. headed by Fazlun Khaled that produces very good educational books and materials.[32]

Muslim countries have created ministries of the environment to educate about and protect it. The campaigns have gone as far as, for example, some scholars in Egypt urging that harming the environment should be considered a criminal act, while other policy makers have urged that loans should not be given to companies that do not protect the environment.[33]

Ecological activism through education within the Islamic faith is not a difficult responsibility. In addition to the theological implications for protecting, bettering, and improving the conditions of God's creation, Muslims follow rituals that make them close to all God's creations. To pray, Muslims need clean water and surroundings free of communicable disease for their communal prayers on Fridays. To fast and celebrate the feasts they need to have a sky clear from pollutants to be able to see the crescent moon. To fulfill the duty of pilgrimage and for it to be accepted, they need to be strong (hence free of disease) and to protect God's creation. Educating Muslims about the relationship between humans and other creations of God is not a complicated theological task, and its practical aspects are clear and easy for all Muslims to understand. The difficult task, however, is to convince Muslims that their activism is required and that they are contributing to the devastation of the environment. It is to this that now I want to turn.

MUSLIM ACTIVISM, ACTION, AND ECOLOGY

The dilemma for those who would awaken Muslim activism to protect the environment does not dwell in the clarity of the spiritual and theological teachings. The quandary lies in providing a persuasive argument demonstrating that some Muslims are contributing to the devastation of the universe, and hence motivating their individual and collective activism as incumbent on them as Muslims. Muslims in both the distant and recent history see themselves as having lost their Golden Age, a time when their actions were respected. Since the time of European colonialism, Muslims have had a vision of themselves as the colonized, oppressed, demonized, and disabled within the larger global perspective. They see the harm that is done to God's creation as being the consequence of the non-Muslims. Dangers that threaten the environment such as industrial and chemical pollution, overconsumption, inequality between the poor and rich, new infectious diseases such as HIV, and even wars are caused by the non-Muslims' having lost sight of the sacred, their greed, and their hunger for power. As such, Muslims regard the destruction of nature as not their doing and believe that God will punish those who are destroying his creation.

Additionally, secular/Western suggestions (including deep ecology) for protecting nature are unacceptable to many Muslim scholars and leaders. This was best exemplified at the United Nations International Conference on Population and Development (ICPD) held in Cairo in 1994, when the official Islamic position opposed the Cairo Platform of Action on slowing population growth to raise the quality of life. Such a call was seen as a "foreign" intervention that has no relevance to the Islamic scheme of life. The entire argument about how the empowered role of women (through education, employment, reduction and spacing of births, etc.) contributes to the welfare of the ecosystem has been perceived as a Western notion that encroaches on the Islamic way of life. As a result the activism of Muslims has taken the form of protecting themselves from the non-Muslims' encroachment on their way of life.

The failure of Muslims to avoid evil and perform good deeds regarding environmental depletion goes against the core of Qur'an and tradition, and in many ways contributes to the corrupted state of the earth. Regardless of who is corrupting and destroying the earth and God's creation, action to protect and improve the environment is incumbent on Muslims. Islam is very clear about the unity—oneness—of God's creation. The Qur'an emphasizes the common origin (and hence the common responsibility) of human creation by stating, "O humankind! We created you male and female and made you into nations and tribes that ye may know each other (not to despise each other). The most honored of you in the sight of Allah is the most Righteous of you" (49:13). This oneness does not differentiate among nationalities or languages. Hence, the Prophet in his last Sermon stated, "People: your

God is one, you all belong to Adam and Adam to earth . . . the most honored is the most pious and there is no difference between an Arab and a foreigner." The Qur'an clearly states that all humans are God's creation by saying, "And among His Signs is the creation of the heavens and the earth and the variations in your languages and colors, verily in that are signs for those who know" (30:2).

Additionally, the empowerment of women (and its related problem of family planning) is not a Western encroachment on Islam. Islam sees women as equal to men. The Qur'an states, "O humankind! Reverence your God who created you from a single soul, created of like nature its mate" (4:1). Part of the Qur'anic vision about women acknowledges the fact that they have been historically (prior to Islam) a disadvantaged group that was treated badly and inhumanely. The Qu'ran never describes women as the seductresses who caused the expulsion from Heaven, but rather it was the devil, *al-Shitan*, who led to such a fate. As such the Qur'an addresses both men and women, "the self surrendering men and the self surrendering women, the believing men and believing women, the obedient men and obedient women (33:35)." It also sees them both as protectors of each other: "[Y]ou are their garments and you are their garments" (2:187); and both are rewarded and responsible for their own actions, "to men allotted what they earn and to women what they earn" (4:32).

The inaction of Muslims can also be seen in the largest world war we have witnessed since World War II, the 1990 "Desert Shield/Desert Storm." More than thirty Muslim nations were involved in this war. It would seem that by adopting a war ethic of negotiations first, Muslims should have been at the forefront of averting a war that environmentalist have dubbed the "Nuclear Winter," because the inaccurate Scud missiles, germ warfare, and the oil fires reduced sunlight and temperatures throughout the region.[34] Unlike Buddhism's nonviolent struggle, Gandhi's concept of non-harm *(satyāgraha)*, or Christ's dictum "to turn the other cheek," Islam considers war as a viable form of struggle against injustice or oppression. One Qur'anic verse says, "[A]nd fight them on until there is no more tumult or oppression, and there prevail justice and faith in God, altogether and every where" (8:39). Nonetheless, as a form of struggle in Islam, war is seen as a last resort. Persuasion and patience should be employed first. According to the Qur'an, first "invite (all) to the way of thy lord with wisdom, and beautiful preaching and argue with them in ways that are best and most gracious" (16:127). If gracious words and arguments do not improve the oppression and distress, another form of nonviolent reaction is recommended, namely, emigration. According to the Qur'an: "He who forsakes his home in the name of God, finds in the earth many refuges, wide and spacious" (4:100).

If nonviolent modes of struggle fail to eliminate tumult and oppression, the Qur'an calls the "Prophet, [to] rouse the faithful to arms" (8:65), "[m]uster against them [the enemies] all the men and cavalry at your disposal" (8:60), and "turn them [the enemies] out from where they turned you out" (2:191). At this stage of war, all Muslims are ordered to join the war in all their capacities. According to the Qur'an: "[F]ighting is obligatory for you, much as you dislike it" (3:200). However, in many wars Muslims fail to follow such steps and often call for war as a first resort. Muslims during the Desert Storm war not only neglected to avert evil and perform good, but they went against clear theological commands of warring.[35]

It is thus important to underscore that Muslims will only be able to perform their role as God's vice-regents who know right from wrong and good from evil if they participate actively in use and protection of the earth/nature. In the last quarter of a century the problem for Muslims has been their acceptance of a hands-off approach regarding a very clear duty toward fulfilling their moral devotional destiny, namely pleasing the one God, Allah.

SUMMARY AND CONCLUSION

Islam has in common with deep ecology its respect for nature and earth. Both Islam and deep ecology view humans as part of this creation and not superior to it. Beyond this commonality the Islamic vision of linking humans to nature, nature and humans to God, and the protection of nature become complex and at many points difficult to compare with deep ecology. Islam, for example does not view creation as sacred in itself. Rather, it is respected as a reflection of sacredness, because it is the creation of God. The distinction of creation from sacredness lies at the heart of the Islamic profession of faith, *Tawhid*. The *Tawhid*, Oneness of God, principle allows for only one sacred entity, namely, Allah. The rest of the entities are created by God and they reflect His sacredness. The fact that nature reflects God's sacredness removes it from the secular domain and places it within the realm of respect and devotion. Yet, this devotion is not of nature itself but of the source of nature, God the Almighty.

Within these devotional layers of linkages between God and nature, humans are appointed as the vice-regents, *Khalifahs*, of God on earth to protect it. They are appointed because they can distinguish between good and evil (91:7–8), are capable of knowing and judging good from evil (90:8–9), and can control harm and corruption (79:40). Humans were also appointed because they were the only ones who accepted such a role. In addition to their appointment as protectors of the earth, humans are asked to use the bounties of the earth as part of their devotion to God's creation. Humans are asked to balance the role of use and protection of the earth as a test of their devotional abilities.

In contrast to some deep ecologists who view action in nature as undesired intervention and corruption, I argue that in Islam action is the only course that fulfills the charge humans were given by God, namely to keep the equilibrium of use and protection of earth. Islam views action to avert evil and do good as the solution to save the corruption of the earth. Although there have been both historical and contemporary actions to avert evil and perform good, there is a need for a more systematic and comprehensive activity to save the environment. The problem in the past quarter-century in Islamic countries and with Muslims has been their hesitation to act against the corruption of the earth, namely because they perceive that they are disempowered, that the corruption is not their own doing, and that they need to protect their own culture from Western encroachment. Such views, however, are in direct opposition to the core teachings of the Qur'an that view all humanity as the creation of God, that call for avoidance of excess, and that mandate respect for women as God's creations. It is the inaction and complacency of Muslims toward protecting the environment that has contributed to such levels of devastation. A retrieval of the action-oriented ethic toward the environment and a systematic program to achieve it would contribute to protecting the earth as a trust, *ammanah*, for the next generations of Muslims and non-Muslims.

NOTES

1. See a new book edited by Harold Coward and Daniel C. Maguire, *Visions of a New Earth: Religious Perspectives on Population, Consumption, and Ecology* (Albany: State University of New York Press, 2000). Initially the book was entitled "A New Theology." However, as the Islamic scholar I argued that there is a clear environmental ethic in Islam and all that is needed is to retrieve it and not to invent it. Most other scholars agreed with my viewpoint and hence the new title.

2. "The Effects of Armed conflict on Girls," *World Vision Report*, 1997.

3. I. al Faruqi, *Islam* (Brentwood, MD: International Graphics, 1984), 53.

4. I use the words *nature, universe, environment,* and *earth* interchangeably. The Qur'an and Arabic generally use earth to denote our universe (the globe)

including the natural and social, and also use the word *Muhit*, which denotes human surroundings. I reflect the linguistic diversity in the Islamic context by using different words at different times in my chapter.

5. The Qur'anic references are cited by chapter and then verse.

6. I have sometimes used Abdullah Yusuf Ali, Holy Qur'an Translation. Often, however, I found the generic word *Insan* or *Nas* translated as Man. Instead, I translated it as Humankind or People, a more accurate translation and more inclusive.

7. Abou Bakr Ahmad Ba Kader et al., *Basic Paper on the Islamic Principles for the Conservation of the Natural Environment* (Gland, Switzerland: IUCN and the Kingdom of Saudi Arabia, 1983), 13.

8. Nawal Ammar, "Islam, Population, and the Environment: A Textual and Juristic View," in *Population, Consumption, and The Environment: Religious and Secular Responses*, ed. Harold Coward (Albany: State University of New York Press, 1995), 123, 124.

9. I. al Faruqi and L. al Faruqi, *The Cultural Atlas of Islam* (New York: Macmillan, 1986).

10. al Faruqi and al Faruqi, *The Cultural Atlas of Islam*; M. Abul-Fadl, "Revisiting the Woman Question: An Islamic Perspective," *The Chicago Theological Seminary Register* 83 (1993), 28–61.

11. al Faruqi and al Faruqi, *The Cultural Atlas of Islam*, 74.

12. Quoted in A. H. Masri, "Islam and Ecology," in *Islam and Ecology*, ed. F. Khalid and J. O'Brien (London: Cassell Publishers Limited, 1992), 18.

13. Ammar, "Islam, Population, and the Environment," 128; S. A. Ismail, *Environment: An Islamic Perspective*, 1993. http://www.igc.apc.org/elaw/mideast/palestine/islamenviro.html.

14. Ammar, "Islam, Population, and the Environment," 129.

15. Ibid.

16. Quoted in M. Rafiq and M. Ajmal, "Islam and the Present Ecologicial Crisis," in *World Religions and the Environment*, ed. O. P. Dwivedi (New Delhi: Gitanjali Publishing House, 1989), 123.

17. al Faruqi and al Faruqi, *The Cultural Atlas of Islam*; M. Izzi Dien, "Islamic Ethics and the Environment," in *Islam and Ecology*, 25–35; and Izzi Dien, *Shari'a and the Environment*, 1993. http://www.igc.apc.org/elaw/mideast/palestine/shariaenviro.html.

18. al Faruqi and al Faruqi, *The Cultural Atlas of Islam*, 316.

19. al Faruqi, *Islam*.

20. For a discussion of free will and predestination with regard to the environment see Ammar, "An Islamic Response to the Manifest Ecological Crisis: Issues of Justice," in *Visions of a New Earth: Religious Perspectives on Population,*

Consumption, and Ecology, ed. Harold Coward and Daniel C. Maguire (Albany: State University of New York Press, 2000), 131–146.

21. Quoted in Masri, "Islam and Ecology," 18.

22. These sayings are commonly known, being among those memorized by Muslims as part of their education.

23. Ammar, "Islam, Population, and the Environment," 130–131.

24. Ibid., 130–133.

25. Izzi Dien, *Shari'a and the Environment.*

26. Ammar, "An Islamic Response to the Manifest Ecological Crisis," 135.

27. See my "An Islamic Response to the Manifest Ecological Crisis."

28. al Faruqi and al Faruqi, *The Cultural Atlas of Islam,* 327.

29. Ammar, "Islam, Population, and the Environment," 133.

30. He stated that the rights of animals upon humans are as follows:

Spend on it (time, money and effort), even if it is aged or diseased such that no benefit is expected from it. The spending should be equal to that on a similar animal useful;

Do not overburden it;

Should not place with it whatsoever what may cause it harm, be it of the same kind or a different species;

Do not slaughter their young within their sight;

Give them different resting shelters and watering places which should all be cleaned regularly;

Should put the male and female in the same place during their mating season.

Should not hunt a wild animal with a tool that breaks bones. (Quoted in Izzi Dien, 5)

31. See A. H. Ba Kader, A. T. S. al Sabbagh, M. S. al-Glejd, and M. U. S. Izzi Dien, *Islamic Principles for the Conservation of the Natural Environment* (MEPA: Saudi Arabia, 1983), 1–25.

32. Fazlun Kahled and Joanne O'Brien have edited a very good book entitled *Islam and Ecology* (New York: Cassell Publishers, 1992).

33. Egypt, for example, created a Ministry of the Environment in the 1990s and it was headed by a woman minister. Indonesia in the summer of 1993 announced that its banks will not grant aide to any industry, firm, or individual that pollutes natural resources.

34. Ammar, "An Islamic Response to the Manifest Ecological Crisis," 133.

35. This war's environmental consequences were grave, including more than two hundred thousand people killed or injured, more than ten thousand Kurds displaced, and many soldiers afflicted with germ warfare ailments.

IO

Protestant Theology and Deep Ecology

JOHN B. COBB JR.

THE FAILURE OF ANTHROPOCENTRISM

ALL OF THE "HIGHER RELIGIONS," when viewed against the background of the primal religions, are anthropocentric and even individualistic. They are religions of human salvation, and they have focused on the salvation of individuals. This salvation has been disconnected from physical well-being and thus from changes in the physical world.

These great traditions all strike other notes as well. In this book, we are emphasizing these other notes. As we have become aware of our historic failures in relation to ecological matters, we have rightly recovered these other elements and sought to give them a central role. These efforts have important contributions to make, but it is best to begin with the acknowledgment that a truly ecological consciousness was far more clearly and effectively present in hunting and gathering societies than in our traditions. When we look for religious versions of deep ecology, it is to them that we should turn.

Although this weakness characterizes all the great world religions, as a Protestant Christian I am impelled to move quickly to the acknowledgment that Protestant theology has been an extreme case. Christianity as a whole has emphasized the interior relation of the individual to God, but the Eastern Church down to the present has kept in view the larger setting of God's relation to the whole of creation. Even in the Western church, in the Patristic and Medieval periods the church's teaching incorporated the whole of society and of the natural world. The Eastern and Roman Catholic traditions have resources today for responding to our new awareness of the ecological crisis that require separate treatment. As a Protestant I will limit myself, as the title of this essay indicates, to the situation of ecumenical Protestantism.

The feature of traditional teaching that disturbed the Reformers and led to their break with Rome had to do quite narrowly with the roles of God, the church, and persons in the salvation of individuals. As a result the writings of the Reformers focused overwhelmingly on these topics. Furthermore, they believed that what they regarded as distortions on these topics came in large part from the broader philosophical traditions incorporated into Christian teaching. Rejecting these led to still further concentration on issues of personal redemption. Calvin built his theology around God and the human soul. The broader creation provided only background and context.

The situation became worse in the nineteenth century. Following Kant, Protestant theologians abandoned the world of nature to the sciences and took history as their only domain, usually emphasizing the moral and spiritual spheres and focusing attention on the individual person. The doctrine of creation that had previously connected Christian thought to the whole of nature was reinterpreted to express the individual's radical dependence on God.

Of course, Protestantism is not a monolithic movement, and many Protestants in the nineteenth and twentieth centuries continued to find God in and through nature. To many of them, creation continued to mean the whole of nature, and the wonder of this nature often grounded their faith in its Creator. Indeed, this appreciation of nature has been more characteristic of popular Protestant piety than was the Kantianism of the theologians. But because it did not receive theoretical expression, its influence on church leadership was negligible. Thus, the Kantian move in theology had enormous effects. What would-be ministers learned in the course of their studies was that attention to nature was sentimental and irrelevant. Their energies should be directed to dealing with the human condition. The options among which they were to choose were alternative ways of understanding human salvation: sociohistorical or otherworldly, psychological or existential, moral or mystical.

My own theological teachers were not Kantian. At the University of Chicago Divinity School we learned that theology should not be separated from the study of the natural world. We learned that there are continuities between natural and historical processes as well as differences. Some of the professors called themselves neonaturalists in order to emphasize this opposition to Kantian theology. Some of them called for deep changes in the Western sensibility.

Nevertheless, we had to learn to operate in the wider theological scene and to express our distinctive views in that context. In that wider scene the spectrum of possibilities was largely defined by Karl Barth's neo-Calvinist theology and Rudolf Bultmann's Christian existentialism. For us it was far easier to relate to Bultmann. In Bultmann's existentialist theology, the focus was on personal decision, and individualistic anthropocentrism reached a pinnacle. Although we sometimes engaged in argument with Bultmann and his followers, his framing of the issues, and the broader neo-Orthodox context tended to shape our agenda and the topics of our reflection. What was happening to the biosphere did not even appear on our radar screen.

At least, this is how it worked out in my case. In the mid-sixties I wrote a book called *A Christian Natural Theology* to express the non-Kantian philosophical theology I had internalized, especially under the influence of the writings of Alfred North Whitehead. But "natural theology" has not been defined in Christian history as reflection about the natural world, although it often included that. It has meant theology within the bounds of reason, that is, independent of appeal to supernatural revelation. The topics I treated were those that were standard in Protestant theology: "man" and God.

I write this to indicate how deeply I was socialized into anthropocentrism by the dominant character of Protestant theology even when the philosophical and theological sources on which I drew offered a very different option. It was not until the end of the sixties, when my eyes were opened to the seriousness of the environmental crisis, that I became aware of this paradox. At that point I realized that my teachers had not been as blind as I. But this openness to the natural world on their part had not affected me, and I think it safe to say that I was not unusual among their students.

When I read Lynn White's famous essay, "The Historical Roots of Our Ecologic Crisis," I saw at once that he was correct, at least as far as the Christian traditions that had informed my thinking were concerned. He extended his charge to the mainstream of the whole of Western Christianity, and despite the fact that pre-Kantian theology was not as extreme in its anthropocentrism as post-Kantian theology, and that Patristic and Medieval Roman Catholic theologies were more inclusive of nature than were the Reformers, I judged then, and I judge now, that he was correct.

White himself pointed out that the tradition included other voices. In particular he pointed to St. Francis as offering another vision, far more suited to our current needs. He wrote as a Protestant layman, calling for reform and suggesting how that could come about.

Western Christianity has always been anthropocentric, and over the centuries it became increasingly so. This is especially true of Protestantism. It was this Protestantism that provided the most important context for the rise of anthropocentric and individualistic philosophy, ethics, economics, and political thought. Together with these, it has supported practices that were consistent with this individualistic anthropocentrism. These practices have changed the face of the Earth. Whatever the failures of the other great religious traditions in these respects, it is our failure that bears the chief responsibility for the degradation of the planet.

THE WAY OF PROCESS THEOLOGY

Fortunately, Christianity is not a static phenomenon. For me its greatest strength is its ability to repent. We Protestants have had much of which to repent, not only in relation to the natural world. Repentance does not mean primarily remorse, although some remorse is no doubt appropriate. It means changing direction. It consists, therefore, of rethinking our theology.

The easiest form of repentance for Protestants is the recovery of neglected biblical themes. The most apparent biblical theme, obviously relevant to our current concern, that has been seriously neglected in mainstream Protestant theology is that of creation. The Bible begins with the account of how God made the heavens and the earth. In the nineteenth century, Protestant theologians dismissed this story to the periphery in order to accent the covenant relation of God with Israel and also to avoid debates with biologists about evolution.

Now the story has been recovered, not for scientific information, but for its clear affirmation of the whole of nature as important to God and as good in God's eyes. What God appreciates, we should appreciate also. Instead of seeing nature as simply a stage on which the human drama is played out, Protestants have been recovering the more biblical vision that the whole of human history takes place in the context of nature and in continuity with nature. What happens in the natural world is of intrinsic importance as well as having vast instrumental importance for human beings.

These teachings are reinforced by the story of the flood. In particular the story of Noah and his ark had been marginalized as a nice story for children. But today we appreciate how it emphasized that human history is interconnected with and dependent upon the conditions of nature. In particular it shows God's concern for the preservation of species, or, in contemporary parlance, for biodiversity.

Once the Kantian spectacles are removed, it is clear that within the Bible the concern for the whole of nature and its interaction with human beings is persistent. Even the eschatological vision, that is, the hope for final salvation, includes the natural world. The salvation that is celebrated is not so much of individual souls from the world as of the world itself, including, of course human beings. Protestant Biblical scholars have reread and reinterpreted extensively.

I speak as a particular type of Protestant theologian, a "process" one. The University of Chicago Divinity School was for many years the chief place where this more naturalistic form of theology was taught. Process theologians have given some leadership in the recovery of creation thinking. In the World Council of Churches, Charles Birch, a biologist as well as a process theologian, provided important leadership in the official affirmation of environmental "sustainability" as a central concern in 1975 at Nairobi. Official acknowledgment of the theological importance of the natural world in Protestant circles dates only from then.

The World Council held a meeting at the Massachusetts Institute of Technology in 1979, on "Faith, Science and the Future." Birch played another role there still more significant for clarifying the distinctiveness of process theology in the Protestant context. The participants were to be divided into groups to discuss diverse issues, such as atomic energy, education, transfer of technology, and economics. Planners recognized that there should also be one group dealing with the underlying theological questions. This they entitled "Faith and Science." Birch proposed an additional group dealing with "nature, humanity, and God." Because of the support of an Eastern Orthodox bishop, this proposal was accepted. I ended up chairing that group.

The difference between the two topics indicates that between Kantian and non-Kantian theology. Under the influence of Kant, most professional Protestant theology had fallen into the modern philosophical bias of defining issues epistemologically. Faith and science are two ways of knowing. The question is, then, how they are related.

Process theology, on the other hand, argues that even epistemology has ontological assumptions; it does not provide a neutral, foundational point of departure. It is just as important to articulate what we believe about the real world as to focus on how we know what we know. Neither approach transcends our always partial perspectives, and, indeed, no such transcendence is possible. This means that process theologians develop our theories about nature and about God as having their reality independently of how they are known by human beings. It also means that we recognized the speculative or hypothetical character of all our affirmations.

The mainstream of Western thought, including the mainstream of Protestant theology, is more comfortable to remain epistemological in focus. Since the epistemological focus is inherently anthropocentric, the mainstream has not adequately overcome anthropocentrism even when it reconnects faith with science. From the perspective of process theologians, the rediscovery of biblical ways of thinking helps to overcome this anthropocentrism of the mainstream, but until the problem with the epistemological starting point is directly faced, the improvement will not have full effect.

These comments indicate that Protestant theology is changing. Process theologians hope that it will change much more. Any sociohistorical movement changes slowly, and those that deal with matters of ultimate concern may be peculiarly slow. There is the danger that the sense of ultimacy be attached to existing beliefs and practices rather than to the object of ultimate devotion.

Nevertheless, change does occur. Protestantism began as change in Christian teaching based on recursion to biblical authority against the way doctrine and practice had developed in fifteen hundred years of tradition. Protestants emphasized the fallibility of human interpretation of God's revelation. Calvinists, especially, insisted that reformation could not be once-for-all; it must be a continuing process. Because the authority of the Bible exceeds for Protestants the authority of any interpretation of the Bible or particular philosophical commitment, changes in biblical interpretation call for changes in doctrine and practice. To whatever extent a concern for creation as a whole is found in the Bible, in principle Protestants must repent of their neglect of this concern. That repentance is far advanced.

From the perspective of process theology, change needs to be embraced on other grounds as well. The Bible itself points us forward to new truth. When Christians encounter wisdom in any source, we should be open to learning. This means that we should assimilate what the natural sciences have to teach us, modifying our teaching accordingly. On the whole, we have done this. It means that we should be open to new understanding coming from the psychological and sociological fields, and changes have occurred in these areas as well. Recently we have been deeply challenged by recognizing that our inherited perspective, including most of that in the Bible, is masculine, and we have been seeking to open ourselves to the different sensibility and insight of women. This has proved more controversial, but much has happened nevertheless. We are now also challenged to learn from other religious traditions as well, including the primal ones.

Much of the change we need in relation to the understanding of the natural world is called for by the Biblical texts themselves. But indirectly the Bible calls us to learn about this from the natural sciences, sociology and psychology, feminists, and other religious traditions as well. To limit ourselves to the biblical texts and what tradition has drawn from them is not truly faithful to the Bible.

PROCESS THEOLOGY AND DEEP ECOLOGY

Theological environmentalism cannot be placed simply under the heading of "shallow ecology." That is usually understood as dealing with particular practical ecological problems in terms of inherited anthropocentric categories. The recognition of the importance of rethinking our intellectual, cultural, and religious heritage is central to current Protestant thought about creation. In this sense it is a form of "deep ecology," and this is especially true of process ecological theology.

Nevertheless, there are tendencies among those who identify themselves as "deep ecologists" that separate Protestant theology, including Protestant process theology, from them. I will identify five such tendencies and indicate why and how Protestant ecological theology, and especially its process form, moves in a different direction. Whether this theology is not "deep ecology" at all, or is a different form of "deep ecology," is a terminological question. But for simplicity's sake, I will use the term "deep ecology" to mean what those who founded this tradition have meant by it.

Writing as a Protestant theologian, I will not only describe the Protestant view but make a case for it. That does not mean that on all points of difference I believe Protestants to be right and deep ecologists wrong. Instead, I believe that there is a place for both approaches and hope for mutual respect.

First, those who have led in defining "deep ecology" often direct attention away from issues of justice and liberation in human relations. Protestant Christians, immersed in the Bible, cannot accept this. Especially from the perspective of process theologians, our concerns can and should extend far beyond the human species to the well-being of God's creation as a whole. But process theologians agree with other Protestants that this must not be allowed to reduce concern for human beings individually and collectively. And concerns for human beings focus on those people who are least able to meet their own needs.

My intention here is not to accuse all deep ecologists of indifference to human suffering and oppression. It is only to say that what is called "deep ecology" usually begins with the condition of the earth and moves from that to the well-being of the human species and its members. This is a rational approach to be fully respected. But it is not the Christian one.

Christians typically begin with the "neighbor" who is in need. A great deal of Christian love is expressed in a very individualistic way. But many Christians have recognized that the condition of the neighbor is bound up with wider systems—political, social, and economic. Accordingly, a great deal of attention is paid also to these systems.

All of this remained, until quite recently as we have seen, limited to the human scene. Prior to the repentance described above, Christian habits, and especially Protestant habits, and still more emphatically those habits informed by Kantian philosophy, paid very little attention to the wider ecological system in which the neighbor lives. For Protestants in general, and process theologians in particular, the shift to include this system as well takes place as an extension of neighbor love.

When this occurs, two positions are possible. Christians may recognize the importance of the ecological system because of human dependence on it. This was all that was necessarily implied when the World Council of Churches affirmed that Christians should be just as concerned that human societies be sustainable as that they be participatory and just. This is the dominant position among those for whom the influence of Kant, consciously or unconsciously, remains strong.

But Christians may recognize that the other creatures that make up the ecosystem are also valuable in themselves and to God, and this is especially emphasized by process theologians. The importance of the well-being of nonhuman creatures is, then, not simply because of their contribution to human beings. This is implied by the shift in World Council rhetoric from the sustainability of human societies to the integrity of creation. For example, the extinction of species is now opposed not only because something of value to human beings may be lost but also because each species is of value to its own members, and each species is of value to God. This leads in the direction of deep ecology.

Nevertheless, the heavy emphasis on humanity remains. The full slogan of the World Council since 1982 has been "peace, justice, and the integrity of creation." The Council knows that sometimes there are tensions among these goals. Efforts to attain justice often disrupt peace, when "peace" means the absence of violent conflict. Virtually all Christians affirm that every effort should be made to attain justice through peaceful means, but most Christians recognize that there are times when violence in the cause of justice is preferable to real alternatives.

More directly relevant to this essay is the fact that there can be tensions between the quest for justice for human beings and the quest to provide for other creatures. For example, to maintain habitat for African animals, poor human beings are sometimes denied the use of lands they need. There are also conflicts between those animal rights organizations that oppose experimentation on animals and supporters of medical research seeking a cure for AIDS by means of such research.

The natural response among Christians is to seek some way of meeting both sets of needs rather than choosing between them. But if a choice must be made, one will expect most Protestants to come down quite consistently for the poor and for sick human beings. Commitment to the human neighbor who is in need has not been significantly compromised by commitment to the integrity of creation.

There are, thus, times when there are tensions between the short-term good of human beings and the health of the natural environment. Tradeoffs are inevitable and, at least for now, most Christians remain sufficiently anthropocentric that they will tend to support meeting the immediate human need. From the perspective of process theology, the dominant Protestant community needs to move farther and become more explicit that human beings should be prepared to make sacrifices for the sake of other animals, but we agree that we should take care that these sacrifices not be imposed on those human beings who are already poor and powerless.

On the other hand, it is a serious mistake to set up the well-being of humanity and that of other creatures dualistically. Far more often, what damages one damages the other, and what helps one helps the other. If we are concerned with the future of the natural world, we must be concerned with peace as well as with justice and participation in human affairs, and if we are concerned with peace as well as justice and participation in human affairs, we must be concerned with the health of the natural world.

For process theologians even that terminology separates humanity too far from nature. It reflects the influence of Kantian dualism rather than deeper Christian traditions. The biblical language of creation unites the human and the natural, and it is with the whole of creation, with its integrity, that we are now to concern ourselves.

Second, whereas Christians see humanity as part of creation, we still see human beings as playing a distinctive role within that creation. The distinction between human beings and the remainder of creation—for convenience I will call it "nature" despite the misleading impression that human beings are not part of nature—continues to be important not only because of our special concern for justice and liberation but also because of our need to reflect about our distinctive role. Deep ecology seems to view the human species as simply one among others in a way that minimizes consideration of its special responsibility for the whole.

Of course, the human species is, for Protestant theology as well, one among others. But for those shaped by the Bible, it is that species that plays the dominant role in the whole and which, therefore, has responsibility for the well-being of the whole. The reality of dominance seems to us confirmed by the actual situation. Indeed, the totality of our dominion over most other species has been realized in truly disturbing ways. Habitable wilderness exists today only where human beings determine that some fragments should survive. The very fact that we have exercised our dominion so disastrously calls us now to exercise it responsibly—not to suppose that we do not have dominion.

Deep ecologists rightly point out that talk of dominion has been part and parcel of an attitude and sensibility that has done enormous harm. They seek a different spirituality, one in which ideas of management and control would be replaced by the sense of connectedness, kinship, and reverence for otherness. They prize letting things be rather than changing them into what suits us. From the point of view of process theologians, they are correct in all this.

But Christians cannot accept the conclusions that deep ecologists sometimes draw from this. The fate of the earth in fact lies in human hands. It is certainly true that unless there are basic changes in the way human beings behave, we are destined for a terrible end. It is also true that this change can only occur if deep-seated attitudes, or our basic spirituality, change. But the change should not be away from responsibility for what happens.

One important way of exercising dominion is to withdraw from controlling presence where that is possible—to leave wilderness alone. But that is an exercise of human responsibility, not the abandonment of the dominant role for which deep ecologists sometimes seem to call. To us it seems that we can counter the still dominant exploitative mentality, if at all, only with a mentality of responsible concern.

Third, deep ecology often speaks of nature or the earth as sacred. Process theologians affirm that against the treatment of other creatures as simply means to human ends this is a valuable reaction. We believe also that for those Protestants who, under the influence of Enlightenment humanism, have become accustomed to speaking of human personality as sacred, this extension of sacredness to all creation is salutary. It is wrong to draw a line between the human and the natural that is supposed also to separate the sacred and the profane. If we connect the sacred with intrinsic value and the profane with instrumental value, we can recognize in this distinction the anthropocentrism that has had such devastating effects. Hence, process theologians can celebrate the growing sense of the sacredness of all creatures.

Nevertheless, that language is, from a historic Protestant perspective, dangerously misleading. Speaking rigorously, the line between the sacred and the profane is better drawn between God and creatures. To place any creatures on the sacred side of the line is to be in danger of idolatry. For many Protestants, including process theologians, the right way to speak is incarnational, immanental, or sacramental. God is present in the world—in every creature. But no creature is divine. Every creature has intrinsic value, but to call it sacred is in danger of attributing to it absolute value. That is wrong.

Deep ecologists in general are not theists. Indeed, with much justification, they see most forms of theism as having directed attention away from the natural world and focused it on the relation of the individual believer to a transcendent Other. The concentration of the sacred in this Other is a major cause of the disenchantment of nature and hence of its ruthless exploitation. The denial of this transcendent God opens the way to the renewed sacralization of nature which inhibits human arrogance in relation to it.

Here, too, the position of deep ecologists is deserving of full respect. Their picture of what has happened and what can happen is correct. But the move they make is one that Protestants, including those in the process traditions, cannot follow. And from the Protestant perspective, it is a dangerous one.

Once something is viewed as sacred, judgments of relative value or importance cease to function. Within Protestantism, we have seen something like this in the thought of Albert Schweitzer. His doctrine of reverence for life precluded any judgments with respect to the relative value of one form of life and another. On the other hand, in practice he made such judgments all the time. He killed bacteria for the sake of the health of his human patients. To nurse a bird back to health, he fed it fish. In these acts he expressed normal Protestant values.

But for most Protestants, and certainly for process theologians, there is an advantage in articulating the principles by which one acts so that they can be criticized and discussed. One problem with having declared human life to be sacred is that it has made very difficult the many decisions that have to be made in the area now known as bioethics. If all human life is sacred, how can we articulate the basis on which we make decisions about which life to save when we must choose?

It seems better to many Protestants, and certainly to process theologians, to affirm that only God is sacred but that God's Spirit is present in every creature. All creatures have intrinsic value. In addition, they have value for God and for other creatures. Recognizing this has the effect of checking our casual exploitation of others for narrowly selfish purposes. But it also allows us to think about the intrinsic value of different creatures, their contributions to the divine life, and their importance in the biosystem as a whole. On the basis of such reflection, we can decide which of the many needs we confront are of greatest urgency.

Fourth, in reaction to anthropocentrism, deep ecology typically opposes all judgments about gradations of value. These gradations are often defined in terms of a hierarchy of value. Hierarchy is associated with power or authority as well as with gradation; so the use of that language has further intensified the opposition of deep ecologists. As one who has sometimes spoken of a hierarchy of value, I acknowledge the appropriateness of the deep ecology critique.

It would be too much to say that Protestants as a whole or through their institutional expressions have dealt clearly with this question. My comments here, more than elsewhere in this essay, project the implication of positions taken rather than explicit affirmations. Furthermore, they do so from the perspective of a process theologian.

Process theologians cannot give up the affirmation of gradations of value. All creatures have intrinsic value, but some have greater intrinsic value than others. That is to say, the inner life of some creatures is more complex, deeper, and richer than that of others. More positive value is lost and more suffering is inflicted in killing a whale than in destroying some plankton. Of course, this is a human judgment, but that does not make it anthropocentric in the way we should avoid. We are called to exercise our best judgment about the consequences of our actions in relation to other creatures.

The charge of anthropocentrism here is often supported by pointing out that we typically judge that creatures more like ourselves have greater value than those that differ greatly from us. There is truth in this account of how judgments work out, but similarity is not as such the basis of judgment. We do know that human beings are capable of remarkable scope and depth of experience, and that, accordingly, human experience often has great intrinsic value. Other creatures that are like us in relevant respects, we judge, also have rich experience and thus great intrinsic value.

But our judgment is about the probable richness of experience of other animals, not about the similarity of their experience to our own.

Because of our limited imagination, this judgment may be distorted by similarities. We may underestimate the richness of a dolphin's experience and overestimate that of a monkey because the latter is more like us. But this would be an error in judgment; it is not built into the basis for judgment.

Furthermore, we judge God's experience to be incomparably richer than our own. If judgments of the intrinsic value of the experience of other animals is to be made on resemblance, it is resemblance to God's perfect inclusion of all that is and creative integration of this into a new whole. An experience that includes more of the world is of greater value than one that includes less. One that integrates this complexity into an effective unity is better than one that is left in discord.

I have chosen the example of whales and plankton so as to bring out a second important point. Intrinsic value is quite different from value for others or for the whole. If whales become extinct, life in the ocean will continue. They play a role in the ecology of the seas, but it is not an essential role. If plankton disappear, the whole system will collapse.

In addition to this practical interdependence, in which some creatures and species are more important than others for the well-being of the whole, there is an ontological interdependence. Each of us is constituted by relationships to all others. Even when we know nothing about the others, what happens to them affects us in some way, however slight. We are, in Paul's language, members one of another.

There are other value considerations as well. For process theologians diversity is valuable in itself. Thus, the loss of a species is important beyond the loss of individual members or the damage to the ecosystem. This is true because the diversity of creatures contributes to some extent to the richness of the experience of all, but decisively and universally to the all-inclusive divine experience.

My point is that responsible action for the sake of the creation must be based on complex judgments of value. These are inhibited by the refusal to acknowledge gradations of value. Since as Protestants we are committed to accepting responsibility for what happens—this is sometimes called stewardship—we also need to reflect on the bases on which we make judgments.

Fifth, as a process theologian I find it necessary to address a question on which thus far very few Protestant institutions have spoken clearly. It is the concern for individual animals, especially for those judged to have significant subjective experience.

The World Council language about the integrity of creation translates into recognition that our concern for the well-being of creation should not be simply anthropocentric and that other species are of importance to God. Thus far, however, the Council has not spelled out the implications for concern about the suffering of individual nonhuman animals.

Deep ecologists, also, for the most part do not attend to the question of individual animal suffering. Their concern for the health of the biosystem leads them to accept animal suffering as the natural course of things. That humans share in inflicting suffering on other animals is not of special importance. Interest in "humane" treatment of domesticated animals seems to many deep ecologists to be sentimental. Their concern is directed chiefly to the wild and to how human beings rightly fit into the order of the wild.

As a Protestant process theologian I am critical of both my fellow Protestants and deep ecologists on this score. I share their concern for the system as a whole and the species that make it up. But that is no reason to be indifferent to the vast amount of unnecessary suffering inflicted by human beings on helpless fellow creatures.

If we had to choose between preserving a viable biosphere and reducing the suffering of domesticated animals, I would accept the priority of the former without question. But neglecting an issue because it is not the *most* important one is a serious mistake. From the point of view of a process theologian, the suffering of our fellow creatures, whether human or not, causes suffering to God. This view has good Biblical warrant. To cause unnecessary pain to others, whether they are human or not, is to inflict pain, unnecessarily, both on them and on God. There is nothing sentimental about the commitment to reduce such pain and suffering.

Since the recent move beyond anthropocentrism in Protestant leadership has not yet expressed itself explicitly in concern for the suffering of individual animals, I have not posed this as a conflict between Protestant theology and deep ecology. Nevertheless, there is a difference that is brought out more clearly in the process form of Protestant theology than elsewhere but is implicit in Protestant thought generally.

Protestants emphasize the subjectivity of the other. When one person relates to another, the other is understood not primarily as what appears in one's sense experience of the other but as a partly independent subject of experience—as a thou. How the thou feels is important. Hence, inflicting unnecessary pain and suffering on another individual human being is self-evidently wrong. Even though there are theoretical issues stemming from traditional doctrines of divine impassability, most Protestants understand from the Bible that God cares about this pain and suffering.

When Protestants affirm, with the Bible, that God's care is not for human beings alone, there is a very natural extension of the concern about individual human suffering to those other creatures about whom God cares. Indeed, until this extension is made explicit, one will have to suspect that the grip of anthropocentric thinking has not been fully broken. Furthermore, millions of Protestants have long since made this move and provide much of the support and even leadership of organizations committed to the betterment of the condition of domesticated animals.

Finally, it is noteworthy that an organization such as the Humane Society of the United States, headed by a former Protestant minister, has expanded its concerns and commitments far beyond the humane treatment of domesticated animals. It now places that concern in a wider context. Just as concern for the individual neighbor has led Protestants to systemic analysis; so concern for individual nonhuman animals is leading to such systemic analysis. Thus far I have not seen a similar move from the side of deep ecology to sympathetic interest in animal suffering.

We find it dangerous, also, to react so strongly against anthropocentrism as to minimize the distinctive value of individual human beings. For those informed by the Bible, individual persons have a special preciousness for God and should be held in that way by other human beings. Repentance for destructive anthropocentrism should not be allowed to reduce our sensitive concern for the human neighbor who is in need.

CONCLUSION

All of these qualifications of the basic agreements with deep ecology often lead deep ecologists to reject our position and to hold that it continues to be anthropocentric. This, too, is a matter of definition. As a Protestant process theologian I reject anthropocentrism in the following ways.

1. God cares for all creatures, not just for human beings, and human beings should follow in that universal care.
2. The value of other creatures is not limited to their value for us. Their value for God, for one another, and for themselves is also important. Human values should sometimes be sacrificed for the sake of others.
3. Reality is what it is in itself and not restricted to how it is experienced by human beings.
4. Individual human beings and even humanity as a whole are not self-contained. We are physically and psychically embedded in a matrix

that includes the other creatures. Our relations to them are internal to our being. Destruction and loss anywhere diminishes me.

As a process Protestant theologian, I retain what deep ecologists call anthropocentrism in the following respects.

1. In all probability individual human beings are the greatest embodiments of intrinsic value on the Earth.

2. Human beings have a responsibility for other creatures in a way that is shared by no other species. A great deal depends on how we exercise that responsibility, and that means that we should acknowledge and affirm it as well as repent of the way we have exercised dominion in the past.

3. In order to exercise our responsibility well, we must make judgments of relative value about other creatures. We know these are human judgments, and this knowledge should lead us to be particularly careful not to make the judgments anthropocentrically. At the same time, there is no basis for making these or any other judgments that does not depend on distinctively human experience.

The accent in this essay has been on places at which Protestant theologians, including Protestant process theologians, disagree with what is usually called deep ecology. But from the point of view of those Protestants who are trying to move Protestant practice to catch up with the best Protestant thinking, the work of deep ecologists is to be celebrated and they are to be thanked for their leadership. We Protestants must do our own thinking out of our own heritage. But in doing that we are indebted to the stimulus of those who stand outside our community, who point out our faults, and who provide alternatives that at least on some issues are far ahead of us.

It is important also to recognize that in the broader scene the differences between us are minor in comparison with the agreements. We cannot merge forces; the differences are too great for that. But on most of the issues that face humankind so urgently today, we *can* and should learn to appreciate one another's contributions.

On many fronts, furthermore, we can work together. No one group of those concerned for the fate of the earth has the power to save it. It is far from clear that even if we work together wherever our agreements allow, pooling our resources to accomplish what most needs to be done, we can succeed. But it is very clear that if we fall into academic habits of endless debate, instead of appreciating one another in our differences and supporting one another's efforts when that is possible, the united forces of exploitation will continue to rape the earth.

II

Deep Ecology, Ecofeminism, and the Bible

ROSEMARY RADFORD RUETHER

HIS ESSAY I want to engage in a three-way dialogue or discussion
:ween deep ecology, ecofeminism, and the Bible. In this dialogue I
pe to mediate several key critiques that have taken place between
ree: the ecofeminist charge that deep ecology is uncritical of sex-
nd implicitly androcentric in the way it critiques anthropocen-
; the charge by deep ecologists that the Bible is anthropocentric
promotes human domination over nature; and the differences
g ecofeminists among themselves, specifically between social
minists and essentialist ecofeminists.

DEEP ECOLOGY AND ECOFEMINISM
ON ANTHROPOCENTRISM

ritique by ecofeminists that deep ecologists have been oblivious to
exist structures of domination over nature seems to me correct.[1]
critique is central to the basic premise of ecofeminism. Ecofemi-
is founded on the basic intuition that there is a fundamental con-
on in Western culture, and in patriarchal cultures generally,
en the domination of women and the domination of nature, both
rally/symbolically and socioeconomically.
mong Western ecofeminists this connection between domination
men and domination of nature is generally made, first, on the cul-
symbolic level. One charts the way in which patriarchal culture

229

has defined women as being "closer to nature," or as being on the nature side of the nature-culture split. This is shown in the way in which women have been identified with the body, earth, sex, the flesh in its mortality, weakness and "sin-proneness," vis-à-vis a construction of masculinity identified with spirit, mind, and sovereign power over both women and nature.

A second level of ecofeminist analysis goes beneath the cultural-symbolic level, and explores the socioeconomic underpinnings of how the domination of women's bodies and women's work interconnects with the exploitation of land, water, and animals. How have women as a gender group been colonized by patriarchy as a legal, economic, social, and political system? How does this colonization of women's bodies and work function as the invisible substructure for the extraction of natural resources? This socioeconomic form of ecofeminist analysis then sees the cultural-symbolic patterns by which both women and nature are inferiorized and identified with each other as an ideological superstructure by which the system of economic and legal domination of women, land, and animals are justified and made to appear "natural" and inevitable within a total patriarchal cosmovision.

To fail to see this connection between domination of women and domination of nature, and to speak of "anthropocentrism" as if this were a generic universal attributable equally to all human beings in all classes, races, and cultures and both genders equally is a fundamentally analytical error that prevents a clear understanding of both the problem and the ways to begin to overcome it. All humans do not dominate nature equally, view themselves as over nature or benefit from such domination. Rather, elite males, in different ways in different cultures, create hierarchies over subjugated humans and nonhumans: men over women, whites over blacks, ruling class over slaves, serfs, and workers.

These structures of domination between humans mediate the domination of elite males over nonhuman nature. Women are subjugated to confine them to the labor of reproduction, childcare, and work that turns the raw materials of nature into consumer and market goods, while being denied access to the education, culture, control of property and political power of the male elite, identified with "human" transcendence over nature.

This means women's inferiority to men is modelled after the inferiorization of nonhuman nature to men. The term *man* is an androcentric false generic which really means the elite male as normal human, with women as lesser human or subhuman, identified as standing between mind and body, human and animal, closer to the lower pole in this dualism than the male.

owever, ecofeminists sometimes engage in their own version of
generics by assuming that the primary or only important division
hierarchy of elite male domination over subjugated humans and
nature is gender division. This is not to say that the sexist division
crucially important. Much of the symbolic structures of domina-
f nature, as well as their social structuring, is built on male domi-
n of women. But ecofeminist analysis needs to be integrated with
f class and race.

ooking at subjugated races and classes, as well as women, as being
nferiorized animals is central to cultural symbols of domination.
as only to think of the great variety of negative animal names
to women: chicks, bitches, nags, sows, etc. But subjugated races
asses are equally inferiorized by identifying them with inferior-
nimals: apes, mules, dogs, etc. This is not simply cultural "preju-
Rather, it signals the right to use these subjugated people as one
l use the subjugated animals, as beasts of burden, as sexual dan-
to be suppressed, as cur to be kicked around, as "dumb" animal
incapable of education and so need not be provided with it.

e also have categories of nature that we regard as demonic and
ng to be destroyed; such as lice, insects, cockroaches, germs, ver-
lirt, or filth. Categories of humans who are demonized, thereby
ing their destruction, are named through analogy to these danger-
rms of nature. The rhetoric of homophobes against homosexuals,
is against Jews, of Christians against heretics, of nations at war
t the members of the enemy nation regularly employ this lan-
thereby justifying the extermination of these despised "others."

elieve we cannot really deal with the full ramifications of male
paration from and domination over nature unless we deal with
complex ways these male elites position themselves over against
ated groups of humans, justify both their exploitative use and
of them and ultimately their right to destroy them when they are
s dangerous to their power. It is not enough to withdraw such
for other humans, We have to deal with the interconnection with
nigration of nature; our contempt, fear, and loathing for the finite
realm and its animal populations, including insects and bacteria.
too are our ancestor, our kin, and part of our own organisms.

DEEP ECOLOGY AND THE BIBLE

cologists have been influenced by Lynn White's famous essay,
listorical Roots of Our Ecologic Crisis,"[2] which identified biblical

teaching on dominion as the key source of Western arrogance and pre-
sumed right to dominate nature. White himself did not dismiss the
Christian tradition altogether, but ended by lifting up what he saw as
some alternative traditions in Christianity, particularly Franciscan nature mysticism, that can counteract the tradition of separation and domination. Some deep ecologists have concluded that the Bible and the
Christian tradition are totally anti-ecological and need to be discarded in
order to create an alternative ecological spirituality, although Bill Devall
and George Sessions included some possible positive contributions of
Christianity in their book.[3] Ecofeminists have often carried this critique
farther, by showing the roots of both male domination and domination
of nature in the Bible. The Bible is seen as the key source of this interconnection of the two dominations; reverence for the Bible the chief
means of perpetuating them.

I don't disagree with these insights into the negative aspects of the
biblical tradition. Indeed my own book, *Gaia and God*, was aimed at
showing how deep these roots are in the biblical tradition, in Mediterranean cultures before the biblical tradition, and in the Greek tradition,
all of which shaped Christianity. But, like Lynn White, I see counter-
vailing traditions not only in an occasional figure, such as Francis of Assisi, but in the Bible itself.[4]

The biblical and Christian traditions do have elements that sacral-
ize domination and negation of body, earth, and woman. But they also
struggled against what they perceived to be injustice and evil and
sought to vindicate the goodness of creation and the body and their ultimate redemption against extreme dualists that saw in the material
world only the manifestation of the demonic. We can reclaim these
more holistic traditions to ground an ecojustice vision of redemption.

Let me be clear about what I am *not* saying by such affirmations. I
am not saying that the biblical and Christian tradition is the sole source
of religious truth, the only way of access to true divinity, and therefore
only here is religious truth to be found. The great Asian religious traditions, as well as the unjustly scorned nature religions of indigenous
peoples, have precious resources that need to be cultivated. An ecological crisis of global proportions can mean nothing less than a true dialogue and mutual enrichment of all spiritual traditions.

Secondly, I am not saying that these biblical and Christian traditions are adequate. They need critique and reinterpretation. But I suspect that this is true of all human spiritual heritages. The global
ecological crisis is a new situation. Until now humans have assumed
that nature's power far transcended puny humans. Even biblical apocalyptic thought did not put the power to destroy the earth in human

. The notion that our power has grown so great that we must now
:sponsibility for preserving the biotic diversity of rain forests and
one layer of the stratosphere was unimaginable in past human
ence.

though biblical and Christian tradition is not the only source for
;ical theology and ethics, it is a source that must be central for
of Christian background. First, there are magnificent themes here
»ire us. Secondly, Christian people and their institutions are a ma-
rld religion and world power. They have been a major cause of
»blems. But they will not be mobilized to conversion unless they
id the mandates for it in those traditions that carry meaning and
:ity for them. Finally, I suspect that none of us work in a healthy
we operate merely out of alienation from our past. We need new
s. But new visions have power when they are not rootless, but are
enced as gathering up and transforming our heritage.

ie ecological theologies of Christian inspiration at this time seem
into two different types, which I call the covenantal and the sacra-
l. Protestants have generally been stronger on the covenantal tra-
that searched for an ecological ethics, while Catholics have
l to stress the sacramental tradition.[5] My view is that these two
ons, covenantal and sacramental, are complementary.

useable ecological theology, spirituality, and ethic must intercon-
iese two traditions. Each supplies elements the other lacks. In the
intal tradition we find the basis for a moral relation to nature and
another that mandates patterns of right relation, enshrining these
elations in law as the final guarantee against abuse. In the sacra-
l tradition we find the heart, the ecstatic experience of I and Thou,
rpersonal communion, without which moral relationships grow
ess and spiritless.

ie notion that the Bible is antinature comes in part from the read-
the Bible popularized by German scholarship of the late nine-
and early twentieth centuries. This scholarship read into the
heir own sharp dualism of history against nature, setting the true
f history against the gods of nature. Although the biblical view of
<presses a transformation of the way God is seen as related to na-
iere is also a lively sense of God's relation to and presence in na-
iat was overlooked in this stress on the God of History "against"

though God is seen as "creating" nature, rather than being an ex-
on of it, nevertheless the nature God creates is alive and enters
/ely relation to God. God delights in the creatures God creates,
e creatures return this rejoicing in joy and praise. Divine blessing

inundates the earth as rain, and the mountains skip like a calf, the hills gird themselves with joy, the valleys deck themselves with grain; they shout and sing together for joy.

This language is typical of Hebrew Scripture. There is no reason to write it off as "mere poetic metaphor," a judgment that reflects the modern loss of the experience of I-Thou relation to what we see around us. The experience of nature, of fields, mountains, streams, birds, and animals, in Hebrew sensibility, while not seen as "divine," is still very much animate, interacting as living beings with their Creator.

The modern nature-history split distorts the biblical view. In the biblical view, all things, whether they happen as human wars and struggles for liberation in and between cities or whether they happen as rain that brings abundant harvests or as drought that brings disaster to the fields upon which humans depend, are "events." In all such events, whether in cities or in fields, Hebrews saw the presence and work of God, as blessing or as judgment.

All such events have moral meaning. If enemies overwhelm the walls of the city or floods break down irrigation channels and destroy the fruits of human labor, God is acting in judgment upon human infidelity. When humans repent and return to fidelity to God, then justice and harmony will reign, not only in the city, but in the relations between humans and animals, the heavens and the earth. The heavens will rain sweet water, and the harvests will come up abundantly. Thus, what modern Western thought has split apart as "nature" and as "history," Hebrew thought sees as one reality fraught with moral warning and promise.

There are problems in reading moral meaning and divine will into events in "nature." We would not wish to see in every flood, drought, volcanic eruption, and tornado the work of divine judgment. But when destructive floods rush down the Himalayan mountains, carrying all before them into the Pakistan delta, or drought sears African lands, we are right to recognize the consequences of human misuse of the land, stripping the forest cover that held back the torrential rains, and overgrazing the semi-arid African soils.

In these disasters today we have to recognize a consequence of human culpability and a call to rectify how we use the land and how we relate to the indigenous people who depend on these lands. As human power expands, colonizing more and more of the planet's natural processes, the line between what was traditionally called "natural evil," and which was ethically neutral, and what should be called sin; that is, the culpable abuse of human freedom and power, also shifts. Hebrew moral sensibility, in which relation to God is the basis for both justice in

ɾ and prosperity in nature, while disobedience to God's com-
; of right relation brings both violence to society and disaster to
, takes on a new dimension of moral truth.

ɨbrew genius saw divine commands of right relation between hu-
ɛings and to the rest of the creation enshrined in a body of law.
ɔf this law did not seem relevant to Christians, who believed that
ɩew relation to God through Christ allowed them to discard a
ɩeal of it. But some elements of this legal tradition take on new
ɩg today, particularly the tradition of sabbatical legislation. These
 laws that mandate periodic rest and restoration of relations be-
humans, animals, and land.

ɨbrew theology of creation rejects the aristocratic split between a
-class divinity and a humanity that serves this divinity through
ɩbor, which was typical of Ancient Near Eastern mythology. In
s God is described as both working and resting and thereby set-
ɛ pattern for all humans and their relations to land and animals
ɩovenant of creation. This pattern of work and rest is set through
 of concentric cycles, of seven days, seven years, and seven times
ɾears.

 the seventh day of each week, not only the farmer, but also his
s and animal work force, are to rest. "On the seventh day you
ɪst, so that your ox and your donkey may have relief, and your
ɔrn slave and your resident alien shall be refreshed" (Exodus
In the seventh year attention is given to the rights of the poor
ʋild animals, as well as to the renewal of the land itself. "For six
ɔu shall sow your land and gather its yield; but the seventh year
 fallow, so the poor of your people may eat, and what they leave
d animals may eat. You shall do the same with your vineyard
ɩr olive orchard" (Exodus 23:10–11). Slaves are to be set free and
; to rest, as well.

ally in the Jubilee year, the fiftieth year, there is to be a great
ɩon of all relationships. Those who have lost their land through
ɛ to be restored to their former property. Debts are to be forgiven,
ɩtives freed. The earth is to lie fallow, and animals and humans
ɛst. All the accumulated inequities of the past seven times seven
ɩetween humans in debt, loss of land and enslavement, and to
n overuse of land and animals, are to be rectified. All is to be re-
ɔ right balance.

; vision of periodic redemption and restoration of right relation
ɛs Jesus' language in the Lord's Prayer. It is a vision of redemp-
ɾe compatible with finitude and human limits than the radical vi-
 the millennium and the once-for-all apocalyptic end of history

through which recent biblical scholarship has read the meaning of the
term "Kingdom of God." Modern revolutionary thinkers would have
done better if they had taken the Jubilee, rather than the millennium and
the apocalyptic future, as their model of historical change. Periodic renewal and restoration of right relations is a more doable and less dangerous vision than final perfection.

The sacramental tradition of Catholic Christianity complements the
covenantal tradition. It starts with the community as a living whole, not
only the human community, but, first of all, the cosmic community. The
human being not only mirrors cosmic community as micro to macrocosm, but also intercommunes with the whole cosmic body. God is seen
not only as over against and "making" this cosmic body, but also as immanent within it. The visible universe is the emanational manifestation
of God, God's sacramental body. God is incarnate in and as the cosmic
body of the universe, although not reduced to it.

Hellenistic Judaism developed this vision of divine Wisdom as the
secondary manifestation of God and God's agent in creating the cosmos, sustaining it, and bringing all things into harmonious unity with
God. Strikingly, Hebrew thought always saw this immanent manifestation of God as female.

> Wisdom . . . pervades and permeates all things. . . . She rises from
> the power of God, the pure effluence of the glory of the Almighty.
> . . . She is the brightness that streams from everlasting light, the
> flawless mirror of the active power of God and the image of his
> goodness. She is one but can do all things, herself unchanging, she
> makes all things new; age after age she enters into holy souls and
> makes them God's friends and prophets. . . . She spans the world in
> power from end to end and orders all things benignly. (Wisdom of
> Solomon: chapter 8)

In the New Testament this cosmogonic Wisdom of God is identified
with Christ. Jesus as the Christ not only embodies, in crucified form, the
future king and redeemer, but also incarnates the cosmogonic principle
through which the cosmos is created, sustained, redeemed, and reconciled with God. In this cosmological Christology, found in the Preface to
the Gospel of John, in the first chapter of Hebrews and in some Pauline
letters, Christ is the beginning and end of all things.

In the letter to the Colossians, the divine Logos that dwelt in Christ
is the same Logos that founded and has sustained the cosmos from the
beginning. "All things have been created through him . . . and in him all
things hold together." This same Logos, through Christ and the Church,
is now bringing the whole cosmos to union with God. "In him all the

s of God was pleased to dwell and through him God is pleased to
ile himself with all things, whether on earth or in heaven."
is theology sought to synthesize cosmogony and eschatology, and
ogether the Hebrew creational and the Greek emanational views
elation of the divine to the cosmic body. Being and Becoming are
ically interconnected. The visible cosmos was seen as the bodying
f the word and spirit of God and in turn being brought to blessed-
rough communing with its own divine "ground" of being.[6]
claiming the covenantal and sacramental traditions are central to
ved understanding of Christian redemptive hope as encompass-
justice. But this needs to be deeply transformed and developed
edding these insights in contemporary knowledge of earth his-
d ecological crisis. This more developed vision then needs to be
entral to Christian teaching and worship and embodied in its soon.

ECOFEMINISMS: DIFFERENT PERSPECTIVES

canvassed the relation of domination of nature and domination
gated humans, and the contributions of the Bible for an ecojustice
y, I turn now to differences of perspective among ecofeminists
ves. I see a sharp distinction between two lines of thought among
nists, even though they may share many common values.
ial ecofeminists see the woman-nature connection as a social
y constructed by patriarchal culture to justify the ownership of
of both women and the natural world as property. Ecofeminism
deconstructing these dualisms, both in regard to women and in
o nature. This critique of the woman-nature connection as a pa-
l cultural construction needs to be used, not to separate women,
1, from the rest of nature, but to call men as much as women to
ie the myth of separation and learn to commune with nature as
mon biotic community, while respecting trees, lakes, wolves,
id insects as beings with their own distinct modes of life and
être apart from our use of them.[7]
cond line of essentialist ecofeminism agrees that this patriar-
man-nature connection justifies their domination and abuse,
believes that there is a deeper truth that has been distorted by
is some deep positive connection between women and nature.
are the life givers, the nurturers, the ones in whom the seed of
rs. Women were the primary food gatherers, the inventors of
ire. Their bodies are in mysterious tune with the cycles of the

moon and the tides of the sea. It was by experiencing women as life givers, both food providers and birthers of children, that early humans made the female the first image of worship, the Goddess, source of all life. Women need to reclaim this affinity between the sacrality of nature and the sacrality of their own sexuality and life-powers. To return to worship the Goddess as the sacred female is to reconnect with our own deep powers.[8]

I find this exaltation of woman and nature as Great Goddess exciting, but also problematic. There are some women for whom the worship of the Goddess means the reclamation of their own lost powers unjustly stolen from them by patriarchy and patriarchal religion, sometimes excluding men from their circles to focus on the own female-based spirituality. A second approach—more popular with men—sees men as appropriating the Goddess as Divine Feminine, the repressed feminine side of their souls which they must reclaim to midwife themselves into androgynous wholeness. But there is a tendency in these circles to demand that women specialize in the feminine as nurturers of the development of a male-centered androgyny.

These "takes" on the meaning of the Goddess and an alternative matricentric world tell us something about where we are and have come from, but in a way that reduplicates the old patterns that have long underlain and reproduced patriarchy. We are still far from the kind of transformed story that will break the cycle both of female maternalism *and* submission, both of male insecurity *and* retaliatory dominance, and found real partnership.

Most problematic for me, much of Western ecofeminism fails to make real connections between the domination of women and classism, racism, and poverty. Relation with nature is thought of in psycho-cultural terms; rituals of self-blessing of the body, experiencing of the sacrality of the rising moon, the seasons of the year. I don't disvalue such ceremonial reconnecting with our bodies and nature. But I believe they must be connected concretely with the realities of overconsumerism and waste by which the top 20 percent of the world enjoys 82 percent of the wealth while the other 80 percent of the world scrape along with 18 percent, and the lowest 80 percent of the world's population, mostly female and young, starve and die early from poisoned waters, soil, and air.

Western ecofeminists must make concrete connections with women at the bottom of the socioeconomic system. We must recognize the devastation of the earth as an integral part of the appropriation of the goods of the earth by a wealthy minority who can enjoy strawberries in winter winged to their glittering supermarkets by a global food procurement

. while those who pick and pack the strawberries lack the money
id and are dying from pesticide poisoning.
re Western ecofeminists can learn from ecofeminists from Asia,
and Latin America,[9] as well as from the struggles of racial-ethnic
; against environmental racism in the United States and other
ialized countries.[10] While there are many differences among
of these many nonwhite and non-affluent contexts, what seems
>asic is that women in Latin America, Asia, and Africa never
hat the base line of domination of women and of nature is im-
hment; the impoverishment of the majority of local people, par-
y women and children, and the impoverishment of the land.
s connection of women and nature in impoverishment is present
rday concrete realities. It means deforestation and women walk-
ce and three times as far each day gathering wood; it means
t and women walking twice and three times as far each day to
ater back to their houses.
en these women talk about how to heal their people and their land
is impoverishment and poisoning, they talk about how to take
ntrol over their resources from the World Bank and the wealthy
They critique the global system of economic power. They also en-
vays of reclaiming some traditional patterns of care for the earth
igenous forms of spirituality, but in a flexible, pragmatic way.
these traditions are not romanticized. African women also
ow women were limited by pollution taboos that forbade them
o forests and kept them from growing their own trees.[11] They
e pragmatically some of the old customs that cared for the wa-
s, and animals with modern understandings of conservation
al right of women to own land and have equal access to agricul-
edit that have come to them from Western liberalism. They are
l ecumenists who know how to cross cultures, to use whatever
om these many cultures to enhance life for all, particularly for
at the bottom of the society.
re are many groups today that are creating powerful syntheses
1 traditional religions and ecological spirituality and praxis. One
is groups of Catholic nuns, who call themselves "sisters for the
who are melding a Christian sacramental cosmology with the
e story of Brian Swimme and Thomas Berry, and incarnating
on into practices of sustainable agriculture and alternative en-
the lands and institutions that they manage.[12]
ther important example is the African earth-keeping churches in
we who have integrated the Shona traditions of ancestral spirits
nand justice and care for the earth with a vision of Christ as

cosmological creator-redeemer. They have incarnated this vision into earth-keeping eucharists that call for repentance for destruction and pollution of the earth followed by communion and then a dispersal into the area around the liturgy to plant trees and clean up polluted waterways.[13]

A third example is the Buddhist network Alternatives to Consumerism, based in Thailand, who fuse a Buddhist critique of greed, hatred, and delusion with a liberation theology call for social and ecological justice. They use this vision to create local communities that resist deforestation and the destruction of habitats of animals for huge gas line projects.[14]

In all these three examples, not only are ancient religious elements, from one or more traditions, reenvisioned in the light of the ecological challenge, but this vision is being used for concrete action to resist destruction of the earth and to restore healthy communities of humans, animals, and land together.

We need the signs of hope that come to us from these examples, for we are facing a new situation, which humans have never faced before; namely, that human species power, actualized by a dominant class, has grown so great that it may destroy the planetary basis of life for all humans and the nonhuman biosphere. While there is no one tradition that has the whole answer to this crisis, many cultures can provide us with clues to a healing culture.

But even as we develop a global dialogue of spiritualities, we need to remain firmly rooted in concrete and practical struggles for life in solidarity with the women of impoverished lands. We must not forget to keep the reality of these women firmly in our mind's eye, as they hold the child dying of dehydration from polluted water, and trek long hours to fetch basic necessities, and also as they continue to struggle to defend life with a tenacity that refuses to be defeated and celebrate with a fullness of spirit that belies the seeming hopelessness of their situation. Only as we learn to connect both our stories and our struggles, in a concrete and authentic way, with women on the underside of the present systems of power and profit, can we begin to glimpse what an ecofeminist theology and ethic might really be all about.

NOTES

1. For example, Marti Kheel, "Ecofeminism and Deep Ecology: Reflections on Identity and Difference," in *Reweaving the World: The Emergence of Ecofeminism*, ed. Irene Diamond and Gloria Orensten (San Francisco: Sierra

90), 128–137; also Ariel Kay Salleh, "Deeper than Deep Ecology: The
nist Connection," *Environmental Ethics* 6 (1984): 339–345.

Lynn White, "The Historical Roots of our Ecologic Crisis," *Science* 155
h 1967): 1203–1207.

See Bill Devall and George Sessions, *Deep Ecology* (Salt Lake City: Pere-
oks, 1985), 44–48, 90–92.

Rosemary Ruether, *Gaia and God: An Ecofeminist Theology of Earth Heal-
Francisco: Harper, 1992).

For a Protestant covenantal perspective, see Richard Austin, *Hope for
Atlanta: John Knox Press, 1988). For Catholic approaches see Matthew
Coming of the Cosmic Christ* (San Francisco: Harper, 1988), and Thomas
eam of the Earth (San Francisco: Sierra Club, 1988).

For the sacramental tradition as it developed in Christian history and
philosophy, see Ruether, *Gaia and God*, 229–253.

A major example of a social ecofeminist is Ynestra King. See her essay
the Wounds: Feminism, Ecology, and the Nature/Culture Dualism" in
and Orensten, *Reweaving the World*, 106–121, and "The Ecology of Fem-
the Feminism of Ecology," in *Healing the Wounds: The Promise of Ecofem-
Judith Plant (Philadelphia: New Society Publishers, 1989), 18–28.

Charlene Spretnak combines essentialist and social elements in her
her essay, "Ecofeminism: Our Roots and Flowering" in Diamond and
Reweaving the World, 3–14.

ee Rosemary Ruether, *Women Healing Earth: Third World Women on
eminism and Religion* (Maryknoll, NY: Orbis Books, 1996).

ee Benjamin Chavis and Charles Lee, eds., *Toxic Wastes and Race in the
ites* (New York: Commission on Racial Justice: United Church of
37) and Benjamin Goldman and Laura Fitton, *Toxic Wastes and Race Re-
Update of the 1987 Report* (Washington, D.C.: Center for Policy Alter-
94); also George Tinker, "Ecojustice and Justice: An American Indian
e," in *Theology for Earth Community: A Field Guide*, ed. Dieter T. Hessel
ll, NY: Orbis Books, 1996), 143–152.

e the essays by Tumani Mutasa Nyajeka, Sara Mvududu, and Isabel
iri in Ruether, *Women Healing Earth*, 135–171.

e coordinating center for "Sisters of the Earth" is the Sisters of Prov-
Mary of the Woods, Indiana.

e main promoter of the African Earthkeeping Churches is Innus Da-
is article "Church and Ecojustice at the African Grassroots," in *Chris-
Ecology*, ed. Dieter Hessel and Rosemary Ruether (Cambridge:
niversity Press, 1999).

r the Alternatives to Consumerism network, see article by Rosemary
hey Meet to Counter Consumerist Evils," *National Catholic Reporter
1998), 19.

12

Ken Wilber's Critique of Ecological Spirituality

Michael E. Zimmerman

FTER MANY NOTEWORTHY achievements, the environmental movement is being confronted by critics who challenge concepts
whose validity used to be taken for granted by most envi-
talists. First of all, and perhaps most startling, many ecological
ts no longer support the ecosystem model, to which environ-
sts and friendly legislators have long appealed as the scientific
r establishing environmental law and policy. Many ecologists
se their work on population dynamics, which assumes that
ale natural processes are not functions of an overarching "sys-
ut rather are the unintended effects of the decisions made by
ss individual organisms seeking to maximize their fitness. In ad-
o denying that ecosystems exist, these ecologists add that nat-
cesses—far from being characterized by stability, integrity, and
—are characterized by chaos, constant flux, and relative unpre-
ity.[1] Indeed, disaster and violent change—such as hurricanes
est fires—seem to be necessary factors in promoting healthy
Important as these insights about environmental perturbations
ulation dynamics may be, caution must be exercised before ac-
the contention that ecosystem thinking is scientifically impotent
levant to contemporary thinking about ecological issues.
h caution is warranted because, in view of these challenges to
m ecology, some critics of environmentalism are now asking:
is subject to and even benefits from constant flux, should we
nsider environmental policies that were designed to protect

supposedly "fragile" ecosystems from human intervention? Isn't it even possible that human intervention into nature can have unintended consequences that are *beneficial* as well as harmful? Of course, many developers and industrialists raise such questions primarily to justify their own plans to clear cut forests or to increase pollution levels. These days, however, the developers can at least claim to have science on their side, even though ecosystem scientists have scarcely thrown in the towel. Because of the enormous stakes involved in this shift away from ecosystem ecology, some environmentalists have been scrambling to find ways to rethink their own positions in light of that shift.[2]

A second challenge is directed at the presupposition that ecological problems are very serious and growing worse. A spate of recent books and articles have contested the gloom-and-doom projections that have characterized the environmental movement since the 1960s.[3] Perhaps the Cold War's end, which lifted the "nuclear shadow" that had loomed over two generations, helps to explain a growing sense of optimism about environmental prospects, at least in some areas. Of course, *some* optimistic pronouncements are plainly part of a politically inspired anti-environmental backlash. Still, lay people without the time or expertise needed to assess the claims made by scientists representing environmental optimism, on the one hand, and environmental pessimism, on the other, face a difficult challenge when it comes to making a decision about the current environmental situation. For better or worse, many people are as skeptical about the claims of the Sierra Club as they are about the claims of Exxon.

These days, however, even well-known environmentalists such as Mark Sagoff argue we are *not* running out of raw materials, food, timber, or energy.[4] As he notes, many environmentalists have simply not understood the extent to which market forces and human inventiveness either develop new ways of extracting/growing needed materials, or else find alternatives to materials that are becoming too expensive. Furthermore, far from requiring a decrease in wealth and material consumption, environmental well-being would seem to require an increase in such consumption on the part of underdeveloped countries. As wealth and consumption increase, in part because oppressive regimes are overthrown, human population growth wanes and the demand for environmental protection (including preservation of animal habitat) waxes. These more optimistic assessments have the virtue of inspiring hope for the future. Nevertheless, many environmentalists insist that a future resulting from the combined consequences of economic globalization and human population growth will scarcely be benign.

ıddition to the challenge to ecosystem ecology, and the challenge ımistic assessments of the environmental situation, yet a third tual challenge faces the environmental movement. This chal- he subject of the present essay, is directed at those radical envi- ıtalists, including some deep ecologists and ecofeminists, who that only a recovery of archaic and/or archetypal beliefs, in- ; the sacredness of Gaia or Mother Earth, can forestall ecological ıphe. In what follows, I will analyze these environmentalists in ıf the writings of Ken Wilber, one of the leading transpersonal s. Wilber believes that today's ecological problems are in part ıms of a spiritual crisis, but also holds that spiritually-oriented :ology (SDE) may not provide the understanding of spirit, hu- ıd, and nature necessary for resolving global ecological prob- t first glance, the issue involved in this third challenge may seem nificant than the issues involved in the other two challenges. I 'ith Wilber, however, that restoring a place for spirituality in the ıdern world is in fact a crucial ingredient in dealing with the personal, social, cultural, and political problems created by ıity. The question is: what kinds of spirituality are most appro- t this moment?

ny spiritually-oriented deep ecologists (SDEs) explain the eco- :risis as the failure of modern people to revere the sacredness of ' The West in particular is said to be governed by an arrogant an- 'entrism, subject-object or humanity-nature dualism, and a con- ;t mentality, which act in concert to disclose nature as nothing ⁊ material for human ends. Some environmentalists maintain ransformation of Christianity would help solve the ecological ut many others contend that Christianity is anthropocentric and :hal, hence, profoundly implicated in Western "man's" attempt inate nature.⁶ Many SDEs maintain that because modern ideals gress" have justified the destruction of nature as well as the ıtion of women, nonwhites, and poor white males, Western must abandon his anthropocentric pretensions and enter into a ıious and respectful relationship with Gaia, understood some- ; the interrelated whole of ecosystemic processes, and at other ; the all-inclusive and sacred Earth Mother. Ostensibly, because peoples were more in tune with the sacred mysteries of nature, 'ing archaic beliefs and practices might enable modern people to ⁊ir dualistic-anthropocentric attitudes, restore contact with the 'orces of nature, and begin to behave in ways that promote eco- ıealth, social harmony, and personal well-being.

Although not a major current in contemporary life, eco-paganism appeals to a number of people who have lost faith both in traditional religions and in the modern world view. There is no denying that modernity has created many problems, ranging from nuclear weapons and ecologically destructive industries, to personal meaninglessness and social nihilism. Despite these drawbacks, modernity has also made important political, scientific, and economic gains for great numbers of people. My own experience with interpreting Heidegger's thought and its relation to National Socialism has made me particularly sensitive to the dangers of antimodernist philosophical and/or spiritual movements.[7] Antimodernist attitudes discernible in some eco-paganism have been criticized as reactionary by modernist ideologues, liberals and socialists alike, who recall that National Socialism was in part a neo-pagan revival and a radical "green" movement, which took dreadful steps to maintain the purity of German "blood and soil." Moreover, Murray Bookchin has castigated deep ecologists, ecofeminists, and others for celebrating a mystical, neo-pagan spirituality, which in its American guise is largely ignorant of the green dimension of National Socialism.[8] Bookchin acknowledges the positive achievements of modernity, even while criticizing it for tolerating hierarchical organizations that run counter to its own emancipatory agenda. Unfortunately, because he has no sympathy for genuine spiritual concerns, included those correctly intuited by SDEs, neither Wilber nor I find his critique of eco-paganism satisfactory.

In my view, a critical appraisal of SDE must take seriously its spiritual dimension. First of all, such an appraisal would agree that there are serious (though, I would hope, not insurmountable) environmental problems, which arise in part because modern "man" is alienated from and exhibits an arrogant, ruthless attitude toward nature, corporeality, emotions, and the female. This appraisal would also hold that modernity's interrelated ecological, social, cultural, economic, and political problems can be resolved by the further development of consciousness, although materialist modernity itself cannot adequately account for consciousness. Having acknowledged all this, the appraisal would express concern that the spiritual cosmology of *some* (by no means all) SDEs is misguided, incomplete, and potentially dangerous: *misguided*, because it tends to regard the Divine as wholly immanent in natural phenomena (the sacred "web of life"), thereby overlooking the transcendent aspect of the Divine; *incomplete*, because it fails to appreciate humankind's role in the cosmic evolutionary process by which the Divine manifests itself as nature and then recovers itself by coming to consciousness through various creatures; and

ally *dangerous*, because at times it involves antimodernist sen-
; that fail to appreciate the positive political and material ac-
;hments of modernity.

ι Wilber's cosmology seeks to preserve the achievements of
lity, while simultaneously criticizing its undeniable shortcom-
preover, he acknowledges the genuine spiritual thirst and eco-
concerns of SDEs, while emphasizing the need for a more
e understanding of "spirit." Perhaps the most striking (and con-
al) aspect of Wilber's critique of SDE is his claim that it exhibits
mensional, "flatland" ontology that has much in common with
ernity of which radical environmentalism is otherwise so criti-
)er's criticism of SDEs "retro-romanticism" is sometimes quite
Although I myself prefer that he would use a kinder, gentler
he maintains that his cutting remarks are motivated by his con-
: some SDEs inadvertently impede environmentalism. They do
; view, by promoting views that are so problematic and politi-
pect, that mainstream thinkers and actors can readily dismiss
t modernity has serious spiritual shortcomings, and that such
lings play a role in generating ecological problems.

:, I should like immediately to emphasize that there are SDEs
ee that the Divine involves both an immanent and a transcen-
tension. Some of these SDEs, including deep ecologists and
ists, as well as thinkers from outside these traditions, have im-
nsights that need to be widely understood. Instead of dismiss-
SDEs as naive and dangerous, as Wilber often does, I believe
ire respectful dialogue is called for. Despite the overall impor-
lis spiritual cosmology, Wilber's critical analysis of spiritually-
deep ecology is marred by a tendency to depict it with a broad
it blurs valid distinctions among various instances of deep
:cofeminism, neo-paganism, and so on.

:r's own version of eco-spirituality acknowledges the inherent
ill beings, emphasizes humankind's dependence on the well-
he biosphere, and insists that conscious awareness places hu-
higher on the cosmic "holarchy" than other (known) beings.
d by thinkers such as Plotinus, Schelling, and Aurobindo,
aintains that humankind is one aspect of the evolutionary
by which spirit returns to self-consciousness after having
:self into matter-energy at the Big Bang. In his view, the solu-
dernity's inadequate conception of the relation among spirit,
d humankind lies not in returning to premodern social rela-
religious beliefs, but rather in moving ahead to a mode of
that reintegrates what modernity has dissociated.

The following examination of Wilber's critique of and alternative to
eco-paganism will restrict itself to two interrelated issues. First, I present Wilber's contention—one that challenges the orthodoxy of many
environmentalists—that even though humankind is dependent *on* the
biosphere (or Gaia), in an important sense humankind is not included
in the biosphere. That is, human consciousness cannot be understood
solely in terms of the physical and biological phenomena that preceded
it and on which it continues to depend. Seeking to renovate the neo-
Platonic "great chain of being," which he now calls the "great holarchy
of being," he maintains that reverence for nature involves acknowledging genuine differences among holonic levels, rather than ignoring
them as part of an impulse to "return" to an undifferentiated unity with
nature. Second, Wilber argues that much of radical environmentalism
exhibits its own version of modernity's one-dimensional ontology, despite radical ecology's critique of other aspects of modernity. According
to Wilber, the modern effort to conquer nature and the environmentalist effort to reconnect with it are misguided efforts to deal with *the* central problem of modernity: the lack of a place for subjectivity in a
cosmos understood solely in terms of physical processes.

In *Up From Eden* (1981), Wilber maintains that death denial and dissociation play central roles in modern man's efforts to control nature. In
more recent works, however, including *Sex, Ecology, Spirituality* (SES)
and *A Brief History of Everything* (BHE), he gives greater emphasis to a
different condition that gives rise to ecological problems.[9] In my reading, Wilber believes that the human subject, having lost its place in the
cosmos, desperately tries to reassert its importance by developing technological agency. According to Wilber, SDEs may rebuke the striving for
such agency, but their own yearning for contact with nature can be understood as yet another way of coping with the same perceived loss of
a place for human subjectivity in the modern cosmos. Let us begin our
examination of Wilber's critique of eco-paganism by considering his
challenge to a staple presupposition of many environmentalist, namely,
that humanity is included within the biosphere.

HOLONIC HIERARCHY

In SES, Wilber offers a cosmology that seeks to rehabilitate the concept
of hierarchy, which many environmentalists criticize for justifying not
only the domination of one class of humans by another, but also the exploitation of nature by various human groups. Some SDEs portray the
biosphere as the sacred whole that gives birth to us and sustains us,

meriting our reverence and care. Even if there were a cosmic hi-
, humans would by no means be at the top. As an alternative to
hical models, many environmentalists use the model of the in-
ndent "web of life," of which all species are threads.[10] Discount-
adequacy of the web of life model, Wilber promotes instead the
a "holonic" cosmic hierarchy. A holon (Arthur Koestler's term)
s within itself features of things that are less complex than it,
n turn included within things that have features that are more
x than it. Janus-faced, holons both include and are included.

ne environmentalists, seeking both to replace atomism with
and to overcome anthropocentric hierarchalism, overlook the
model, which includes both individual holons and social holons.
following systems theory, such environmentalists interpret
1al organisms as temporary phenomena arising out of the larger
whole, the biosphere, or *Gaia*. In Wilber's view, holistic ap-
s typically do not adequately appreciate the difference between
holon (for example, a human society) and a compound individ-
n (for example, an individual person living in that society). If
1l holon is considered more comprehensive and important than
ridual holon, one can justify sacrificing the well-being of the in-
for the sake of the well-being of the whole. In modern politi-
;, this approach is known as fascism (though state socialism has
1aved in much the same way). Because some radical ecologists
that ecosystems are more important than individuals (human
wise), modernist critics often label radical environmentalists
s as ecofascists.[11]

ems theory has much to contribute to understanding organic-
1l processes, as Wilber shows by calling on the insightful work
antsch, who himself develops a hierarchical model. According
r, Jantsch—following Lynn Margulis and James Lovelock—
; Gaia as "the social holon composed primarily of the individ-
1s of prokaryotes" (SES, 85). In addition to mediating atmos-
:changes, the prokaryotes "form a global and interconnected
[or system] with all other prokaryotes—the overall Gaia sys-
;, 86). Because this system arose more than a billion years ago,
irmous *breadth*, such that all life since then (including human
nds on it. Far from standing at the top of Earth's holonic hier-
vever, as many SDEs suggest, the ecosystem emerges early on
l holon constituted by the relationship of simple organisms.
s remarkable breadth, however, the Gaia network in and of it-
not have much depth when compared to the individual or-
1nd social structures that have evolved since then. To explain

what he means by "depth," Wilber reminds us that a complex holon "includes" or "embraces" the less complex holons that compose it. For example, a molecule contains atoms, but is itself contained by organelles. An organelle is more complex than any molecule and thus stands higher in the holonic hierarchy. But the organelle is itself included in something still higher, the cell, which appears very early in organic evolution and is thus less complex than many of the compound organisms that will arise later. In this sense, the organelle is deeper than the cells that compose it, even though the organelle depends on cells for its very existence.

In going on to make the seemingly controversial claim that the biosphere is itself included in or embraced by more complex individual holons, such as plants and animals, Wilber finds himself on the side of many ecological scientists, who have challenged the once-predominant ecosystem view, according to which individual organisms are "included" in (and thus are holonically lower than) the overarching ecosystem.[12] Wilber insists that the "noosphere," i.e., human consciousness, far from being included "in" the biosphere, *contains* it, as well as the holonic levels achieved by other complex organisms.

Obviously, humans depend for survival on a functioning biosphere, and clearly do not physically "contain" it. Wilber insists, however, that as highly complex humans include all the levels of complexity achieved by atoms and molecules, not to mention one-celled organisms, plants, and animals, which themselves *already* contain (and are thus holonically higher, in the sense of more comprehensive than) the biosphere. The totality of atoms, molecules, cells, and organisms are far greater in sheer number, mass, expanse, or "span" than human beings, but the noosphere has a deeper and more comprehensive cosmic "embrace" than these other holons. Indeed, according to Wilber, one fully enlightened human being can "contain" the entire cosmos, in the sense of including and manifesting all its possible holonic levels. Although sympathetic regarding the motives of those environmentalists calling for ecological holism (SES, 90), Wilber maintains that such holism is usually confused. A holonic analysis reveals that holons with the greatest sheer numbers are the simplest (e.g., atoms). As things become more complex, there are fewer of them in comparison with the lower level holons. There are fewer multicelled organisms than cells, for example. The sheer span of the biosphere is vaster than any organism, including humankind, but is less complex than and thus holonically lower than an organism. By putting the biosphere at the top of the terrestrial holonic hierarchy, ecological holists fail to consider that the span of higher holons becomes ever smaller, not larger. What stands at

should be comparatively smaller, especially in comparison
mething as vast as the biosphere.

ber acknowledges that the higher depends on the lower for its
ce. If the lower is destroyed, the higher perishes, but not the
ay around. For example, if one destroys the cells in an organism,
nism cannot survive, but in many cases cells can survive the de-
n of the organism. The cells are part of the organism, which
survive without them. Many eco-holists, with the aim of tem-
human arrogance, maintain that humans are merely part of the
re, just as cells are part of the organism. Wilber asserts, however,
just the other way around.

we have seen, if the noosphere were really a *part* of the bio-
here, then if we destroyed the noosphere the biosphere would
sappear, and that is clearly not the case. An atom is genuinely a
rt of a molecule, and thus if we destroy the atoms we also de-
oy the molecule: the whole needs its part. Just so, if the noos-
ere were really a part of the biosphere, then destroying the
osphere [i.e., humankind] would eliminate the biosphere, and
t it is just the other way around: destroy the biosphere, and the
osphere is gone, precisely because *the biosphere is part of the noos-
*re, and not vice versa.[13] (SES, 90; my emphasis)

ead, humankind includes *within* itself, but also *transcends* all the
lready achieved by material-organic evolution. Many environ-
sts, whether spiritually oriented or not, complain that humans
hubris by portraying themselves as special, rather than simply
trand in the biospheric web. Wilber contends, however, that this
akes a category mistake, by failing to see that human conscious-
an *emergent* property that is more complex than anything
d hitherto in terrestrial evolution (at least, so far as we know).
ough such consciousness has co-evolved with other forms of
nan consciousness arguably exhibits a degree of intricacy, self-
reness, and capacity for moral judgment that distinguishes
ty from other life forms. The mythic lore of traditional so-
ften acknowledges the strangeness of human life, whose self-
usness and mortality-awareness distinguishes humans from
nimals, but also makes humans capable of evil acts unknown in
nal realm. Whereas many traditions describe the emergence of
sciousness as a kind of fall from a relatively pristine condition,
om Eden Wilber maintains that this fall was a fall "upward," the
ng of the evolution of consciousness that manifests itself in hu-
tory.

Some ancient traditions maintain that the fully awakened human being amounts to the "microcosm" that contains or adequately mirrors the entire cosmos ("macrocosm"), but many SDEs dismiss such traditions as anthropocentric and ecologically misinformed. Yet when Bill Devall and George Sessions praise the "perennial philosophy" as a source for the deep ecology perspective, they do not seem to recognize that this philosophy is consistent with Wilber's holonic hierarchy.[14] Likewise, the phrase "self-realization for all beings!" which Arne Naess promotes as the crucial maxim for his own approach to deep ecology, owes much both to Spinozism and to Advaita Vedanta, which involve hierarchical cosmologies, according to which humans are endowed with a very high-level mode of "selfhood." In my reading of Wilber, he would agree with deep ecology's laudable goal of encouraging self-realization *for all beings*, although he would insist that the notion of self-realization must acknowledge holonic hierarchy, as does the "perennial philosophy." The perennial philosophy, including Wilber's version of it, in no way justifies heedless destruction or abuse of nonhuman life forms; indeed, a self-realized person would exhibit universal compassion and respect for all beings.

Like Heidegger, Wilber defines humankind as the site through which entities can manifest themselves and thus "be," in a way that they cannot "be" for creatures lacking the transcendental consciousness that defines humankind. Saying this does not deny that other creatures have their own modes of awareness, each of which contributes in its own way to the extraordinarily complexity of a conscious cosmos, as has recently been suggested both by David Abrams and by Stan Grof.[15] Unlike Heidegger, however, who renounced cosmological and cosmogenic narratives, Wilber develops a story of divine emanation and return, involution and evolution, even while acknowledging the limitations of all such narratives. The story of what Wilber calls "Spirit" has something in common with neo-Platonism, neo-Hegelianism, Vajrayana Buddhism, Advaita Vedanta, and aspects of contemporary cosmology. Like Aristotle and Whitehead, Wilber describes Spirit as the cosmic "lure" or Eros that draws entities toward ever more complex and conscious modes of manifestation, that is, toward the actualization of the potential of Spirit that emptied itself into matter-energy at the moment of the Big Bang. Spirit is not only fully present in each level of creation, but is also active in the unfolding of new levels that give increasingly adequate expression to Spirit. Humankind plays a leading (but by no means the only!) role in this actualization process at this point in time and space, but human consciousness in its current modern modes will be superseded by more integrative modes. Moreover, con-

peings in other eras and other solar systems may already have
l far beyond humankind's current mode of personal awareness.
1 emphasizing the uniqueness of human existence, Wilber does
ert that only humans have inherent value or that all other beings
iable solely as raw material for human ends. *All* beings contain
ie ground value; all are authentic manifestations of Spirit. But
ianifests itself in many different ways, some of which are more
hensive than others. Hence, Wilber's "holonic hierarchy" ac-
dges the inherent worth of all beings, on the one hand, while ac-
dging the legitimate differences among kinds of beings, on the
or him, animals deserve more consideration than plants, be-
ws *do* scream louder than carrots. Cows and other animals have
eveloped sentience than plants, and humans have the most re-
nd of sentience yet discovered.

is may protest that Wilber simply reinstates anthropocentrism
subtle terms, but he insists that only by taking seriously hu-
d's distinctness can today's mistreatment of the biosphere be
Such mistreatment occurs within a social context that has been
ted and defined by the communicative agency of human be-
ily by transforming this social context, for example, by ending
oppression and militarism, and by educating people about the
sequences of ecological misbehavior, can people begin altering
iavior. In Wilber's view, these alterations occur more readily in
democracies than in authoritarian regimes, as can be seen by
ch worse environmental conditions were in the former Soviet
1d its satellite states than they were in Western Europe and the
states during the 1980s. For Wilber, the greatest revolution in
day would be the worldwide consolidation of rational-egoic
sness along with the institutions needed to sustain it, including
tic politics and such universal human rights as personal free-
ucation, health care, and basic material necessities. Such a
ansformation would rid the world of the authoritarianism,
m, and militarism that are responsible for so many environ-
roblems.

is regard, at least some neo-pagan SDEs would agree with
ius diZerega, for instance, a political philosopher and Wiccan
efers democratic governments not least because they do not go
ith one another.[16] Other environmentally destructive practices,
those carried out by multinational corporations, would have to
ted by a democratic world citizenry, which would have a better
revealing and countering such practices than would people
der authoritarian regimes. In addition to globally consolidating

democratic practices, what is needed in today's materialistic world is a new cosmology that takes into account modern science, even while simultaneously providing a place for subjectivity, interiority, soul, or spirit.

Beyond Flatland Ontology

Wilber argues that SDEs and modernists alike have more in common than either group might think, because members of both groups adhere to what Wilber calls modernity's one-dimensional or "flatland" ontology that has no place for subjectivity, interiority, soul, or spirit. Many environmentalists adhere to some version of ecosystem theory, which describes biospheric systems in terms of enormously complex and interconnected energy flows. For some SDEs, ecosystem theory in particular and systems theory in general overcomes the one-dimensional and reductionist ontology of scientific modernity, and thereby enables people once again to discern nature's sacred dimension. Wilber argues, however, that systems theory does *not* overcome scientific reductionism, because systems theory fails adequately to distinguish among the three most basic levels of the holonic hierarchy: the It, the Personal, and the Spiritual. Systems theory does an excellent job at the It level, the material level that lacks conscious agency and the capacity for dialogue, but cannot adequately address either the Personal level, which involves such agency, or the Spiritual level, which is simultaneously immanent in the It and the Personal, while transcending both of them. Although SDEs seek to end the domination of nature by appealing to systems theory, more than a few environmentalists have complained that ecosystem theory itself—despite the scientific ammunition it has contributed to the environmental movement—is not only a variation of the abstract, quantitative scientific reductionism that has gone hand in glove with industrialism, but is also responsible for displacing earlier scientific views of the natural world (including those that spoke of natural "communities") that are arguably more congenial with efforts to resacralize nature.

Just as many SDEs resist the notion of transcendent spirituality because it has been used to justify the domination of nature, so many moderns resist the same notion because it discourages such domination, insofar as otherworldly people pay insufficient attention to finding ways to improve life on Earth through mastering natural processes. Neither SDEs nor modernists are able adequately to account for their own subjectivity and interiority in terms of the principles of reductionist science. But if SDEs seek to recover and to legitimate such subjectivity by reenchanting nature and becoming aligned with it, modernists seek to demonstrate the reality of human agency (if not full-blown subjectivity) by dominating nature through the use of rationality, science, technology, and industry. By dominating nature, "man" convinces himself that he has a certain dignity, power, and agency unknown in nature.

Wilber places the environmentalist versus modernist debate within the context of the longstanding battle between Ascenders and Descenders, "the *central* and *defining* conflict in the Western mind" (BHE, 258). For the Ascenders, including St. Augustine, God was transcendental, incorporeal, not of this world. Tending toward asceticism and monasticism, Ascenders sought to rise above the corrupt and manifold material plane in order to unite with the eternal One. For the Descenders, in contrast, God was not the One but the Many. Worshipping the incredibly diverse, visible, sensible, sensual God/Goddess, Descenders "delighted in a creation-centered spirituality that saw each sunrise, each moonrise, as the visible blessing of the Divine" (BHE, 258). Sometimes SDEs try to portray Enlightenment moderns as continuing the Ascent tradition, insofar as moderns emphasize Reason. Wilber maintains, however, that in fact the Age of Reason represents the triumph of the *Descent* tradition in the West:

> Salvation in the modern world—whether offered by politics, or science, or revivals of earth religion, or Marxism, or industrialization, or retribalism, or sexuality, or horticultural revivals, or scientific materialism, or earth goddess embrace, or ecophilosophies, you name it—salvation can be found only on earth, only in the phenomena, only in manifestations, only in the world of Form, only in pure *immanence*, only in the Descended grid. There is no higher truth, no Ascending current, nothing *transcendental* whatsoever. In fact, anything "higher" or "transcendental" is now the Devil. . . . And all of modernity and postmodernity moves fundamentally and almost entirely within this Descended grid, the grid of flatland. (BHE, 260)

Partly out of disappointment in Christian dogmatism and oppression, modern humankind turned away from seeking an otherworldly heaven and sought to erect a paradise on Earth. Although the death of the otherworldly God helped to liberate humanity from the chains of religious dogmatism and political despotism, on the one hand, and freed humankind to address previously intractable material and political problems, on the other, the this-worldly turn (Descent) had untoward consequences, not least of which was the meaninglessness that follows when the cosmos and humankind are viewed through the

monological lens of mechanistic materialism. Many twentieth
philosophers have protested against reducing humans to the
complex mechanisms. Modern science can study humans as
phenomena, but can neither explain nor fully acknowledge t
sonal, interpersonal, interior, and spiritual dimensions, since tl
not be made the object of material inquiry.

Wilber depicts the mood of modernity as irony, "the bitter
of a world that cannot tell the truth about the substantive dep
Kosmos. . ." (BHE, 275). Writing more than sixty years earlie
Heidegger concluded that the mood of modernity is twofold: l
and horror. Moderns are bored because the one-dimensional
of mechanistic materialism has emptied humans and things
substance; instead of being endowed with a transcendent di
that allows things to manifest themselves and thus "be," hum
become clever animals competing for power and security. Mo
horrified because they surmise the utter meaninglessness of e
such an ontologically poverty-stricken world.[17] What Wilber
mood of irony may be how moderns have learned to transr
grimmer mood of horror.

Like Heidegger, Wilber contends that the monological
mechanistic materialism, according to which to be means to be
that can be understood by natural science, amounts to an indu
tology. "It is industrialization that holds flatland in place, that l
objective world of simple location as the primary reality, that c
and dominates the interiors and reduces them to instrumenta
in the great web of observable surfaces. That 'nature alone is re
is the voice of the industrial grid" (BHE, 273–274). According t
"The religion of Gaia, the worship of nature, is simply one of
forms of industrial religion, of industrial spirituality, and in per
the industrial paradigm" (BHE, 275).

Obviously, SDEs would be shocked to hear that their rever
sacred Earth unwittingly helps to maintain the grip of the indu
tology that is responsible for violating the earth! Wilber insis
ever, that because SDEs (including eco-romantics) failed to inte
transcendent dimension, they perpetuate in their own way th
logical Descent tradition. Eco-romantics "think transcenden
stroying Gaia, whereas transcendence is the only way fragmen
joined and integrated and thereby saved" (BHE, 277). For Wilt
scendence is made otherworldly by Ascenders who fear natu
and emotions, but genuine transcendence is always integrated
manence in the non-dual embrace described in Mahayana Buc
dictum that Samsara is not other than Nirvana.

ause Wilber so sharply criticizes their views, SDEs may con-
1at he is just another modernist with no interest in the natural
but in fact he expresses deep concern about current mistreat-
 the biosphere; indeed, he does not seem to share the ecological
m that I mentioned at the outset. He writes that "[t]he planet, in-
 headed for disaster, and it is now possible, for the first time in
history, that owing *entirely* to manmade circumstances, not one
ill survive to tell the tale. If the Earth is indeed our body and
then in destroying it we are committing a slow and gruesome
" (SES, 4). Moreover, he sympathizes with SDEs who yearn for
1 union in a world threatened, fractured, and made meaningless
elentless industrialism of modernity. There are two reasons, un-
tely, why otherwise well-intended SDEs actually reinforce the
dustrialism that they despise.

t, by conceiving of the sacred in nature as wholly immanent, as
sed interconnectivity of the world-system, SDEs accept moder-
lescent orientation, which basically lopped off the upper reaches
reat holarchy of being. Unintentionally, then, some branches of
ecology participate in the process of portraying the cosmos in
llogically one-dimensional manner. Well-meaning efforts to re-
t the world by neo-pagan ideas and practices cannot fully restore
lodernity has eliminated, namely, the interior dimension of per-
d, soul, and spirit. Second, by calling for the return of various
f neo-pagan nature worship, some people may fall prey to what
calls the "pre/trans fallacy."[18] It is a fallacy to confuse *surrender-*
ional-egoic consciousness by regressing to a more primitive, pre-
us state with *transcending* egoic consciousness by moving
 an authentically transpersonal state. Wilber acknowledges that
ve egoic integration, as well as to encourage the development of
-logic"—the final stage before the emergence of genuinely trans-
1l awareness—individuals may need to explore and to integrate
ed forms of consciousness. He disagrees, however, with the
hat recovering archaic tribal consciousness and engaging in a
r of New Paradigm practices will contribute to achieving gen-
transpersonal consciousness.

 Wilber, the spiritual vacuum of modernity can be overcome in
 demonstrating that the positive achievements of modernity
ite an important stage in the evolutionary development of
1-the-world. Balancing criticism of modernity's ecologically de-
e practices and of the industrial ontology that gave rise to them,
cknowledgment of the authentic contributions of modernity
emancipation of humankind from material want and political

oppression, Wilber seeks to persuade moderns to take seriously the need for a postindustrial ontology that restores depth to the cosmos by reintegrating what has been dissociated, i.e., the interior, subjective domains. Following Habermas, Wilber emphasizes that modernity's great achievement was differentiating three domains:

1. consciousness, subjectivity, self, and self-expression (including art), whose mode of truth involves truthfulness and sincerity;
2. ethics, morality, world view, culture, intersubjective meaning, whose mode of truth involves justice;
3. science, technology, objective nature, whose mode of truth involves correct propositions. (BHE, 123)

Differentiating the "Big Three" created the social-cognitive space necessary for democratic politics and new art forms, for liberation movements of all varieties, ranging from the antislavery movement to feminism, and for modern science. In such a differentiated world-space, the individual could develop his or her own views, take part in democratic political movements, and express himself/herself artistically to some extent without being constrained by social-cultural powers, including mythologically based religions and regimes that had previously limited individual freedom of decision and expression. In the domain of morality and politics, worldcentric views that promoted rights for *all* people supplanted moral doctrines based on racial or tribal exclusivity. Distinguishing between the biological domain (studied by science) and the subjective and social-cultural domains (enacted by persons and institutions), moderns denied that some people were biologically "fit" to be slaves, or that women were "naturally" unsuited for public life. Finally, science could explore the natural universe without the constraints imposed by ecclesiastic authority. Such exploration gave rise to the enormous advances in medicine, agriculture, industry, communication, and transportation.

Unfortunately, as Wilber points out, modernity did not adequately integrate the Big Three that it had differentiated. Since the modes of knowledge in the personal-artistic and cultural-moral domains are relatively more difficult to achieve in comparison with empirical scientific knowledge, and since scientific knowledge brought such important material gains, scientific modes of knowledge marginalized the other two kinds. Natural science could not even notice, much less study, selfhood, interiority, culture, and morality, since empirical inquiry is suited for material phenomena, not for personal and social phenomena. Far from representing nature as a sum of disconnected atoms, as some environ-

ists have complained, modern science represented nature as "a
y *harmonious and interrelated system*, a great-it-system, and knowl-
insisted in patiently and empirically mapping this it-system"
28). Modern science unified the cosmos in terms of the "great
life' conception, a great interlocking order of beings, each mutu-
rwoven with all others" (BHE, 129). As noted earlier, when SDEs
iat humanity must learn to live within the great "web of life,"
: repeating an eighteenth-century idea that is crucial to the in-
ontology of which environmentalists are otherwise so critical.
iough their solution may be misguided, at least SDEs have
riously the problem of the split between humanity and nature,
iat for many moderns became an effort for the rational mind to
:e nature. The rational ego sought to disenchant nature, not only
to eliminate any lingering concerns about violating Mother Na-
t also in order to achieve modernity's ideal of rational and
jectivity. So long as one's reasoning processes are influenced by
al factors (e.g., emotions), so long as one's moral judgment is
iy personal, familial, tribal, or racial factors, one is not truly ra-
npartial, and thus fully human. Following Kant's lead, the
ego sought to transcend the domain of particularity and corpo-
i order to attain the perfection of universality and impartiality.
quest for transcendence had two major problems. First, it was
y short-circuited by the fact that moderns could not really ad-
lomain transcending the material plane; hence, the ego was left
of transcendental limbo that was made increasingly untenable
elentlessly reductive processes of scientific materialism. To
for its own conceptual erasure, the modern ego engages in ex-
iry, nature-dominating *agency*. To demonstrate its own exis-
other words, the ego set out to subjugate the material domain,
ily domain that supposedly exists. Heidegger wrote that mod-
's striving for world domination shows that he had become an
eking power and security, but so far as I can tell, Wilber holds
fferent view: the striving for world domination represents, at
irt, an effort at self-assertion on the part of persons who *intuit*
(interior and interpersonal) reality, but who cannot find any
conceptual expression for it. Hence, when Marx said that the
hilosophy is not to reflect on the world, but rather to change
ght in part to reemphasize the power of human agency in a
t was increasingly mechanized and devoid of subjectivity. A
ter, Michel Foucault spoke of "the disappearance of man" in
i with the dramatic eclipse of subjectivity in the modern sci-
rld.

The second problem with the modern quest for transcendence was that the justifiable differentiation between mind and body ended up in unjustifiable *dissociation:*

> The rational ego wanted to rise above nature and its own bodily impulses, so as to achieve a more universal compassion found nowhere in nature, but it often simply repressed these natural impulses instead: repressed its own biosphere; repressed its own life juices; repressed its own vital roots. The Ego tended to *repress* both external nature and its own internal nature (the id). And this repression, no doubt, would have something to do with the emergence of a Sigmund Freud, sent exactly at this time (and never before this time) to doctor the dissociations of modernity. (BHE, 284)

The romantic reaction against rational modernity's humanity-nature split, and against the repression that follows from it, was justified, for something serious was amiss. Nevertheless, efforts made by romantics and SDEs to overcome this split went astray, according to Wilber, because they had two different conceptions of nature. The first conception was the modernist view that nature is the all-encompassing, interrelated whole, the great life-stream or web-of-life. Supposedly, modernity had lost touch with this web-of-life, despite the fact that everything is completely enclosed and flows within it. In positing that culture has deviated from or split off from nature, however, the romantics posited a *second* conception of nature: a nature from which humankind *can* deviate. Wilber asks: "[W]hat is the relation of this Nature with a capital N that embraces *everything,* versus this nature that is *different* from culture because it is getting ruined by culture?" (BHE, 287). Romanticism foundered because it could not reconcile these conflicting views of nature. Great romantics, such as Schelling, sought to reconcile this conflict by saying that "Nature with a big N is Spirit, because all-embracing Spirit does indeed *transcend* and *include* both culture and nature" (BHE, 287). Most Romantics, however, were so committed to the Descent path, that

> they simply identified Nature with nature. They identified Spirit with sensory nature. And here they went up in smoke, a spectacularly narcissistic, egocentric, flamboyant explosion—because the closer you get to nature, the more egocentric you become. And in search of Nature, the Romantics headed back to nature, and disappeared into a black hole of their own selfhood, while claiming to speak for the ultimately Divine—divine egoism, it sadly turned out. (BHE, 287)

Vilber is right, the "back to nature" dimension of SDE is a
of this failed romantic effort to overcome the humanity-nature
I]nstead of moving *forward* in *evolution* to the emergence of a
or Spirit (or World Soul) that would indeed unify the differen-
nind and nature, [SDEs] simply recommend 'back to nature'"
88). Such a view invites psychological and social regression for
owing reason: if nature/biosphere is the "fundamental reality"
ss/Gaia), that which deviates from nature threatens nature. If
'is the ultimately Real, then culture must be the original Crime"
!88). The goal, then, must be to dismantle culture, in order to
: a lost paradise involving unconscious unity with pristine na-
:pression is to be cured by regression, as some Earth First!ers
dicated in their call for a return to the Pleistocene age (BHE,
ich a yearning for primal unity with divine nature is tempting,
entially disastrous.[19]
ber says that misguided eco-sentimentalism will never halt eco-
y destructive industrial processes. What is needed instead is the
ment of "mutual understanding and mutual agreement based
  worldcentric moral perspective concerning the global com-
But such an achievement requires "interior growth and tran-
ace," not surrender to the beauties of this or that ecosystem
$11). To escape ecological destruction, then, a genuinely post-
 humanity must overcome its fear and loathing of transcen-
since such transcendence alone can integrate what modernity
;ociated in the process of generating industrial ontology.

CRITICAL APPRAISAL

gh largely in agreement with Wilber's insightful ideas about
 hierarchy, cosmic evolution, and the complex relation of moder-
d eco-paganism, I do have some reservations about his views.[20]
: thing, he has more confidence in his grand narrative than I do,
lly in an age that is so skeptical of them. Alternative narratives,
f which are quite appealing, offer different interpretations of the
d present, and different visions of the future. For another thing,
doesn't always acknowledge nuanced differences among radical
imentalists and SDEs, although he promises to do so in a forth-
; book. Of course, to cover such a vast amount of territory, he
:glect certain distinctions, some of which matter more than oth-
vertheless, I have sympathy for some SDEs who demand that
 provide specific examples of texts which or of authors who

equate spiritually-oriented deep ecology as involving little more than seeking undifferentiated union with nature.

Critics have also charged that Wilber does not understand the importance of recovering insights from archaic and pagan spirituality. Jürgen W. Kremer has argued that Wilber virtually ignores indigenous people, their cultures, and their religious beliefs. By failing to take seriously the possibility that such people have something important to say to contemporary humanity, Wilber supposedly continues the error made by many other white Eurocentric thinkers, who justified colonialism on the basis of the notion that Western culture is at the cutting edge of human evolution. From this evolutionary perspective, indigenous people may merit protection, but are of little world-historical importance, since they are on the fringes of evolutionary-historical processes that are closely involved with the *real* developments taking place globally. According to Kremer, failing to integrate the insights of indigenous people represents "the shadow of evolutionary thinking."[21] Despite asserting that his thought springs from a kind of "vision-logic" that integrates perspectives that to others seem incompatible, then, Wilber's work allegedly remains unintegrated, since it leaves out the experience of so many cultures, including those with ideas of spirituality that would seem irreconcilable with what he regards as spirituality consistent with the emergence of a new level of consciousness: vision-logic, the capacity to adopt various perspectives regarding many different issues.

Certainly Wilber is influenced by Western thought, especially the idea of evolutionary progress, but he is also heavily informed by Asian religion and philosophy. Indeed, he could scarcely have developed his particular reading of Western thought and history apart from his study of many varieties of Buddhism, Vedanta, and other non-Western traditions. He has been particularly inspired by Sri Aurobindo's effort to integrate the Western evolutionary perspective with the Eastern spiritual perspective, but Wilber has also attempted to interpret the Hellenstic thinker, Plotinus, as anticipating many of Aurobindo's insights. Of course, one could argue that Aurobindo himself, living in colonized India, was infected with Eurocentric ideas, but he was also a staunch Indian nationalist. If Aurobindo was influenced by Western ideas, Plotinus was apparently influenced by *Eastern* thought. In the future, I suspect, using terms such as *Eurocentric* will become increasingly uninformative, since a global culture is emerging in which individuals will inevitably be shaped by many different perspectives. In view of Europe's important achievements, moreover, one should scarcely wonder that European values and practices have such a planetary influence.

ıfluences would have spread, albeit more slowly, even without
s unfortunate colonial history, which helps to explain suspicion
urocentrism on the part of many Third World and Euro-Ameri-
cs of modernity.

ıaps it would be advisable for Wilber to engage more often the
s and ideas of indigenous people, some of whom may have
l views that are at least partly in agreement with his own. De-
iisting that "we all want to honor and acknowledge the many
:omplishments of past cultures the world over, *and attempt to re-
incorporate as much of their wisdom as we can*" (BHE, 50—my em-
Wilber is concerned that some efforts to recover insights from
:eligions invite regression to less differentiated psychological
al states. In reply, Gus diZerega argues that if such efforts are
ıut responsibly, something important can come out of them.[22]
ıe, one problem in this debate is that our understanding of ar-
igions is limited. The beliefs and practices of contemporary in-
s peoples are not equivalent to the outlook of tribal societies
m several centuries ago. Hence, in attempting to "recover"
ipiritual pathways, well-intended people may go astray, espe-
hey conjure up a "spirituality" that is virtually entirely imma-
, for in so doing they would be repeating in different guise the
nade by radically this-worldly moderns.

far as many SDEs join modernity in denying the transcendent
ın, they risk excluding important aspects of spirituality. It is
:o name either a tribal or a world religious tradition that does
: reference to a hidden domain, or to an invisible generative
/irtually all spiritual traditions take for granted realms that
l the material plane, even if those realms are somehow "intra-
Hence, SDEs who propose a totally physio-biological, web-of-
ɔgy as the basis for their spiritual path are not in a position to
heir path is somehow aligned with traditional paths, and cer-
: with the perennial wisdom. In fact, a number of adherents to
ıism freely acknowledge there are ontological realms, includ-
: in which the Goddess dwells, that transcend the material
en though such realms are somehow related to the material
her informative book, *Nature Religion in America*, Catherine L.
maintains that today's neo-pagan Goddess "functions at the
ın immanentist transcendentalism that puts earth—as earth—
in the camp of heaven."[23] Although the Goddess is "of the
nanent in all that exists," She "*is as transcendental as Emerson-
:m had been*. Magic happens through human imagination:
other words, creates the Goddess's world."[24] The Goddess

expresses the Transcendentalists' ambiguity: "Pushed one way, she celebrates the reality, the concreteness of matter. [....] Pushed another way, though, she tell us that matter is only a form of spirit, that it can be shifted and changed by spirit."[25] Albanese also quotes the noted Wiccan priestess, Starhawk, as saying that "[t]he flesh, the material world, are not sundered from the Goddess, they are the manifestation of the divine. Union with the Goddess comes through embracing the material world."[26] Further, in an essay on her experience with shamanism, for example, Gloria Feman Orenstein, writes:

> It is arrogant of Westerners to think that if we have not identified something with our modern instruments, it does not exist. This also negates the powers and intelligence of native people. By our arrogance, by our insistence on labeling those whose wisdom was acquired without Western technology as "primitive," we open ourselves to great dangers from elements and entities of *other dimensions* that we have chosen to ignore. In this way we have trivialized the spirit world and attributed all agency in human affairs to humans alone.[27]

Later on, warning against dualism, she writes: "We must *remember* that in Shamanism, spirit resides in matter, and all that exists is sacred. We must also resist thinking in hierarchies, privileging the spirit world and its entities over the material world and its inhabitants."[28]

Although sharing Wilber's aversion to Ascent-oriented otherworldliness, she doubts that a holarchy that acknowledges that spirit is more complex than matter can avoid being a dominator hierarchy. By saying that spirit resides *in* matter, she hopes to avoid otherworldliness. Wilber maintains, however, that matter is embraced by spirit. No belittling of matter is meant by speaking of such an embrace. In Wilber's view, then, despite her references to entities from "other dimensions," Orenstein's exploration of shamanism fails to appreciate sufficiently the *depth* dimension of the cosmos.[29] Though he would agree with aspects of Orenstein's critique of modern materialism, Wilber's concerns about the possibility of regression leads him to be suspicious of many such efforts aimed at recovering archaic spirituality. Critics such as diZerega, however, maintain that Wilber has such deep reservations about and even hostility toward the material world, that he overemphasizes the transcendent dimension. To resolve these complex issues, serious dialogue between Wilber and his critics is needed.

A careful reader will see that Wilber has considerable sympathy for many of the claims made by radical environmentalists and by people exploring nature-oriented religions. He understands that some people

explore previously repressed areas in order to become better in-
. Conceivably, he might even regard some of current interest in
ism as a potentially promising development, provided that
actices are explored in the right spirit, i.e., with the goal of mov-
ard by first looping back, and in a way that does not require the
of *critical* forms of consciousness. Arguably, Wilber's real con-
h contemporary interest in nature religions is not so much that
ıvite psychological or social regression, but rather that it will
dicule of *all* efforts to resolve serious ecological problems by
ating the spiritual dimension in the postmodern age. Most
ıns, for example, are either too attached to traditional religions,
ɔo far down the road of secular modernity to take seriously
ism, neo-paganism, Earth-based religiosity, and SDE. If the ed-
ɔublic concludes that contemporary Wiccans and SDEs consti-
"spiritual" approach to addressing ecological problems, that
ıay conclude that spirituality has nothing to recommend itself
ɛgard.

ı Wilber's viewpoint, however, and from mine as well, this
e a very unfortunate development. His evolutionary approach
uality could gain a far more sympathetic hearing from many
ɔorary people, than does the approach offered by *some*—though
y no means all—SDEs. By praising the achievements of moder-
ile also maintaining that the ecological crisis is a symptom of
humanity's loss of spiritual awareness, Wilber wants to create
t in which moderns can think seriously about spiritual matters,
hey have abandoned traditional religious formations, partly be-
ey *do* so often seem otherworldly. Wilber does not conceive of
 scendent in an otherworldly way, or in a manner that devalues
ɛct of the material world. This is why in SES he so emphasized
's attack on the world-despising Gnostics. Moreover, like Ma-
Buddhists, Wilber affirms that samsara *is* nirvana, that the
f suffering *is* the perfect world, seen with the awakened mind.
ılar moderns abandoned traditional religions in part because
med insufficiently interested in improving material circum-
Wilber, however, embraces Enlightenment modernity's revolu-
ɔroposal to transform the human condition by ending hunger,
lisease, resisting despotism, encouraging knowledge, and re-
g dogmatism. In this way, he aligns himself not only with
ıty, but also with the Jewish, Christian, and Islamic proclama-
: humankind must do God's work on earth, not only by over-
social injustice and oppression, but also by resisting the wanton
ion of Creation. He believes that by demonstrating that his

perennial philosophical conception of spirit is compatible both with social justice and with environmental issues, some moderns will become interested in his related idea that modernity's emancipatory impulse is a crucial stage in the evolutionary development of spirituality. Modernity's promise is to end dogmatism by differentiating among human realms, including natural science, religion, morality, and personal judgment. Modernity's agony is that its initial differentiation failed, insofar as the methods and truth claims of natural science marginalized the methods and truth claims of the other realms. As a result, a new version of dogmatism emerged. In his most recent book, *The Marriage of Sense and Soul,* Wilber criticizes this collapse of differentiation, while arguing that spiritual practices reliably generate experiences that confirm the truth claims made by religious traditions, including claims that there are domains that transcend the material domain studied by natural science.[30]

Secular moderns are perhaps less likely to become interested in the intertwinement of spirituality, social justice, and environmentalism, if SDEs are allowed to define that intertwinement. SDEs often reinforce the conviction among many moderns that modernity's positive achievements—scientific, political, economic—are currently threatened by irrational forces, which calls for a return to benighted religious beliefs and premodern social formations. Many modernists and postmodernists whom Wilber hopes to reach are already incapable of embracing the Christianity and Judaism of their elders, in part because those religions contain mythological dimensions that cannot be reconciled with contemporary modes of thought. For many moderns/postmoderns, embracing a revitalized neo-paganism is simply out of the question.

Nature-oriented religiosity and SDE have a relatively small following, but they receive enough press coverage to convince some moderns not even to pick up Wilber's *Sex, Ecology, Spirituality,* since they assume that it involves neo-paganism. Indeed, it is often stocked in the "Metaphysics," "Occult," and "New Age" sections of bookstores. Wilber is so critical of "eco-romanticism," then, partly because he regards it as involving an inadequate understanding of spirituality, and partly because he is concerned that it prevents his own voice from being heard by the people who need to hear it. In his view, SDE and New Age spirituality alike may promise a genuine *transformation* of consciousness, but deliver more effective modes of *translation* within the existing mode of consciousness. That is to say, "they do not offer effective means to utterly dismantle the self, but merely ways for the self to think differently."[31] Even worse, allegedly transformational movements may encourage the regression of consciousness to premodern stages. At

o the consternation of critics and supporters alike, Wilber's
regarding SDEs is harsh, although at other times his rhetoric is
couraging and compassionate. He explains his rhetorical strat-
ecessary to tell the truth about the aim of all spirituality, namely,
ver "my Master is my Self, and that Self is the Kosmos at large,
Kosmos is my Soul."[32]
ng the skillful means at his disposal, he attempts to foster a mode
uality that is consistent with the best of contemporary science,
uided by the notion of biological, cultural, and personal evolu-
it includes what is valid about Descent-oriented SDEs and As-
ented Christian monotheists, and that seeks to reconcile Ascent
cent in nonduality. Given the remarkably ambitious character of
rt, one can expect Wilber to make mistakes. In my view, however,
t deserves critical appropriation by all who are concerned about
the biosphere by transforming human consciousness and culture.

NOTES

See Donald Worster, "The Ecology of Order and Chaos," in *Environ-
thics*, ed. Susan J. Armstrong and Richard G. Botzler (New York:
-Hill, 1993), 39–43. See my essay, "The Postmodern Challenge to Envi-
alism," *Terra Nova* 1, no. 2 (spring 1996): 131–140.

See J. Baird Callicott, "Do Deconstructive Ecology and Sociobiology
ne Leopold's Land Ethic?" *Environmental Ethics* 18, no. 4 (winter 1996):

For example, see Gregg Easterbrook, *A Moment on the Earth: The Coming
vironmental Optimism* (New York: Viking Press, 1995) (though some en-
ntalists have criticized it for containing many inaccuracies); Ronald
l., *The True State of the Planet* (New York: Free Press, 1995); *Green Delu-
Environmentalist Critique of Radical Environmentalism* (Durham: Duke
ty Press, 1992); Julian Simon, ed., *The State of Humanity* (Cambridge,
:kwell/Cato Institute, 1995).

See Mark Sagoff, "Do We Consume Too Much?" *Atlantic Monthly*, 279
ne 1997), 80–97. See the rebuttal, "No Middle Way on the Environ-
y Paul R. Ehrlich, Gretchen C. Daily, Scott C. Daily, Norman Myers,
s Salzman, in *Atlantic Monthly* 280, no. 6 (December 1997), 98–104, and
off's counter-rebuttal in the *Atlantic Monthly* (March 1998), 8–9.

The literature by and about SDEs is large and growing, though of un-
lity. A sampling of the better literature includes Carol J. Adams, ed.,
ism and the Sacred* (New York: Continuum, 1994); Allan Hunt Badiner,
ma Gaia* (Berkeley: Parallax Press, 1990); Charlene Spretnak, *States of*

Grace (San Francisco: HarperCollins, 1991); Roger S. Gottlieb, ed., *This Sacred Earth: Religion, Nature, Environment* (New York: Routledge, 1996); and Shirley Nicholson and Brenda Rosen, *Gaia's Hidden Life* (Wheaton, IL: Quest Books, 1992).

6. Whenever I use the term *man*, I have in mind the class of patriarchal males who have typically exercised social control in Western history.

7. See Michael E. Zimmerman, *Heidegger's Confrontation with Modernity: Technology, Politics, Art* (Bloomington: Indiana University Press, 1990); *Contesting Earth's Future: Radical Ecology and Postmodernity* (Berkeley and Los Angeles: University of California Press, 1994); and "Ecofascism: A Threat to American Environmentalism?" in Roger S. Gottlieb, *The Ecological Community* (New York: Routledge, 1997), 229–254.

8. See Murray Bookchin, *The Philosophy of Social Ecology* (Montréal and New York: Black Rose Books, 1990).

9. Ken Wilber, *Up From Eden: A Transpersonal View of Human Evolution* (Boston: Shambhala, 1981); *Sex, Ecology, Spirituality: The Spirit of Evolution* (Boston and London: Shambhala, 1995); and *A Brief History of Everything* (Boston and London: Shambhala, 1996).

10. See Fritjof Capra, *The Web of Life* (Anchor Books, 1996).

11. On this topic, see my essay, "Ecofascism," which discusses the ecofascist tendencies of one of J. Baird Callicott's early writings.

12. See Worster, "The Ecology of Order and Chaos."

13. Wilber, *Sex, Ecology, Spirituality*, 90.

14. Bill Devall and George Sessions, *Deep Ecology* (Salt Lake City: Peregrine Smith Books, 1985), 80–81.

15. David Abrams, *The Spell of the Sensuous* (New York: Pantheon Books, 1996); Stan Grof, *The Cosmic Game* (Albany: State University of New York Press, 1998).

16. See Gus diZerega, "Democracies and Peace," the *Review of Politics* 57 (1995): 279–308.

17. See Martin Heidegger, *Die Grundbegriffe der Metaphysik*, ed. Friedrich-Wilhelm von Hermann, *Gesamtausgabe* 29–30 (Frankfurt am Main: Vittorio Klostermann, 1983); Michael E. Zimmerman, "Ontical Craving versus Ontological Desire," in *From Phenomenology to Thought, Errancy, and Desire*, ed. Babette E. Babich (Dordrecht: Kluwer, 1995).

18. Ken Wilber, "The Pre/Trans Fallacy," in *Eye to Eye: The Search for the New Paradigm* (Boston: Shambhala, 1996), 198–243.

19. In *Masculinities* (Berkeley and Los Angeles: University of California Press, 1995), 134–137, R. W. Connell describes an instance of apparent psychological regression in the case of Bill Lindeman, a young man heavily involved in Australian counterculturalism and radical environmentalism. Adopting a philosophy emphasizing "undifferentiated wholeness," Lindeman came to expe-

passive-receptive attitude toward nature and a "wonderfully clear, ing" of communion with it. When speaking of his efforts to change his osophy, however, Lindeman's language became unstructured "with ents and commentary tumbling out together." Connell comments that follows Julia Kristeva's arguments that separation from the mother advent of Oedipal castration awareness are connected with a particu- e in language, where subject and object are separated and propositions ments arise (the 'thetic' phase), Peter's shift in speech would make the sign of an attempt to undo Oedipal masculinity." Peter's effort to uct his masculinity by developing "an open, non-assertive self risks io self at all; it courts annihilation." Wilber would argue that Peter Lin- effort to dissociate himself from masculine personhood and to em- unmediated union with nature, achieved not a transpersonal mode of isness but a prepersonal one.

See my essay, "A Transpersonal Diagnosis of the Ecological Crisis," in *er and the Future of Transpersonal Inquiry: A Spectrum of Views, Part I*, ed. Rothberg and Sean M. Kelly, *ReVision* 18, no. 4 (spring 1996): 38–48.

Jürgen W. Kremer, "The Shadow of Evolutionary Thinking," *ReVision*, *er and the Future of Transpersonal Inquiry, Part II* 19, no. 1 (summer 1996):

Gus diZerega, "A Critique of Ken Wilber's Account of Deep Ecology ture Religions," *The Trumpeter* 13, no. 2 (spring 1996): 52–71.

Catherine L. Albanese, *Nature Religions in America: From the Algonkian to the New Age* (Chicago: University of Chicago Press, 1990), 178.

Ibid., 179. My emphasis.

Ibid.

Ibid., 181.

Gloria Feman Orenstein, "Toward an Ecofeminist Ethic of Shamanism Sacred," in *Ecofeminism and the Sacred*, ed. Carol J. Adams (New York: ium, 1993), 172–190; citation is from 180. My emphasis.

Ibid., 189.

Wilber would probably say that what Orenstein calls "spirit" refers to chic or perhaps subtle domain. He asserts that entities encountered in periences "actually exist. They have real referents. But these referents do st in the sensorimotor worldspace [or in rational or existential world- . . . Rather, they *exist* in the subtle worldspace, and evidence for them can tifully found *there*" (BHE, 212).

. Ken Wilber, *The Marriage of Sense and Soul* (New York: Random House,

. Ken Wilber, "A Spirituality that Transforms," *What Is Enlightenment?*, fall/winter 1997): 23–32. Citation is from 29.

. Ibid., 32.

Bibliography

Edward. *The Monkey Wrench Gang*. New York: Fawcett, 1974.

, David. *The Spell of the Sensuous: Perception and Language in a More-Than-Human World*. New York: Pantheon Books, 1996.

adl, M. "Revisiting the Woman Question: An Islamic Perspective," *Chicago Theological Seminary Register* 83, no. 1 and 83, no. 2 (1993): 28–61.

, Carol J., ed. *Ecofeminism and the Sacred*. New York: Continuum, 1994.

l, Anil, and Sunita Narain. "Dying Wisdom: The Decline and Revival of Traditional Water Harvesting Systems in India." *Ecologist* 27, no. 3 (1997): 112–116.

dli M.S. *The Enlightened Jewels in Islam and Environmental Protection*. In Arabic, *al-jawahir al-mudia'h fi al-Islam wa Himaiat al-bia'h*. Cairo, Egypt: Dar al-nahda al-arabiah, 1995.

nese, Catherine L. *Nature Religions in America: From the Algonkian Indians to the New Age*. Chicago: University of Chicago Press, 1990.

ruqi, I. *Islam*. Brentwood, MD: International Graphics, 1984.

ruqi, I., and al Faruqi L. *The Cultural Atlas of Islam*. New York: Macmillan, 1986.

. Y. *The Holy Quran: Text, Translation and Commentary*. Brentwood, MD: Amana Press, 1989.

n, E. L. "The Hebrew View of Nature," *Journal of Jewish Studies* 2: 2 (1951): 100–104.

ers, Antony. *Maori Myths and Tribal Legends*. Auckland: Longman Paul, 1964.

es, Roger. "Taoism and the Nature of Nature," *Environmental Ethics* 8 (1986): 317–350; retitled "Putting the Te back into Taoism" in Callicott and Ames, 113–144.

mar, N. "An Islamic Response to the Manifest Ecological Crisis: Issues of Justice." In *Visions of a New Earth: Religious Perspectives on Population, Consumption, and Ecology*, ed. H. Coward and D. Maquire, 131–146. Albany: State University of New York Press, 2000.

———. "Islam, Population, and the Environment: A Textual and Juristic View." In *Population, Consumption, and The Environment: Religious and Secular Responses*, ed. Harold Coward, 123–136. Albany: State University of New York Press, 1995.

Anderson, Charles R., ed. *Thoreau's Vision: The Major Essays*. Englewood Cliffs, NJ: Prentice-Hall, 1973.

Apffel-Marglin, Frederique. "Sacred Groves: Regenerating the Body, the Land, the Community." In *Global Ecology: A New Arena of Political Conflict*, ed. Wolfgang Sachs, 197–207. London: Zed Books, 1993.

Austin, Richard. *Hope for the Land*. Atlanta: John Knox Press, 1988.

Badiner, Allan Hunt, ed. *Dharma Gaia*. Berkeley: Parallax Press, 1990.

Bailey, Ronald, ed. *The True State of the Planet*. New York: Free Press, 1995.

Ba Kader, Abou Bakr Ahmad, et al. *Basic Paper on the Islamic Principles for the Conservation of the Natural Environment*. Gland, Switzerland: IUCN and the Kingdom of Saudi Arabia, 1983.

Banwari. Pancavati. *Indian Approach to Environment*. Translated by Asha Vora. Delhi: Shri Vinayaka Publications, 1992.

Barnhill, David Landis. "Great Earth Sangha: Gary Snyder's View of Nature as Community." In *Buddhism and Ecology: The Interconnection of Dharma and Deeds*, ed. Mary Evelyn Tucker and Duncan Ryūkan Williams, 187– 218. Cambridge: Harvard University Center of the Study of World Religions, 1997.

———. "Indra's Net as Food Chain: Gary Snyder's Ecological Vision," *Ten Directions* 11, no. 1 (1990): 20–28.

Basso, Kieth H. "'Stalking with Stories': Names, Places, and Moral Narratives among the Western Apache." In *Text, Play, and Story: The Construction and Reconstruction of Self and Society*, ed. Edward M. Brunner. Proceedings of the American Ethnological Society, 1983.

Berry, Thomas. *Dream of the Earth*. San Francisco: Sierra Club, 1988.

———. *The Great Work*. New York: Bell Tower/Random House, 1999.

Birdwhistell, Anne. *Li Yong (1627–1705) and Epistemological Dimensions of Confucian Philosophy*. Stanford: Stanford University Press, 1996.

Bookchin, Murray. *The Philosophy of Social Ecology*. Montréal and New York: Black Rose Books, 1990.

Bordo, Jonathan. "Ecological Peril, Modern Technology and the Postmodern Sublime." In *Shadow of Spirit: Postmodernism and Religion*, ed. P. Berry and A. Wernick. New York: Routledge, 1993.

Brennan, Andrew. *Thinking About Nature: An Investigation of Nature, Value, and Ecology*. Athens, GA: University of Georgia Press, 1988.

Cajete, Gregory. *Look to the Mountains: An Ecology of Indigenous Education*. Durango, CO: Kivaki Press, 1994.

Callicott, J. Baird. "Do Deconstructive Ecology and Sociobiology Undermine Leopold's Land Ethic?" *Environmental Ethics* 18 (winter 1996): 353–372.

———. *Earth's Insights: A Multicultural Survey of Ecological Ethics from the Mediterranean Basin to the Australian Outback*. Berkeley: University of California Press, 1994.

———. *In Defense of the Land Ethic: Essays in Environmental Philosophy*. Albany: State University of New York Press, 1989.

J. Baird, and Roger T. Ames. *Nature in Asian Traditions of Thought: Es-*
.ys in Environmental Philosophy. Albany: State University of New York
.ess, 1989.

.ritjof. *The Web of Life.* Anchor Books, 1996.

.ing-tsit, trans. *A Source Book in Chinese Philosophy.* Princeton: Princeton
.niversity Press, 1963.

.Garma C. C. *The Buddhist Teaching of Totality: The Philosophy of Hwa Yen*
.uddhism. University Park: Pennsylvania State University Press, 1971.

.e, Christopher Key. "India's Earth Consciousness." In *The Soul of Nature:*
.isions of a Living Earth, ed. Michael Tobias and Georgianne Cowan,
.45–151. New York: Continuum, 1994.

Nonviolence to Animals, Earth, and Self in Asian Traditions. Albany: State
.Jniversity of New York Press, 1993.

. "Toward an Indigenous Indian Environmentalism." In *Purifying the*
Earthly Body of God: Religion and Ecology in Hindu India, ed. Lance E. Nel-
.son, 13–38. Albany: State University of New York Press, 1998.

.le, Christopher, and Yogi Anand Viraj (Eugene P. Kelly Jr.). *The Yoga*
Sūtras of Patanjali: An Analysis of the Sanskrit with English Translation.
Delhi: Satguru Publications, 1990.

., Chung-ying. "On the Environmental Ethics of the Tao and the Ch'i," *En-*
vironmental Ethics 8 (1986): 351–370.

—. "Chinese Philosophy and Symbolic Reference." In *New Dimensions of*
Confucian and Neo-Confucian Thought, 165–184. Albany: State University
of New York Press, 1991.

.g, Julia. "What is Confucian Spirituality?" In *Confucianism: The Dynamics of*
Tradition, ed. Irene Eber, 63–80. New York: Macmillan, 1986.

.c, John. "A Social Ecology." In *Environmental Philosophy: From Animal Rights*
to Radical Ecology (2nd edition), ed. Michael E. Zimmerman et al.,
416–440. Upper Saddle River, NJ: Prentice-Hall, 1998.

—. *The Anarchist Movement: Reflections on Culture, Nature, and Power.* Montréal: Black Rose Books, 1984.

.ry, Thomas. *Entry into the Inconceivable: An Introduction to Hua-yen Bud-*
dhism. Honolulu: University of Hawaii Press, 1983.

—. *Entry Into the Realm of Reality: The Text.* Boulder: Shambhala, 1987.

.nell, R. W. *Masculinities.* Berkeley and Los Angeles: University of California Press, 1995.

.ok, Francis. *Hua-yen Buddhism: The Jewel Net of Indra.* University Park: Pennsylvania State University Press, 1977.

.rtin, Dean. "Dōgen, Deep Ecology, and the Ecological Self," *Environmental*
Ethics 16 (1994): 195–213.

.neel, Innus. "Church and Ecojustice at the African Grassroots." In *Christian-*
ity and Ecology, ed. Dieter Hessel and Rosemary Ruether. Cambridge:
Harvard University Press, 1999.

. Bary, William Theodore. *The Liberal Tradition in China.* New York: Columbia
University Press, 1983.

―――. *The Trouble with Confucianism*. Cambridge: Harvard University Press, 1991.

―――, ed. *The Unfolding of Confucianism*. New York: Columbia University Press, 1975.

de Bary, William, and Irene Bloom, eds. *Principle and Practicality*. New York: Columbia University Press, 1979.

―――. *Sources of Chinese Tradition*, vol. 1. New York: Columbia University Press, 1999.

Deloria Jr., Vine. *For This Land: Writings on Religion in America*. New York: Routledge, 1999.

Devall, Bill, and George Sessions. *Deep Ecology: Living as if Nature Mattered*. Salt Lake City: Peregrine Smith Books, 1985.

diZerega, Gus. "A Critique of Ken Wilber's Account of Deep Ecology and Nature Religions," *The Trumpeter* 13, no. 2 (spring 1996): 52–71.

―――. "Democracies and Peace," *Review of Politics* 57 (1995): 279–308.

Dwivedi, O. P. *India's Environmental Policies, Programmes and Stewardship*. London: MacMillan Press, 1997.

Dwivedi, O. P., and B. N. Tiwari. *Environmental Crisis and Hindu Religion*. New Delhi: Gitanjali Publishing House, 1987.

Eagle, Luther Standing. *Land of the Spotted Eagle*. Boston: Houghton Mifflin, 1933.

Easterbrook, Gregg. *A Moment on the Earth: The Coming Age of Environmental Optimism*. New York: Viking Press, 1995.

Ehrlich, Paul R., et al. "No Middle Way on the Environment," *Atlantic Monthly* 280, no. 6 (December, 1997): 98–104.

Emett, Carolyn. "The Tree Man," *Resurgence: An International Forum for Ecological and Spiritual Thinking*, no. 183 (July/August 1997).

Fisher, William F. *Toward Sustainable Development: Struggling Over India's Narmada River*. Armonk, NY: M. E. Sharpe, 1995.

Flannery, Tim. *Future Eaters*. Sidney, Australia: Brazillier, 1994.

Flinders, Carol Lee. *At the Root of This Longing: Reconciling a Spiritual Hunger and a Feminist Thirst*. San Francisco: HarperSanFrancisco, 1998.

Forbes, Jack D. "Nature and Culture: Problematic Concepts for Native Americans." In *Indigenous Traditions and Ecology*. Cambridge, Harvard University Press for the Harvard University Center for the Study of World Religions, forthcoming.

Foreman, Dave. *Confessions of an Eco-Warrior*. New York: Harmony Books, 1992.

Fox, Matthew. *The Coming of the Cosmic Christ*. San Francisco: Harper, 1988.

Fox, Warwick. *Toward a Transpersonal Ecology: Developing New Foundations for Environmentalism*. Boston: Shambhala, 1990.

Freudenstein, Eric G. "Ecology and the Jewish Tradition," *Judaism* 19 (1970): 406–414.

Gadgil, Madhav, and Ramachandra Guha. *This Fissured Land: An Ecological History of India*. Delhi: Oxford University Press, 1992.

Glasser, Harold. "On Warwick Fox's Assessment of Deep Ecology," *Environmental Ethics* 19, no. 1 (spring 1997): 69–85.

ı, Benjamin, and Laura Fitton. *Toxic Wastes and Race Revisited: An Update* the 1987 Report. Washington, DC: Center for Policy Alternatives, 1994.

Robert. "Judaism and the Environment," *Congress Monthly* 57, no. 6 eptember/October 1990): 10.

Roger S. "Spiritual Deep Ecology and the Left." In *This Sacred Earth: ligion, Nature, Environment*, ed. Roger S. Gottlieb, 516–531. New York: utledge, 1996.

A Spirituality of Resistance: Finding a Peaceful Heart and Protecting the rth. New York: Crossroad: 1999.

:d. *This Sacred Earth: Religion, Nature, Environment*. New York: Rout-dge, 1996.

A. C. Graham. *Disputers of the Tao*. La Salle, IL: Open Court, 1989.

:orge. *Nga Mahi o Nga Tupuna*. Fourth edition. Wellington: A. H. and . W. Reed, 1971.

lliam. "Anthropocentrism and Deep Ecology," *Australasian Journal of hilosophy* 71, no. 4 (December 1993): 463–473.

Marcel. *Ogotemmeli*. New York: Oxford University Press, 1975.

Donald A., and Bruce E. Johansen. *Ecocide of Native America: Environ-ental Destruction of Indian Lands and People*. Santa Fe, NM: Clear Light,)95.

ın. *The Cosmic Game*. Albany: State University of New York Press, 1998.

Jeil. *Nga Pepeha a Nga Tupuna*. Second edition. Wellington: Department f Maori Studies, Victoria University of Wellington, 1984.

Lamachandra. "Radical American Environmentalism and Wilderness reservation: A Third World Critique." In *Ethical Perspectives on Environ-ental Issues in India*, ed. George A. James, 115–130. New Delhi: A. P. H. ublishing, 1999.

avid M. *To Weave and Sing: Art, Symbol, and Narrative in the South Ameri-n Rain Forest*. Berkeley: University of California Press, 1989.

ıvid L. "On Seeking a Change of Environment." In *Nature in Asian Tra-itions of Thought: Essays in Environmental Philosophy*, ed. J. Baird Callicott nd Roger T. Ames, 99–112. Albany: State University of New York Press, 989.

ell, A. Irving. "Ojibwa Ontology, Behavior, and World View." In *Culture nd History: Essays in Honor of Paul Radin*, ed. Stanley Diamond, 207–244. Jew York: Columbia University Press, 1960.

Ian. "Getting To Grips With Buddhist Environmentalism: A Provisional ypology," *Journal of Buddhist Ethics* 2 (1995): 173–190.

ger, Martin. *Die Grundbegriffe der Metaphysik*. Ed. Friedrich-Wilhelm von Jermann, Gesamtausgabe 29–30. Frankfurt am Main: Vittorio Kloster-nann, 1983.

eung. "Taoism and the Foundation of Environmental Ethics." In *Religion nd the Environmental Crisis*, ed. Eugene C. Hargrove, 94–106. Athens: Jniversity of Georgia Press, 1986.

Ismail, S. A. *Environment: An Islamic Perspective.* 1993. http://www.igc.apc.org/elaw/mideast/palestine/islamenviro.html.

Ives, Christopher. *Zen Awakening and Society.* Honolulu: University of Hawaii Press, 1992.

Izzi Dien, M. "Islamic Ethics and the Environment." In *Islam and Ecology*, ed. F. Khalid and J. O'Brien, 25–35. London: Cassell Publishers Limited, 1992.

———. *Shari'a and the Environment.* 1993. http://www.igc.apc.org/elaw/mideast/palestine/shariaenviro.html.

James, George A., ed. *Ethical Perspectives on Environmental Issues in India.* New Delhi: A. P. H. Publishing, 1999.

Jarvenpa, Robert. *Northern Passage: Ethnography and Apprenticeship Among the Subartic Dene.* Prospect Heights, IL: Waveland Press, 1998.

Katz, Eric. *Nature as Subject: Human Obligation and Natural Community.* Lanham, MD: Rowman and Littlefield, 1997.

Katz, Eric, Andrew Light, and David Rothenberg, eds. *Beneath the Surface: Critical Essays in Philosophy of Deep Ecology.* Cambridge, MA: MIT Press, 2000.

Kaza, Stephanie. *The Attentive Heart: Conversations with Trees.* New York: Ballantine, 1993.

Kellert, Stephen R. and E. O. Wilson, eds. *The Biophilia Hypothesis.* Washington, DC: Island Press, 1993.

Kheel, Marti. "Ecofeminism and Deep Ecology: Reflections on Identity and Difference." In *Reweaving the World: The Emergence of Ecofeminism*, ed. Irene Diamond and Gloria Orensten, 128–137. San Francisco: Sierra Club, 1990.

King, Sallie B. *Buddha Nature.* Albany: State University of New York Press, 1991.

King, Ynestra. "Healing the Wounds: Feminism, Ecology, and the Nature/Culture Dualism." In *Reweaving the World*, ed. Irene Diamond and Gloria Orenstein, 106–121. San Francisco: Sierra Club, 1990.

———. "The Ecology of Feminism and the Feminism of Ecology." In *Healing the Wounds: The Promise of Ecofeminism*, ed. Judith Plant, 18–28. Philadelphia: New Society Publishers, 1989.

Klein, Anne Carolyn. *Meeting the Great Bliss Queen: Buddhists, Feminists, and the Art of the Self.* Boston: Beacon Press, 1995.

Kremer, Jürgen W. "The Shadow of Evolutionary Thinking," *ReVision, Ken Wilber and the Future of Transpersonal Inquiry*, Part II, 19, no. 1 (summer 1996): 41–48.

LaChance, Albert, and John E. Carroll. *Embracing Earth: Catholic Approaches to Ecology.* New York: Orbis Books, 1994.

LaChapelle, Dolores. *Sacred Land Sacred Sex—Rapture of the Deep: Concerning Deep Ecology and Celebrating Life.* Silverton, CO: Finn Hill Arts, 1988.

Lamm, Norman. "Ecology and Jewish Law and Theology." In *Faith and Doubt*, 162–185. New York: KTAV, 1971.

Le Blanc, Charles. *Huai-Nan Tzu and Philosophical Synthesis in Early Han Thought.* Hong Kong: Hong Kong University Press, 1983.

Leopold, Aldo. *A Sand County Almanac.* New York: Oxford University Press, 1949.

lartin W. *Green Delusions: An Environmentalist Critique of Radical Envi-nmentalism*. Durham: Duke University Press, 1992.

ieorg. *History and Class Consciousness*. Cambridge, MA: MIT Press, 1971.

anna. *World as Lover, World as Self*. Berkeley: Parallax, 1994.

ı, Robert. *Derrida on the Mend*. West Lafayette, IN: Purdue University ress, 1984.

ıhn. *Heaven and Earth in Early Han Thought*. Albany: State University of lew York Press, 1993.

l, Peter. *Nature's Web: Rethinking Our Place on Earth*. New York: Paragon Iouse, 1994 (1992).

ı. H. "Islam and Ecology." In *Islam and Ecology*, ed. F. Khalid and O'Brien, 1–23. London: Cassell Publishers Limited, 1992.

ɪs, Freya. "Conservation and Self-Realization," *Environmental Ethics* 10, .o. 4 (1988): 347–356.

"Ecofeminism and Deep Ecology." In *Ecology*, ed. Carolyn Merchant, 35–247. Atlantic Highlands, NJ: Humanities Press, 1994.

The Ecological Self. Savage, MD: Barnes and Noble, 1991.

an, John. "Nondual Ecology," *Tricycle: The Buddhist Review* 3, no. 2 (win-er 1993): 58–65.

ıen, Bill. *Hope, Human and Wild: True Stories of Living Lightly on the Earth*. iaint Paul: Hungry Mind Press, 1995.

The End of Nature. New York: Random House, 1989.

ghlin, Andrew. "The Heart of Deep Ecology." In *Deep Ecology for the 21st Century*, ed. George Sessions, 85–93. Boston: Shambhala, 1995.

Regarding Nature: Industrialism and Deep Ecology. Albany: State Univer-sity of New York Press, 1993.

ey, James. *Holy Wind in Navajo Philosophy*. Tucson: University of Arizona Press, 1981.

ɪson, Dennis, and J. Douglas Rabb. *Indian from the Inside: A Study in Ethno-Metaphysics*. Thunder Bay, Ontario: Lakehead University, Centre for Northern Studies, 1993.

ɪ, Rosemary, trans. *Deep Words, Miura Baien's System of Natural Philosophy*. Leiden: E. J. Brill, 1991.

, Joan. *New Growth from Old: The Whanau in the Modern World*. Wellington: Victoria University Press, 1995.

Baien. "An Answer to Taka Bokkyo." Trans. Gino K. Piovesana, S.M. *Monumenta Nipponica* 20 (1965): 442.

ı, Melinda A. "The Kerala House as a Hindu Cosmos." In *India Through Hindu Categories*, ed. McKim Marriott, 169–202. New Delhi: Sage Publi-cations, 1990.

ɔ, Donald. *Images of Human Nature: A Sung Portrait*. Princeton: Princeton University Press, 1988.

, Arne. "The Deep Ecological Movement: Some Philosophical Aspects." In *Environmental Philosophy*, ed. Michael Zimmerman et al., 193–212. Engle-wood Cliffs, NJ: Prentice-Hall, 1993.

————. *Ecology, Community, and Lifestyle: Outline of an Ecosophy.* Trans. David Rothenberg. Cambridge: Cambridge University Press, 1989.

————. "Gestalt Thinking and Buddhism." 1983. Unpublished paper.

————. "Identification as a Source of Deep Ecological Attitudes." In *Deep Ecology,* ed. Michael Tobias. San Diego: Avant Books, 1985.

————. "The Shallow and the Deep, Long Range Ecology Movement. A Summary," *Inquiry* 16 (1973): 95–100.

Nagarajan, Vijaya Rettakudi. "The Earth as Goddess Bhu Devi: Toward a Theory of 'Embedded Ecologies' in Folk Hinduism." In *Purifying the Earthly Body of God: Religion and Ecology in Hindu India,* ed. Lance Nelson, 269–296. Albany: State University of New York Press, 1998.

Nakai, Kate. "The Naturalization of Confucianism in Tokugawa Japan: The Problem of Sinocentrisim," *Harvard Journal of Asiatic Studies* 40 (1980): 157–199.

Nakamura Hajime. *Ways of Thinking of Eastern Peoples.* Trans. Philip P. Wiener. Honolulu: East-West Center Press, 1964.

Narayanan, Vasudha. "One Tree is Equal to Ten Sons: Hindu Responses to the Problems of Ecology, Population, and Consumption," *Journal of the American Academy of Religion* 65, no. 2 (January 1997): 291–332.

Nelson, Lance, ed. *Purifying the Earthly Body of God: Religion and Ecology in Hindu India.* Albany: State University of New York Press, 1998.

New Mexico Bishops. "Reclaiming the Vocation to Care for the Earth: Pastoral Letter of Archbishop Michael Sheehan of Santa Fe, Bishop Ricardo Ramirez of Las Cruces, and Bishop Donald Pelotte of Gallup." In *Origins: CNS Documentary News Service,* Vol. 28, no. 4 (11 June 1998).

Ng, Benjamin Wai-ming. "Quantitative Notes on I Ching Scholarship in Tokugawa Japan," *The Japan Foundation Newsletter* 23, no. 5 (February 1996).

————. "Study and Uses of the *I Ching* in Tokugawa Japan," *Sino-Japanese Studies* 9, no. 2 (April 1997).

Nicholson, Shirley, and Brenda Rosen. *Gaia's Hidden Life.* Wheaton, IL: Quest Books, 1992.

Odin, Steve. *Process Metaphysics and Hua-Yen Buddhism: A Critical Study of Cumulative Penetration versus Interpenetration.* Albany: State University of New York Press, 1982.

Orenstein, Gloria Feman. "Toward an Ecofeminist Ethic of Shamanism and the Sacred." In *Ecofeminism and the Sacred,* ed. Carol J. Adams, 172–190. New York: Continuum, 1993.

Paper, Jordan. *Chinese Religion Illustrated (CD-ROM).* Belmont, CA: Wadsworth Publishing, 1998.

————. *The Fu-tzu: A Post-Han Confucian Text.* Leiden: E. J. Brill, 1987 (1971).

————. "Mediums and Modernity: The Institutionalization of Ecstatic Religious Functionaries in Taiwan," *Journal of Chinese Religion* 24 (1996): 105–130.

————. *The Spirits are Drunk: Comparative Approaches to Chinese Religion.* Albany: State University of New York Press, 1995.

Through the Earth Darkly: Female Spirituality in Comparative Perspective. ew York: Continuum, 1997.

rdan, and Li Chuang Paper. "Chinese Religions, Population, and the nvironment." In *Population, Consumption, and the Environment: Religious 1d Secular Responses,* ed. Harold Coward, 173–191. Albany: State University of New York Press, 1995.

rdan, and Lawrence G. Thompson, eds. *The Chinese Way in Religion.* elmont, CA: Wadsworth Publishing, 1998.

Graham. "Human/Nature in Nietzsche and Taoism." In *Nature in Asian raditions of Thought: Essays in Environmental Philosophy,* ed. J. Baird Callicott and Roger T. Ames, 79–98. Albany: State University of New York 'ress, 1989.

ngimarie Rose. *Ako: Concepts and Learning in the Maori Tradition.* Hamilton: University of Waikato, 1982.

Moozhikkulam Chandrasekharam. *Mannarassala: The Serpent Temple.* Translated by Ayyappa Panikker. Harippad: Manasa Publication, 1991.

na, Gino. "Miura Baien: 1723–1789," *Monumenta Nipponica* 20 (1965).

ood, Val. "Ecosocial Feminism as a General Theory of Oppression." In *Ecology,* ed. Carolyn Merchant, 207–219. Atlantic Highlands, NJ: Humanities Press, 1994.

"Nature, Self, and Gender." In *Environmental Philosophy: From Animal Rights to Radical Ecology* (2nd edition), ed. Michael E. Zimmerman et al., 291–314. Upper Saddle River, NJ: Prentice-Hall, 1998.

, James J. *Cult of the Goddess: Social and Religious Change in a Hindu Temple.* Prospect Heights, IL: Waveland Press, 1985.

Ranchor. *Hinduism and Ecology: Seeds of Truth.* London: Cassell, 1992.

M., and M. Ajmal. "Islam and the Present Ecologicial Crisis." In *World Religions and the Environment,* ed. O. P. Dwivedi. New Delhi: Gitanjali Publishing House, 1989.

R Victor. *The Hindu Connection: Roots of the New Age.* Saint Louis: Concordia Publishing House, 1995.

rajan, Mahesh. *Fencing the Forest: Conservation and Ecological Change in India's Central Provinces 1860–1914.* Delhi: Oxford University Press, 1961.

rt of the Sub-Commission on Prevention of Discrimination and Protection of Minorities on its Forty-Sixth Session." Geneva 1–26, August, 1994: Draft United Nations Declaration on the Rights of Indigenous Peoples.

an, John. "The Liberation of Nature?" *Inquiry* 20 (1977): 83–131.

Richard, O.F.M. *Simplicity: The Art of Living.* New York: Crossroad, 1992.

n III, Holmes. "Can the East Help the West to Value Nature?" *Philosophy East and West* 37 (1987): 172–190.

—. *Environmental Ethics: Duties to and Values in the Natural World.* Philadelphia: Temple University Press, 1988.

nan, Marina. *Healing Sounds from the Malaysian Rainforest: Temiar Music and Medicine.* Berkeley: University of California Press, 1993.

Ruether, Rosemary Radford. *Gaia and God: An Ecofeminist Theology of Earth Healing*. San Francisco: Harper, 1992.

———. "They Meet to Counter Consumerist Evils," *National Catholic Reporter* (30 January 1998).

———. *Women Healing Earth: Third World Women on Ecology, Feminism and Religion*. Maryknoll, NY: Orbis Books, 1996.

Ryusaku Tsunoda, Wm. Theodore de Bary, and Donald Keene, eds. *Sources of Japanese Tradition*. New York: Columbia University Press, 1958.

Sagoff, Mark. "Do We Consume Too Much?" *Atlantic Monthly* 279, no. 3 (June 1997): 80–97.

Salleh, Ariel Kay. "Deeper than Deep Ecology: The Ecofeminist Connection," *Environmental Ethics* 6 (1984): 339–345.

Sampat, Payal. "What Does India Want?" *World Watch* 11, no. 4 (July/August 1998): 29–38.

Saso, Michael. *Blue Dragon, White Tiger: Taoist Rites of Passage*. Washington, DC: The Taoist Center, 1990.

Schama, Simon. *Landscape and Memory*. New York: Alfred A. Knopf, 1995.

Schipper, Kristopher. *The Taoist Body*. Trans. Karen Duval. Berkeley: University of California Press, 1993.

Schrempp, Gregory. *Magical Arrows: The Maori, The Greeks, and the Folklore of the Universe*. Madison: University of Wisconsin Press, 1992.

Schwartz, Eilon. "Bal Tashchit: A Jewish Environmental Precept," *Environmental Ethics* 19 (1997): 355–374.

Seed, John. "Anthropocentrism." In Bill Devall and George Sessions, *Deep Ecology*, 243–246. Salt Lake City: Peregrine Smith Books, 1985.

———. "Spirit of the Earth: A Battle-Weary Rainforest Activist Journeys to India to Renew His Soul," *Yoga Journal*, no. 138 (January/February 1998): 69–71; 132–136.

Sen, Geeti, ed. *Indigenous Vision: Peoples of India Attitudes to the Environment*. New Delhi: Sage Publications, 1992.

Shaner, David, and Shannon Duval. "Conservation Ethics and the Japanese Intellectual Tradition," *Environmental Ethics* 11 (1989): 197–214.

Shepard, Paul. *Nature and Madness*. San Francisco: Sierra Club, 1982,.

Simon, Julian, ed. *The State of Humanity*. Cambridge, MA: Blackwell/Cato Institute, 1995.

Slicer, Deborah. "Is There an Ecofeminism-Deep Ecology 'Debate'?" *Environmental Ethics* 17, no. 2 (summer 1995): 151–170.

Smil, Vaclav. *The Bad Earth*. Armonk, NY: M. E. Sharpe, 1984.

———. *China's Environmental Crisis: An Inquiry into the Limits of National Development*. Armonk, NY: M. E. Sharpe, 1993.

Smith, Kidder, Peter Bol, Joseph Adler, and Don Wyatt. *Sung Dynasty Use of the I Ching*. Princeton: Princeton University Press, 1990.

Snyder, Gary. *A Place in Space: Ethics, Aesthetics, and Watersheds*. Washington, DC: Counterpoint, 1996.

*arth House Hold: Technical Notes and Queries to Fellow Dharma Revolu-
maries.* New York: New Directions, 1969.

The Practice of the Wild. San Francisco: North Point Press, 1990.

The Real Work: Interviews and Talks, 1964–1979. New York: New Direc-
ons, 1980.

, Charlene. "Ecofeminism: Our Roots and Flowering." In *Reweaving the
World,* ed. Irene Diamond and Gloria Feman Orenstein, 3–14. San Fran-
sco: Sierra Club, 1990.

"Radical Nonduality in Ecofeminist Philosophy." In *Ecofeminism:
Women, Culture, Nature,* ed. Karen J. Warren, 425–436. Bloomington: In-
iana University Press, 1997.

States of Grace. San Francisco: HarperCollins, 1991.

David, and Eileen Spring, eds. *Ecology and Religion in History.* New York:
Harper Torchbooks, 1974.

David, and Peter Knudtson. *Wisdom of the Elders: Sacred Native Stories of
Nature.* New York: Bantam Books, 1992.

Richard. "A Critique of Deep Ecology," *Radical Philosophy* 40 (summer
1985): 2–11 and *Radical Philosophy* 41 (autumn 1985): 10–22.

Richard, and David Bennett. *The Greening of Ethics.* Tucson: University
of Arizona Press, 1994.

to, Okada. "Yamazaki Ansai and Kaibara Ekken." In *Principle and Practicality,* ed. Wm. Theodore de Bary and Irene Bloom, 231–306. New York:
Columbia University Press, 1979.

Bron. "Earth First! And Global Narratives of Popular Ecological Resistance." In *Ecological Resistance Movements: The Global Emergence of Radical
and Popular Environmentalism,* ed. Bron Taylor, 11–34. Albany: State University of New York Press, 1995.

. "Earth First! From Primal Spirituality to Ecological Resistance." In *This
Sacred Earth,* ed. Roger Gottlieb, 545–557. New York and London: Routledge, 1995.

. "Earth First!'s Religious Radicalism." In *Ecological Prospects: Scientific,
Religious, and Aesthetic Perspectives,* ed. Christopher Chapple, 185–209.
Albany: State University of New York Press, 1994.

. "Earthen Spirituality or Cultural Genocide? Radical Environmentalism's Appropriation of Native American Spirituality," *Religion* 27 (1997):
183–215.

, Paul. *Respect for Nature: A Theory of Environmental Ethics.* Princeton:
Princeton University Press, 1986.

rd de Chardin, Pierre. *Red Earth, White Lies: Native Americans and the Myth
of Scientific Fact.* New York: Scribner, 1995.

. *The Heart of Matter.* Translated by Rene Hague. New York: Harcourt
Brace Jovanovich, 1979.

. *The Phenomenon of Man.* Translated by Bernard Wall. New York: Harper
& Row, 1959.

Thomashow, Mitchell. *Ecological Identity: Becoming a Reflective Environmentalist.* Cambridge, MA: MIT Press, 1995.

Thompson, Lawrence. *Chinese Religion: An Introduction.* Belmont, CA: Wadsworth, 1996 (1973).

Tinker, George. "An American Indian Theological Response to Ecojustice." In *Defending Mother Earth,* ed. Jace Weaver, 153–176. Maryknoll, NY: Orbis, 1996.

———. "Ecojustice and Justice: An American Indian Perspective." In *Theology for Earth Community: A Field Guide,* ed. Dieter T. Hessel, 143–152. Maryknoll, NY: Orbis Books, 1996.

Tu, Weiming. *Centrality and Commonality.* Albany: State University of New York Press, 1989.

Tuan, Yi-Fu. "Discrepancies between Environmental Attitude and Behaviour: Examples from Europe and China." In *Ecology and Religion in History,* ed. David Spring and Eileen Spring, 91–113. New York: Harper Torchbooks, 1974.

Tucker, Mary Evelyn. *Moral and Spiritual Cultivation in Japanese Neo-Confuciansm: The Life and Thought of Kaibara Ekken 1630–1714.* Albany: State University of New York Press, 1989.

Tucker, Mary Evelyn, and John Berthrong, eds. *Confucianism and Ecology.* Cambridge: Center for the Study of World Religions and Harvard University Press, 1997.

Turner, Nancy, Randy Bouchard, and Dorothy Kennedy. *Ethnobotany of the Okanagan-Colville Indians of British Columbia and Washington.* No. 21, Occasional Paper Series. British Columbia Provincial Museum, Victoria, 1980.

van Wyck, Peter C. *Primitives in the Wilderness: Deep Ecology and the Missing Human Subject.* Albany: State University of New York Press, 1997.

Waller, David. "Friendly Fire: When Environmentalists Dehumanize American Indians," *American Indian Culture and Research Journal* 20, no.2 (1996): 107–126.

Wang, Aihe. "Cosmology and the Transformation of Political Culture in Early China." Ph.D. Thesis, Harvard University, Cambridge, MA, 1995.

Wang Yangming. "Inquiry on the Great Learning." In *Instructions for Practical Living and Other Neo-Confucian Writings by Wang Yang-ming,* trans. Wing-tsit Chan. New York: Columbia University Press, 1963.

Weaver, Jace, ed. *Defending Mother Earth: Native American Perspectives on Environmental Justice.* Maryknoll, NY: Orbis, 1996.

Weurthner, George. "An Ecological View of the Indian," *Earth First!* 7, no. 7 (August 1987).

White Jr., Lynn. "The Historical Roots of our Ecologic Crisis," *Science* 155 (10 March 1967): 1203–1207.

Wilber, Ken. *A Brief History of Everything.* Boston and London: Shambhala, 1996.

———. *Eye to Eye: The Search for the New Paradigm.* Boston: Shambhala, 1996.

———. *The Marriage of Sense and Soul.* New York: Random House, 1998.

5ex, Ecology, Spirituality: The Spirit of Evolution. Boston and London: 1ambhala, 1995.

'A Spirituality that Transforms," *What Is Enlightenment?* 12 (fall/winter,)97): 23–32.

Up From Eden: A Transpersonal View of Human Evolution. Boston: Shamhala, 1981.

Jeanette. "Ecological Risk Assessment and Management: Their Failure) Value Indigenous Traditional Ecological Knowledge and Protect Tribal Iomelands," *American Indian Culture and Research Journal* 22, no. 2 (1998): 51–169.

, Donald. "The Ecology of Order and Chaos." In *Environmental Ethics,* d. Susan J. Armstrong and Richard G. Botzler, 39–43. New York: AcGraw-Hill, 1993.

Arthur, ed. *Confucianism and Chinese Civilization.* Stanford: Stanford University Press, 1964.

ga, Toshinobu. *Andō Shōeki: Social and Ecological Philosopher of Eighteenth-Century Japan.* New York: Weatherhill, 1992.

rman, Michael. *Contesting Earth's Future: Radical Ecology and Postmodernity.* Berkeley and Los Angeles: University of California Press, 1994.

"Ecofascism: A Threat to American Environmentalism?" In *The Ecological Community,* ed. Roger S. Gottlieb, 229–254. New York: Routledge, 1997.

. *Heidegger's Confrontation with Modernity: Technology, Politics, Art.* Bloomington: Indiana University Press, 1990.

. "Ontical Craving versus Ontological Desire." In *From Phenomenology to Thought, Errancy, and Desire,* ed. Babette E. Babich. Dordrecht: Kluwer, 1995.

. "The Postmodern Challenge to Environmentalism," *Terra Nova* 1.2 (spring 1996): 131–140.

. "A Transpersonal Diagnosis of the Ecological Crisis." In *Ken Wilber and the Future of Transpersonal Inquiry: A Spectrum of Views,* Part I, ed. Donald Rothberg and Sean M. Kelly. *ReVision* 18, No. 4 (spring 1996): 38–48.

Contributors

ѦMMAR is associate professor of justice studies at Kent State University.
is an Egyptian-American who was born in Beirut, Lebanon. She has a
ι sociocultural anthropology and her areas of research have focused on
ssues for women including Muslim and Arab women, Islam and ecol-
l restorative justice. Some of Nawal's recent publications include articles
emic journals: "Simplistic Stereotyping and Complex Reality of Arab-
an Immigrant Identity: Consequences and Future Strategies in Policing
attery" and "In the Shadow of the Pyramids: Domestic Violence in
' In addition she has published essays in various edited volumes:
rative Justice in Qur'anic/ Legal Context"; "Ecojustice and Human
for Women in Islam"; "Islam and the Environment: Issues of Justice";
ιn's Grassroots Movements in Egypt: Legal and Social Democratization"
.eila Lababidy); and "Discrimination against Women under the Nation-
ιws: Case Studies from Egypt and Lebanon."

LANDIS BARNHILL is director of interdisciplinary studies and Dana Profes-
intercultural studies and religious studies at Guilford College. He has
an anthology of American nature writing, *At Home on the Earth: Becoming
to Our Place*, and published articles on the Japanese nature poet Matsuo
and the American Buddhist poet Gary Snyder. He also has served as
r of the Religion and Ecology Group of the American Academy of Reli-
He is currently working on an anthology of American nature writing in-
ed by Asian culture, as well as a book on the significance of Buddhism for
mmental and social issues.

ł. CARROLL, professor of environmental conservation at the University of
Hampshire, has edited or coedited three books in the field of ecological
ιiritual values: *Embracing Earth: Catholic Approaches to Ecology; The Green-
Faith: God, the Environment, and the Good Life;* and *Ecology and Religion: Sci-
Speak.* He has published many articles and papers in the area of ecology
ιligion, and is assisting the Catholic bishops of New England on a pastoral

address on ecology and Catholicism. He also has authored books in international environmental diplomacy and is a Kellogg Foundation National Fellow. He teaches ecological ethics and values at both the graduate and undergraduate levels and has guided a number of theses and dissertations in this area.

CHRISTOPHER KEY CHAPPLE is professor of theological studies and director of Asian and Pacific studies at Loyola Marymount University in Los Angeles. He has published several books, including *Karma and Creativity*, a cotranslation of the *Yoga Sutras of Patanjali*, and *Nonviolence to Animals, Earth, and Self in Asian Traditions*. He has also edited several volumes of collected essays, including *Ecological Prospects: Scientific, Religious, and Aesthetic Perspectives* as well as *Hinduism and Ecology* and *Jainism and Ecology*, which arose from a series of conferences on Religion and Ecology held at Harvard University's Center for the Study of World Religions.

JOHN B. COBB JR. is professor emeritus of theology in the Claremont School of Theology and of Religion in Claremont Graduate University. Among his publications are *Is It Too Late? A Theology of Ecology, The Liberation of Life, Beyond Dialogue: Toward a Mutual Transformation of Christianity and Buddhism, The Earthist Challenge to Economism: A Theological Critique of the World Bank, Sustainability: Economics, Ecology, and Justice*, and *Sustaining the Common Good: A Christian Perspective on the Global Economy*.

ROGER S. GOTTLIEB is professor of philosophy at Worcester Polytechnic Institute. He is the author or editor of ten books whose subjects include nineteenth- and twentieth-century-political philosophy, feminism, contemporary spirituality, environmental politics, ecotheology, and the Holocaust. His essays have appeared in leading scholarly journals (including *Ethics, Journal of Philosophy, Journal of the American Academy of Religion, Cross Currents, Science and Society*) and in general interest publications (*Boston Sunday Globe, Sierra, Orion Afield*). He is "Reading Spirit" columnist for *Tikkun* Magazine, where he focuses on general issues of religious interest; and he serves on the editorial boards of *Social Theory and Practice* and *Capitalism, Nature, Socialism: A Journal of Socialist Ecology*. His most recent books are *A Spirituality of Resistance: Finding a Peaceful Heart and Protecting the Earth* and *This Sacred Earth: Religion, Nature, Environment*.

JOHN A. GRIM is a professor and chair in the Department of Religion at Bucknell University. As a historian of religions, John undertakes annual field studies in American Indian lifeways among the Apsaalooke/Crow peoples of Montana and the Swy-ahl-puh/Salish peoples of the Columbia River Plateau in eastern Washington. Raised in the Missouri drift prairies of North Dakota, John went to the urban environs of the Bronx to study with Thomas Berry at Fordham University. There, he completed a doctoral dissertation on Anishinaabe/Ojibway healing practitioners published in 1983 by the University of Oklahoma Press as *The Shaman: Patterns of Religious Healing Among the Ojibway Indians*. With his wife, Mary Evelyn Tucker, he has co-edited *Worldviews and Ecology*, a book dis-

>erspectives on the environmental crisis from world religions and con-
ry philosophy. John co-organized, with Mary Evelyn Tucker, a series of
conferences on "Religions of the World and Ecology" held at Harvard
ty's Center for the Study of World Religions from the spring of 1996 to
of 1998. The culminating conferences in this series were held at the
Nations on 20 October 1998, and the American Museum of Natural His-
21 October 1998. This work continues as the Forum on Religion and
John is also president of the American Teilhard Association. This orga-
explores issues in religion and science especially in light of the thought
 Teilhard de Chardin and the late-twentieth-century reworking of Teil-
hought by Thomas Berry and Brian Swimme.

TZ is an associate professor of philosophy and director of the Science,
ogy, and Society Program at the New Jersey Institute of Technology. He
uthor of *Nature as Subject: Human Obligation and Natural Community*,
r of *Environmental Pragmatism*, and *Beneath the Surface: Critical Essays in*
psophy of Deep Ecology.

PAPER teaches in the Religious and East Asian Studies Programs, as well
ts dissertations in the Faculty of Environmental Studies and the School
nen's Studies, at York University in Toronto. His books include *Offering*
The Sacred Pipe and Native American Religion, The Spirits Are Drunk: Com-
e Approaches to Chinese Religion, and *Through the Earth Darkly: Female Spir-*
in Comparative Perspective. He is currently writing a comparative study of
stic experience and a book on polytheistic theology.

ARY RADFORD RUETHER is a Catholic feminist theologian teaching at Garrett
ogical Seminary and is a member of the Graduate Faculty of Northwest-
niversity. Among her many books are *Sexism and God-talk: Toward a Femi-*
heology; *Gaia and God: An Ecofeminist Theology of Earth Healing; Women*
g Earth: Third World Women on Feminism, Religion, and Ecology; New Woman
arth: Sexist Ideologies and Human Liberation; Introducing Redemption in Chris-
minism*; and *Gender and Redemption: A Theological History*.

EVELYN TUCKER is a professor of religion at Bucknell University in Lewis-
Pennsylvania, where she teaches courses in world religions, Asian reli-
, and religion and ecology. She received her Ph.D. from Columbia
ersity in the history of religions, specializing in Confucianism in Japan. She
author of *Moral and Spiritual Cultivation in Japanese Neo-Confucianism*, and
edited *Worldviews and Ecology, Buddhism and Ecology*, and *Confucianism and*
gy. She and her husband, John Grim, have directed a series of ten confer-
 on World Religions and Ecology at the Harvard University Center for the
y of World Religions from 1996–1998. They are the series editors for the ten
mes that are being published from the conferences by the center and Har-
University Press. They are also editors of a book series on Ecology and Jus-
rom Orbis Press. In addition, they are now coordinating an ongoing Forum

on Religion and Ecology (FORE). Mary Evelyn has been a committee member of the Environmental Sabbath program at the United Nations Environment Programme (UNEP) since 1986 and is vice president of the American Teilhard Association.

MICHAEL E. ZIMMERMAN is professor and chair of philosophy at Tulane University. In addition to many academic articles, he has authored *Contesting Earth's Future: Radical Ecology and Postmodernity* and edited the anthology *Environmental Philosophy: From Animal Rights to Radical Ecology*. He also has written *Heidegger's Confrontation with Modernity, Technology, Politics, and Art*, and *Eclipse of the Self: The Development of Heidegger's Concept of Authenticity*.

Index

Printed in the United States
19805LVS00002B/231